Deadly Clerics

Deadly Clerics explains why some Muslim clerics adopt the ideology of militant jihadism while most do not. The book explores multiple pathways of cleric radicalization and shows that the interplay of academic, religious, and political institutions has influenced the rise of modern jihadism through a mechanism of blocked ambition. As long as clerics' academic ambitions remain attainable, they are unlikely to espouse violent jihad. Clerics who are forced out of academia are more likely to turn to jihad for two reasons: jihadist ideas are attractive to those who see the system as turning against them, and preaching a jihad ideology can help these outsider clerics attract supporters and funds. The book draws on evidence from various sources, including large-scale statistical analysis of texts and network data obtained from the Internet, case studies of clerics' lives, and ethnographic participant observations at sites in Cairo, Egypt.

Richard A. Nielsen is an Associate Professor in the Department of Political Science at the Massachusetts Institute of Technology, where he studies and teaches on Islam, political violence, human rights, economic development, and research design. His research has been published in the *American Journal of Political Science, International Studies Quarterly, Political Analysis,* and *Sociological Methods and Research.* He holds a PhD in government (2013) and an AM in statistics (2010) from Harvard University, and a BA in political science (2007) from Brigham Young University.

T0384764

Cambridge Studies in Comparative Politics

Other Books in the Series

Christopher Adolph, *Bankers, Bureaucrats, and Central Bank Politics: The Myth of Neutrality*

Michael Albertus, *Autocracy and Redistribution: The Politics of Land Reform*

Ben W. Ansell, *From the Ballot to the Blackboard: The Redistributive Political Economy of Education*

Ben W. Ansell, David J. Samuels, *Inequality and Democratization: An Elite-Competition Approach*

Leonardo R. Arriola, *Multi-Ethnic Coalitions in Africa: Business Financing of Opposition Election Campaigns*

David Austen-Smith, Jeffry A. Frieden, Miriam A. Golden, Karl Ove Moene, and Adam Przeworski,eds., *Selected Works of Michael Wallerstein: The Political Economy of Inequality, Unions, and Social Democracy*

Andy Baker, *The Market and the Masses in Latin America: Policy Reform and Consumption in Liberalizing Economies*

Continued after index

Deadly Clerics

Blocked Ambition and the Paths to Jihad

RICHARD A. NIELSEN
Massachusetts Institute of Technology

CAMBRIDGE
UNIVERSITY PRESS

CAMBRIDGE
UNIVERSITY PRESS

University Printing House, Cambridge CB2 8BS, United Kingdom

One Liberty Plaza, 20th Floor, New York, NY 10006, USA

477 Williamstown Road, Port Melbourne, VIC 3207, Australia

314–321, 3rd Floor, Plot 3, Splendor Forum, Jasola District Centre, New Delhi – 110025, India

79 Anson Road, #06-04/06, Singapore 079906

Cambridge University Press is part of the University of Cambridge.

It furthers the University's mission by disseminating knowledge in the pursuit of education, learning, and research at the highest international levels of excellence.

www.cambridge.org
Information on this title: www.cambridge.org/9781108416689
DOI: 10.1017/9781108241700

First published 2017

Printed in the United Kingdom by Clays, St Ives plc

A catalogue record for this publication is available from the British Library.

ISBN 978-1-108-41668-9 Hardback
ISBN 978-1-108-40405-1 Paperback

Contents

List of Figures		*page* vi
List of Tables		vii
Acknowledgments		ix
1	Why Clerics Turn Deadly	1
2	Muslim Clerics	27
3	Paths to Preaching Jihad	51
4	Meet the Clerics	82
5	Recognizing Jihadists from Their Writings	106
6	Networks, Careers, and Jihadist Ideology	131
7	Conclusion	169
	Appendix A Syllabus of Hamid al-Ali	187
	Appendix B Technical Appendix	202
Bibliography		213
Index		229

Figures

2.1	The topics of a large fatwa corpus.	*page* 44
3.1	Students engaging a cleric after a lesson.	67
4.1	Four clusters of cleric biographies.	98
4.2	Countries mentioned in cleric biographies.	102
4.3	Higher education attainment and year of birth.	103
5.1	Proportions of topic use in a jihadist corpus by author.	118
5.2	A word cloud representation of the jihad score classifier.	120
5.3	Jihad scores for clerics with benchmark texts.	122
5.4	Jihadist clerics ranked by jihad scores.	124
5.5	Validation of jihad scores.	127
5.6	Jihadist image: scholars of falsehood.	129
6.1	Correlation between networks, insider appointments, and jihad scores.	138
6.2	Cleric jihad scores and imprisonment.	164

Tables

4.1	Academic terms in cleric biographies.	*page* 103
5.1	Top words for five topics in a jihadist corpus.	117
5.2	Texts that are representative of five topics in a jihadist corpus.	117
6.1	Percentage of jihadi clerics by number of teachers and career path.	140
6.2	Number of teachers and career path predict jihadism.	148
6.3	Summary of case studies of fifteen jihadist clerics.	156
6.4	Summary of case studies of fifteen jihadist clerics (*continued*).	157
6.5	Summary of case studies of fifteen jihadist clerics (*continued*).	158
6.6	Jihadist fatwas are popular with Salafis.	163
B.1	Top words for five topics in a jihadist corpus.	205
B.2	Texts that are representative of five topics in a jihadist corpus.	207

Tables

Acknowledgments

This is a book about jihadists as academics. It tells stories of scholars experiencing the benefits and constraints of academia, relying on their scholarly networks to get ahead or finding them unequal to the task, of academic success and failure, and the ways that the disappointment of having one's academic ambitions blocked can push some people to embrace violent ideas and urge heinous actions. I do not mean this by way of analogy. Jihadist clerics are not "like" academics, but rather they *are* academics, although their academic personalities are often overshadowed by the dreadful consequences of their ideas. Writing about networks of scholars in Islamic legal academia has forced me to repeatedly contemplate my own academic networks and recognize just how fortunate I have been. Without the people thanked here, and many more that I'm sure I have failed to recall, it would not have been possible for me to write this book.

While I was a Mormon missionary in Alaska, I spent many hours at the house of an elderly man named Gene Rutledge who had little interest in religion but was willing to talk to me if I would help him organize his papers – a lifetime of snippets from a career spent in science, including a role in the Manhattan Project. The last time I saw him, in 2004, he told me, "When you write your first book, send me a copy." At the time, I merely smiled politely. It wasn't until years later that I realized he had been right: inevitably I was going to try to write a book. The confidence implicit in his request carried me through some of the self-doubt of writing, for which I am deeply grateful. I looked him up some years ago and found his obituary in a local Anchorage newspaper. I wish I could have written more quickly so that I could have sent this book to him before his passing.

I was introduced to the vocation of political science by Daniel Nielson, who taught my first class in social science research design in the summer of 2005 and then, upon encountering me working as the campus security guard for a *Harry*

Potter book release party, asked if I might prefer a job as a research assistant. Working closely with him and others in Brigham Young University's Political Science program – especially Jeremy Pope, Jay Goodliffe, Donna Lee Bowen, Darren Hawkins, and Sven Wilson – set me on the path to writing this book.

The first draft of this book was a dissertation in the Department of Government at Harvard University. My dissertation committee – Beth Simmons, Gary King, Robert Bates, Tarek Masoud, and Adam Glynn – has been everything that a committee should be. My first conversation with Beth was a chance encounter in 2006 in which she generously spent the better part of an hour trying to figure out what an undergraduate student from Utah was doing at the New England Political Science Association's annual conference. She has been a peerless advisor ever since. At a crucial turning point, Beth urged me to pursue this project instead of the more standard international political economy topics I was considering. It felt like the project was impossible, but she was right.

At the other end of the process, Lew Bateman and Robert Dreesen were excellent editors. From our first conversation at a Polmeth poster session in 2011, Lew was passionate about the project, and he helped me refine it through a series of meetings over four years. He retired just as I was finally ready to submit the manuscript for review, but I hope he is satisfied to see the finished book. Robert shepherded me through the review process and recruited three careful, critical, and conscientious reviewers who improved the manuscript substantially.

I owe a great deal to my teachers over the years. Arabic is a hard language for me and it has been crucial for all of the research reported in the pages that follow. My first Arabic instruction was with Doug Bradford, dubbed *al-jaysh* by the class because of his demand for military precision. Doug, Shareen Salah, and Dil Parkinson at BYU, and later Bill Granara at Harvard, all tried to instill proper grammar with varying degrees of success. For essential training in statistics I thank Jeremy Pope, Adam Glynn, Gary King, Kevin Quinn, Edo Airoldi, Xiao-Li Meng, and especially Joe Blitzstein, whose Statistics 110 class at Harvard is perhaps the best I have ever taken. Don Rubin was particularly generous with his time and support during my time as a master's student in the Harvard Statistics Department. Jon Bischof's morose humor buoyed me through the many statistics classes we took together, and I also benefited from the camaraderie and mathematical prowess of Patrick Lam, Maya Sen, and Omar Wasow.

While in graduate school, Brandon Stewart, Yuri Zhukov, Jeff Friedman, and Iain Osgood were a crucial brain trust that shaped the early course of this project. I benefited immensely from conversations with other graduate student colleagues: Ashley Anderson, Tyson Belanger, Oliver Bevan, Matt Blackwell, Brett Carter, Amy Catalinac, Josh Cherniss, Andrew Coe, Andrew Eggers, Noam Gidron, Justin Grimmer, Jens Hainmueller, Masha Hedberg, Alisha Holland, Sean Ingham, Didi Kuo, Matt Landauer, Jennifer Larson, Danial Lashkari, Yascha Mounk, Clayton Nall, Vipin Narang, Jennifer Pan, Eleanor

Powell, Jonathan Renshon, Molly Roberts, Shahrzad Sabet, Evann Smith, Chiara Superti, Elina Treyger, Brandon Van Dyck, Jane Vaynman, Joseph Williams, and Miya Woolfalk. A number of Harvard faculty members were very generous with their time and comments, including Jeffry Frieden, Nahomi Ichino, Peter Hall, Iain Johnston, Dustin Tingley, Arthur Spirling, Prerna Singh, Baber Johansen, Jocelyne Cesari, and Daniel Ziblatt.

Outside of Harvard, I received crucial feedback on the research in this book from too many people to adequately thank, but I was particularly influenced by comments from Amaney Jamal, Dan Corstange, Rob Blair, Jesse Driscoll, Justin Gest, Josh Gubler, David Laitin, Marc Lynch, Will McCants, Harris Mylonas, and Gabriel Koehler-Derrick. Lisa Blaydes has helped me in many ways over the years. Scott Gehlbach wandered into a poster session where I was presenting and asked some especially perceptive questions. Brian Haggerty helped me understand how scholars of religion write about Islam. Jillian Schwedler has always asked me hard questions and forced me to answer them well. Thomas Hegghammer is responsible for the most intellectually stimulating afternoon I've ever spent at the Boston airport. I have pages and pages of remarkably helpful notes, without adequate names, from presentations I gave to audiences at the University of Michigan, New York University, University of Washington, University of California Berkeley, Northwestern University, and the annual meetings of the American Political Science Association and the Association for Analytical Learning about Islam and Muslim Societies. I gave a particularly memorable talk at the home of John and Cindy Reed, who invited me to share this research with a distinguished group. Bob Millard's comments to me at the end of the night were especially encouraging.

As a graduate student at Harvard, I received funding from the Institute for Quantitative Social Science and the Weatherhead Center for International Affairs, both at Harvard University. Some of this research was conducted while I was a predoctoral fellow at the Harvard Academy for International and Area Studies, where I deeply enjoyed the intellectual environment. The National Science Foundation has supported this project twice while I was in graduate school: first through a Graduate Research Fellowship that provided me with stipendiary support for three years of graduate work, and again through a Doctoral Dissertation Improvement Grant (number 1159298) in the final stages of completion. Without these resources, my time in graduate school would have been substantially more difficult and this project would have been impossible. I am fully cognizant that this represents a substantial investment in my early career by the taxpayers of the United States; I hope that my work is of sufficient importance to merit this trust.

The Massachusetts Institute of Technology has generously supported my research since 2013. MIT's Center for International Studies, Security Studies Program, and International Policy Lab have provided financial and intellectual support. My colleagues in the Political Science Department are magnificent. Fotini Christia and Taylor Fravel gave me comments on the entire manuscript;

Taylor and Vipin Narang helped with crucial advice about book publishing; Suzanne Berger, Dick Samuels, and Barry Posen have given me the opportunity to present to influential audiences; Chap Lawson helped me make the hard call to trim some extraneous material; and everyone in the department has improved this book through countless conversations in the hallway and over lunch. A research leave from MIT in 2015–2016 was especially helpful as I was finishing the manuscript. I spent my leave year at the Crown Center for Middle East Studies at Brandeis University, led by Shai Feldman, where I benefited immensely from exchanges with Pascal Menoret, Eva Bellin, Hikmet Kocamaner, Naghmeh Sohrabi, and a number of others. David Patel offered crucial wit and wisdom as we each hammered out our manuscripts. These conversations at the Crown Center, interspersed with productive periods of time to focus on my writing, were crucial for completing the manuscript.

In the fall of 2015, I had an amazing book conference with Carrie Wickham, Melani Cammett, Malika Zeghal, Tom Pepinsky, Tarek Masoud, and long-distance comments from Ron Hassner. I'm indebted to each of them for providing detailed comments on the entire manuscript. Tom drove through the night from Ithaca after the weather grounded his plane, a sacrifice I won't soon forget.

I've had excellent research assistance on various parts of this project. Marsin Alshamary provided some translations, read and coded a large number of Wikipedia articles, took notes at my book conference, and did a million other things between 2012 and 2016. Emma Smith helped with text classification over the summer of 2014 and entertained me with interesting conversations about the coincidental relation of her name to Mormon history. Over the summer of 2015, Vincent Bauer collected and organized the writings of clerics. Michael Freedman helped with curating the replication materials, and Elisha Cohen helped with various odds and ends.

I'm grateful for friends I made during my fieldwork in Egypt, especially Diaa, Salman, Fahmi, and Ismail. Everyone at the al-Azhar mosque was kind and welcoming, and many were exceptionally patient with my questions and generous with their answers.

Closer to home, my remarkable friends in Cambridge got me through the book-writing process. I love the Outstitute crew more than I can express. Dan Hadley put up with endless musings about this project on the way to surf breaks. Peter McMurray memorized portions of the Quran with me every morning for a year, and he and Ari Schriber were excellent Arabic reading companions. Later, the Second Sunday reading group led by Zachary Davis and Laurel Ulrich read the introduction and made a number of helpful comments.

My family has been my biggest source of support. Life would have been far less interesting without my creative and talented siblings. Rebecca's suggestion that I take Scott Cooper's introductory international relations class put me on the path to becoming a political scientist, and her encouragement has been essential ever since. My mother, a professional writer, read much of the manuscript and attempted to improve my infelicitous writing style. My children, Jonas and Willa, have been patient with my absences. My wife, Leslie, has supported me from the beginning to the end of this project. It is to her that I dedicate this book.

Note on Arabic transliteration: Throughout, I use *International Journal of Middle East Studies* standards for transliteration. Accordingly, I use "ʿ" for *ayin* (a voiced pharyngeal fricative) and "ʾ" for *hamza* (a glottal stop). I do not include these diacritics for proper names of people.

This material is based on work supported by the National Science Foundation under a Doctoral Dissertation Improvement Grant (1159298) and the National Science Foundation Graduate Research Fellowship Program. Any opinions, findings, and conclusions or recommendations expressed in this material are those of the author and do not necessarily reflect the views of the National Science Foundation.

Why Clerics Turn Deadly

In July 2010, the media wing of al-Qaeda interviewed the American-born jihadist[1] cleric[2] Anwar al-Awlaki from a secret location in Yemen. One striking element of the resulting video is that throughout, al-Awlaki's remarks reflect the trappings of academia. Rather than emphasizing his violent credentials, the introductory frames recount al-Awlaki's curriculum vitae, including a BA from the University of Colorado and a master's from San Diego State University.[3] After welcoming him, the interviewer asks what al-Awlaki's role was in inciting Major Nidal Hasan to carry out the Fort Hood shooting in November 2009. His response? "Yes, Nidal Hasan was a *student* of mine and I am honored by this" (emphasis mine, na'am, niḍāl ḥasan min ṭulābī, wa ānā ātasharaf bidhalik), revealing that when portraying himself to his fellow jihadists, al-Awlaki defines himself primarily as a scholar and teacher rather than as a fighter or dissident.[4]

---

[1] Jihadist ideology is a set of ideas organized around the central claim that Islam should be the organizing principle of human affairs and that violence is an acceptable means for pursuing this goal. I use the terms "jihadi" and "jihadist" to denote a person, thing, or organization that is associated with jihadist ideology. These are the most common terms for these individuals and organizations in academic literature, and are literal translations of the term that these actors prefer. Hegghammer (2009) and Hegghammer (2010a) propose alternative terms based on the variety of jihadists' goals and methods.

[2] There is no uncontested definition of the term "cleric" when applied to Muslim religious elites. For my purposes, a cleric is a person who produces Islamic literature and who may or may not claim a lineage of scholarly authority. I defend my definition in detail in Chapter 2.

[3] It appears that al-Awlaki is inflating his credentials. He started but never finished a degree at San Diego State University.

[4] "Anwar Al Awlaki Al Malahem Interview FULL ENGLISH Translation," YouTube video, posted July 20, 2014, www.youtube.com/watch?v=eInGfXV3YvY, min. 8:13, accessed July 27, 2015, and archived at http://dx.doi.org/10.7910/DVN/PG4A7K.

Al-Awlaki is not the only jihadist who styles himself an academic. Abu Bakr al-Baghdadi, leader of the Islamic State in Iraq and Syria (ISIS), released a curriculum vitae that was vague on details but touted his PhD from the University of Baghdad and his purported reputation as a knowledgeable scholar of Islamic law. Ayman al-Zawahiri, the current leader of al-Qaeda, writes prodigious tomes with scores of academic-style citations. Like any citation-obsessed academic, Abu Muhammad al-Maqdisi, one of the most prominent jihadist theoreticians, crowed about being identified in a 2006 RAND study as the most influential living jihadist thinker based on citations by featuring the study on his website. And even Usama Bin Laden, the now-deceased leader of al-Qaeda, imitated the academic pretension of taking photographs in front of bookshelves to convey learned authority.[5]

This book explores the academic culture of jihadist clerics to illuminate how jihadist ideology is produced and reproduced among the elites of the jihadist movement. Scholars of Islamic law such as Zeghal (1996, 34) understand that Muslim clerics are academics who strive for a life of pious learning, often with professional titles that exactly mirror those of academics in other settings. However, scholarship on political violence has frequently overlooked the academic identities of jihadist clerics, instead conceptualizing them primarily as religious leaders, preachers, writers, extremists, and militants. Clerics can turn to violence for a variety of reasons, but I focus on two major pathways. The first way to become a jihadist cleric is to become a jihadist first and a cleric later. As I show later, these *jihadists-turned-clerics* can be understood through existing models of lay Muslim radicalization.

The second pathway to jihadism that I describe highlights an overlooked aspect of cleric radicalization: a surprisingly mundane set of academic career pressures that can push clerics toward militant jihadist ideas. My core argument is that *blocked ambition* – the inability of an actor to achieve a substantial, deeply held goal – nudges clerics toward jihadism. Blocked ambition is a common human experience and has been suggested as a cause of radicalization in other contexts. When the ambition of a cleric to become an academic is blocked by failure on the cleric job market or by state repression, those clerics whose ambitions are blocked are at much greater risk of becoming jihadist. To put the argument colloquially, I offer a disgruntled-graduate-student theory of jihad.

The divide is stark: clerics who find gainful employment in state-dominated academic, religious, and political institutions in the Middle East are extremely unlikely to preach violent jihad, while those who work outside of this system are more likely to end up preaching violence. Of course, it may be the case that some clerics with state-funded jobs secretly endorse jihadism, but secretly held beliefs are not my concern. Instead, I seek to understand those clerics who openly preach and incite political violence.

---

5   http://ichef.bbci.co.uk/news/660/media/images/83127000/jpg/_83127737_83127321.jpg, accessed February 9, 2017, and archived at http://dx.doi.org/10.7910/DVN/PG4A7K.

Proving that some clerics become jihadists because their academic ambitions are blocked is not an easy task. In the chapters that follow, I demonstrate that indicators of blocked ambition in the lives of would-be clerics – weak graduate school networks, nonacademic jobs, and removal from academic posts – are highly correlated with whether clerics preach jihadist ideas. Of course, there are other plausible explanations for this outcome: some would-be clerics develop jihadist ideas early and never seek a traditional academic career, and even if they do, they may be shut out of traditional academic circles precisely because their ideas are already too radical. Sorting out the various pathways to jihadism is difficult, and even though I provide a substantial amount of new quantitative and qualitative data on jihadist clerics, the evidence I can provide remains circumstantial. However, it represents the outer frontier of what is currently knowable about why some clerics advocate jihadism.

This introductory chapter lays the groundwork for the remainder of the book by previewing the argument and the evidence. In Section 1.1, I lay out the terms of the debate surrounding the rise of modern jihadism and consider whether the causes of radicalization identified in other contexts might also explain why clerics turn to violent jihad. Section 1.2 sketches the theory of blocked ambition. I first provide contextual information about how the norms, practices, and politics of Islamic legal academia deeply pervade the lives of Muslim clerics. I then explain how the ambition of clerics to advance within academia shapes their behavior and expression, and how finding this ambition blocked can put them on a path to jihadism. Section 1.3 describes how I use a combination of methods ranging from ethnography to statistics to test my argument. Section 1.4 considers the ethics of researching militant jihadism, and Section 1.5 concludes by summarizing the plan of the book and the content of the subsequent chapters.

1.1 UNDERSTANDING THE RISE OF MODERN JIHADISM

Few ideologies have influenced international affairs in the twenty-first century more than militant jihadism. Modern jihadism is a movement founded around an ideology that claims to hearken back to the founding doctrines of Islam but is in fact a relatively recent phenomenon. At its core, jihadism is violent Islamism. It is Islamism because jihadist ideology holds that society should be governed by Islamic doctrines (according to jihadists' interpretation of Islam). It is inherently violent because jihadists hold that violence is a legitimate means for achieving the society and government they desire. Modern jihadists reach these conclusions by drawing a doctrinal connection between the foundational Islamic concept of God's sovereignty to the violent imposition of the society and government that jihadists believe God desires. For jihadists, God's sovereignty requires that only God's laws be followed, so any form of government that does not take God's laws as its own should be resisted and replaced, violently if necessary. From this foundational claim, jihadist apologists work to develop interpretations of Islamic law that permit violence in a variety of circumstances to achieve jihadist political goals, though jihadists differ about precisely how these goals should be pursued and what form an ideal Islamic government should take.

Modern jihadism has been developing by fits and starts over the past century. Abu al-Ala Mawdudi (1903–1979), Hassan al-Banna (1906–1949), and Sayyid Qutb (1906–1966) each developed and refined ideas that would come to constitute the framing principles of modern jihadism. Still, modern jihadism did not really come into existence until the intellectual development provided by Abdullah Azzam (1941–1989) and the violent Egyptian Islamism of the 1980s and 1990s. In fact, Hegghammer dates the dawn of the modern jihadist era to as recently as 1979 or 1980 (Hegghammer 2010a, 3).

Observers at the end of the twentieth century might be forgiven for overlooking signs that names like "Bin Laden" and the "Islamic State" would become household terms. Data from the Google n-grams project shows that the term "jihad" was relatively infrequent in English-language books until 1950, when its use began to rise dramatically.[6] By the eve of the September 11, 2001, attack on the World Trade Center and targets in Washington, DC, and Pennsylvania, the term "jihad" was being used seven times as often as in 1950. Usama Bin Laden's name does not register until 1998, the year in which he directed attacks against the US embassy in Nairobi, Kenya, and came to the attention of the American public for the first time. Even then, Flagg Miller writes, "Bin Laden's role in global affairs was not immediately apparent to Muslim audiences familiar with his career" (Miller 2015, 9). Then, in 2001, the September 11 attack catapulted jihadism and Bin Laden to the fore of American consciousness and foreign policy. Reference to "jihad" in English-language books approximately tripled from its 2000 value, and Bin Laden's name became roughly nine times more frequent, exceeding references to "jihad" itself. On the day of his death, Bin Laden was the subject of virtually every headline and a substantial amount of web activity.[7]

Today, militant jihadism is perhaps the most widely influential revolutionary ideology in the international system, having shaped world events over the last twenty years and still posing a remarkably durable challenge to the existing international order. Nationalist strains of jihadism have fueled tenacious territorial conflicts in Palestine, Chechnya, and elsewhere. Transnational jihadists have called for the complete overthrow of the existing international system and virtually all of the norms that undergird it (Mendelsohn 2009), and have followed through with dramatic acts of political violence. As a result, US

---

[6] The Google n-grams project tracks the frequency of words in approximately 15 percent of all English-language books ever published. I obtain data on the use of the word "jihad" from https://books.google.com/ngrams/graph?direct_url=t1%3B%2Cjihad%3B%2Cco, archived.

[7] Google search trends for "bin laden" show a dramatic spike on the day of his death: www.google.com/trends/explore?date=all&q=bin%20laden, archived.

foreign policy has been dominated by the specter of jihadism in a way that few anticipated even during the tense weeks following the September 11 attacks. By October 2001, the US military was striking targets in Afghanistan in a war that would officially last thirteen years. In 2003, the United States launched a second war against Iraq, lasting almost nine years. Although the initial impetus for war was not to root out jihadists, the administration of President George W. Bush consistently referred to Iraq as a front in the "war on terror,"[8] and the power vacuum that ensued after American forces toppled the government of Saddam Hussein was filled, in part, by a tenacious jihadist insurgency aimed at both ousting American forces and settling scores with Shia militias.

Even after the official end of the Iraq war, the remnants of this insurgency haunt US foreign policy interests in the Middle East. After apparent defeat in 2007, an insurgent group named the Islamic State of Iraq grasped the opportunities offered by the neighboring Syrian civil war, reinvented itself as the Islamic State of Iraq and Syria, and declared itself a jihadist state under Emir Abu Bakr al-Baghdadi. A 2014 RAND Corporation study reports that "beginning in 2010, there was a rise in the number of Salafi-jihadist groups and fighters, particularly in Syria and North Africa. There was also an increase in the number of attacks perpetrated by al-Qa'ida and its affiliates" (Jones 2014, x). Despite US efforts to pivot away from the Middle East after fifteen years of fighting jihadists, the next decade of American foreign policy is likely to be as dominated by counter-jihadism as the last.

What explains the rise and persistence of modern jihadism? Broadly speaking, scholars have taken two approaches to answering this question. The first approach attempts to develop general theories to explain rebellion and then applies these theories to understand jihadist movements (see, for example, Della Porta 2013). A key debate in this scholarship is whether rebellion is primarily caused by the grievances of those who rebel or by structural conditions that provide opportunities for violent collective action. This approach results in parsimonious theories of rebellion, but these explanations sometimes struggle to explain specific aspects of jihadist violence. A second approach starts from the specific circumstances and details of jihadist movements and traces the apparent causes of their rise using the tools of history, sociology, and anthropology. This work is especially well attuned to the nuance and texture of jihadists and their social movements, but these explanations are often contextually specific and refer to unique historical moments and the idiosyncrasies of individuals.

My argument in this book draws on both of these approaches. I explain the choices of some Muslim clerics to preach jihad using a theory of blocked ambition that hearkens back to general theories of grievance and rebellion, but

---

8 Garamone, Jim. "Iraq Part of Global War on Terrorism, Rumsfeld Says." DoD News. http://archive.defense.gov/news/newsarticle.aspx?id=43444, accessed February 9, 2017, and archived at http://dx.doi.org/10.7910/DVN/PG4A7K.

I highlight particular forms of blocked ambition that are specific to the context of modern jihadism.

Among the scholarship that develops general theories of rebellion, the argument of Gurr (1970) that grievances motivate rebels is the most direct predecessor to my theory of blocked ambition. There has been a great deal of work before and since, but Gurr's *Why Men Rebel* remains one of the clearest applications of the frustration-aggression hypothesis (Dollard et al. 1939) to the problem of political violence. Gurr focuses on the choice of individuals to rebel and argues that individuals get angry when they feel they should be getting more resources and opportunities than they are. This sense of mismatch between expectations and outcomes can arise because individuals have higher expectations than before, or because their ability to realize those expectations is lower, or both (Gurr 1970, 46). In Gurr's argument, if people become angry enough because of their relative deprivation in society, they will rebel when the opportunity presents itself.

This argument is a predecessor to my own argument that clerics' blocked ambitions can push them toward the violent ideas of militant jihadism. The novel aspect of my argument is in detailing the specific features of blocked ambition for clerics. Although Gurr is theorizing about the psychology of frustrated individuals, he tends to focus on sources of relative deprivation relevant to broad societal groups across many contexts: discrimination, economic decline, and repression (Gurr and Duvall 1973, 138–139). I focus instead on a form of blocked ambition that is specific to individuals who would like to become Muslim clerics in the specific context of the modern Middle East and Muslim world.

I am not the first scholar to propose the idea that jihadists are inspired by a mismatch between their circumstances and their expectations. Many scholars have pointed to poverty and marginalization as possible explanations for the rise of jihadist violence. For example, Ansari (1984, 141) examines the jihadist assassins of Anwar Sadat in Egypt and concludes that "the militant view is confined to a segment of the population on the margin of urban society. ... For this segment of the population which is experiencing an acute sense of deprivation, the resort to Islam was more a sign of social protest than a way of life." Kepel (1984, 128), also speaking of Egypt, says that, "In the ramshackle dwellings of the suburbs ringing the large Egyptian cities, people by-passed by the progress and development turned towards other, more radical tendencies of the Islamicist movement." Ayubi (2003) agrees that the dissatisfactions of the middle class in the Middle East explain the surprising number of students and professionals involved in the jihadist movement in Sadat's Egypt. "While the middle strata have been expanding in size and in proportion in most Arab societies, their rising expectations (stimulated in particular by the acquisition of higher education and by the move to urban centres), are being severely frustrated because of the constrained nature of economic development in these societies" (Ayubi 2003, 159–160).

However, grievance-based explanations have drawn substantial criticism on a number of grounds and are somewhat out of fashion in the current literature on political violence. Gurr's argument was criticized by Tilly (1978, 23) for "neglect[ing] the analysis of organization and mobilization in favor of a view of collective action as a resultant of interest plus opportunity," and Oberschall (1978, 300) says it "lacks explanatory power." These critics follow the logic of Trotsky, that "the mere existence of privations is not enough to cause an insurrection; if it were, the masses would be always in revolt" (Trotsky 1932, 353). Hafez (2003, 9–15) applies these critiques of grievance-based theories to the problem of jihadist militancy, pointing out that conditions of disappointing economic underperformance and tumultuous social change have been endemic to Muslim-majority states in the Middle East, but levels of violence in these countries have varied substantially. These critics have tended to support explanations that focus on the ways social movements facilitate collective action.

The second approach to understanding the rise of jihadism has been to start from the phenomenon itself and to propose more limited, short-range theories and explanations. Scholars in this tradition emphasize the influence of human agency on the rise and course of the jihadi movement. Hegghammer (2010a, 10), for example, argues that structural accounts have only limited ability to explain jihadist violence in Saudi Arabia since 1980 because "violent contestation requires actors who can mobilize followers and operationalise intentions." Hegghammer therefore focuses a great deal on individuals, amassing an impressive collection of Saudi militant biographies and highlighting the unique roles of individuals such as Abdullah Azzam and Hamud al-Shu'aybi.

Another example of this approach is Madawi Al-Rasheed's (2007) analysis of religious protest and violence in Saudi Arabia. Al-Rasheed highlights many potential causes but argues that, fundamentally, the adoption of Wahhabist[9] ideology – a form of conservative, revivalist Islam – by the authoritarian Saudi state fueled the rise of various strains of Wahhabism. When the state came under pressure from forces of globalization, it lost control of Wahhabist discourse, and jihadism emerged as one extension of Wahhabist ideas.

The main challenge to these explanations is that they are too context dependent to be useful as theoretical explanations, and the scholars writing these accounts focus on descriptions of how jihadism developed in a particular time and place, rather than exploring the deeper causes that might be common to many contexts. For example, while it is true that charisma and force of will of individuals like Abdullah Azzam and Usama Bin Laden are important for the development of modern jihadism, this explanation is unsatisfying in its

---

9   Wahhabism is a form of conservative, revivalist Islam that is intellectually tied to the teachings and legacy of Muhammad Abd al-Wahhab (1703–1792) in Saudi Arabia. It is related to, though not wholly synonymous with, Salafism (Commins 2015).

specificity. Would jihadism have come to Saudi Arabia if Bin Laden had taken a different life course? These explanations cannot say.

Beyond the scholarship that is focused on jihadism, I use a wide-ranging literature on Islamism and Islamist[10] mobilization to develop my theory of blocked ambition (e.g., Wickham 2002; Blaydes and Linzer 2008; Brown 2012; Pepinsky, Liddle, and Mujani 2012; Cammett and Luong 2014; Masoud 2014. Much of this work examines Islamist moderation and radicalization: Can formerly militant Islamist groups decide to participate in politics as "normal" actors if they are brought into the formal political system (Schwedler 2011, 2007)? If so, does inclusion lead to moderation because the individuals who lead Islamist groups change their minds (Wickham 2013)? Or do Islamists moderate because political structure compels them to change their behavior, even if their ideology remains the same (El-Ghobashy 2005, 375)? My argument and evidence weigh in on this debate about whether inclusion leads to moderation: I find that those individuals with careers inside state-supervised educational and religions institutions are far less likely to preach violence than those who are turned away from such careers.

I am not alone in drawing on both general theories of rebellion and specific examinations of the jihadist phenomenon to proffer an account of why people become violent jihadists. In addition to the scholarship already noted, recent accounts of jihadist radicalization by scholars such as Sageman (2004) and Wiktorowicz (2005b) incorporate insights from broad theories of rebellion and the specific literature on jihadists. My aim in this book is not to replace existing accounts of the rise of modern jihadism but rather to enrich them by exploring the choices of individual clerics to preach jihadism. Recent scholarship demonstrates that individuals can dramatically affect international relations (Byman and Pollack 2001; Chiozza and Goemans 2011; Horowitz, Stam, and Ellis 2015), a finding that stands in contrast with earlier work that minimized the role of individuals (e.g., Waltz 1979). Examining the choices of individual clerics addresses a recent critique that, "despite over a decade of government funding and thousands of newcomers to the field," scholars are "no closer to answering the simple question of 'What leads a person to turn to political violence?'" (Sageman 2014, 565). Despite the challenges of studying the choices of individuals (Stern 2014), insight as to why individuals turn to violence, or in this case to preaching violence, will be most forthcoming from studies that take individuals as the primary unit of analysis.

Are jihadist clerics important to jihadist movements? If not, then offering an explanation of why some people become jihadist clerics will not advance the broader agenda of explaining jihadism. Jihadist clerics matter because

[10] In scholarship on political Islam, the term "Islamist" refers to actors who believe that Islam should be the organizing principle of society and the basis of its laws, and who are engaged in political action to achieve this aim. Jihadists are Islamists who approve of violence, but most Islamists reject political violence and are thus not jihadists.

they are the idea entrepreneurs whose beliefs and teachings provide doctrine and framing for jihadist social movements. Existing scholarship suggests that clerics play a crucial role in motivating lay Muslims who perpetrate violence (Sageman 2004; Wiktorowicz 2005*b*). Those perpetrating jihadist violence have repeatedly invoked the ideas of clerics, and jihadists tend to commit violence in ways consistent with the beliefs they profess (Hegghammer 2013). Counterterrorism officials see jihadist preachers as grave threats, going so far as to call one of them, Anwar al-Awlaki, "the most dangerous man in the world" in 2010.[11] Jihadist terrorists who have carried out attacks in the United States appear to have been influenced by preachers such as al-Awlaki.[12] And according to commentators such as Greame Wood (2015) and Will McCants (2015), the religious ideas promoted by jihadist clerics are fundamental to the motivations of jihadist groups and their visions for the future.

However, the assertion that jihadist violence is caused by religious ideas has stirred controversy (Cottee 2017), and some question whether the ideas of jihadist clerics are relevant for understanding the rise of the jihadist movement. Foust, for example, has argued that the importance of the ideas jihadist clerics preach is overstated: "Ideology is a woefully incomplete explanation for why terrorists chose to commit terror."[13]

The contention that jihadist ideology is largely irrelevant to the jihadist movement, and thus to world affairs, comes in two flavors. First, the obvious congruence between the forms of jihadi violence and the professed beliefs of jihadists could merely demonstrate that jihadists will say anything to justify their actions. There are limits to how plastic Islamic law can be, but jihadists have a track record of issuing Islamic legal rulings supporting extreme violence that is normally forbidden. For example, to justify their burning of a Jordanian fighter pilot, the Islamic State issued a fatwa, quoted in Chapter 2 of this book,

---

[11] Cole, Matthew and Aaron Ketersky. "Awlaki: 'The Most Dangerous Man in The World'" ABC News. http://abcnews.go.com/Blotter/awlaki-dangerous-man-world/story?id= 12109217, accessed February 9, 2017, and archived at http://dx.doi.org/10.7910/DVN/ PG4A7K.

[12] "Investigators believe OSU attacker self-radicalized, inspired by ISIS propaganda." FoxNews.com. www.foxnews.com/us/2016/11/29/investigators-believe-osu-attacker-self-radi calized-inspired-by-isis-propaganda.html, accessed February 11, 2017, and archived; Serrano, Richard. "Boston bombing indictment: Dzhokhar Tsarnaev inspired by Al Qaeda." *Los Angeles Times.* http://articles.latimes.com/2013/jun/27/nation/la-na-nn-boston-marathon-bombing-suspect-indictment-20130627, accessed February 11, 2017, and archived; *United States of America vs. Dzhohar Tsarnaev,* indictment, United States District Court, Massachusetts, https://assets.documentcloud.org/documents/718914/tsarnaev-indictment. pdf, accessed February 11, 2017, and archived.

[13] See Foust, Joshua. "GUEST POST: Some Inchoate Thoughts on Ideology." Jihadology.net. http://jihadology.net/2011/01/19/guest-post-some-inchoate-thoughts-on-ideology, accessed July 31, 2015; Foust, Joshua. "GUEST POST: Jihadi Ideology Is Not As Important As We Think." http://jihadology.net/2011/01/25/guest-post-jihadi-ideology-is-not-as-important-as-we-think, accessed July 31, 2015. Both articles are archived at http://dx.doi.org/ 10.7910/DVN/PG4A7K.

in which they make an argument that clearly runs counter to the traditional Islamic legal view that punishment by fire belongs only to God.

Second, even if jihadist ideas cause the form of violence, ideas may not cause violence itself. If jihadism did not exist, the argument goes, then structural factors such as persistent authoritarianism, poor economic opportunity, and long-term demographic trends would cause disaffected young men in the Middle East to rebel under the banner of communism, pan-Arabism, or some other ideology.[14] Of course, world history cannot be run twice, once with jihadism and once without it, so this is a difficult claim to either prove or disprove. More generally, because it is impossible to directly perceive the mental states of other individuals, it is difficult to conclusively demonstrate that ideas have a causal impact on politics (O'Mahoney 2015).

A large research tradition takes up the challenge of showing that ideas shape political outcomes in various domains (Reich 1988; Hall 1989; Goldstein and Keohane 1993; Blyth 1997; Wendt 1999; Blyth 2001; Philpott 2001; Blyth 2003; Chwieroth 2007; Culpepper 2008; Jacobs 2009; Mehta 2011; Nelson 2014), with a particular focus on the role of religious ideas, such as jihadism, in international affairs (Fox 2000; Hasenclever and Rittberger 2000; Philpott 2000; Fox 2003; Toft 2007; Horowitz 2009; Hassner 2009; Hassner and Horowitz 2010; Hassner 2011; Toft, Philpott, and Shah 2011; Hassner 2016). The dominant approach is to link ideas to political outcomes using reports from the actors involved. For example, Wagemakers (2012, 22) studies the influence of jihadist ideologue Abu Muhammad al-Maqdisi by following citations to al-Maqdisi's work, tracking unattributed intellectual borrowing of his ideas, and interviewing Islamists about his influence. However, this approach can only assess influence in a thin, scholarly sense: other jihadists may be influenced by al-Maqdisi, as evidenced by citations and intellectual borrowing, but this does not mean that these individuals were originally drawn to jihadism *because* of al-Maqdisi. And it does little to disprove the claim that just as much violence would have occurred in a counterfactual world where al-Maqdisi had never written anything. Most available evidence of the importance of ideas for jihadists is similarly circumstantial: jihadists who commit violence claim to follow the teachings of jihadist clerics and assert that these teachings inspire them to fight.[15]

---

14 David Laitin, personal communication.

15 In a survey of fifty fighting jihadists in Syria, Mironova, Mrie, and Whitt (2014) ask, "Have you heard or read the Islamic teachings of any of the following?" followed by a list of current official scholars from the fighters' group Jabhat al-Nusra, and four prominent jihadist ideologues from outside the group. By and large, these clerics were widely recognized by fighters: Abu Musab al-Suri 84 percent recognition, Abu Qatada al-Filistini 59 percent, Abu Muhammad al-Maqdisi 49 percent, Abu Maria al-Qahtani (al-Nusra) 47 percent, Sulayman Bin Nasr al-Ulwan 41 percent, Abu Sulayman al-Muhajir (al-Nusra) 35 percent, and Sami al-Oraidi (al-Nusra) 35 percent. Sixty-three percent of these fighters selected the statement "fatwas by the Ulama affect my decision to fight" as one of their reasons for fighting.

Other scholars have used quantitative data to suggest that ideas matter. Using an experimental design, Masoud, Jamal, and Nugent (2016) show that exposing Egyptian survey participants to a quotation from the Quran framed as an argument in favor of women's political equality increases their support for gender equality. And using an experiment in Kenya, McClendon and Riedl (2015) demonstrate that appeals to religious ideas can cause more or less political participation.

However, it is difficult to use experiments to study the effects of ideas on political violence in an ethical way. Instead, some scholars have turned to "natural experiment" designs that exploit random variation in access to media during episodes of political violence to show that access to media influences the violent actions of individuals and groups. Yanagizawa-Drott (2014) examines the effects of radio propaganda on violence during the 1994 Rwandan genocide by comparing violence in villages where radio signal was available to villages where radio was blocked by natural variation in Rwanda's topography. This comparison shows that up to 51,000 perpetrators of violence are attributable to the effect of radio, comprising 10 percent of the total violence. Another study by Adena et al. (2015) uses similar variation in radio signal to link Nazi radio broadcasts to violence against Jews in pre–World War II Germany. Because such "natural experiments" are the result of historical accident, it is difficult to design such a study on jihadism specifically, but it is likely that if ideas motivate political violence in other settings, they motivate jihadists as well.

Despite the key role of revolutionary ideas in political violence, their origins and production are not always well understood because the effort to conclusively demonstrate that ideas "matter" has distracted the field from the question of where ideas come from and how they spread. The large literature on jihadism[16] offers relatively few solid conjectures about which factors cause some clerics to preach violent jihadist activism because the focus has been on the fighters, not the preachers.

1.2 THE RADICALIZATION OF JIHADIST CLERICS

Why do some individuals become jihadist clerics? To answer this question, we must first ask *when* the individuals in question radicalized. Did the individual become a jihadist first and a cleric later, or a cleric first and a jihadist later? The likely paths to jihadism for these two categories of people are quite different.

Those who become jihadists first and clerics later often follow a trajectory that may be familiar to most readers: an angst-ridden young man finds a radical mentor, typically through his network of friends, and then comes to believe and

---

[16] Wiktorowicz (2001*b*); Gerges (2005); Devji (2005); McCants (2006); Habeck (2006); Lia (2008); Brachman (2009); Mendelsohn (2009); Hegghammer (2010*a,b*); Lahoud (2010); Moghadam and Fishman (2011); Wagemakers (2012); Deol and Kazmi (2012); Hegghammer (2013); Shapiro (2013).

act upon violent religious ideas. The career of Abu Muhammad al-Maqdisi, perhaps the most influential living jihadist theologian, fits this mold: al-Maqdisi was exposed to Islamist teaching through a Muslim Brotherhood member at his local mosque and gradually sought out additional teachers, each more jihadist than the last, until he wholly embraced Salafi[17] jihadism. After attempting to fight in Afghanistan, al-Maqdisi concluded that his talents were more suited to scholarship and turned to writing a now-influential body of scholarly apologia for jihadism.

This pathway to jihadism is familiar because it has been observed repeatedly in the literature on lay Muslim radicalization, which generally points to poverty,[18] psychology,[19] and socialization[20] as important factors. For future clerics who radicalize before deciding to become clerics, the critical period of radicalization occurs while they are still lay Muslims, so it is no surprise that these existing theories of lay radicalization would generally apply.

My argument applies to the second category, those who become clerics first and jihadists second. I argue that pursuing a career as a Muslim cleric creates a new set of ambitions, incentives, and constraints that changes the processes through which an individual is most likely to be radicalized. For these individuals, a cleric-specific theory of radicalization is necessary – one that acknowledges the particular set of incentives and trade-offs that would-be clerics face as members of an academic culture.

Consider the story of Nasr al-Fahd. In the early 1990s, al-Fahd was a star in Saudi academia. Appointed as a dean at Umm al-Qura University in 1992, his research interests tended more toward strict interpretations of historical authors rather than the *Sahwa* Islamist wave sweeping through Saudi Arabia. However, he did risk some political activity and landed in jail for writing a poem that insulted one of the Saudi prince's wives. Unfortunately for al-Fahd, his offense coincided with a Saudi crackdown on Islamist leaders, which included harsh prison sentences for those the government viewed as offenders. While the imprisoned Islamist leaders gained respect among the leaders of the Sahwa movement as a result of their political imprisonment, al-Fahd did not. The

---

[17] Salafism is a reform movement within Islam that seeks to return to the supposed practices and beliefs of the first three generations of pious Muslims. Jihadists are almost invariably Salafi Sunnis, though most Salafi Sunnis are not jihadists. For a discussion of the bifurcation between violent and nonviolent traditions in Salafism, see Wiktorowicz (2005c). For a general overview of Salafism, see Meijer (2009). It is also important to note that Islam is bifurcated into two main sects: a majority Sunni sect and a minority Shi'i sect. These traditions have developed along different lines since their split during a seventh-century succession crisis in Islam. Because of differences in the nature of religious authority in Sunni and Shi'i Islam, my argument applies only to Sunni clerics.

[18] See Keefer and Loayza (2008); Krueger (2007); Krueger and Maleckova (2003); and Enders, Hoover, and Sandler (2014).

[19] See Victoroff (2005); Post et al. (2009); Lester, Yang, and Lindsay (2004); and King and Taylor (2011).

[20] See Wiktorowicz (2005b) and Sageman (2004).

leaders of these Islamists were later released and the Saudi state placed them back in positions of relative scholarly comfort and security as a way of buying their acquiescence to the regime's authority. But al-Fahd was not given his position back. With academia permanently closed to him, this former star of the scholarly world turned his talents toward justifying the actions of al-Qaeda and became one of its top clerics during the late 1990s and early 2000s. As of this writing, he is imprisoned in Saudi Arabia.

The trajectory of al-Fahd's career illustrates what I call *blocked ambition*, in which the thwarted goals of an individual nudge him toward extreme stances and actions. Blocked ambition has been recognized to some extent in existing accounts of lay Muslim radicalization, often as the "shock" that turns a lay Muslim toward radical preachers. But for clerics, blocked ambition takes on a particularly academic flavor that deserves special attention.

My argument about blocked ambition highlights the academic identities of jihadist clerics rather than their identities as militants, terrorists, preachers, and plotters, which have been the focus of prior research on jihadism. An academic is a person whose professional life is within academe and whose behavior is influenced by its institutions and culture.[21] Academia places many normative constraints on individuals: "Academic systems are symbolically rich, with participants devoted to bodies of specific symbols, and often uncommonly bounded by affect despite elaborate pretensions to the contrary" (Clark 1983, 74).

The inculcation of academic norms by academics happens as a routine part of scholarly training (Jungert 2013). "There is in each field a way of life into which new members are gradually inducted. Physicists, economists, and historians of art are socialized into their particular fields as students and later through on-the-job interaction with disciplinary peers. As recruits to different academic specialties, they enter different cultural houses, there to share beliefs about theory, methodology, techniques, and problems" (Clark 1983, 76). Although the purpose of scholarly training may be to pass on knowledge, one of its signature by-products is the reproduction of existing scholarly norms among scholars in training. These norms shape both "categories of thought" and "related codes of conduct" into what Clark (1983, 76) calls a "knowledge tradition." An academic life is thus constructed (Richardson 1997) by placing oneself within the constraints of formal and informal academic institutions and adopting, at least to some extent, the goals, behaviors, and mannerisms encouraged by these institutions.

Academics signal that they belong by deploying a set of symbols, including credentials such as doctorates, special clothing for academic ceremonies, hierarchies of seniority based on scholarship and teaching, and formatting

---

21   Academe, originally the name of the grove in which Plato taught (Blau 1994, 1), has come to signify a set of institutions developed for the goal of identifying, curating, and transmitting human knowledge.

of academic curricula vitae. Individuals who see themselves as academics but lack the ability to deploy some of these symbols may compensate with others (Wicklund and Gollwitzer 1981, 90). For example, psychologists in US academia who lack research prominence and hold lower-ranking appointments are more likely to compensate by signing their name "John Doe, PhD" in emails (Harmon-Jones, Schmeichel, and Harmon-Jones 2009). Patterns of language are a crucial part of academic norms. As Clark (1983, 79) notes, "everywhere at the core of a disciplinary substructure we find a 'common vocabulary,' one increasingly so arcane that outsiders find it mystifying and call it jargon." Common vocabularies are closely linked to academic writing genres; producing work in these genres is a clear marker of an academically oriented individual (Flowerdew 2002, 23).

Muslim clerics often understand themselves to be academics and deploy a variety of symbols to signal their belonging to and status within Islamic legal academe. Many of the symbols used by Muslim clerics to communicate their academic identities are similar to those in other academic settings. For example, clerics write a *sīra dhātiyya* (autobiography), *tarjima dhātiyya* (curriculum vitae), or *nabdha* (abstract), which is quite similar to a curriculum vitae in Western academia. Like their counterparts in other academic disciplines, Muslim clerics write their CVs in ways intended to enhance their scholarly authority, prominently listing their connections to famous teachers and occasionally touting the speed with which they memorized the Quran. The culture of Islamic legal academia influences how clerics see themselves, how they present themselves to others, and the nature of the books, articles, fatwas, videos, and other works they produce. All clerics are affected by these norms to some degree, regardless of their ideological inclinations.

The norms of Islamic academic culture naturally give individuals academic ambitions – aspirations to attain status and recognition within the academic community. When would-be academics have their ambitions blocked, either by forces within the academic system or by intervention from the state, they are at greater risk of turning to jihadist ideology. Those who achieve their academic ambitions are disciplined by the state not to adopt jihadist ideas, an argument that echoes Said's classic essay on orientalism in which he documents the ways in which "fields of learning are constrained and acted upon by society ... and by governments" (Said 1978, 201). This argument also reflects the observation of Bourdieu (1984) that the academy reflects, reproduces, and sometimes shapes the power relations of society.

My argument draws attention to the *political economy* of the religious sphere in countries where clerics train and preach. A growing body of work provides tools for theorizing about the political economy of religion in a variety of settings (Iannaccone 1988, 1994, 1995; Gill 1998; Iannaccone 1998; Iannaccone and Berman 2006; Berman and Laitin 2008; Trejo 2009; Clingingsmith, Khwaja, and Kremer 2009; Kuran 2011; Cosgel, Miceli, and Rubin 2012; Trejo 2012; Chaney 2013), with some working directly on the question of how politics and religion intersect in the modern Middle East (Taylor 2008; Patel 2012). A core claim of this literature is that religious actors and institutions can often be thought of as firms providing religious products in a market of instrumentally rational religious seekers. Rather than being innate and fixed, religious ideas and practices are influenced by the supply and demand of religious goods. In showing how the political economy of Islamic academia can shape what clerics preach, my research applies this logic to the domain of jihadism.

How does politics in the religious sphere shape what Muslim clerics preach? Clerics face a set of career constraints in Islamic legal academia that can influence their eventual political ideologies. In Muslim-majority countries in the Middle East, mosques and universities are partially (or wholly) controlled by the ministries of religion and education and government officials appoint and pay clerics to teach religious classes in the mosques, preach in Friday services, and teach in religious schools and colleges. The idealized career trajectory for a Muslim cleric in the late twentieth and early twenty-first centuries involves early memorization of the Quran, training in the Islamic sciences at the hands of the most prominent professors and clerics, and advanced degrees in theology and jurisprudence, followed by state appointment to a clerical position funded by the government ministries. Clerics on this path, which I call the *insider* track, can expect a high-status, well-compensated career.

Clerics who have their ambitions to gain the insider track blocked by personal failing, government interference, or some other factor may still want to use their clerical training to earn a living. The *outsider* career paths open to these individuals are varied, but the unifying feature is that these individuals still produce material in cleric genres while supporting themselves financially, often through private teaching or donations. Clerics who would have liked to pursue an insider's academic career but lose the opportunity face blocked ambition.

The door to an insider career can close at different junctures. One such juncture occurs when clerics transition from Islamic graduate training to seeking their first appointment. Graduating students with strong connections to prominent teachers in Islamic academic networks can often leverage these connections to improve their prospects on the cleric job market. Clerics with the recommendations and endorsement of influential teachers will be more likely to gain access to academic positions at elite, state-funded Islamic universities. From these academic positions, clerics find opportunities for appointments within government ministries, opportunities for "shariah consulting," and other prestigious and lucrative options. On the other hand, clerics with few connections to teachers will be disadvantaged in the competition for elite cleric jobs. If these clerics fail to successfully enter the academic track, they search for other ways to build a career that uses their human capital investments in the Islamic sciences.

Clerics can also find themselves unexpectedly outside of Islamic legal academia after they have started a career as an insider. I find that the most important of these junctures happens when a cleric holds an academic position but then loses it, typically because they have run afoul of political authorities. The governments of the Middle East are largely authoritarian, and academic freedom is far from guaranteed in many of the universities and countries where clerics work. Continued employment is ultimately subject to favorable opinions by political elites. Where red lines of unacceptable dissent are uncertain or shifting, politically minded clerics can land themselves in trouble with political authorities and have their academic positions revoked. Often, this summary dismissal is also coupled with a jail sentence of some kind. I find that a number of clerics who adopted jihadist ideology in the late 1990s did so following a sequence of harsh treatment in which they were fired from their university positions and imprisoned because of Islamist leanings, only to emerge far more jihadist than when they entered.

Many options are available to outsider clerics, but with the traditional academic career closed, some clerics find a move toward radical jihadi ideology an attractive option. Jihadism is a viable career option for several reasons. One may be that it allows clerics to draw financial support from constituencies of lay Muslims who distrust the regime-sanctioned clerics. Jihadist clerics are better able to attract the support of these constituents than other clerics because their jihadist positions credibly differentiate them from regime-supported clerics. In sum, I argue that the divergence of insider and outsider pathways is the key to understanding cleric radicalization.

Of course, idiosyncratic personality features and life experiences play a role in a cleric's turn to jihadism, and perhaps most clerics themselves would attribute their choices about ideology to personal conviction. As I show below, blocked ambition is not the only pathway to jihad for clerics, and probably only explains about 30 percent of them. Nevertheless, I demonstrate a strong empirical regularity of insider clerics rejecting jihadist ideas, while some outsiders adopt it. This is not to say that all outsiders become jihadists, but rather that being an outsider substantially increases the chances that a cleric will preach militant jihad. These findings suggest that clerics are influenced by a set of structural factors that arise from the system of cleric education and training in the modern Middle East, especially Saudi Arabia and Egypt.

1.3 GATHERING EVIDENCE

I look for evidence about the reasons individuals become jihadist clerics using a variety of methods and data sources, including statistical analysis of text and network data obtained from the Internet, case studies of clerics' lives, and ethnographic participant observation at sites in Cairo, Egypt. Throughout, I try to report what I have observed with what Pearlman (2015, 138) calls an "ethnographic sensibility." Although employing "mixed methods" is common in many social science disciplines, my particular combination of ethnographic and statistical approaches is unusual and deserves explanation.

Throughout the book, I use statistics to summarize and interpret data that are too numerous or complex to feasibly approach in other ways. My move to quantification is both scientifically motivated and pragmatic. In some parts of the book, quantification assists me in reporting statistically representative evidence about the culture and behavior of clerics. Previous scholarship on jihadists has often fallen into the research design trap of "selection on the dependent variable" – looking only at jihadists to understand the causes of jihadism when a comparison with non-jihadists would be more appropriate. I avoid this problem by collecting a novel data set of *all* Arabic-speaking Muslim clerics online – 10,000 total – and then sampling 200 for statistical analysis. I also make pragmatic use of statistical text analysis methods to analyze approximately 150,000 pieces of writing produced by these clerics. Although close reading would certainly be preferable, it is infeasible. When presenting statistical results, I have tried to limit my use of jargon and any unnecessary discussion of technical details. Interested readers can find the details in Appendix B and in replication materials that I have placed online.[22]

My research also relies on qualitative observations about the behavior of clerics in the virtual space of the Internet. Studying jihadists "in the field" is difficult (Dolnik 2013). Jihadists have learned not to congregate in physical space in order to avoid drone strikes and government surveillance, and even when they do, physical safety is a serious concern for any researcher trying to reach them. Instead, I visited the online "field" of jihadism by following updates to websites, web libraries, and message boards (see Boellstorff et al. (2012) for a discussion of ethnography in virtual spaces). For ethical reasons, I tended to only observe and record, not contribute or interject. Silent observers – "lurkers" in Internet parlance – still change and shape the environments they enter because jihadists write online with the assumption that governments and researchers are watching, but by not participating, I minimize the risk of my research inadvertently contributing to the jihadist movement.

I also spent approximately four weeks immersed in the life of the mosque at al-Azhar University in Cairo, Egypt, in 2011 and 2012. This is arguably the greatest teaching mosque in the Muslim world, and I selected it as a site for fieldwork because of its prominence and because Egypt readily hosts many Western academics who are conducting research across a variety of disciplines. While at al-Azhar, I conducted roughly twenty interviews that inform my analysis below. However, the bulk of my time was spent visiting and observing the mosque itself, the rhythms of religious ritual, the comings and goings of teachers and students, and the process of clerical instruction. I spent a substantial amount of this time sitting in the public teaching circles of al-Azhar clerics. I also sat in the study circles of al-Azhar students, talked with students one-on-one, and occasionally interviewed clerics. Where I deemed it

---

[22] Replication materials are available at http://dx.doi.org/10.7910/DVN/PG4A7K (Nielsen 2017).

appropriate, I participated in religious rituals and practices, including group prayer and Friday worship.

I began memorizing the Quran while at al-Azhar and persisted until I could recite half of the final section, from sura 83 (al-Mutaffafin) until the end. The process was taxing. While at al-Azhar, I would sit in the open courtyard with others also reading or memorizing the Quran and try to force myself to both learn and memorize the meanings and sounds of an Arabic dialect with only a familial resemblance to either the modern standard Arabic taught in Azhari schools or the Egyptian colloquial spoken in the streets. Many of the words in the Quran are unique to that text, so even native Arabic speakers learn new words through the memorization process. A student at al-Azhar gleefully recounted a faith-promoting rumor in which an Indonesian won a Quran recitation competition by reciting its entirety flawlessly, but when congratulated in Arabic, it became clear that "he could not understand a word, *mā shā> allāh*." On days when my Arabic was particularly slow and clumsy, I could relate.

Quranic quotations infuse clerical speech. My memorization allowed me to recognize deeper levels of meaning while listening or reading, although there is a great deal I missed by not having an even greater mastery. My attempts to memorize the Quran also had the unintended but welcome side effect of opening doors with informants – the individuals who helped me gain insights into their culture. I realized this on my second day in Cairo when, while at the al-Hussein mosque (across from al-Azhar), a young man quizzed me, somewhat skeptically, about my reasons for being there. As a crowd gathered, my initial interlocutor dared me to prove my genuine interest in Islam by reciting the first sura of the Quran, the *Fatihah*, which is always recited as part of prayer. When I nervously but successfully rendered a passable recitation, the mood changed dramatically: "*mā shā> allāh, yā ustādh!*" (O teacher! See what God has wrought!). Immediately, about five cell phones appeared and I had to recite again several times to satiate their desire to document this curiosity, and the young man who had initially been suspicious gave me his cell number and asked to meet the next day.

While at al-Azhar, I also participated in prayer and other religious practices as much as I believed appropriate for a non-Muslim community outsider. Many of my informants wished me to convert to Islam, and they were eager for me to participate. My first prayer instruction was from Essam, a guard at the gate of the al-Azhar campus adjoining the mosque. I had gotten to know Essam when, on my first day in Cairo, I attempted to walk onto campus and was promptly stopped by him and three others who never allowed me unfettered access to the campus, but did befriend me and show me around. They seemed entertained by my company and throughout my stay I made a point of returning to update them about my exploits and ask questions. When I asked Essam about prayer, he gave me a practicum, leading me through *wuḍū>* (ablution) in the bathroom of one of the campus buildings and then praying the evening prayer on rugs in the darkening walkway by the campus gate. His handwritten prayer instructions in my field book are among my most prized possessions from this time in Cairo.

Despite instruction, some of my attempts to participate in religious rituals were failures. In one instance, while exploring Cairo's *al-qarāfa*, the city of the dead, I ended up at the *al-ʿAshīra al-Muhammadiyya* mosque during prayer time and proceeded to thoroughly embarrass myself by making egregious errors in my prayer movements. In this, and all other settings where I erred, those around me generously welcomed my participation and attempted to correct my mistakes. At other times, my religious participation made me fairly invisible to those around me. By and large, Western tourists walk into al-Azhar with shorts or skirts and T-shirts and hastily draped headscarves leaving large swaths of hair uncovered, all immodest in Azhari culture. They do not pray. I dressed in work pants, faded plaid shirts, and ragged Adidas sneakers that I removed and carried around the mosque like the other congregants. Clothing at al-Azhar is varied, but this attire did not place me outside of the norm, nor did it signal my affinity with any particular strain of Sunni Islam. My participation in the religious practices of the mosque often led people to assume that I belonged.

Four weeks is not very long, especially for any sort of political ethnography. For personal reasons, long research trips to Cairo were not possible, so I opted for short, intense visits to al-Azhar.[23] While my methods were ethnographic, I relied on a modified version of participant observation that Bernard (1995, 139–140) calls "rapid assessment." With rapid assessment, an ethnographer abbreviates fieldwork by shortening or eliminating the process of building rapport with informants in the field, instead getting in, getting "the data," and getting out. This approach has obvious limitations: Bernard cites Naroll's (1962) finding that anthropologists who stayed in the field for over a year were more likely to report on sensitive issues than those whose fieldwork was limited to less than a year. I made close friends in my short time and felt surprisingly invisible in the mosque after only a few days of semiconstant presence there, but I was not aware of meeting any jihadists in Cairo so I cannot claim that these trips give me direct insight into the culture of jihadism. Instead, I use data collected in the field for greater insight about the broader culture of Islamic academia in which jihadists are entangled.[24]

Statistics and ethnography are not often combined because many researchers find the orientations of these methods to be at odds. Statistics is associated with a *positivist* orientation that treats social reality as objectively knowable through experience, while ethnography is often, though not always, associated with an *interpretive* orientation that views social reality as a human construct that can only be subjectively observed by a particular researcher. Ahmed and Sil (2012,

---

[23] See similar issues mentioned by Carpenter (2012, 368).

[24] Access to informants does not necessarily solve the difficult problems of studying jihadism. Menoret (2014, 26–36) was able to meet jihadists in Saudi Arabia but nevertheless found it difficult to pursue work on Islamism.

942) suggest that mixing statistical analysis with interpretive ethnography is difficult and possibly logically inconsistent.

However, logical consistency may not the appropriate criterion for evaluating whether mixing methods is fruitful. After all, the methods are not "mixing" in a literal sense in the text of this book. Rather, the combination of inferences from multiple methods happens in the minds of the researcher and the reader, so perhaps a better criterion is whether my argument is more persuasive because I support it with evidence from multiple methods with different orientations.[25]

It is not the case that the quantitative portions of this book are uniformly positivist while the qualitative portions are necessarily interpretive. In the first part of this book, I use both qualitative and quantitative methods to interpret the culture of jihadist scholars and the broader culture of Sunni Islamic academia in which they are embedded. When I turn to testing hypotheses about the causes of clerics' divergent pathways in this culture, I turn to positivism, but maintain my reliance on both qualitative and quantitative data. Rather than seeing these as contradictory, I share Wedeen's (2010, 257) aspiration "that interpretive social science does not have to forswear generalizations or causal explanations and that ethnographic methods can be used in the service of establishing them. Rather than taking flight from abstractions, ethnographies can and should help ground them."

The ways in which my fieldwork grounds my findings are sometimes subtle. My fieldwork at al-Azhar and online was crucial for developing the theoretical propositions in the book and provides vignettes to illustrate key points throughout. Like Bernard (1995, 141), I find that "participant observation gives you an intuitive sense of what's going on in a culture and allows you to speak with confidence about the meaning of the data." My approach provides an example of what might be termed "grounded analysis of big data."

Also, much of the primary source material in this study comes from texts I encountered online or in conversations from the field. In some places, I have erred on the side of quoting heavily from primary sources. Block quotations are my attempt to help the reader understand the ideology of jihadist and non-jihadist clerics by directly engaging the same sources I have.

Many of the texts I have used are difficult to adequately cite. Most of the jihadist material I draw from is available primarily via the Internet, and could be removed at any time; in fact, during the writing of this book, the largest jihadist web library in the world, a resource which I use throughout, went offline. The tenuous accessibility of jihadist output does not mean that the texts are ephemeral or unimportant, however; these are the texts that have shaped the face of Islamism, both jihadist and not. However, it is difficult to point readers to stable sources where these works are located, especially as counterterrorism units work to take them out of circulation. In addition to providing original

---

[25] For another example of recent research on the Middle East that combines positivist and interpretive approaches, see Jones (2017).

URL addresses for Internet materials, my solution was to download and save Internet materials to storage devices that I control, which allows me to provide readers with both the original URL addresses as well as stable URL addresses to these archived sources (when legal limits permit).

Finally, it is worth considering a methodological approach I do not employ: why not just ask clerics why they support jihad? Clerics' own accounts of the reasons for their ideological positions are worth considering, but they are likely to be aimed at reinforcing the legitimacy of their life choices rather than offering a true description of the process of ideological change. I therefore follow Wedeen (2010), who urges political scientists to move beyond interpretations of informant self-narratives that take their words at face value. Wickham makes an even broader observation in her exploration of ideological change in the Egyptian Muslim Brotherhood: "Any claims [from any method] about the motives driving an actor's observable rhetoric and behavior will always fail to meet the standard of scientific 'proof,' as those motives are by definition inaccessible to an outside observer" (2013, 73).

Even if jihadists do attempt to honestly portray the causes of their decisions, people have poor recall. Bernard (1995, 114) summarizes the literature on informant accuracy: "A great deal of research has shown that about a third to a half of everything informants report about their behavior is not true. If you ask people what they eat, they'll tell you, but it may have no useful resemblance to what they actually eat."

A deeper reason that jihadists' accounts cannot be accepted uncritically is that they themselves may not know why they embraced jihadism. While humans *believe* they can introspectively report why they made particular choices, findings by Nisbett and Wilson (1977) show that in fact humans cannot accurately report why they make particular choices because the brain does not have the capacity for true introspection. Rather, self-reporters draw on mental models of why such a choice might occur and then infer that their choice must have been caused by the features of this mental model. When humans are correct about the reasons for their choices, this is because their mental models are roughly accurate. However, this is often not the case. Thus, inner motivations are not only inaccessible to outside observers, they are also often inaccessible to the actors themselves. As a result, I agree with Milgram (1975, 44) who writes, "While we must take very seriously everything the subject says, we need not necessarily think that he fully understands the causes of his own behavior. A line must be drawn between listening carefully to what the subject says and mistaking it for the full story."

1.4 WHY STUDY JIHADISM?

"Focusing on jihad is just like an American and not a good idea. If you look at any book of jihad, the definitions are clear." This was the reaction of Said, a student at the al-Azhar mosque, as I described my research. It was only the beginning. "Let me talk for seven minutes," he interjected, and then gave an extended explanation for why my focus on jihad was a mistake.[26] He argued that jihad was purely defensive, was misunderstood by non-Muslims, and that by focusing on it, I was reinforcing violent stereotypes about Islam while ignoring the concerns that matter to scholars at al-Azhar. Said was particularly vocal, but he was not alone. My 2011 notes record that four Azhari students who had invited me back to their flat "ask[ed] why I was so focused on [Yusuf] al-Qaradawi and al-Qaeda, as if these two things aren't important to them and they found the choice strange."[27] Since these conversations occurred, I have had many further opportunities to reflect on the question: why study jihadism?

On a personal level, my suspicion is that I was nudged toward studying jihadism because the September 11, 2001, attacks happened during a remarkably formative time in my life: the second week of my first year of college. But all researchers have personal experiences that draw them toward the objects of their study. It remains necessary to consider the scientific merit of any proposed topic. In my case, why study jihadism? And what of the ethics of producing yet another addition to an already saturated market of books returning again and again to the question of violence in Islam?

On the question of scientific merit, I find that the reproduction of jihadist ideology by Muslim clerics is an ideal place to study the dynamics of idea adoption among elites. It is a good case because, to a first approximation, jihadists' ideas can be expected to "matter," which allows me to largely bracket that question in favor of other, less tilled ground: how do actors come to adopt certain ideas?

Also, though I wish it were not so, knowledge about jihadism is, and is likely to remain, a vital piece of human understanding about the political world. When possible, I believe that scientists should work on problems that concern society.

Choosing to research violent jihadism bears the risk of perpetuating a form of neo-Orientalism that typifies some Muslim "other" as quintessentially exotic, violent, and irrational (Said 1978; Tuastad 2003; Lockman 2004). It is difficult to see bias in one's own work so I cannot definitively rule out this possibility. My intention, however, is that my research will challenge orientalist misconceptions about the subjects of my study and present them as complex human beings, rather than abstract, essentialized Others. My findings cut against the tendency to characterize jihadists as inherently irrational or exotic. I show that, far from being innate and irrational, the turn to embrace jihadist ideology is at least partially influenced by rational calculations that clerics make within the constraints of a professional system.

---

[26] This is recorded in my 2012 field notes, p. 17, archived at http://dx.doi.org/10.7910/DVN/PG4A7K.

[27] This is recorded in my 2011 field notes, p. 30, archived at http://dx.doi.org/10.7910/DVN/PG4A7K.

Some readers may be concerned that focusing on violent jihadism improperly elevates its importance within the Muslim faith tradition at the expense of alternative understandings that better represent Islam's core principles. As Orsi (2005, 179) describes, "People want to be reassured that the men who flew their planes into the World Trade Center on September 11, 2001, were not representatives of 'real' or 'good' Islam."

The assertion that jihadism is not "real" Islam, and therefore should not dominate scholarly attention, comes from an admirable desire not to hold the varied adherents of a diverse global religion culpable for violence perpetrated by a marginal subgroup of co-religionists, and to avoid reinforcing colonial structures of power that legitimize control and domination of Muslim bodies by casting them as intrinsically violent, exotic, or alien (Said 1978). However, subterranean power structures in fields of knowledge are more complex than this anticolonial critique admits because the act of defining jihadists as "bad" or "untrue" Islam is itself a reflection of power. Unless we "excavate our hidden moral and political history ... the distinctions that we make will merely be the reiteration of unacknowledged assumptions, prejudices, and implications in power" (Orsi 2005, 180).[28]

With the implicit power dynamics of defining "true" Islam clearly in view, it is no longer surprising that the subjects of my study, as well as readers, disagree about the role of jihad in Islam. The jihadists argue that violent jihad *is* an essential part of Islam and represents a "forgotten duty" of all Muslims (Faraj 1981). Non-jihadists argue that the only important jihad in the modern era is the struggle to purify one's soul. My research attempts not to take a side in the power struggle for the essence of Islam, although I realize my attempt may be quixotic. Instead, I attempt to represent the subjects of my study – jihadists and non-jihadists alike – with enough fidelity that they might recognize themselves in my descriptions.

1.5 PLAN OF THE BOOK

The remainder of this book lays out the arguments and evidence I have introduced in this chapter. The broad arc of the book is this: I introduce Muslim clerics in Chapter 2 and then explain my theoretical arguments about the pathways clerics take to become jihadists in Chapter 3. In Chapters 4 through 6, I offer empirical evidence to support my claims, primarily by collecting a sample of clerics, determining which ones are jihadists, and then testing whether events in the lives of these clerics predict which ones will become jihadists. In the final chapter, I summarize my analysis and then discuss how this research might be of use to others: first, by suggesting what lessons policy-makers might draw

---

[28] See also Wiktorowicz (2005a, 208) for further discussion of why the rhetorical effort to brand jihadists as "bad" Muslims has "little or no grounding in the realities of Islam or the Muslim world."

from the analysis and second, by describing how the theory and methods I use might be profitably deployed and extended by other scholars.

I now describe each of the chapters in more detail. Any argument about the decisions of Muslim clerics requires a clear definition of who is and is not a member of this group. I begin the next chapter by explaining my definition of who counts as a Muslim cleric and clarifying how my definition differs from the definitions other scholars have used. Next, I draw on my own observations as well as primary sources and secondary literature to describe how clerics are trained and what they do. To illustrate clerical training for the reader, I parse the syllabus of a jihadist cleric detailing a ten-year program of study to become a scholar. I then describe some genres of work that clerics produce – websites, academic and popular writing, sermons, and fatwas – in order to analyze what these types of intellectual production reveal about the self-conception of clerics.

With this background information in place, in Chapter 3 I develop my theoretical arguments about why some individuals might become jihadist clerics. I make a distinction between individuals who radicalize first and become clerics later and those who become clerics first and jihadists later. I then explain why existing theories of lay Muslim radicalization apply to the first set but not the second. To understand the radicalization of individuals who become clerics first and jihadists later, I focus on the role of academic career incentives in clerics' choices and how blocked ambition at various stages of academic advancement turns clerics toward jihadist ideology. I argue that clerics with better academic networks usually go on to have traditional academic careers and avoid radicalization, while less networked clerics face tougher academic prospects and are more likely to radicalize. Similarly, clerics who build insider careers and then find themselves abruptly on the outside, often because of government repression, are at particular risk of radicalizing.

After presenting my theory, I turn to collecting data with which to test it. Chapter 4 introduces a representative sample of Sunni Muslim clerics with a substantial online presence, describes how I constructed this sample from Internet sources, and presents summaries of clerics' biographical information. These data are unique because I conducted a comprehensive census of Arabic-speaking Muslim clerics on the Internet to form a sampling frame and then sampled 200 clerics at random for inclusion in a quantitative data set. To my knowledge, this is the first sample of Muslim clerics that is representative of Sunni Muslim clerics online. The benefit of this random sampling is that the patterns I uncover in the data are likely to be present in the broader population and are unlikely to be spurious correlations caused by ad hoc sampling. I describe the biographies I collected for the 200 clerics in my sample and report data coded from these biographies showing trends in the mobility, education, and careers of these clerics. This biographical data forms the first half of the data set I will use to test competing arguments about why some clerics become jihadists.

In Chapter 5, I describe how I determine which of the 200 clerics in my sample are jihadists. Detecting jihadists requires conceptual clarity on jihadist ideology itself. To identify the key features of jihadist ideology that my coding must capture, I couple close reading of important jihadist texts with statistical text analysis of a large jihadist corpus. This analysis shows that almost all of jihadist ideology flows from a particular conception of God's sovereignty, called *tawḥīd*. I explain this concept, show how jihadist conceptions of *tawḥīd* differ from non-jihadist conceptions, and trace the logic by which the jihadist version of *tawḥīd* leads them to excommunicate others, reject contemporary regimes in the Middle East, reject notions of state sovereignty, decry democracy, and justify violence against others, both combatant and noncombatant and Muslim and non-Muslim.

In the remainder of Chapter 5, I collect all of the writings I can find for the 200 clerics in my sample and use these to determine which clerics express jihadist ideology when they write. Because these clerics have produced far more writing than I can possibly read – almost 150,000 documents total – I develop a statistical text analysis model that distinguishes jihadist writing from non-jihadist writing based on patterns of word use. I apply this method to measure the jihadism of each cleric and then verify the results of the model by comparing them to statements about clerics' ideological positions in their biographies, the scholarly literature, and the opinions of other jihadists. I find that the model provides accurate assessments of the degree to which a cleric's writing expresses jihadist ideology, and has the advantage of being transparent and scalable.

I bring the data developed in Chapters 4 and 5 together in Chapter 6 to show that the educational networks and career paths of clerics strongly predict which clerics will be more jihadist, even when accounting for alternative explanations statistically. I also provide evidence that jihadism may give clerics credibility; I analyze page views of fatwas on a large Salafi website and find that jihadist-leaning fatwas are more popular than non-jihadist fatwas. I next present brief case studies that examine turning points in the lives of several jihadist clerics. These case studies complement the statistical analysis by illustrating the theoretical mechanisms at work and providing a rough estimate of which pathways to becoming a jihadist cleric are most common.

Chapter 7 concludes the book. After reviewing the argument and evidence, I offer some suggestions for what policy-makers might learn from my study. I highlight two suggestions that cut against the grain of current thinking: first, that involvement in Islamic education may not be as likely to radicalize people as some have claimed and second, that the attempts of many governments in the Middle East to pacify and dominate the religious sphere have backfired. I then consider what scholars should take away from this study. I first make the case that blocked ambition should be considered as a candidate cause of political choices by individuals in a number of settings far beyond Islamic legal academia. Next, I suggest that the data sources and methods I employ in this book could open new avenues for the study of Islam and Muslim societies. Although there have been a few forays into quantitative approaches, particularly by those working on Islamic "digital humanities" (Muhanna 2016), the full potential of these research methods has not yet been realized. My advocacy for these new methods does not disparage more traditional methods; in fact I argue that old and new approaches are complementary and hope that together they can offer new insights into the causes of radicalization and other crucial questions of our time.

2

Muslim Clerics

I am sitting on a thin mattress on the floor in the spartan apartment of Fahmi, a student at al-Azhar, as we eat small green bananas and I ask him questions about his motivation for becoming a cleric. Not all of my informants at al-Azhar are well positioned to talk about becoming clerics as most are not entirely sure why they are there or what their job prospects will be after they graduate. Many of the students I talk to seem to be on autopilot, pursuing a degree from al-Azhar merely because it buys them time off from thinking about adulthood and the challenges of life in a country with 25 percent unemployment. Fahmi is the exception. He strikes me as sharp and motivated. He wants to become a *faqīh* (one who studies and teaches *fiqh*, or Islamic jurisprudence) and he seems to know what it takes to get there. He is flattered and pleased when I tell him that I think he has the charisma of an al-Azhar sheikh such as Ahmad al-Riyan, whose study circle we attended before going back to Fahmi's house.

Fahmi does not consider jihadists to be *ʿulamāʾ*, a commonly used Arabic word for clerics, apparently because he disagrees with their doctrinal positions and believes their training is suspect. "Because of the Internet and television, anyone can call themselves a cleric now and the masses aren't smart enough to know better. People just read a few books and declare themselves to be *ʿulamāʾ*."[1] Fahmi is so bothered that he specifically asks me to stop using the word *ʿulamāʾ* while referring to jihadists. He asks me whom I consider to be famous jihadist clerics, so I rattle off the name of Abu Muhammad al-Maqdisi, one of the most influential living jihadists and the administrator of a large online jihadist library. He says he doesn't know of him. "Who said that he is important or famous?"

---

[1]   From my 2012 field notes, p. 25, archived at http://dx.doi.org/10.7910/DVN/PG4A7K.

This illustrates a dynamic that I have observed repeatedly in writings about Muslim clerics, in conversations, and in online debates: clerical authority matters, so people who care about the influence of clerical authority are very careful to define religious figures with whom they agree as "clerics" and exclude others.

There is no uncontested definition of a "cleric." Few have enough legitimacy that their status as a cleric is unassailable, thus opposing scholars frequently attempt to undermine each other's religious authority. Azharis (people affiliated with al-Azhar University) deride those who lack formal education and credentials while jihadis criticize Azharis for their cozy relationship to the Egyptian regime, intimating that no true cleric can ever be too proximate to political power. Clerics who teach in traditional study circles derisively refer to those with large Internet followings as "YouTube" or "Google" sheikhs, even though they themselves often have websites, Facebook pages, and Twitter accounts. This chaotic contest over authority is possible because Sunni Islam lacks an undisputed religious hierarchy. As a result, because the label of "cleric" confers authority, defining who is and is not a cleric in Islam invites a political fight.

The plan of this chapter is as follows. I first define, for the purposes of this study, a Muslim cleric as someone who produces Islamic materials. I conclude by examining how people become clerics and what they do once they get there.

2.1 WHO COUNTS AS A CLERIC?

In English, the word cleric refers to someone who is "of the clergy" – traditionally someone who holds priesthood within Christianity. This definition becomes complicated when applied to Islam, which does not replicate Christian notions of sacerdotal authority, and thus there is no body with official say over who is a member of the "priesthood." As Bagader (1983, 3) puts it, "Muslims strongly deny the existence of an ecclesia class in Islam." However, I follow Mouline (2014, 3) who argues "the ulama were the genuine guardians of what the ancient Greeks referred to as *klerôs* – that is, the patrimony and heritage, spiritual and profane, of classical Islam. They therefore can be described as clerics."

Turning to internal definitions within Islam, there are several words that Arabic-speakers use to refer to clerics. Perhaps most common is the word *shaykh*, which is in common use throughout most of the Arab world, although in the small Gulf states a "shaykh" can also refer to a political ruler. The word "shaykh" is often preceded by the honorifics *faḍīla* or *samāḥa* (honorable or virtuous). Taken literally, the word "shaykh" suggests that age might have something to do with the Arabic definition of a cleric but in practice there can be relatively young shaykhs. Clerics are also referred to generally as *rijāl al-dīn* (men of religion), suggesting an emphasis on a career of devotion to sacred things as a marker of clerics.

The other general term that is used most often in Arabic is *ʿālim* (pl. *ʿulamāʾ*), which connotes learning. It is this term specifically that Fahmi, my informant, objected to, perhaps because it implies a level of scholarship he feels jihadists have not obtained. Of course, the logic here is often circular, as some at al-Azhar would consider adoption of jihadism a mark of ignorance no matter how learned the scholar.

Muslim clerics may also be referred to using titles for their roles in religious society rather than their qualifications: *imām* (one who gets up before the congregation), *khatīb* (one who gives the *khutba*, or sermon during worship), *muftī* (one who issues fatwas), *qārī* (one who recites the Quran), *faqīh* (an expert in jurisprudence), *qāḍī* (a judge), and a *mū'zin* (one who issues the call to prayer). This list inspires my own criteria for determining who is and is not a cleric. In this study, individuals who perform clerical activities count as clerics, while those who do not are left out. Specifically, *Muslim clerics are individuals who produce religious content for public consumption within an Islamic tradition*. This content can be varied – a judgment, a lesson, a recitation, a song – but it must recognizably fit into one of the culturally prescribed genres of religious production in Islam, which I discuss in detail below.

This definition is different from some definitions used by other scholars of Islam, most notably because I include as clerics individuals who cannot claim traditional pedigrees of scholarly training.[2] For example, I include figures such as Usama Bin Laden and Sayyid Qutb, both of whom lacked formal training but who produced documents that they claimed were fatwas (Bin Laden) and Quranic exegesis (Qutb).

Just as Fahmi rejected the notion of calling jihadists "clerics," many Muslims consider Bin Laden's "fatwas" to be illegitimate, in part because he lacks traditional clerical qualifications. The former head cleric in Saudi Arabia, Abd al-Aziz Bin Baz, said that "Bin Laden is among those who corrupt the earth, and explores the ways of corrupt wickedness and rebellion against rightful rulers." Bin Baz's successor, Abd al-Aziz Bin Abdullah Al al-Sheikh, reiterated that Bin Laden and his associates "are a source of sin and corruption. They have lost their way." And summarizing many others, Muqbil Bin Hadi al-Wada'i stated succinctly, "His works are evil."[3] Other jihadists are similarly dismissed. As one

---

[2] For example, Zaman (2012) defines the ulama as "representatives of the Islamic religious and scholarly tradition" (p. 2) whose "identity and authority rest, more than anything else, on a continuous engagement with the historically articulated Islamic religious and especially the juristic tradition" (p. 46). Whether this matches my definition is somewhat ambiguous, but it seems that individuals who lack the formal training of the traditional ulama might not qualify. In other work, Zaman (2005, 93) contrasts "ulama" with "modernists, Islamists, and other 'new' religious intellectuals," which are all categories that I consider clerics, provided they produce Islamic material. Similarly, Brinton (2016, 67) sets up ulama and "preachers" as different categories, but I consider both categories to be clerics. Bagader (1983, 3) defines an *alim* as "a person who sets himself in public to teach Islamics, most probably in the traditional Islamic learning style," and says "he is usually [a] graduate of an accredited traditional Islamic school, with certification ('Ijaza') from some celebrated Ulama." Note that this discussion applies primarily to Sunni clerics. For a discussion on what constitutes clericism in Shi'i Islam, see Nasr (2007, 70).

[3] These quotes are taken from a collection of anti-Bin Laden fatwas gathered at www.qataru. com/vb/showthread.php?t=61658 and accessed July 10, 2015. Unfortunately, this forum now

leading Sunni scholar said while refuting the teachings of jihadist ideologue Abu Qatada al-Filistini: "This man, as you know, did not study at the hands of the scholars" (al-Jazairi 2007, 13).[4]

While these debates about who "counts" as a cleric are important, I cannot simply rely on them to determine which individuals should fall within the scope of this study and which fall outside. These arguments about who qualifies as a cleric are embedded in the very politics that I describe in this book. Drawing a categorical distinction between "clerics" and "jihadists" without acknowledging that some individuals are both would obscure, rather than clarify, the reasons why some religious elites come to preach violent jihad while others do not. I will not argue that Fahmi, or anyone else, should accept jihadists as legitimate religious leaders, but for the purposes of this book, it is important that I treat jihadists and non-jihadists who perform the same religious duties for their respective followers as analytically comparable types of people. My shorthand for this is to refer to all of them as clerics.

One instructive way to probe the boundaries of my definition of the term "cleric" is to consider ambiguous cases. Easily one of the most unusual clerics I have encountered is Adnan al-Tarsha, who started his career as a martial artist and now writes about Islam.[5] His website includes side-by-side links to a "Section on the Art of Kyokushin Fighting"[6] and an "Islamic Section,"[7] featuring his religious writings on topics such as *What Allah Likes and Dislikes* (tenth edition), *The Satanic Nakedness* ("The plan that Satan uses step-by-step to undress a woman"), and *Why Fajr Prayer?*. While he certainly does not have the training that my informant Fahmi believes is essential to qualify an individual as a cleric, his writing in an Islamic tradition clearly makes him a cleric by my definition.

Another example of a nontraditional cleric who nevertheless fits my definition is Yemni Zakaria, whose writings and biography are posted on the Islamic aggregator website Alukah.[8] His biography leans against classifying him as a cleric: he is primarily a psychologist focusing on children with

requires credentials to access the web page, but a similar post is available at www.muslm.org/ vb/showthread.php?290050, accessed February 9, 2017, and al-Wada'i's statement is available at www.muqbel.net/fatwa.php?fatwa_id=3101, accessed February 9, 2017. Both are archived at http://dx.doi.org/10.7910/DVN/PG4A7K.

4   This source can be accessed at http://download.salafimanhaj.com/pdf/SalafiManhajQataadah. pdf, as of February 9, 2017. I have archived it at http://dx.doi.org/10.7910/DVN/PG4A7K.

5   Adnan al-Tarsha's biography is available in Arabic at www.adnantarsha.com/HomePage.htm, accessed February 9, 2017, and archived at http://dx.doi.org/10.7910/DVN/PG4A7K.

6   www.adnantarsha.com/Karate_MainPage.htm, accessed February 9, 2017, and archived at http://dx.doi.org/10.7910/DVN/PG4A7K.

7   www.adnantarsha.com/IslamicPage.htm, accessed February 9, 2017, and archived at http://dx. doi.org/10.7910/DVN/PG4A7K.

8   www.alukah.net/authors/view/home/6469, accessed February 9, 2017, and archived at http: //dx.doi.org/10.7910/DVN/PG4A7K.

cognitive impairments. In a very uncharacteristic move for a cleric, he finishes his biography by describing interests outside of the religious sphere: "Reading, walking, art of several types (such as: painting, needlework, crochet, origami)." However, Zakaria writes works with religious content in an Islamic tradition, including an advice article titled, "The Way of Example for Calling Children to God."[9]

Contrast this with the case of Nufal Abd al-Hadi al-Masari, who also has writings on Alukah but does not fit my definition of a cleric.[10] Although al-Masari is a prolific writer whose articles are posted to Islamic websites such as Alukah, his genre is self-help, not religion. Some clerics write religiously themed self-help books and it is something of a judgment call to decide when this writing passes into the realm of religious production, but al-Masari's does not. His work has the goal of developing "an innovative model for change and development named [the] Nofal Model, to help people find self-leadership, manage change, and discover their potential."[11] While this may be of interest to many Muslims, it does not fall within a traditional genre of Muslim clerical production.

Having offered a concrete definition of "cleric" for the purpose of my research program, I now turn to an examination of clerics' backgrounds and roles. There is a large literature spanning several disciplines on the roles clerics play in Islam, their training, their preaching, and their politics (see, among others, Antoun 1989; Abu-Zahra 1997; Zaman 2002; Al-Rasheed 2007; Hatina 2010; Zaman 2012; Al-Rasheed 2013; Mouline 2014; al Rasheed 2015; Brinton 2016). This chapter cannot comprehensively cover all aspects of the lives of Muslim clerics, but my goal in the following sections is to introduce the reader to the general types of training that clerics might receive and the religious material they might subsequently produce. This information serves as necessary background for understanding why some Muslim clerics turn to jihadism and why some jihadists decide to become clerics.

2.2 WHAT A CLERIC SHOULD KNOW

The syllabus[12] of jihadist cleric Hamid al-Ali opens modestly:

This is a small thesis that can place in the hands of the student of religious knowledge, with blessings from God, a complete curriculum for learning how to seek knowledge of Sharia Studies based on the salafi school of thought. I have provided this hastily, based

---

9 www.alukah.net/fatawa_counsels/0/71833, accessed February 9, 2017, and archived at http://dx.doi.org/10.7910/DVN/PG4A7K.
10 www.alukah.net/authors/view/home/636, accessed February 9, 2017, and archived at http://dx.doi.org/10.7910/DVN/PG4A7K.
11 This quote is from al-Masari's CV, almusarea.com/?page_id=498, last bullet point. I last accessed this page on February 21, 2017, and archived it at http://dx.doi.org/10.7910/DVN/PG4A7K.
12 As of February 9, 2015, this syllabus is available a number of places online, including at al-Ali's website (www.h-alali.net/b_open.php?id=913b735c-fb6b-1029-a701-0010dc91cf69) and on islamway.net (http://ar.islamway.net/book/955). It is archived at http://dx.doi.org/10.7910/DVN/PG4A7K and a full translation is in Appendix B.

on the desires of students from about nine years ago. It found, with God's grace, wide approval from students, and many of them have informed me that they have benefited from it. Then, when the first edition copies ran out, some students urged me to re-publish it with edits, additions, and re-structuring so that the program becomes more clear and easy in organization. So I did as they asked me, while seeking God's aid and relying on him.

Syllabi are a tedious genre of academic writing and even the revolutionary promise of Salafi-jihadi ideology cannot rescue al-Ali's syllabus from becoming tiresome as he fills twenty-seven pages with details of a ten-year program of study, citation by citation.[13] Perhaps the implicit first lesson for the eager student is that Salafi jihadism is a serious academic subject with a depth and technicality not reflected in the fiery slogans of YouTube jihadists. If ISIS has mastered the use of media for attracting youth to jihadism, then al-Ali's syllabus is the opposite: a deterrent meant to screen out all but the most dedicated of followers.

The second lesson implicit in al-Ali's syllabus is that becoming a cleric is going to take a long time.

Other scholars have described the training of clerics, including Mouline (2014, 185), who details the training and apprenticeship of clerics who eventually become high-ranking members of the Saudi religious establishment, and Zeghal (1996), who describes the training at the al-Azhar mosque in Cairo. These excellent works provide a level of detail that I cannot hope to reproduce here. Instead, the purpose of this section is to offer a unique view of cleric culture by considering the elements of al-Ali's training manual for becoming a Salafi scholar.

Al-Ali's program of study requires completing five levels over a period of ten years. In this span of time, the student memorizes the Quran and reads 186 works. Some of the required readings are exceedingly lengthy; the final reading assignment of the fifth level is a thirty-seven-volume compilation of fatwas by the medieval cleric Ibn Taymiyya, a work that occupies seven linear feet of shelf space in the mosque library at al-Azhar. Becoming a classically trained cleric is not for the faint of heart.

The following excerpt describing the first (and shortest) level gives a flavor of Hamid al-Ali's syllabus:

I. The first level lasts one and a half years.

   a. In it he memorizes the last six parts of the Quran.
   b. In Theology, he should read:

      i. The Scholar al-Uthaymeen's *explanation of the three Principles of Jurisprudence and the four Rules.*
      ii. *The book of the Doctrine of Oneness with the Right Opinion.*
      iii. Imam Muhammad Bin Abd al-Wahhab's *Uncovering Suspicions.*

---

[13] See Appendix A for a full translation of al-Ali's Salafi-jihadi syllabus.

c. In Jurisprudence, he should read: *An Easy Explanation of the Most Important Laws* by al-Bassam. With it he should learn the proper way to pray from contemporary, summarized publications like those by the scholar Abd al-Aziz Bin Baz (may God grant him mercy) or by the scholar al-Uthaymeen or *The Characteristics of Prayer* by the scholar al-Albani, may God grant him mercy.

d. In Hadith, he should read:

i. The 40 hadiths from al-Nawwawi's book.
ii. *The Gardens of the Good*
iii. *The Brightest Lantern*

e. In the Study of Hadith: the book *Explaining Hadith*

f. In Disciplining Behavior, he should read:

i. *The Sufficient Answer* by Ibn al-Qayyim
ii. The summary of *The Curriculum of the Seekers*
iii. *Knowledge that You Have to Act On* by al-Hafez al-Baghdadi

g. In Language Studies, he should read: *Al-Igrumiya and Its Explanation: The Sunni Treasure.*

h. In Biography and History, he should read: *The Sealed Honey*

Memorization of the Quran is the foundation of al-Ali's syllabus: it comes first in the listing of tasks for each level and, in the front material, the sheikh emphasizes that the student "should take very good care of the Quran and increase his recitation and memorization of it." This is not accidental. Memorizing the Quran in its entirety is a critical skill for many, though not all, who become clerics and it confers status as a *ḥāfiẓ*, "one who preserves" the Quran in their memory.

This tradition hearkens back to the initial transmission of the Quran, in which Muhammad received the revelations and then recited them back to his devotees until they too could recite them from memory. In fact, many will say that the Quran is not a book at all but rather a recitation. According to mainstream Sunni tradition, textual copies of the Quran were not systematically collected and produced until after the battle of Yamama in 633 CE (a year after Muhammad's death), when seventy Muslims who had memorized the Quran were killed, sparking concern in the Caliph Abu Bakr that parts of the Quran could be lost if the remaining memorizers were killed (Sahih al-Bukhari, 4986).

Because Quran memorization is greatly respected and conveys substantial religious credibility, many clerics list it among their credentials. Cleric biographies tend to highlight the early age and great speed with which clerics completed the task. For example, the biography of Abd al-Rahman al-Dawsary states, "It was amazing that he was able to memorize the entire Noble Quran in his seventh year,[14] as he says himself (God have mercy on him): 'I memorized the Noble Quran in two months. I cut myself off from people and locked

---

14 The Arabic original suggests that he means his seventh year of age here.

myself in my library and didn't come out except for prayers.'"[15] The Quran is approximately 77,430 words long,[16] so this rate of memorization would be 1,290 words per day.

This focus on memorization has also spread to Islamic education more generally. For example, Abd al-Rahman Bin Nasr al-Barak has an entire section of his website biography entitled "Memorizations"; here he lists nine books that he has memorized. In an interview, Sulayman Bin Nasr al-Ulwan answered a question about his study habits by stating, "I read more than 15 hours per day, divided between memorization, recall, and reading."[17]

What is the quality of this memorization? In sermons and lessons, some clerics display remarkable facility with the Quranic text and are able to recite seemingly endless passages. On the other hand, one of my informants who insisted on helping me memorize the first page of the al-Baqara chapter of the Quran had clearly memorized it but as he recited, his eyes would bounce off the page at regular intervals, seeking some visual cue to jog his memory. I was not sure he could have done it without.

The Quran is divided into thirty universally recognized divisions (*juz*, pl. *ajzā*ʾ) of equal length. The careful observer of al-Ali's syllabus will note that he requires students to memorize the Quran out of order, starting from the final sections and then moving backward for the first four years, then starting from the beginning section and going forward for the remaining six years. My observations at al-Azhar indicate that this is a common, though not universal, approach. The Quran is organized by length, from longest chapter to shortest, and many new students find it substantially more manageable to begin with the short and poetic chapters at the end rather than with the second sura, which stretches to 200 pages in the official Saudi printing.

Apart from Quran memorization, al-Ali's syllabus makes clear the topics in which a cleric should be expert: assigned readings are organized into categories of theology, jurisprudence, hadith (the collected sayings of the Prophet Muhammad), Quranic studies, behavior, language, biography, history, and fatwas. The assigned readings are dense, serious books. Few of the works are overtly political despite al-Ali's inclusion of his own political inclinations in his work. Although al-Ali is a known jihadist, the reading list includes none of the names Westerners associate with the jihadist movement. Usama Bin Laden is nowhere to be found, for example, nor any other clerics in al-Qaeda's orbit. Muhammad Qutb does make an appearance – al-Ali assigns his book, *An Islamic Vision in Our Contemporary Reality* – but apart from this, the

15 http://ar.islamway.net/scholar/376, accessed February 9, 2017, and archived at http://dx.doi.org/10.7910/DVN/PG4A7K.

16 See Dukes, Kais. "RE: Number of Unique Words in the Quran." mail-archive.com. www.mail-archive.com/comp-quran@comp.leeds.ac.uk/msg00223.html, accessed February 9, 2017, and archived at http://dx.doi.org/10.7910/DVN/PG4A7K.

17 http://ar.islamway.net/scholar/245, accessed February 9, 2017, and archived at http://dx.doi.org/10.7910/DVN/PG4A7K.

usual jihadist suspects are not here. This is a jihadist's syllabus that contains surprisingly little jihad.

Rather, al-Ali tends to assign two types of authors. First, he assigns works by authors who are seen as foundational to the Salafi movement. Salafis have long found legal foundations for their positions in the writings of medieval scholars such as Ibn Taymiyya (b. 1263 CE) and his student Ibn al-Qayyim (b. 1292 CE). The syllabus assigns thirteen works by Ibn Taymiyya and ten by Ibn al-Qayyim, sending the message that classics are worth reading in full and that the relatively inflexible and sometimes anachronistic teachings of these scholars remain relevant. Al-Ali's exuberance for these authors is unbounded: "It is incumbent upon the student to collect any of their work that he lays his eyes on, for in them there are so many blessings for knowledge (only God knows how great). Whoever is diligent in reading these publications will have God put light in his heart and open his eyes and bless him in his work."

Second, and a more surprising feature of al-Ali's syllabus, is his inclusion of contemporary Saudi clerics who are deeply critical of jihadism: Abd al-Aziz Bin Baz, Muhammad Ibn al-Uthaymeen, and Muhammad al-Albani. By including a generous sampling of their work on the syllabus, al-Ali acknowledges that despite their political positions these authors are the foremost scholars in their respective subfields of the Islamic sciences. Apart from the assigned readings, al-Ali also suggests that their books are important in any scholar's library, although he does not endorse them with the same enthusiasm as he does Ibn Taymiyya and Ibn al-Qayyim.

The implicit lesson from al-Ali's syllabus choices is that quality counts. Al-Ali seems intent on assigning the most rigorous treatments available, provided that they are consistent with a Salafi viewpoint. A firebrand student seeking polemical training would be bored here, and perhaps that is the point. To become a cleric is to discipline oneself and, thereby, enter the discipline of the Islamic sciences.

2.3 WHAT CLERICS PRODUCE

Another way to understand the cultural milieu of Muslim clerics is to examine their efforts to produce Islamic-tradition academic and religious material for each other and for lay Muslims. There are multiple genres of clerical production, aimed at different audiences. Here, I describe the most important and common of these genres, though a full excavation of the work of modern Muslim clerics in the age of the Internet deserves an entire study in its own right.

I focus on websites, traditional academic production (dissertations, scholarly books, and conference papers), popular production (articles and popular books), religious production (sermons, fatwas), lessons, and lectures. Although clerics produce recordings, music, and visual materials, I do not focus on these because the clerics who tend to produce them often do not produce written work expressing their ideological stances. The most prominent of these are *talawiyyat*, recitations of the Quran. Clerics who produce recordings of Quran recitation tend to specialize primarily in this craft and are called *qārī*. I do not analyze many reciters in this study primarily because, although they fit my definition for clerics, they do not produce text with their own ideas and thus there is no way to tell where their ideological allegiances lie. The same is true for clerics who primarily record Islamic songs, called *nashīd*. Finally, "Islamic Flashes" (*al-filāshāt al-islāmiyya*) – animated Quran verses and hadith set to Islam-themed backgrounds and music – are a remarkably entertaining genre of Islamic religious production that deserves further treatment but is not my focus in this study.[18]

2.3.1 Cleric Websites

Many of the clerics I study create and curate websites where they share information about themselves, promote their writings, and cultivate their images. Cleric websites offer an extraordinary window into the lives of contemporary Muslim clerics. As I discovered at al-Azhar, even clerics who are somewhat private and aloof in person can become gregarious and unguarded online. Perhaps in this way clerics are not much different from most other users of Internet-based social media.

Cleric websites come in several forms. The most complete form is generally a website that a cleric personally owns and administers, with content that is primarily their own. In many ways, these websites resemble academic websites by scholars in Western academia. They are primarily places for clerics to disseminate their research and ideas, and for people interested in their work to learn more about them. The URLs to these websites are almost always some transliteration of the cleric's name with the internet suffix ".com." These websites typically have navigation bars for five to ten categories, including "CV," "Books," "Fatwas," "Lessons," "Audio Clips," "Video Clips," "Map of the Site," "Contact Us," and "Record of Visitors" (where website users can leave comments).

Some clerics appear to put substantial effort into these websites and update them relatively frequently. Others appear to have created them once, typically in the late 2000s, and then abandoned them. Cleric websites go down fairly frequently because clerics fail to pay hosting fees or do not know how to keep up with advances in Internet technology. Managing a website is not always a straightforward task for octogenarian clerics; I have found at least one instance of a junior cleric mentioning his role in managing the website of a more senior associate.[19] All this gives even the most elaborate of cleric websites a somewhat ephemeral quality; it could all be gone tomorrow.

---

[18] For examples, see http://ar.islamway.net/flashes/new, accessed February 9, 2017, and archived at http://dx.doi.org/10.7910/DVN/PG4A7K.

[19] http://anassarmini.blogspot.com/2012/12/blog-post_3640.html, accessed February 9, 2017, and archived at http://dx.doi.org/10.7910/DVN/PG4A7K.

A number of clerics at academic institutions have websites hosted by their university. In most cases, these are simply a single page with the university's visual branding that hosts a photo of the cleric, a short biographical statement, a list of classes he teaches, and links to some of his recent published work. In some cases, this university website is more elaborate, serving the functions of a stand-alone cleric website. The primary purpose of these websites for clerics seems to be to comply with university requirements that everyone in a particular academic unit have a web page with some information that is accessible from the university homepage.

Facebook is a popular social media website that allows users to share content with friends and followers online. Many clerics have one or more Facebook pages that they use in place of or alongside their "real" websites. Often, these will be labeled "the Official Website of Sheikh so-and-so" (*mawqaᶜ rasmiyya*) to alert readers that this is the web space that the cleric in question most actively updates. Facebook seems to be easier for some clerics to manage than a website and more to their liking. Rather than having to learn new software to create a website or hire someone, clerics can simply use Facebook's web architecture to disseminate their writings.

Facebook is also host to many pages managed by the students and followers of a cleric. These have titles like "Admirers of Sheikh so-and-so" to distinguish them from the cleric's official page. These pages can help increase a cleric's profile by disseminating their writings and making them seem influential and trustworthy (after all, they have "admirers"). On the other hand, "unofficial" fan websites can challenge clerics' attempts to control their online image. One cleric goes so far as to post a statement on his official website noting, "Only fatwas from this website are valid, and anything found anywhere else isn't valid."[20]

Writings by clerics are also sometimes available on Islamic aggregator websites that collect and host the work of many clerics under a single web domain. Some clerics use these as their "official" website and post a biography to go along with their collection of writings. Others do not seem involved; their writings are most likely reposted at the behest of an Islamic aggregator site administrator. Some clerics have turned their own websites into Islamic aggregator sites, such as Salman al-Awda, whose website, "Islam Today" (www.islamtoday.net), has sections devoted to current events and to the advice and fatwas of other clerics.

It is easy to overlook cleric websites as a type of clerical production because, as in Western academia, cleric websites are not usually seen as scholarly output in their own right. To an outsider, however, these websites are crucial for understanding what clerics do and how they see themselves because they provide unparalleled access to the scholarly lives of their creators and reveal the inner workings of cleric life in both explicit and implicit ways.

---

[20] www.shankeety.net, accessed January 2, 2012, and archived at http://dx.doi.org/10.7910/DVN/PG4A7K.

2.3.2 Academic and Popular Writing

Academic writing by clerics needs relatively little description. Anyone who has ever completed a thesis or dissertation in a Western academic setting will recognize an Islamic academic thesis as essentially the same animal. For example, Sheikh Sa'ad al-Sabr describes his dissertation defense as follows:

He completed a doctorate at the High Institute for Judges of the Department of Comparative Jurisprudence at the University of Imam Muhammad Bin Saud; the qualifying discussion of the doctoral thesis has been completed, the title of which was "Hanafi Doctrinal Differences in Almsgiving and Fasting, in Teaching and in Practice."

The Committee formed to discuss the doctorate of Dr. Sa'ad included:

   1. Prof. Aqeel Bin Abdulrahman al-Aqeel, Supervisor and Chairman of the Committee.
   2. Prof. Ibrahim Nasser Bin Hamoud, Committee Member. A member of the Council for Study at the High Institute for Judges of the Department of Comparative Jurisprudence at the Islamic University of Imam Muhammad Bin Saud.
   3. Prof. Mohammed Bin Abdullah Shanqeeti, Committee Member. President of the Division of Justice at the University of Nayef Bin Abdul Aziz, God bless him.

The open defense was completed on Tuesday 1435/2/21 after sunset prayers in the Hall of the High Institute for Judges of Imam Muhammad Bin Saud Islamic University, and Dr. Sa'ad received his doctorate cum laude with honors.[21]

Clerics also produce scholarly books. Often, as in Western academia, their first book is a revised version of their doctoral dissertation.

In addition, clerics write popular books, such as A'id al-Qarni's widely circulating *lā taḥzan* (*Don't Be Sad*), which is an Islamic pop-psychology book "full of practical advice on how to replace sadness with a pragmatic and ultimately satisfying Islamic outlook on life."[22] Topics in this book range from the largely scientific ("Depression may lead to suicide") to the overtly religious ("When you ask, ask Allah"), all with a generous sprinkling of quotes from the Quran and in accessible, advice-column language (al Qarni 2005, 207, 423). Many of these books are in a genre that could be described as Islamic self-help (Kenney 2015).

---

[21] I accessed and translated this passage from www.alsaber.net/articles.php?action=show&id=206 in the summer of 2015, but as of February 9, 2017, the link is broken and I cannot locate the original source online. This event also received a small write-up in the local news. Zila', Yahya. "Doctorate for Sa'ad al-Sabr." Alriyadh.com. www.alriyadh.com/906205 as of February 9, 2017, and archived at http://dx.doi.org/10.7910/DVN/PG4A7K.

[22] Abu Hisham. "Don't Be Sad." Islamic Books Free Download. http://download-islamic-book.blogspot.com/2014/02/dont-be-sad-al-qarni.html, accessed February 9, 2017, and archived at http://dx.doi.org/10.7910/DVN/PG4A7K.

Clerics also write articles (*maqālāt*) in both academic and popular styles. Not surprisingly, on websites that report user statistics and ratings for content, such as islamway.net, accessible articles on controversial topics are far more widely read than dry writing on arcane academic points.

One way of assessing the importance of different genres of writing to Muslim clerics is to examine their libraries. While at al-Azhar, I was given free rein of the mosque library, subject only to the constraints of somewhat sporadic hours of operation and the requirement that I present an ID and sign in each time. The library is relatively spacious; aerial photographs of al-Azhar allow me to estimate that it occupies approximately one-fifteenth of the overall floor plan of the mosque. The ceiling is tall, with intricately painted woodwork. An ornate *miḥrāb*, or prayer nook, commands the east wall. The room looks like it was redone at some point in the last thirty years but has become cluttered (the back corner had a pile of Hostess Ho Hos boxes filled with dusty, torn books topped with an overturned blue plastic stool).[23]

The walls are lined with thirty-one wooden bookshelves, between four and six feet high and generally about seven feet wide. Forty-six more bookshelves are arranged in the middle of the room, mostly in clusters of two or four. Most bookshelves have a label; I count the frequency of genres by counting the shelf space devoted to that genre. This is not a perfect measure of the reading or writing priorities of clerics because some genres require more shelf space than others and some books are read much more frequently than others (a fact made evident by coatings of dust on some volumes). Still, it is useful to know what one would encounter most if they were to read the entire mosque library at al-Azhar. Of the seventy-seven bookshelves, the genres of writing were, from most frequent to least: Quranic exegesis (thirteen shelves), hadith (thirteen), *fiqh* (jurisprudence)[24] (ten), Islamic history (five), biographies of the Prophet (four), biographies of others (three), Quranic sciences (two full shelves plus one empty), *qānūn* (law) (three), and then creed, philosophy, landmarks and mosques, fatwas, journals, and conference proceedings, each of which occupy a single shelf.[25]

2.3.3 Sermons

Clerics also produce content that is primarily religious rather than academic. A major role of Muslim clerics is to deliver sermons during Friday group prayer and they take this task seriously. Clerics denote their role as sermon givers

---

23 Several photographs of the library are archived at http://dx.doi.org/10.7910/DVN/PG4A7K.

24 *Fiqh*, often translated as "jurisprudence," is the human understanding of the divine law of God (*sharica*) as developed by Muslim scholars through legal rulings and theory.

25 This accounts for fifty-nine of the seventy-seven bookshelves. The remaining shelves were either unoccupied, unlabeled, or in disarray. The map of the room I drew in my field notes is archived at http://dx.doi.org/10.7910/DVN/PG4A7K.

(*khaṭīb*) on their CVs and often place collections of their sermons in prominent subsections of their websites. Writing and delivering sermons at a large mosque is an honor and a feather in the cap for even the most accomplished clerics. In Egypt, few sermon venues are more prominent than Friday prayers at al-Azhar.

The first time I heard the sermon at al-Azhar, I had been at the mosque all morning, sitting in the shade of the pillars around the open white-marble courtyard for which al-Azhar is famous.[26] The prayer space at al-Azhar is vast but when attending a Friday sermon, it is best to arrive early because it is thronged with congregants. Prayer did not start until approximately noon, but by 11 a.m., people were beginning to enter the prayer space.

To enter and pray, one must perform *wuḍūʾ*, a ritual cleansing that puts the participant into a state of purity required for prayer. The fountains for performing *wuḍūʾ* are outside of the mosque, to the north side, inside the gate. Since many mosque goers, myself included, have removed their shoes, a pile of wooden sandals with leather or plastic straps sits piled outside the north entrance for congregants to use while walking to the fountains. Wearing these shoes is a clumsy and entertaining experience; mosque regulars seem to take subtle pride in using them instead of their own shoes to signal that they are a mosque regular (and thus do not have their shoes with them) and that they perform *wuḍūʾ* often (and are well practiced with the wooden sandals). I was not well practiced and I tripped several times while clunking my way loudly to the place of *wuḍūʾ*.

Wuḍūʾ involves wiping water in a pattern over one's body and I returned to enter the prayer space refreshed and with my ears still wet. The prayer space was built at two different times and comprises a vast rectangular room that is immediately adjoined to a slightly smaller, but still vast, rectangular annex that one enters by stepping up about a foot at the dividing point. The door to the prayer space is at the center back, so everyone enters there and then disperses throughout to find seating. The roof is supported by more than 100 pillars and arches. The floor is carpeted in a burgundy pattern with white and gold prayer mats printed every six inches or so. Each prayer-mat pattern is rectangular at the bottom and shaped like an arched window at the top, with two minarets framed at the top and two columns running down the side. I did not see a similar prayer-mat pattern at any of the other mosques that I visited. The prayer-mat pattern offered a way to approximately guess the number of congregants; walking the perimeter, I calculated that there were 3,786 prayer-mat patterns in thirty-six rows. No one actually spaces out according to the pattern, so with the hall full, there are approximately two people for every prayer-mat pattern. On this day, my best guess is that approximately 7,600 people attended the sermon.

The front was filling up and I was self-conscious of making mistakes while praying, so I sat down against a column in the middle of the prayer space. Unfortunately, this gave me an excellent view of the *mihrāb*, the arched nook

---

[26] My fieldwork notes from this event are archived at http://dx.doi.org/10.7910/DVN/PG4A7K.

from which the imam normally leads prayers, but placed a column directly in my line of sight to the *minbar*, the stepped wooden pulpit from which the imam delivers the sermon. This is not unusual at al-Azhar, where the multitude of columns means that almost nobody gets a perfect view. My proximity to a pillar also meant that I garnered more attention, not less. Unknown to me, it is common custom for people to carry their shoes with them into the prayer space after removing them at the mosque entrance. Worshipers cannot pray with shoes in their hands and it is disrespectful to place them on the carpet where worshipers press their foreheads in prayer, so shoes pile up at the columns where a marble base juts out approximately a foot. As shoes collected around my column, I collected stares. A shock of blond hair is not common at al-Azhar.

The sermon was preceded by a long recitation from the Quran, sung by a cleric at the front whom I couldn't see. After this, most people (but not everyone) arose and prayed two *rukūʿa* (prostrations), after which some jostling at the front indicated the sermon was about to begin.

Sermons are divided into two parts. The first must begin with the *hamdallah*, an expression of praise for God, and is immediately followed by a set piece that asks for blessings upon Muhammad, his family, and the faithful. Then the imam transitions to the core of the sermon, mingling Quranic recitation with exhortation to righteous living. This sermon was about purity ("Oh my Muslim brothers, what is purity? Light!"), and was apolitical. The second sermon was more political and exhorted congregants to support the righteous cause of protestors (not yet rebels) in Homs, Syria, and Sanaa', Yemen. Both sermons were loud and passionate; the amplification system distorted and my ears hurt during the loudest parts. It lasted about thirty-five minutes, and both the sermon and group prayer that followed were over by 12:50, at which point the people streamed back out and into the street.

In some countries, a state ministry of religious affairs suggests sermon topics or directly writes sermons that clerics must deliver. Sermons in Turkey, for instance, are distributed by the Ministry of Religious Affairs and are to be read verbatim by clerics. They are also remarkably more boring than other sermons I have encountered. After the 2013 overthrow of President Muhammad Mursi, the Egyptian government, led by Abd El-Fattah al-Sisi, moved to regulate Friday sermons in a similar fashion, hoping to avoid sermons that incite political action.

2.3.4 Lessons, Lectures, and Recordings

Clerics also give lessons and lectures. The mosque has been the traditional setting for this type of teaching but increasingly these lessons are recorded and placed online by the cleric's followers. Some clerics primarily distribute their lectures online through sites such as YouTube.

At al-Azhar, these lessons happen throughout the day and are most frequent in the afternoon (perhaps not coincidentally, this is also the preferred teaching schedule of many academics in the United States). Lesson times are posted sometimes on the mosque door and sometimes on the al-Azhar Facebook page and website. Sometimes after leading the midday prayer, the imam leading the prayer will stay after to lecture. Some mosque regulars will sit in on whatever lesson happens to be starting; this was my method of finding lessons to attend because I could not seem to figure out the schedule.

Some lessons are one-off sessions that have no prerequisites. Others are sessions of long-running classes and students bring their books and follow along with the lecturing sheikh. At al-Azhar, the sheikh typically sits in a large, comfortable chair brought out in front of the center *miḥrāb*. Students sit on the ground in concentric half-circles, with the most dedicated students vying for the front and mosque cleaning staff taking a break around the edges. This is the modern incarnation of the traditional Islamic *ḥalaqa*, the teaching circle of a sheikh. Many students place recording devices on a table next to the sheikh while others record on cell phones. I am perennially uncomfortable sitting cross-legged on the floor, but apparently I am the only one who minds because I readjust my body much more frequently than the others in the circle. Perhaps people like me who are uncomfortable on the floor are not meant to become clerics.

In general, lessons are not interactive. The sheikh typically gives the lesson from prepared notes without interruption, although some clerics do engage in a call-and-response type of review as they talk about concepts that were, apparently, previously covered. Every mention of the Prophet also evokes a response from the circled students as they rush to say *ṣalā allāhu ʿalayhim wa-salam* (peace and prayers be upon him) so as to secure the blessings specified in the hadith tradition for doing so. Lessons are often followed by a question and answer period that is more interactive.

2.3.5 Fatwas

In Islam, questions of religious belief are brought by lay Muslims to a member of the ʿulamāʾ, who answers in the form of a fatwa. A fatwa is a nonbinding legal opinion that serves an advisory role for the recipient and possibly for other Muslims as well.[27] As Agrama (2010) shows, the apparent authority of fatwas deserves explanation. On one hand, the nonbinding nature of fatwas makes their status as law somewhat tenuous. A colleague of mine at Harvard once taped a sign to their door that modified a line from the movie *The Big Lebowski* to read "A fatwa ... that's just, like, your opinion man." And they are. Individuals do not face legal repercussions for ignoring any particular fatwa.

On the other hand, the system of Islamic law can be binding in that individuals bind themselves to follow the fatwas that they seek. In some cases, the intent of those seeking a fatwa can be perverse. The Islamic scholar Tariq Ramadan told a story in my hearing of a young man who came to him asking for

---

[27] A volume edited by Masud, Messick, and Powers (1996) provides an overview and collects some of the latest work on fatwas in both recent history and the distant past.

guidance about listening to music. Ramadan gave him multiple viewpoints and justifications by many jurists for and against, with a somewhat chilly reception. A few days later, the youth reported to Ramadan that he had asked another cleric who had simply said that music was forbidden in Islam; this was the answer he wanted to hear. "Well, are you going to stop listening to music?" Ramadan asked, to which the young man replied, "No." Such is the world of fatwas.[28]

The term "fatwa" is often misunderstood to be some form of Islamic death sentence. A very small number of fatwas do condemn people to death, and these tend to garner substantial publicity. Perhaps the most infamous is the fatwa issued by Iranian Supreme Leader Ayatollah Khomeini calling for the death of author Salman Rushdie because of perceived blasphemy in Rushdie's novel, *The Satanic Verses*. However, such fatwas are a rare minority, less than one in a thousand. Most fatwas are about personal matters of faith, religious practice, proper management of family relations, dietary law, and moral codes. Fatwas generally deal with matters that might seem mundane: whether it is permissible to eat food remnants caught in one's teeth (permissible if removed by the tongue but not if removed with a toothpick because swallowing blood is forbidden),[29] whether the angels have seen God (no, they see screens of light),[30] or the ruling on someone who dies on the toilet (it does not affect their prospects in the afterlife).[31] The most viewed fatwa on the Islamic website Islam Way (islamway.com) is titled, "How do you advise one addicted to pornography?"; it has been viewed more than 1.3 million times.[32]

To provide an accurate sense of the topical content of fatwas, I collected roughly 105,000 Arabic-language fatwas issued by the scholars' council of the website Islam Web (www.islamweb.net) from the date of the website's creation in 2001 through 2010.[33] These fatwas are responses to questions posed by users

28 For an ethnographic perspective on how fatwas influence the lives of those who request them, see Abu-Zahra (1997, 171–204).

29 "Eating food remnants stuck between teeth." Islamweb English. www.islamweb.net/ emainpage/index.php?page=showfatwa&Option=FatwaId&Id=199225, first accessed March 12, 2013, last accessed February 9, 2017, and archived at http://dx.doi.org/10.7910/DVN/ PG4A7K.

30 "Can the angels see Allaah The Almighty?" Islamweb English. www.islamweb.net/emainpage/ index.php?page=showfatwa&Option=FatwaId&Id=34304, first accessed March 12, 2013, last accessed February 9, 2017, and archived at http://dx.doi.org/10.7910/DVN/PG4A7K.

31 "Ruling on people who die in toilet." Islamway English. www.islamweb.net/emainpage/index. php?page=showfatwa&Option=FatwaId&Id=157823, first accessed March 12, 2013, last accessed February 9, 2017, and archived at http://dx.doi.org/10.7910/DVN/PG4A7K.

32 "How do you advise one addicted to pornography?" Islamway.net. http://ar.islamway.net/ fatwa/3386?ref=p-top, accessed February 10, 2017, and archived at http://dx.doi.org/10.7910/ DVN/PG4A7K. On February 10, 2017, this fatwa had 1,323,858 page views according to the website counter.

33 The fatwas are available at http://islamweb.net/fatwa/index.php, as of February 10, 2017. As of this writing, there are more than 300,000 fatwas in Arabic, with a much smaller number in English, Spanish, French, and German. I originally conducted this analysis in 2010.

Fatwa topic

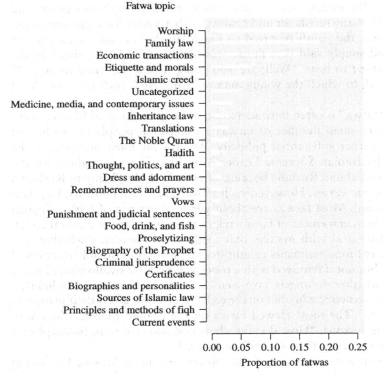

FIGURE 2.1. The topics of a large fatwa corpus.

Notes: The topics used by the website Islam Web to categorize 105,000 fatwas issued by its scholars' council between 2001 and 2010. The topics are defined by the website administrators and each fatwa is assigned to a single category.

of the website, so the topics are driven by what users ask. There is no evidence that the fatwa council selects particular questions to answer and avoids others, provided that the questions are posed sincerely. After the questions are posed, the anonymous council of scholars provides a fatwa that is then posted to the website. When the fatwa is posted, the site administrators classify it into one of twenty-five categories (listed in Figure 2.1). These, and the fatwas assigned to them, are selected by the site administrators for the purpose of allowing readers to find fatwas using a hierarchical set of indexes and subindexes. These categories represent how at least some Muslims think about the content of fatwas.

Figure 2.1 shows the proportion of fatwas (out of 105,000) devoted to each of the twenty-five categories. The results paint a very different picture of the genre than popular perceptions among Western non-Muslims. Over half of the fatwas – 55 percent – fall into just three categories: worship, family law, and economic transactions. This suggests that when lay Muslims are driving the fatwa process, their primary concerns and uncertainties revolve around very practical matters: how to properly worship, interact with family, and conduct economic exchange. The long tail of topics suggests that fatwas can be about anything, in keeping with the belief of many Muslims that divine law governs all human action. On the other hand, clerics may artificially constrain the range of topics in their own output, either by selectively answering questions about a particular topic or by posing questions to themselves that they would like to answer rather than waiting for a follower to ask (Masud, Messick, and Powers 1996).

The topics in the Islam Web collection are similar to the organization of traditional fatwa collections. The order of headings in these traditional collections is customarily the same, in deference to a theological hierarchy of topics. For example, the thirty-seven-volume compilation of fatwas by Ibn Taymiyya at the end of Hamid al-Ali's syllabus is divided thus:[34]

Volume 1: Introduction and Tawhid of Divinity, 267 pp.
Volume 2: Tawhid of Lordship, 306 pp.
Volumes 3–4: The Beliefs of the Salaf (the first three generations of Muslims), 614 pp.
Volumes 5–6: Names and Attributes of God, 718 pp.
Volume 7: Faith, 428 pp.
Volume 8: Power (of God), 335 pp.
Volume 9: Logic, 176 pp.
Volume 10: Behavior, 428 pp.
Volume 11: Mysticism, 395 pp.
Volume 12: The Quran, the True Word of God, 331 pp.
Volume 13: Introduction to Quranic Exegesis, 238 pp.
Volumes 14–17: Quranic Exegisis, 1,198 pp.
Volume 18: Hadith (sayings of the Prophet), 228 pp.
Volumes 19–20: Roots of Jurisprudence, 501 pp.
Volume 21: Jurisprudence – Purity, 368 pp.
Volume 22–23: Jurisprudence – Prayer, 240 pp.
Volume 24: Jurisprudence – "Prayer" through "Zakat" (alms), 219 pp.
Volume 25: Jurisprudence – "Zakat" through "Fasting," 184 pp.
Volume 26: Jurisprudence – Pilgrimage, 172 pp.
Volume 27: Jurisprudence – Travel, 276 pp.
Volume 28: Jurisprudence – Jihad, 372 pp.
Volume 29: Jurisprudence – Selling, 320 pp.
Volume 30: Jurisprudence – Waqf (religious endowments), 238 pp.
Volume 31: Jurisprudence – "Waqf" through "Marriage," 238 pp.
Volume 32: Jurisprudence – Marriage, 238 pp.

34 Translated from https://archive.org/details/mjftitdrwf by the author in 2015. Last accessed February 10, 2017.

Volume 33: Jurisprudence – Divorce, 148 pp.
Volume 34: Jurisprudence – "Pre-Islamic Customs" through "Killing Prostitutes," 170 pp.
Volume 35: Jurisprudence – "Killing Prostitutes" through "Confessions," 262 pp.
Volume 36–37: Index, 1,311 pp.

Comparing the page counts devoted to particular topics in Ibn Taymiyya's compilation reveals that he writes substantially less on some topics (e.g., family law) than the clerics at islamweb.net. Both collections convey that fatwas can cover virtually every topic imaginable.

Because the ostensible purpose of the fatwa genre is to answer questions from lay Muslims about proper worship and living, fatwas by even the most extreme jihadists can seem remarkably mundane and sometimes tedious. In February 2015, a self-reported resident of the Islamic State named Abu Umar al-Masri tweeted images of thirty-two fatwas taken from a larger collection distributed by the Council for Research and Fatwas of the Islamic State (in Iraq and Syria) as a stapled paper handout with the Islamic State logo on top. Cole Bunzel translates and analyzes these fatwas in a post at the Jihadica blog. Some fatwas are directly related to jihadist fighting and are quite horrifying:

No. 60, January 20, 2015
Q. Is it permissible to burn an unbeliever till he dies?
A. The Hanafi and Shafi'i schools of Islamic law judged immolation to be permissible, while some scholars judged it to be forbidden. At all events, it is permissible on the basis of reciprocity (mumathala), as when the Prophet gouged out the eyes of the 'Uraniyyin.[35]

No. 68, January 31, 2015
Q. Is it permissible for Muslims in need to take from the organs of an apostate prisoner?
A. Yes. It is permissible to transplant the healthy organs of the body of an apostate to the body of a Muslim, in order to save the latter's life or improve his condition if he has lost organs. The jurists of the Shafi'i and Hanbali schools of Islamic law, among others, permitted killing belligerent unbelievers or apostates and eating their flesh as a life-saving measure. The case of organ transplantation as a life-saving measure is similar. Moreover, it is established that the lives and organs of apostates are fundamentally licit. Their organs may thus be taken, whether or not the apostates are alive or already dead, and whether or not doing so results in their death.[36]

---

35 Bunzel, Cole. "32 Islamic State Fatwas." Jihadica.com. www.jihadica.com/32-islamic-state-fatwas, accessed February 9, 2017, and archived at http://dx.doi.org/10.7910/DVN/PG4A7K. The 'Uraniyyin are, according to the hadith tradition, eight men from the tribe of Uraynah who came to Medina, became sick, were cured, and then murdered those who helped cure them. Muhammad ordered them to be mutilated and left for dead in the desert as a retributive punishment. See al-Bukhari, Sahih, vol. 1, no. 234.
36 Bunzel, Cole. "32 Islamic State Fatwas." Jihadica.com. www.jihadica.com/32-islamic-state-fatwas, accessed February 9, 2017, and archived at http://dx.doi.org/10.7910/DVN/PG4A7K.

Other fatwas from this same collection reveal the banality of religious and political governance in the Islamic State: "Q: Is it permissible to play foosball? A: Yes, but on several conditions." "Q: Is it permissible for women to bleach their eyebrows? A: Yes." Some even deal with rumors that seem quite harmless, but which the Islamic State feels the need to address:

No. 67, January 29, 2015
Q. Many have asked about the truth of the Arabic numerals (٣ , ٢, ١, etc.), including the claim that they are Indian in origin and are the ones used in the Latin alphabet (1, 2, 3, etc.). We ask for clarification on this matter.
A. The historians have more than one position on this issue, but the best opinion is that the Arabic numerals are ٣ , ٢, ١, etc. The Arabs, not the Indians, introduced these numbers. The Arabs only borrowed from the Indians the idea of the decimal numeral system, not the shape of the numbers. So it is wrong to say that the Arabs took these numbers from the Indians.[37]

Although most of the fatwas in this book are from online sources, the vast majority of fatwas are not placed online or even publicly recorded. Rather, most fatwas are issued by a cleric for a specific person, with the expectation that the fatwa is primarily for personal guidance (Messick 1996, 311–312). To develop an understanding of who seeks personal fatwas and the process by which they are delivered, I visited two fatwa-giving offices in Egypt.

The Egyptian *Dar al-Ifta* – literally the "House of Fatwa-giving" – is a government ministry devoted to providing fatwas, and it provides a number of fatwas on its website, www.dar-alifta.org. The website features an image of the *mushaykha*, an ostentatious building in the Mansouria district of Cairo that serves as the office of the head cleric of Egypt. However, getting a personal fatwa from this building is impossible; it is intended for issuing official fatwas meant for Egyptian Muslims generally. Instead, if private citizens would like a fatwa, they travel two buildings down and enter a smaller, unimposing building with a small waiting area and a single attendant (the mushaykha has a large lobby with about five guards), where they meet with a state cleric who issues a ruling, often writing it on a piece of paper for the recipient. It is actually this building that Egyptians refer to as the government Dar al-Ifta, even though it is not represented this way online.

To learn about the process of fatwa giving, I visited the Egyptian Dar al-Ifta. Door guards at both the mushaykha and the building where citizens request fatwas did not allow me inside to observe any part of the fatwa-giving process. The caginess of the state ministry seems to be due to suspicion about a foreigner snooping around a government ministry, even one as innocuous as the fatwa office. Thus I observed what I could from the outside.

The Dar al-Ifta is a white, two-story building located on a frontage road by the Salah Salam Highway on the eastern edge of the old Islamic district in Cairo,

---

37 Bunzel, Cole. "32 Islamic State Fatwas." Jihadica.com. www.jihadica.com/32-islamic-state-fatwas, accessed February 9, 2017, and archived at http://dx.doi.org/10.7910/DVN/PG4A7K.

in a block of government buildings that serves as a buffer between the crowded neighborhoods near al-Hussein square and the desolate expanse of tombs and make shift dwellings that comprises Cairo's City of the Dead. The Dar al-Ifta is overshadowed by two imposing government buildings immediately behind it: the mushaykha, a six-story stone building built in neo-Islamic style, and the off-site library of al-Azhar (distinct from the mosque library), an imposing fourteen-story monolith of brutalist concrete. By contrast, the Dar al-Ifta looks like part of Cairo. Air conditioning units hang out of rough-cut holes in the exterior walls and the wooden shutters are dusty and sit at odd angles. Passersby on the highway could be forgiven for thinking that the large sign on the building bearing the symbol of the Egyptian Ministry of Justice and proclaiming "The Egyptian House of Fatwa-giving" was a billboard referring to the buildings behind. Only a small blue sign over the door reading "Council of Fatwas" betrays that this is the location where government-appointed muftis answer religious questions for the public.[38]

In general, the Egyptian Dar al-Ifta was busy and visits by patrons were fairly brief, perhaps ten minutes.[39] By observing entrants to the Dar al-Ifta, I got a sense of the types of people who seek fatwas there. I noticed no clear pattern in the demographics of those entering the office. Of fifty-five people who entered (in thirty groups), twenty-seven were men, twenty-one were women, and seven were children. Patron dress ranged from fully Western attire (two individuals) to a niqab covering the face (one individual). All but one woman entering the office were veiled to at least some extent, but this did not strike me as unusual for Egyptian Muslims. Four of the twenty-seven men were overtly Salafi (identifiable by their beards). Overall, the office appeared to serve Egyptian Muslims from a variety of backgrounds.

Down the street, the clerics at al-Azhar mosque also issue fatwas in a room near the main entrance to the mosque. Unlike the Dar al-Ifta, there is no signage on the street. Patrons must know by reputation alone that al-Azhar has a fatwa office. Once inside the mosque, a small-ish, faded sign rendered

---

[38] Photographs of these buildings from my first visit in 2011 are archived at http://dx.doi.org/10.7910/DVN/PG4A7K.

[39] To calculate this figure, I stationed myself outside of the *Dar al-Ifta* and observed who entered and exited on two occasions, Saturday, June 4, 2011, from 12:58–1:12 p.m., and Saturday, April 21, 2012, from 12:58–1:26 p.m. My intent was to combine what anthropologists might call *continuous monitoring* with *spot sampling* by randomly selecting periods of time and days of the week and observing who entered the Dar al-Ifta for a half hour each time (Bernard 1995, 311, 322). However, on both occasions doormen posted at the fatwa office were quite sensitive to my presence and eventually told me to move on. As a result, I have no variation on the time of day or day of the week. Still, the limited data are useful for demonstrating a few general features of the clientele of the fatwa office. In the first observation period, I counted eighteen individuals or groups entering the office and twenty people leaving in just fourteen minutes. On the second occasion, I recorded thirty distinct groups of people entering and later exiting the office over the course of twenty-eight minutes. If the office were this busy throughout an eight-hour workday, then it would issue about 500 fatwas per day. These figures come from my 2012 field notes, p. 6, archived at http://dx.doi.org/10.7910/DVN/PG4A7K.

in a tacky, shadowed font directs fatwa seekers to a hallway with the words, "The Noble al-Azhar, gathering Islamic research, faith, and exhortation, Fatwa Council of the Noble al-Azhar." The older, painted inscription on the lintel reads "Undertake prayer first" (*aqāma al-ṣalāt awalā*), suggesting that the room was once a prayer space that has been converted. In the dark hallway to the office, older signs remain, one affixed over the other, announcing that al-Azhar's fatwas are "for all citizens" and "free and without fees."[40] The clerics at al-Azhar were quite willing to allow me to enter the room where they issued fatwas, observe silently, and speak with a cleric when my turn came.

The fatwa office at al-Azhar is a rectangular room, perhaps eighteen feet by fourteen feet, with four couches along the walls of the room and four tables in front of the couches. A cleric sits in each corner with a book spread out in front of him at the table, and the fatwa seeker sits in a folding chair on the other side of the table. When a fatwa seeker is called, he or she simply goes to the next available cleric (there is no ability to select which cleric). The cleric first listens to the question and then issues a ruling, often with some exchange back and forth so that the cleric fully understands the situation and the recipient understands the answer. There is no independent verification of the situation posed by the fatwa seeker – the fatwa is issued under the assumption that the facts are correct. After the recipient leaves, the cleric writes a very brief description of the fatwa in his ledger. One of the clerics showed me his ledger and explained it briefly, noting that four of the ten entries on his current page related to divorce. Agrama (2010) provides entertaining accounts of interactions in this same office.[41]

When I asked various interlocutors in the vicinity of al-Hussein square (across from al-Azhar and a few blocks from the Dar al-Ifta), I found few strong opinions about whether it was preferable to seek a fatwa from al-Azhar or Dar al-Ifta; several respondents assumed that I would get similar fatwas from both. My impression is that these private fatwas are deemed to be straightforward and prosaic. Traditionally, a cleric was more likely to publish a fatwa or make it public if it required original scholarship, took an original position, addressed a novel question, or weighed in on a controversial issue. Personal fatwas, meanwhile, frequently addressed issues of direct relevance to an individual's life, such as music, hygiene, and divorce. This is still probably true in general, but the Internet has created a new forum for fatwa giving that provides a more permanent digital record of the types of mundane fatwas that previously would have been related orally but not recorded. Many of the clerics in my study now issue such fatwas through their websites and these appear in my corpus of texts.

---

[40] Photographs of these signs are archived at http://dx.doi.org/10.7910/DVN/PG4A7K.
[41] Again I counted patrons, this time from 12:40 p.m. to 1:05 p.m. on Tuesday, April 24, 2012. Traffic was markedly slower than at the Dar al-Ifta – eight patrons in twenty-five minutes – though this is partially attributable to the day of the week. These figures are from my 2012 field notes, p. 18, archived at http://dx.doi.org/10.7910/DVN/PG4A7K.

2.4 SUMMARY

This chapter explores who clerics are. In a departure from much of the scholarly literature on Islam, I do not focus on credentials or academic lineages of teachers as the primary marker of a cleric. The politics of these credentials and lineages are at the heart of the theory of blocked ambition that I will lay out in the next chapter, so limiting my analysis to only "properly" credentialed clerics would be analytically self-defeating. Instead, for the purposes of this study, I define a "Muslim cleric" as someone who produces religious content for public consumption within an Islamic tradition.

The rest of the chapter introduces key ideas about what clerics ought to know and the types of Islamic literature they produce. Rather than trying to describe the training of clerics comprehensively or offer a complete taxonomy of the content they produce, I focus on the areas where I can add new data not already extant in the secondary literature on Muslim clerics. I give a sense of what clerics should know and how they are trained through a detailed description of a syllabus by a jihadist Salafi, Hamid al-Ali, that to my knowledge has never before been described or translated into English. To describe what clerics produce, I focus on primary source materials from cleric websites and online fatwa banks, as well as ethnographic observations of the mosque library, lessons, and Friday sermons at the al-Azhar mosque. Readers seeking more depth should consult the works on Muslim clerics by Zaman (2002), Zeghal (1996), and Mouline (2015).

Overall, this chapter shows that clerics must know a variety of scholarly disciplines arising from an Islamic tradition, and they produce pious academic material in these same genres. Most clerics experience very little conflict between the scholarly and religious aspects of clerical production, although there are differences in style. Jihadists, we will find in the next chapter, see more tension between the demands of religious and academic spheres because they perceive the incorporation of religious elites into state-funded academic institutions as a tool of government discipline and control. Still, jihadists are likewise constrained by the academic flavor of modern Sunni clericism in ways that are profound and sometimes surprising.

3

Paths to Preaching Jihad

In 2001, Anwar al-Awlaki appeared to be a moderate American cleric with a gift for inspired preaching. He was the imam of a mosque near Falls Church, Virginia, and the Muslim chaplain at George Washington University. After the attacks of September 11, 2001, he was invited by Pentagon officials to Washington, DC, for several events, where he served as a representative of Islam. At the same time, he was studying in a doctoral program in human resource development at George Washington University that his father hoped that would credential him for a desirable position with Sanaa University or the Yemeni government (Shane 2015, 123). Yet in 2002, al-Awlaki left the United States and his budding career as an imam, and between 2004 and 2006 completely reinvented himself as one of militant jihad's most outspoken advocates. By 2010, he had been approved by the administration of US President Barack Obama for extrajudicial killing, which eventually occurred in a drone strike in 2011. What happened to turn al-Awlaki into a vociferous proponent of jihadist violence?

Some have suggested that al-Awlaki had always harbored sympathy for a militant brand of jihadism and that his decision to leave the United States was prompted by heavy-handed US surveillance of Muslims in Northern Virginia, where he lived, which stoked his fury and completed his radicalization (see Shane 2015, 102–104). But this narrative is probably incorrect. Although there were hints of jihadist sympathies earlier in life, al-Awlaki's turn to full-blown jihadism seems to have been precipitated by the imminent derailment of his career as a cleric in the United States, in 2002. According to Shane (2015, 118–119), al-Awlaki was planning to stay in the United States until March 2002, when he told his brother Ammar, "I was told that the FBI has a file on me, and this file could destroy my life." Unbeknownst to most, al-Awlaki had a secret vice: he frequented prostitutes, meeting them most often in area motels. A manager of an escort service he used had tipped him off that a US government agent had come around, asking detailed questions. Shane (2015, 120) concludes, "Awlaki would have realized for the first time that his many visits to prostitutes had been monitored by the FBI … [and] that they knew a great deal about his extra-clerical activities."

The looming threat of having his career abruptly and embarrassingly ended if the FBI revealed his sexual improprieties was likely the trigger for al-Awlaki's radical rethinking of his place as a moderate Muslim cleric in the United States and his flight from the country:

His aspiration to serve as a bridge between America and Islam, already challenged by the Operation Green Quest raids and the growing tension between the authorities and many Muslims, was over. He could no longer function as an American imam, living every day under the shadow of his own hypocrisy and the FBI's knowledge of it. He would have to find something else to do with his life. (Shane 2015, 121)

In short, while his career prospects as a mainstream cleric were bright, al-Awlaki did not explore jihadism. Once that career path was looking less promising, he struck out on a new path, advocating and eventually organizing jihadist violence.

There are many paths to becoming a jihadist cleric. Usama Bin Laden, for instance, was a jihadi who twice left Saudi Arabia to fight in the Afghani jihad, first against the Soviet Union and later against the United States. After creating the al-Qaeda organization, he found it useful to act in a clerical role, issuing fatwas among his other communiques. Anwar al-Awlaki abruptly left his position as the imam of a mosque in Northern Virginia and abandoned his ambition to serve as a bridge linking Islam and the West to travel to Yemen, where he reemerged as a leader in al-Qaeda in the Arabian Peninsula. Ayman al-Zawahiri was only 14 when the execution of Sayyid Qutb by the Egyptian government spurred him to form a resistance group that was the start of his lifelong participation in violent Islamist causes.

While the specific details of the paths that lead individuals to the role of jihadi cleric do vary, my goal in this chapter is to reveal common patterns on this path. To do so, I begin by extending existing theories of jihadist radicalization to clerics. The radicalization of jihadist clerics is not well theorized in the academic literature on modern jihadism. Studies have instead tended to focus either on the radicalization of lay jihadists (rather than religious elites) or have tried to explain broad trends in jihadist ideology, such as the timing of the jihadist movement or the evolution of its ideas. In order to understand why certain individuals become jihadist clerics, I must extend existing theories or develop new ones.

Becoming a jihadist cleric involves both a choice to become a jihadist and a choice to become a cleric. These may be related choices, but not necessarily, and either choice can precede the other. In this chapter, I argue that existing theories of lay Muslim radicalization are most likely to explain the radicalization of future jihadist clerics if radicalization takes place before the choice to become a cleric. Prior to pursuing a clerical career, an individual is, by definition, a lay Muslim to whom existing theories should apply. However, once individuals begin pursuing a career as a Muslim cleric, they are exposed to new ideas, incentives, and socialization that potentially change the processes by which they are most likely to become radicalized. In these cases, existing theories of lay radicalization need to be amended to account for the incentives that Muslim clerics face.

3.1 JIHADISTS WHO BECOME CLERICS

Many jihadist clerics are individuals who become jihadists first and only turn to clerical activities later. Because these individuals radicalize as lay Muslims, rather than as religious figures, I turn to the literature on individual radicalization.

The theories that attempt to explain why some lay Muslims become violent jihadists come in two varieties: those that emphasize the psychology of an individual turning to violence, and those that emphasize an individual's embeddedness in social networks that facilitate violent collective action. Psychological theories come in many varieties, but those that find the most empirical evidence suggest that economic and social hardship trigger individuals to harbor grievances that motivate their turn to violence. Social network theories acknowledge that individuals use grievances to justify the idea of political violence, but suggest that social connections to violent actors are the primary factor distinguishing those who choose to act on violent ideas from those who do not.

For casual observers, it is easy to wonder whether deviant psychology explains why some actors endorse, plan, and carry out senseless acts of terrorism and political violence. Psychologists have examined a number of psychological explanations for participation in terrorism (Horgan 2003; Victoroff 2005; Loza 2007; Post et al. 2009; Lester, Yang, and Lindsay 2004; King and Taylor 2011), including antisocial personality disorder (Martens 2004) and narcissism (Pearlstein 1991). However, there is little evidence that conditions such as narcissism are common among terrorists (Crenshaw 1993). Sageman (2004) collects information about the childhoods of sixty-one jihadists and finds that only five had troubled backgrounds characterized by childhood trauma or behavioral issues. Experts on the psychology of terrorism generally reject the notion that there is a "terrorist personality" (Horgan 2003, 5–14) or that terrorists "are people who have a pathological attraction for violence and for inflicting harm on others" (Silke 2003, 30). In fact, Horgan (2003, 16) argues that the evidence supports the psychological "normality" of terrorists, meaning that, other than their participation in political violence, there is no clear pattern of clinically diagnosable psychological disorders among terrorists.

While abnormal psychology offers a surprisingly weak explanation for individual participation in political violence, theories drawing on normal human psychology have been more successful. In *Why Men Rebel*, Gurr (1970) proposes that individuals turn to violence when they become disillusioned by the gap between their aspirations and their reality, a gap caused by rising expectations, diminished opportunities, or both. Gurr calls this gap "relative deprivation," which he defines as an "actor's perception of discrepancy between their value expectations and their value capabilities," where value expectations are "the goods and conditions of life to which people believe they are rightfully entitled," and value capabilities are "the goods and conditions they think they are capable of getting" (24). In other words, Gurr describes relative deprivation as the "the tension that develops from a discrepancy between the 'ought' and the 'is'... that disposes men to violence" (23). Gurr links his theory of relative deprivation to concepts of dissonance, social conflict, and Dirkheim's anomie, but ultimately grounds its microfoundations in the frustration-aggression hypothesis proposed by Dollard et al. (1939) and Miller (1941), and extended by Pastore (1952), Berkowitz (1962), Berkowitz (1978), and Berkowitz (1989), among others.

In his 1970 book, and in related work, Gurr focuses on general economic and societal frustrations, such as economic inequality and discrimination against social groups (Gurr 1968*a,b*), as do other proponents of relative deprivation theory (Davies 1969). Empirically, it does seem that political violence arises disproportionately in impoverished areas where poor economic conditions leave the population undereducated, underemployed, and undernourished (Piazza 2006; Abadie 2006; Keefer and Loayza 2008; Krueger 2007; Krueger and Maleckova 2003; Mousseau 2011; Fair et al. 2013; Enders, Hoover, and Sandler 2014). However, many terrorists are not themselves poor, even when they come from poor societies. This observation has created vigorous debate about whether economic deprivation can be a source of terrorism even if terrorists themselves are relatively well educated and well employed (Maleckova 2005; Bueno de Mesquita 2005; Benmelech and Berrebi 2007; Lee 2011). Of course, relative deprivation theory can still explain political violence by those who are objectively relatively well-off as long as they *feel* deprived of opportunity. Crenshaw (1981, 384) notes, "Many terrorists today are young, well-educated, and middle class in background. Such students or young professionals, with prior political experience, are disillusioned with the prospects of changing society and see little chance of access to the system despite their privileged status." In the face of such marginalization, individuals may turn to terrorism either to right perceived wrongs or as a quest for personal significance (Kruglanski et al. 2009), similar to "the pleasure of together changing unjust social structures through intentional action" that Wood (2003, 235) identifies as an important motivator for rebels in El Salvador.

Relative deprivation theory has been deployed to explain why individuals participate in jihadist violence by a number of scholars, including Ansari

(1984, 141), Ayubi (2003, 159–162), and Sullivan (2007), and it has also been proposed as an explanation for the nonviolent "Arab Spring" uprisings in the Middle East (Campante and Chor 2012). In an argument that parallels aspects of my own, Gambetta and Hertog (2016) offer a relative deprivation argument to explain what they see as the "curious connection between violent extremism and education." Gambetta and Hertog present data showing that engineers are dramatically overrepresented in a sample of 335 members of violent Islamist groups active in the Muslim world since the 1970s (6–13). To explain this puzzle, they argue that engineers in the Muslim-majority Middle East have faced "frustrated ambitions" (34) because of economic stagnation. As a result, engineers in Egypt and elsewhere "fell from the highest perch in terms of expectations and formed or joined Islamist movements that in previous decades had been led by lower-status graduates" (159).

Although many scholars find relative deprivation theory useful, it has faced criticism and is currently somewhat out of fashion among scholars of political violence and terrorism. In 2010, Gurr himself acknowledged the limitations of his argument, saying, "I think the core of the *Why Men Rebel* model remains valid but is incomplete" (Gurr 2010, x). The most persistent criticism of relative deprivation arguments has been that these theories overpredict participation in political violence. As Silke (2003, 33) points out, many people face some form of marginalization or frustrated ambition but only a few turn to political violence. "The question has always been, why did these particular individuals engage in terrorism when most of their compatriots did not?"

Scholars have turned to sociological theories of violent collective action as an alternative to psychological theories that operate primarily at the individual level (Tilly 1978; Skocpol 1979; Tilly, McAdam, and Tarrow 2001; Tilly 2003; Tarrow 2011; Della Porta 2013; Alimi, Bosi, and Demetriou 2015). These scholars acknowledge psychological factors but focus on the social and political structures that encourage participation in terrorism. As Silke writes, "Before an individual will be prepared to join a terrorist group, he or she first needs to belong to that section of society which supports or shares the aims, grievances, and ambitions of the terrorist group" (Silke 2003, 37). In the case of jihadists, this places attention on specific social structures that might lead young Muslim males to radicalize.

The most promising effort to explain the radicalization of lay Muslims is a socialization model proposed by Wiktorowicz (2005b) and Sageman (2004) that incorporates psychological factors but places more weight on social connections (see also Moghaddam 2005). In this account of radicalization, relatively nonreligious lay Muslims face personal hardship or societal alienation that induces frustration and leads them to seek new paradigms for understanding the world. However, most such individuals will not become jihadists. Those that do are likely to be those who found social support in the company of other individuals under the guidance of a spiritual leader who convinces them that a violent interpretation of Islam is correct. Previously nonreligious individuals are most susceptible because they lack confidence to question the claims of religious figures and are willing to adopt extreme positions to demonstrate their new found commitment to the faith (Wiktorowicz 2005b, 102). With religious credibility established, the extremist leader indoctrinates individuals to believe that militant jihad is an essential religious duty that will help them achieve the salvation prioritized by their new religious conviction.

The initial conditions in this sequence are a combination of psychological and experiential factors that make particular individuals susceptible to radicalization. According to Wiktorowicz, cultural and social isolation are among many possible sources of stress that lead to "cognitive opening," in which an individual becomes receptive to new and potentially radical ideas (2005b). Sageman also relies on this mechanism to explain the initial conditions that allow for radicalization. He focuses specifically on relative economic deprivation, discrimination, and the inability to find adequate work as the key sources of individual frustration that lead to cognitive opening and religious seeking (2004).[1] Sageman argues that individuals who become economically or socially isolated seek out groups and organizations that can provide them with camaraderie, friendship, and purpose. At least some alienated individuals find social support in the company of other individuals under the guidance of a radical or radicalizing spiritual leader, who subsequently prepares and recruits these individuals for jihad.

Another permissive factor in this socialization theory is a lack of religious expertise or training (Fair, Goldstein, and Hamza 2017). Lay Muslims who are less religious are more susceptible to jihadi radicalization than Muslims who are deeply embedded in their faith. In a comparison to members and nonmembers of the Britain-based extremist group al-Muhajiroun, Wiktorowicz (2005b) finds that "most al-Muhajiroun activists were irreligious prior to their seeking and involvement in the movement" and "were unlikely to have adopted a religious identity" (102). In comparison, nonjoiners "view themselves first and foremost as Muslims" (102–103). This lack of identification with or knowledge about Islam makes individuals susceptible to radicalization for several interrelated reasons. A low level of religious knowledge means that individuals are less equipped to discriminate between moderate and extreme versions of Islam. Simultaneously, individuals with little prior religious knowledge who turn to Islam are more easily influenced by religious elites with expert knowledge. When this religious elite espouses radical views, these individuals are likely to adopt them as well.

For individuals who become jihadists first and clerics later, these theories offer the best starting point for understanding their radicalization. If these theories are operative, then I expect that radicalization of these individuals will

---

[1]   This claim has empirical support. For example, Dawson and Amarasingam (2017) find evidence that "poor prospects" are part of the reason some individuals in Europe decide to join the Islamic State.

generally happen fairly early in life, to individuals who are marginalized in some way or seeking camaraderie, and that their radicalization trajectories will follow the arc proposed by Sageman (2004) and Wiktorowicz (2005*b*).

After radicalization, the puzzle remains why most jihadists remain lay Muslims while some decide to become clerics. Here, the literature on jihadist radicalization is largely silent. It is generally assumed that there is a need for clerics within jihadist organizations and that some individuals will rise to the call, but I am not aware of theories that offer predictions about which individuals will become clerics instead of, say, fighters. I expect that scholarly predispositions and prior interests are likely to be factors pushing some individuals toward participating in jihadist movements as a cleric. However, I do not investigate this question further and it remains for future research.

3.2 CLERICS WHO BECOME JIHADISTS

Individuals who have decided to become Muslim clerics are, by definition, no longer quite the same as lay Muslims because of their intent to pursue a position as a religious figure. Chapter 2 has already painted a picture of what this pursuit entails in terms of the training they might receive, the religious and academic roles they will fill, and the activities they will perform. The anticipation or realization of becoming a religious elite creates new incentives and constraints for clerics, and many of the explanations for lay Muslim radicalization described previously are likely to be less salient for individuals who are seeking to become clerics or have already done so.

I argue that the unique incentives and constraints that clerics face require revision of existing theories of jihadist radicalization. In this section, I describe a particular, cleric-specific pathway of jihadist radicalization that I call *blocked ambition*. My argument builds directly on the grievance-based theory of Gurr (1970); in fact, I mean the phrase "blocked ambition" in a way that is synonymous with Gurr's "relative deprivation" and Gambetta and Hertog's "frustrated ambition."[2] I prefer the term "blocked ambition" because I feel it emphasizes most clearly the psychological mechanism I am proposing.

Ambition has been defined in the psychological literature as "the persistent and generalized striving for success, attainment, and accomplishment" (Judge and Kammeyer-Mueller 2012, 759), though in the discussion that follows, I often use "ambition" to refer to pursuit of a specific goal, rather than general striving. Humans are ambitious creatures, seeking to accomplish a dizzying range of short- and long-term goals, using nearly every means imaginable. Inevitably, some ambitions are stymied. This is blocked ambition – the inability

---

[2] Gurr himself has moved away from the term " relative deprivation." In the front material of the fortieth-anniversary edition of *Why Men Rebel*, he writes, "Is 'relative deprivation' the best concept …? In my own later research, I have used the words *grievances* and *sense of injustice* to capture the essence of the state of mind that motivates people to political action. Whichever phrase is used, the essential first step in analysis is to understand what people's grievances are and where they come from" (Gurr 2010, x).

to realize a deeply held goal. I argue that the blocked ambitions of would-be clerics can push them toward adopting and preaching jihadist ideology.

To explain what is unique about the blocked ambitions of clerics that differentiates my argument from the work of Gurr and others, I first lay out the range of likely ambitions that clerics might hold, focusing on ambitions for stable, rewarding careers, in addition to more lofty goals of piety and scholarship. I then describe how the state controls the careers of clerics and how the current arrangement between political elites and clerics came to be. This system makes some clerics insiders and some outsiders, and professional networks are an important part of how clerics navigate this divide. Insider and outsider careers influence the incentives that clerics face when choosing whether to preach jihadist ideas, and I argue that blocked ambition plays a role in this choice.

3.2.1 The Ambitions of Muslim Clerics

Like any large group of people defined by their commitment to a profession, Muslim clerics have a variety of ambitions, both professional and personal, so any blanket statement about the ambitions of clerics will necessarily be untrue for some individuals. However, it is possible to speculate in general terms about the benefits that clerics gain from their chosen profession and their motivations for pursuing a clerical career.

Clerics are religious leaders, and like many religious leaders they are motivated by altruism, a desire to help others, and a feeling of deep passion for their religious tradition. As a result, clerics are likely to have some ambition to make a difference in the world, perhaps by leading others to righteousness, encouraging piety and good works, and producing scholarship that gives insight into the mysteries of the divine. These ambitions tend toward activism, so we may suppose that many clerics are, in some sense, predisposed to be activists.

Clerics are also scholars and have scholarly ambitions. As scholars, clerics often seek the esteem of their peers and thus devote time and energy to develop their scholarly reputations. For clerics as for other academics, reputation is based largely on how one's writings and rulings are regarded by members of one's discipline – in this case, other clerics. In essence, "The society of the imams acknowledges (or not) the legitimacy of the religious capital of a colleague ... [via] peer review" (Cherribi 2010, 114).

Clerics may also aspire to a measure of fame and popular following. This may lead them to seek certain types of positions, such as imam or *khatīb* (sermon-giver) at a prominent mosque. Cherribi suggests that "success of the imam in the eyes of the public ... measured by the number of followers" is an important metric for cleric status (Cherribi 2010, 114).

Finally, clerics may aspire to stable, well-compensated positions. This compensation allows them to make a career out of their chosen profession as clerics, devoting all their efforts to pious scholarship rather than dividing their time between unpaid work as a cleric and paid work in some other profession. Some cleric compensation is informal, and clerics often benefit from social norms in Muslim societies that encourage private citizens to provide material support to the religious class. For example, Abu-Zahra describes the Egyptian tradition of putting money and jewelry in the donation boxes of the al-Sayyida shrine during a holiday honoring the Muslim saint Al-Sayyida al-Nafisa:

A fixed proportion of the money is distributed to the workers and officials at each mosque ... It would be too simplistic to conclude that the Azharite officials of the mosque support the common beliefs in and the traditions of al-Sayyida because of the material benefits this generates, though this may partially reinforce their love. (Abu-Zahra 1997, 128)

However, in the modern era, formal salaries from state coffers are the source of a great deal of cleric compensation, as most clerics are paid with government funds administered through state ministries of religious affairs and education, which oversee appointments to mosques, universities, and other Islamic institutions controlled by the government. Clerics who progress in their careers to these positions can typically make enough money to support themselves and their families, while clerics whose careers fail must find other lines of work. Thus, the ambition of many clerics is to obtain a well-paid position in a religious or academic institution where they can pursue their vocation and simultaneously support themselves.

The fact that many clerics seek to draw salaries from government coffers fundamentally shapes the religious field in the Sunni world. Before describing the implications of state control of the religious sphere for the career paths of clerics, I first describe how it came about.

3.2.2 How Clerical Careers Are Controlled by the State

Rulers of Muslim-majority polities have recognized since the early days of Islam that religious leaders can either support or threaten their ability to rule.[3] Because of this, they have repeatedly intervened in the religious sphere to shape the incentives of clerics and mold their ambitions in ways that reinforce rather than undermine the interests and power of political elites.

In the nineteenth and twentieth centuries, the Middle East went through a period of dramatic political and social change, resulting in the modern states of the region today. As part of this process, venerable religious institutions were coopted by political elites and brought under the aegis of the state (Crecelius 1967; Gaffney 1991; Zeghal 1996; Taylor 2008; Fabbe 2012) in what Hermassi calls the "nationalization of the religious sphere" (Hermassi 1994, 91). In Egypt, for example, this meant that the famous and previously independent al-Azhar University became a state institution, a process that was completed with the Nasser-era reform of al-Azhar in 1961 (Zeghal 1996, 25). Where it previously was supported by an independent financial endowment, now it was re-funded under the government ministry of endowments. Most clerics

---

3 For evidence that governments accommodated powerful religious leaders, see Chaney (2013).

at al-Azhar and throughout Egypt became government employees. They still led mosques, taught in schools, and issued advice and fatwas, but rather than drawing support from independent financial sources such as *waqfs* (Islamic endowments), they were paid by the government, often through the newly created Ministry of Waqfs. Career advancement and appointments were now regulated by the state rather than being the sole purview of the community of ʿulamāʾ. This process was more or less replicated in Saudi Arabia (Haykel, Hegghammer, and Lacroix 2015), Morocco (Zeghal 1996, 35), Jordan (Antoun 2006; Wiktorowicz 2001a, ch. 2), and elsewhere throughout the Middle East and North Africa.

The purpose of this cooptation was to grant political elites religious legitimacy through connections to the ʿulamāʾ. During the process of regime-led modernization that took place in Egypt and Saudi Arabia in the nineteenth and twentieth centuries, the rulers found that allying with clerics or coopting them provided religious cover for the contested politics of modernization (Zeghal 1996, 27). The importance of this religious legitimacy continues for these states today, and when political expediency dictates, the state will lean on its clerics to rule in favor of its latest political project.

By taking control of the previously independent financial endowments for the most important religious institutions, political leaders gained leverage over the clerical class through their control of funding (Fabbe 2012). Even the most respected and prestigious clerics have conceded to the demands of the state in order to maintain their careers within the state-dominated system of religious institutions. For example, Abd al-Aziz Bin Baz was widely viewed as one of the most important living clerics before his death in 1999. Despite his importance and the widespread respect afforded him as the Grand Mufti of Saudi Arabia from 1993 to 1999, he was widely seen as having compromised Islamic legal principles for political expediency when he issued a fatwa authorizing the basing of US warplanes on Saudi soil during the 1991 Gulf War (Masud, Messick, and Powers 1996). By controlling funding, political leaders have found that they can simultaneously neutralize potential rebellion from clerics and lean on them to issue rulings legitimating controversial political projects.

Often, the religious elites were not particularly pleased with these arrangements. Several scholarly works have traced how the state takeover of religious institutions effectively sidelined the previously powerful clerical elite (Crecelius 1972, 190–191). Zeghal (1996, 26) reports that "the modernization of al-Azhar was accompanied, in effect, by a close surveillance of the members of the institution, who had to respond to the needs of Nasserist propaganda."[4] Without independent sources of funding, the cost to religious elites of expressing opposition to state policies was significantly higher.

---

4 The original quote is in French: "*La modernisation d'Al Azhar s'accompagne en effet d'une surveillance étroite des membres de l'institution, qui se doivent de répondre aux besoins de la propagande nassérienne.*"

Thus clerics have faced a paradox: their political power as a class has decreased even as their involvement in politics has increased. Nevertheless, individual clerics generally do not have the opportunity or incentive to change the status quo. The state rewards its clerics well, providing them with substantial resources if they side with the state when called upon. States have succeeded in coopting the clerical elite, partly by leaving previously existing clerical structures intact. This means that the most widely recognized and respected clerics rise to the top of the state-dominated hierarchy. New clerics entering the system face the choice of moving up within this hierarchy or attempting to build a career outside of it. The combination of material rewards, prestige, and popular following that accrues to state clerics makes it very difficult for young clerics to resist this option, even when they are skeptical about forming close ties to the state.

3.2.3 Insiders and Outsiders

Because of government intervention in the religious sphere, clerics face two general career paths: an *insider* career in the state-dominated religious system or an *outsider* career (Zeghal 1996, 47–49). Insider careers are primarily defined by the persistent occupation of positions appointed, controlled, or regulated by the state.

Throughout the Middle East, and especially in Egypt and Saudi Arabia, the two countries that produce the vast majority of Arabic-speaking clerics, the appointment of imams and preachers in mosques is state regulated and usually state funded. It is difficult to get precise salaries of clerics, but in 2013, the Egyptian state newspaper, *Al-Ahram*, reported that Ministry of Religious Endowments officials were requesting that entry-level imams be paid at least LE1,800 (approximately $250) per month, and that senior imams receive as much as LE2,500.[5] Senior officials in the Ministry of Religious Endowments were asking for as much as LE4,000 per month, meaning that as one climbs through the hierarchy in the Egyptian ministry, positions become quite well compensated. In a country where over a quarter of inhabitants live on less than $500 a year, these salaries can support a comfortable lifestyle.[6]

Many insider careers are in Islamic legal academia in the Middle East, with clerics holding tenured or tenure-track positions at Islamic universities. Academic positions may not seem like political appointments, but the governments in the Middle East have worked hard to manage the ideology of faculty at

---

5 "Egypt considering pay rises for imams." AhramOnline. http://english.ahram.org.eg/ NewsContent/3/0/89385/Business/0/Egypt-considering-pay-rises-for-imams.aspx, accessed December 9, 2015, and archived at http://dx.doi.org/10.7910/DVN/PG4A7K.

6 "Minimum wage rules set for Egyptian public sector; fate of private sector uncertain." AhramOnline. http://english.ahram.org.eg/NewsContent/3/0/85278/Business/ 0/Minimum-wage-rules-set-for-Egyptian-public-sector;.aspx, accessed December 9, 2015, and archived at http://dx.doi.org/10.7910/DVN/PG4A7K.

Islamic universities. Universities have a long history of revolutionary thought in both the West and East, so the governments of Egypt and Saudi Arabia attempt to regulate who is on faculty, partly by appointing university presidents who will purge radical individuals. Some academic positions are explicitly controlled by the highest levels of the government. For example, the biography of Abd al-Muhsin bin Hamad al-Ibad notes, "In 1393H he was appointed vice president of the Islamic University. He was chosen for this position by his Royal Highness King Faisal."[7]

The trajectory and responsibilities of an academic career for a cleric will be very recognizable to readers familiar with Western academia. Many insider clerics hold formal academic positions with titles such as "Associate Professor at the University al-Imam, College of Shariah, Department of Fiqh" (Yusuf Bin Abdullah al-Ahmad), and "chaired professor" (Rabi'a Bin Hadi al-Madkhali).[8] Clerics advance from rank to rank, and sometimes move from one university to another, as this excerpt from the biography of Sheikh Abd al-Rahman Bin Nasr al-Barak illustrates:

The sheikh worked as a teacher in the finishing school in the city of Riyadh for 3 years from 1379 to 1381H. Then, he moved after that to teach in the College of Shariah of Riyadh. When the College of *Usūl al-Dīn* opened, he moved to it in the Department of *Aqīda* and worked in it until his retirement in 1420H, during which time he advised scores of theses (Masters and Doctorate).[9]

Another category of insider career is that of a government bureaucrat. Academic careers can be a feeder track for the state clerical bureaucracy (Mazawi 2005, 224), with former professors transitioning to serve as leaders of government ministries and advisors on various government counsels.

In addition to drawing a salary from the state, clerics with insider careers often profit from "shariah consulting," in which a cleric serves on the advisory board of a company and provides opinions on the (Islamic) legality of activities the firm would like to undertake. Although it is theoretically possible for outsider clerics to have these roles, it tends to be insiders – academics and government appointees – who are invited to serve in an advisory capacity because of their prestige and connections (for more discussion, see Mouline 2014, 196–197). For example, Sheikh Saud Bin Abdullah al-Funaysan reports

7   "*Al-Shaykh ʿAbd al-Muḥsin bin Ḥamad al-ʿIbād.*" Islamway.net. http://ar.islamway.net/scholar/461, accessed April 14, 2014, and archived at http://dx.doi.org/10.7910/DVN/PG4A7K.
8   "*Tarjima Mawjiza l-al-Shaykh al-ʿUlāma Rabiʿ bin Hādī ʿAmir al-Madkhālī.*" rabee.net. www.rabee.net/profile.aspx, accessed March 1, 2012, and archived at http://dx.doi.org/10.7910/DVN/PG4A7K. As of this writing, the page seems to have moved to www.rabee.net/ar/sharticles.php?cat=10&id=55, also archived.
9   "*Nabdha ʿan al-Shaykh.*" *Mawqiʿ Faḍilat al-Shaykh al-ʿUlāma ʿAbd al-Rahman bin Nāṣr al-Barāk.* http://albarrak.islamlight.net/index.php?option=content&task=view&id=1364&Itemid=45, accessed December 31, 2011, and archived at http://dx.doi.org/10.7910/DVN/PG4A7K.

"serving as Chairman of the Sharia Supervisory Board in Takaful Malaysia (an Islamic insurance company) for three years" as item thirteen of his employment history.[10]

An *outsider career* is the alternative for clerics who do not follow an insider career path, whether or not this is their preference. I consider an outsider to be any cleric who is not compensated substantially by state institutions and whose professional position is not controlled by the government.

One way for outsider clerics to support themselves is to seek financial support directly from lay Muslims rather than the state. Clerics naturally tend to gravitate toward outsider careers that make use of their substantial human capital investments. Many clerics teach in their homes or at mosques where they do not hold official positions. Sulayman Bin Nasr al-Ulwan began his career "teaching and mentoring in his house in the year 1410 H, and then in 1411 H moved to mentoring and teaching the mosque. His lessons were throughout the week after dawn, noon, and evening prayers, and sometimes on Friday."[11]

In addition to teaching locally, there is an international Islamic conference circuit and some outsider clerics make a career out of public speaking. Others fund themselves with publishing. Yasir Birhami, for instance, "participated with the sheikhs of the salafi School of Alexandria in a number of proselytizing magazines."[12]

The alternative to seeking pay from lay Muslims for performing religious roles, be it through teaching, speaking, or publishing, is to have a day job, perhaps as a dentist (this is the occupation of the Egyptian cleric Ahmad Hutayaba[13]) or an engineer.

The contrast between insider and outsider careers is a product of state domination of the religious sphere. For the most part, the most famous, academically respected, and well-paid clerics are those at the top of the state-run religious institutions, so clerics with ambitions for a stable, well-compensated career will generally aspire to an insider career. In this way, the policy of the state to funnel resources to clerics who toe the party line through state-controlled institutions affects the incentives for clerics to pursue certain types of career paths.[14]

---

10   "*Al-Sīra al-Dhātiyya al-Shaykh.*" alfunisan.com. www.alfunisan.com/dsf-cv.html, accessed December 30, 2011, and archived at http://dx.doi.org/10.7910/DVN/PG4A7K.

11   This is from the biography of al-Ulwan, "*Nabdha ʿan al-Shaykh – al-Shaykh Sulaymān bin Nāṣr al-ʿUlwān,*" formerly hosted at http://salalwan.com/catsmktba-15.html, accessed January 25, 2012, and archived at http://dx.doi.org/10.7910/DVN/PG4A7K. The biography is still available at http://ar.islamway.net/scholar/245 as of February 10, 2017.

12   "*Tarjima al-Shaykh al-Duktūr Yāssir Birhāmī.*" *Ṣawt al-Salaf.* www.salafvoice.com/moshref_resume.php, accessed January 16, 2012, and archived at http://dx.doi.org/10.7910/DVN/PG4A7K. This link is now broken.

13   "*Aḥmad Ḥuṭayba.*" Shamela.ws. http://shamela.ws/index.php/author/2333, accessed April 14, 2014, and archived at http://dx.doi.org/10.7910/DVN/PG4A7K.

14   The contrasting careers of religious leaders who are supported by their followers and those who are supported by the state, or some other endowment, is noted by none other than Adam Smith in his famous *Wealth of Nations* (Smith and Nicholson 1887): "The institutions for the

3.2.4 Professional Networks and Academic Careers

The path to becoming an insider cleric is long and there are many places at which ambition can be blocked. Blocked ambition is most likely to nudge clerics toward jihadism when it comes in the late stages of the road to an insider career, but I start from the beginning of the process for clarity. In the following discussion, I also highlight alternative causal processes that might induce a relationship between career paths and ideology, but through different mechanisms than blocked ambition. In the following chapters, I test my argument against these alternatives.

Future clerics get their start when families choose one of their children, almost always a son, to receive specialized religious training and enroll them in a *kutāb*, a school intended to teach literacy, basic arithmetic, and the Quran. Students in the *kutāb* learn to pronounce and recite the Quran (an Islamic science called *tajwīd*) and most will work to memorize the entire Quran while in the *kutāb*. Many students will not perform well at this stage and will never become clerics, but this rarely represents a serious blocking of ambition because the students have not yet invested very much in the prospect of becoming a cleric

instruction of people of all ages are chiefly those for religious instruction. This is a species of instruction of which the object is not so much to render the people good citizens in this world, as to prepare them for another and a better world in a life to come. The teachers of the doctrine which contains this instruction, in the same manner as other teachers, may either depend altogether for their subsistence upon the voluntary contributions of their hearers, or they may derive it from some other fund to which the law of their country may entitle them; such as a landed estate, a tithe or land-tax, an established salary or stipend. Their exertion, their zeal and industry, are likely to be much greater in the former situation than in the latter. In this respect the teachers of new religions have always had a considerable advantage in attacking those ancient and established systems of which the clergy, reposing themselves upon their benefices, had neglected to keep up the fervour of faith and devotion in the great body of the people, and having given themselves up to indolence, were become altogether incapable of making any vigorous exertion in defence even of their own establishment" (The Wealth of Nations, book V, ch. I, pt. III, article III). Smith goes on to quote Hume, who explicitly argues, as I do below, that self-supporting religious preachers are more likely to preach violence: "Each ghostly practitioner, in order to render himself more precious and sacred in the eyes of his retainers, will inspire them with the most violent abhorrence of all other sects, and continually endeavor, by some novelty, to excite the languid devotion of his audience. No regard will be paid to truth, morals, or decency in the doctrines inculcated. Every tenet will be adopted that best suits the disorderly affections of the human frame. Customers will be drawn to each conventicle by new industry and address in practising on the passions and credulity of the populace. And in the end, the civil magistrate will find that he has dearly paid for his pretended frugality, in saving a fixed establishment for the priests; and that in reality the most decent and advantageous composition which he can make with the spiritual guides, is to bribe their indolence by assigning stated salaries to their profession, and rendering it superfluous for them to be farther active than merely to prevent their flock from straying in quest of new pastures. And in this manner ecclesiastical establishments, though commonly they arose at first from religious views, prove in the end advantageous to the political interests of society" (ibid.).

at this early point in their lives and they have the remainder of their schooling ahead of them to train for an alternative career.

Students who show promise proceed through primary and secondary schools, usually in their home village, before heading to a religious finishing school (*ma*ᶜ*hid* ᶜ*ilmī*) in a major city (often Cairo, Riyadh, or Mecca) during their midteens. It is at this point that future clerics begin to develop ambition for a clerical career. One sign of this is that their biographies mention close ties to specific clerics at this stage of their education. This suggests that these early ties constitute the beginnings of their educational social networks. Typically, teachers in the finishing schools are not well known or influential clerics, but my reading of cleric biographies shows that students feel particularly loyal to these less prominent teachers, often noting the affiliation with pride. It is rare however for clerics to list more than one important teacher from their finishing school, suggesting that these are not the most important network connections for opening subsequent career opportunities.

After religious finishing school, students typically enroll in an Islamic university. University attendance was not universal for clerics born prior to 1950, but since that time, virtually all clerics have attended a university of some sort. In the past fifty years, the most popular schools for Salafi clerics are al-Azhar University in Cairo, King Saud University in Riyadh, and the Islamic University of Medina al-Munawara, although clerics have attended a number of other schools and some have degrees from multiple universities. Students are internationally mobile – al-Azhar University has a large number of students from Indonesia, for example – but Saudi students tend to study at Saudi schools and Egyptians at Egyptian schools.

Although enrolling in a university is now de rigueur for future clerics, attending classes is not. Thus, at the university, the major obstacle for would-be clerics is not whether they can complete their formal schoolwork but rather whether they can develop connections to prominent clerics that will help them get ahead. In fact, clerics develop more extensive educational networks by skipping their formal courses to instead sit in the informal study circles (*ḥalaqāt*) of the most prominent clerics in their university's mosque. This is due in part to the inflexibility of the traditional Islamic education system, which relies heavily on memorization.[15] An Azhari student told me directly that "often the best students don't actually go to class because it is so rigid. The not-so-good students often just do the memorization." During my time at the mosque of al-Azhar University, I found that the best students did indeed spend substantial amounts of time in informal study circles while appearing to spend very little time on their nominally required studies. Identifying the

---

[15] The degree to which Islamic education prizes memorization can hardly be overstated. In June 2011, I sat with a study circle of al-Azhar students from the College of Shariah and Law as they tested each other on their word-for-word memorization of a 300-page, third-year textbook. See 2011 field work notes, archived at http://dx.doi.org/10.7910/DVN/PG4A7K. See also Boyle (2004).

most ambitious students was not easy, partly because norms of appropriateness dictate that one should not come right out and state one's aspirations of someday becoming an important sheikh.[16] However, once I identified a few of the most serious students, I found that they spent between three and eight hours of each day at the mosque rather than in class.[17]

Many of these study circles are public and being part of them does not imply any special connection to the teacher. The public study circles at al-Azhar, for instance, are advertised throughout the week on a series of paper schedules. The teacher's loyal students will likely be in attendance, but so will a number of other individuals ranging from curious students at the university to the mosque cleaning staff. As a result, simply attending these open study circles does not provide special access to the teacher or constitute a mentoring relationship.

Instead, mentoring relationships are most strongly reinforced in private study circles that clerics hold but do not advertise except to their current circle of students. Teachers typically invite a student to come to these private sessions once they have assessed the student's quality in other settings. It is these circles that allow students to claim particular clerics as their teachers and advisors. At the end of a series of study circles on a particular topic, a teacher might issue an *ijaza* to each of his students – a specialized certificate or letter of reference noting that the student is approved by the teacher in the specific area of study covered in the sessions. These credentials from clerics are often more important for cleric career advancement than the formal university degrees that students receive. As Mouline (2014, 186) reports, "Following these *halaqat*, the disciple submitted an *istid'a'* – that is, a request for *ijaza* corresponding to the works he had studied and the prophetic traditions he had learned by heart. The most brilliant disciples became assistants to the master, a step that opened the door for them to becoming professors or judges. Their careers were thus launched."

The importance of connections to prestigious teachers is evident in the ways that potential students attempt to curry favor with the most prominent and well-connected clerics. One tactic of eager students is to attend prayers at the mosque during the day and hope that a prominent cleric will lead the prayers. Sometimes this is known in advance, particularly for noon prayers at al-Azhar, where the prayer leader will often lecture for about twenty minutes following the prayer. Afterward, potential students throng the cleric as he seeks to exit the prayer space, kissing him on the hand and then attempting to seek permission to attend a class or ask some perspicacious question (see Figure 3.1).[18] Similarly, students seeking to join the private study circle of a cleric will attend his public

---

16   See 2012 field notes, pp. 19–21, and my electronic notes from an interview with a former al-Azhar student, both archived at http://dx.doi.org/10.7910/DVN/PG4A7K.

17   See 2012 field notes, p. 26, archived at http://dx.doi.org/10.7910/DVN/PG4A7K.

18   Also, see my 2012 field notes, p. 27, archived at http://dx.doi.org/10.7910/DVN/PG4A7K.

FIGURE 3.1. Students engaging a cleric after a lesson.

Notes: A photograph by the author of students attempting to engage a prominent teacher, Ahmad al-Riyan, after a lesson following midday prayers at the al-Azhar on May 7, 2012.

study circles, sit in the front row, and be quite vocal during the question and answer session at the end of the lecture.

Students flock to the most famous and prominent clerics. At al-Azhar, a lecture by an unknown visitor will gather only a handful of serious listeners while famous, well-established clerics will have audiences as large as 50 or 100 in their public lectures and they will find themselves recorded by as many as twenty audio recorders and quite possibly uploaded to the Internet.

The following selection from the biography of Hamud al-Shu'aybi provides a flavor of how clerics actually describe their educational network.

"While in finishing school, the College of Shariah, and other settings, the Sheikh [al-Shu'aybi] studied at the hands of the greatest of the Sheikhs, including Sheikh Abd al-Aziz Bin Baz, from whom he studied *tawḥīd* and *ḥadīth*, Sheikh Abd al-Rahman al-Afriqi (in *ḥadīth* also), Sheikh Abd al-Aziz al-Rashid in *fiqh*."[19]

---

[19] "*Sīra al-Shaykh al-ᶜUlāma: Ḥamūd bin ᶜUqalāʾ al-Shuᶜaybī Raḥamahu Allah.*" alajman.net. www.alajman.net/vb/showthread.php?t=71621, accessed February 10, 2017, and archived at http://dx.doi.org/10.7910/DVN/PG4A7K.

Al-Shu'aybi's biography conforms to the prevalent norm of listing one's associations with the most prestigious clerics first. Here, al-Shu'aybi lists Sheikh Abd al-Aziz Bin Baz, arguably the most famous Salafi cleric of the past fifty years, before his other teachers, despite the fact that Bin Baz was probably not his primary advisor.

Clerics' career trajectories are often determined by whom they know, and the friendship and endorsement of prominent clerics is extremely valuable. Although it is not an ironclad rule, clerics are often promoted because they are the successful students of clerics who are in a position to recommend and endorse their promotion. This means that equally talented and intelligent would-be clerics can face very different career paths depending on their access to training with the most famous and well-connected clerics. Individuals who do not have these connections have a higher chance of having their academic ambitions blocked.

Specifically, I argue that clerics who are well connected in a particular way have distinct advantages when seeking insider appointments. Simply having many teachers is neither necessary nor sufficient for gaining preferential access to career opportunities. Rather, what matters is that a cleric's teachers are themselves well connected, meaning that they can leverage their connections to get jobs for their students. Ideally, a cleric will be well connected to well-connected teachers, who also had well-connected teachers, and so on.

The biographies of clerics illustrate the significance of their networks in determining their career trajectories. For instance, the biography of Hamud al-Shu'aybi describes a series of government appointments, including an appointment to a judgeship that is curiously canceled:

When he graduated from the College of Sharia, he was appointed to be a judge in Wādī al-Dawāsir, but this appointment was subsequently canceled by the intervention of Sheikh Muhammad al-Amin al-Shanqiti as was previously mentioned. He was thus appointed as a teacher in the finishing school for a single year (1375H) and then moved to the College where he taught for forty years.[20]

Reading between the lines, what we learn is that al-Shu'aybi was probably not happy with his initial appointment in an outlying province in Saudi Arabia, so he leveraged his connection to a well-connected and influential teacher, Muhammad al-Amin al-Shanqiti, to gain a different appointment that kept him in the city. This suggests that connectedness is very helpful for clerics attempting to optimize their career path.

The biography of Sheikh Abd al-Muhsin Bin Hamad al-Ibad likewise illustrates how his professional network influenced his insider career. He writes,

---

[20]   "*Sīra al-Shaykh al-ʿUlāma: Ḥamūd bin ʿUqalāʾ al-Shuʿaybī Raḥamahu Allah.*" alajman.net. www.alajman.net/vb/showthread.php?t=71621, accessed February 10, 2017, and archived at http://dx.doi.org/10.7910/DVN/PG4A7K.

"When the Islamic University of the City of the Prophet was established, and the first College to be established in it was the College of Shariah, the noble Sheikh Muhammad Bin Ibrahim Al al-Sheikh chose him to work in it as a teacher."[21] It is not coincidental that he lists Muhammad Bin Ibrahim Al al-Sheikh among his mentors.

My conversations with students at al-Azhar demonstrate that students are well aware that they need well-connected teachers in order to fulfill their career ambitions. When I asked an al-Azhar University student how to become a cleric, he responded, "It's really all about trying to study with the prominent sheikhs and getting some kind of *ijāza* [certificate] from them if you can. You just try to get into people's networks." Another told me that he had moved from the famous school of al-Zaytuna in Tunis because "al-Zaytuna has fewer big sheikhs, so I am here."[22] Speaking specifically of how one might go about being promoted as a cleric in contemporary Egypt, a third student explained:

Being in Ali Goma's crew [then Grand Mufti of Egypt] is really the way to move up right now. That's how you get appointed to teach, how you get a position in the Dar al-Ifta [Egyptian Fatwa Ministry], which gets you a nice car. He has lots of students, and he'll often favor them in promotions.[23]

These quotes suggest that students understand that those with extensive educational networks are more likely to fulfill their career ambitions within the cleric hierarchy.

Once ensconced in the insider career path, clerics are likely to remain insiders for their entire careers. For example, the CV of Sheikh Ahmad al-Riyan indicates that, upon graduation from al-Azhar university, he was appointed teacher of comparative fiqh at the College of Shariah and Law in 1975, assistant professor at the College of Shariah and Law in 1980, and professor at the College of Shariah and Law from 1985–present – a career path that means he has been on the state payroll for his entire working life.[24]

On the other hand, clerics who are forced out of insider positions unexpectedly are likely to face career trouble. This is a particularly acute form of blocked ambition because it occurs after a cleric has invested heavily in his career and has much to lose from his inability to continue in his chosen career path.

---

21 "Al-Shaykh ʿAbd al-Muḥsin bin Ḥamad al-ʿIbād." Islamway.net. www.islamway.com/?iw_s= Scholar&iw_a=info&scholar_id=461, accessed January 1, 2012, now at http://ar.islamway. net/scholar/461, accessed February 10, 2017, and archived at http://dx.doi.org/10.7910/DVN/ PG4A7K.

22 See my 2012 field notes, p. 27, archived at http://dx.doi.org/10.7910/DVN/PG4A7K.

23 Interview with al-Azhar student, September 25, 2011, archived at http://dx.doi.org/10.7910/ DVN/PG4A7K.

24 "Tarjima Mukhtaṣara l-al-Duktūr Aḥmad Ṭaha Riyān." *Multaqa Ahl al-Ḥadīth.* www. ahlalhdeeth.com/vb/showthread.php?t=262939, accessed February 10, 2017, and archived at http://dx.doi.org/10.7910/DVN/PG4A7K.

Theoretically, this type of midcareer derailment could occur for a variety of reasons, but in most cases it is the intervention of the state that closes the door.

3.2.5 Career Paths and Radicalization

A key reason for state cooptation of Muslim clerics is to neutralize their potential for coordinating antiregime political action, so it is hardly a surprise that the state discourages insider clerics from preaching jihad. The state attempts to ensure that clerics' teachings and writings are acceptable to the political rulers, keeping those in its employ in line with both the promise of reward and the threat of punishment.

This cooptation is usually successful. Clerics who are government appointees generally avoid commenting on topics that directly oppose the government, including jihad. For example, as I sat in the study circle of Sheikh Ahmad al-Riyan in the al-Azhar mosque of Cairo, a student asked for his opinion on the controversial visit of the Grand Mufti of Egypt, Ali Gomaa, on April 18, 2012, to the al-Aqsa mosque, located in the old city of Jerusalem. Gomaa's visit violated a long-standing practice of not visiting the mosque as long as the territory is held by Israel. Other clerics, particularly jihadists, had been quite vocal in their condemnation because they viewed the visit as legitimating Israel and undermining the Palestinian jihad. But Sheikh al-Riyan is a career appointee at al-Azhar where he has taught since 1974 and where he has enjoyed several promotions. In response to this sensitive question, Sheikh al-Riyan chuckled, paused, and replied, "I don't like to speak about politics."[25] Other observers have remarked on similar patterns of compliance. For example, Al Aswany (2011, 153) writes of Egypt, "The government's clerics are civil servants who receive their salaries and perquisites from the government and hence select from Islam everything that supports the wishes of the ruler, however corrupt or oppressive he may be."

---

[25] The lecture, including this exchange, was recorded and is viewable on YouTube at AzharTV, "*Sharḥ Kitāb Riyāḍ al-Ṣāliḥīn al-Ḥalaqa 16 Tābiᶜ Bāb al-Murāqiba l-al-Duktūr Aḥmad Ṭaha al-Riyān*," YouTube. www.youtube.com/watch?v=GgJiCFxBfvA#t=5900s, min. 1:38:18, accessed February 10, 2017, and archived at http://dx.doi.org/10.7910/DVN/PG4A7K. Ali Gomaa himself has asserted that affiliation with al-Azhar keeps people from turning to jihadism. "It would take a team of sociologists and psychologists to analyze this phenomenon – how come anyone who becomes religious outside of the religious establishment turns out violent? In al-Azhar University, there are 400,000 people, and 20 million people worldwide are affiliated with it – and not a single one of them ever committed a terrorist act. ... How come not a single al-Azhar scholar came up with this idea [of terrorism]? We are talking about 20 million ... Even Omar Abd Al-Rahman is the exception that proves the rule. He himself never participated in terrorist acts. Even when his ideology became deviant he did not participate in acts of terrorism." "In Interview, Egyptian Mufti Ali Gum'a Questioned On Treatment of Women in Islam, Blames 'Secularists' For Terrorism Worldwide." Middle East Media Research Institute. www.memri.org/report/en/0/0/0/0/0/0/2446.htm, accessed February 10, 2017, and archived at http://dx.doi.org/10.7910/DVN/PG4A7K.

The few state-appointed clerics to openly endorse jihadi ideology have been investigated by the state and relieved of their appointments (Lacroix 2011; Brachman 2009). For example, *Al-Ahram* reported in 2014 that "Egypt's main Islamic university has suspended a controversial preacher and professor over allegations he incited violence and violated the parameters of his job. ... A video was published on social media websites last month of a speech by Shaaban in which he referred to ISIS as fellow Muslims who had 'made mistakes and whom we are obliged to guide and mentor'."[26] Even remaining silent can get clerics into trouble. In the summer of 2014, *Al-Ahram* reported that "Saudi Arabia's Islamic Affairs Ministry is investigating 17 mosque imams in the capital Riyadh for not using their Friday sermons to denounce an al Qaeda attack this month."[27]

The deterrence the state wields against endorsing jihadi ideology extends beyond the threat of losing one's job to actual imprisonment. Clerics who have turned drastically toward jihadism, or political Islamism more generally, have faced jail time. In a set of events that produced many of jihadism's current clerics, a number of academic clerics associated with the Salafi Sahwa (Awakening) movement in Saudi Arabia in the 1980s and 1990s began to adopt political views that made the Saudi monarchy uncomfortable. These were generally Islamist calls for changes to the political system rather than full-blown jihadism, but the Saudi government reacted harshly (perhaps more harshly than expected) and a number of these scholars were let go from their state sinecures and imprisoned. Three of these clerics – A'id al-Qarni, Safar al-Hawali, and Salman al-Awda – were ultimately brought back into the state fold after renouncing jihad, probably because they were viewed as influential enough that the Saudi regime found it worthwhile to buy them off. For those who were not brought back in, this effectively ended their academic careers, potentially forcing them to cast about for new ways to support themselves as clerics.

The monitoring and punishment of insider clerics who step out of line has the obvious result of discouraging jihadi ideology among clerics who are trying to make a living while working their way through the ranks of the state system.

Could it be that insider clerics secretly harbor jihadist sympathies? Possibly, but if so, it does not matter much. Clerics who are secretly jihadist are not likely to inspire political violence. If they do, they will likely be discovered

---

26 "Al-Azhar suspends controversial preacher Mahmoud Shaaban." AzharOnline. http://english.ahram.org.eg/NewsContent/1/64/114629/Egypt/Politics-/AlAzhar-suspends-cont roversial-preacher-Mahmoud-Sh.aspx, accessed December 9, 2015, and archived at http://dx.doi.org/ 10.7910/DVN/PG4A7K.

27 "Saudi Arabia investigates imams who did not condemn al Qaeda attack." AhramOnline. http://english.ahram.org.eg/NewsContent/2/8/106641/World/Region/Saudi-Arabia-investigates-imams-who-did-not-condem.aspx, accessed December 9, 2015, and archived at http://dx.doi.org/10.7910/DVN/PG4A7K.

and thus lose the position that was the reason for adopting secrecy in the first place. Thus, any preaching or action would have to be either exceptionally small scale or exceptionally clandestine to avoid the gaze of state authorities. Moreover, jihadism as an ideology is generally predisposed to despise clerics who dissemble about their true beliefs in order to draw a steady paycheck. Such a cleric would face an uphill battle to prove that his secret jihadist leanings were in fact real.

While insider clerics discipline themselves to avoid jeopardizing their means of livelihood, outsider clerics are less constrained because their financial support comes from lay Muslims who are not necessarily opposed to jihadi ideology. This alone suggests that more jihadists will come from the ranks of outsider clerics, as will more clerics with other nonstandard ideologies. Higher variance in the ideology of outsider clerics implies more clerics who fall "in the tails" of the ideology distribution.

3.2.6 How Blocked Ambition Nudges Clerics to Preach Jihad

There are a number of reasons to believe that blocked ambition might lead to a substantial shift in an individual's goals and ideology. First, blocked ambition creates disappointment, which may in turn nudge some outsider clerics toward jihadism. Disappointment is a psychological mechanism that "originate[s] in a comparison process in which the outcome obtained is compared to an outcome that might have been" (Zeelenberg et al. 2000, 522), so clerics who experience disappointment after failing to gain access to an insider career are mentally comparing their current circumstances to an imagined career path that they might have achieved had circumstances been different. A focus on circumstances, rather than personal failings, is key to disappointment. Zeelenberg et al. (1998) show that while regret is linked to a rethinking of one's own actions, disappointment is linked to a desire to change the circumstances that led to an undesired outcome (see also Zeelenberg, van Dijk, Manstead, and van der Pligt 1998). Behaviorally, disappointment has been shown to cause goal abandonment and complaining to others about the circumstances that led to failure, whereas regret leads individuals to persist in pursuing their original goals while changing their own behavior to achieve better outcomes (Zeelenberg and Pieters 1999; Zeelenberg et al. 2000, 528). Thus, for clerics who experience disappointment as a result of blocked ambition, vociferous opposition to the system and attempts to change it might be expected.

Second, disappointed individuals display *hindsight bias* after positive events fail to come to pass, meaning that they revise their previous estimates of the event's probability downward after it fails to happen (Pezzo and Beckstead 2008). For would-be clerics, this could translate into a feeling that the system was rigged against them from the start, breeding resentment.

Disappointment is more likely and more intense when failure occurs after individuals have exerted extensive effort to achieve their goals (van Dijk, van der Pligt, and Zeelenberg 1999), so blocked ambition will be harshest for individuals who were far along the path to achieving their ambitions. Ambitions can come to define one's identity over time, and aspiring clerics who have sacrificed substantially to achieve their goals will be especially frustrated if they are stymied just before the finish line. While an undergraduate student at al-Azhar University's School of Shariah and Law may merely shrug at having his clerical ambitions blocked, a doctoral student from the same school who realizes he will be denied the position he desires after a decade of scholarship will be more likely to feel deeply disappointed and thus respond in a volatile way. Those who have already gained access to insider careers and then have them taken away will be the most likely to turn to extreme measures.

Why are disappointed aspiring insiders willing to sometimes turn to making violent calls against the state itself? For clerics who have had their hopes for a well-paid clerical career dashed by state intervention, jihadism offers a readily available ideology for articulating anger against the state. Correctly or not, they believe that they might have enjoyed a comfortable career as a cleric had they not been treated unjustly by political authorities, and thus feel justified in their anger. It is not too much of a leap to imagine at least a few clerics who face blocked ambition turning to jihadist ideology as a way of understanding the perceived injustice and railing against it.

There is also a sociological mechanism through which blocked ambitions can lead to cleric radicalization. Blocked ambition may incline some clerics to preach jihadist ideas because this path offers a track to fame and popularity outside of the state-administered religious institutions. Preaching jihadist ideas can draw a considerable following among lay Salafi Muslims, and this can in turn provide some of the benefits for clerics that they would have enjoyed as insiders: large audiences and financial support. Salafis are one of several large demographics of lay Muslims motivated to support independent clerics. They form a substantial minority in almost all of the Arab Middle East and are particularly interested in proper clerical interpretation. Clerics appeal to Salafis by adopting the conservative Salafi ideology and practicing the Salafi methodology (*al-manhaj al-salafi*) of favoring direct interpretation of the Quran and *sunna* (the sayings of Muhammad) over the consensus of later Muslim jurists. Clerics compete to demonstrate their integrity and to persuade others that their rulings represent an accurate interpretation of Islam as intended in the original sources.

In this somewhat cramped marketplace of clerics, each cleric faces competition for followers. To attract support, outsider clerics try to send signals that they are theologically expert and ideologically independent. Jihadi ideology can serve as a credible signal of independence because it clearly differs from the stances of establishment clerics and it is costly to adopt because of government repression. Thus, some clerics outside the state system adopt jihadi ideology in order to gain popular support and advance their careers. This is not necessarily because jihadi ideology is popular with most Salafi Muslims, although at some times and some places it has been popular.[28] Rather, clerics gain religious credibility because they have demonstrated that they will speak their mind even when it is costly.

Jihadists are quite deliberate in their attempt to tap into the discomfort lay Muslims feel about the close relationship between clerics and the state. In his famous work, *The Religion of Abraham*, jihadist Abu Muhammad al-Maqdisi is thoroughly critical of the modern academic system, the alliance between clerics and the state, and the personal fame that follows. He bitterly criticizes the members of the modern Salafi establishment who "graduate from 'The Faculties of Political Sciences and Rights,'" "come and seek the entrance of the Sultan," and seek "fame and the applause of their followers" (al-Maqdisi 1984, 65). al-Maqdisi's argument is that these practices are un-Islamic because they were not practiced by the righteous Companions of the Prophet Muhammad. For him, the state clerics' connections to the political elite are a departure from precedent that undermines their legitimacy. Similarly, jihadist cleric Abu Yahya al-Libi says of the state clerics, "These muftis have become experts in perverting the source texts and are accustomed to bending them and don't even see anything wrong with occasionally breaking them if they refuse to be flexible."[29]

Similar thinking is evident among jihadist clerics in the West who are responsible for sending youth as foreign fighters to the Islamic State. As documented by Ben Taub in *The New Yorker*, a firebrand cleric in Belgium, Fouad Belkacem, founded a group called Sharia4Belgium and began indoctrinating followers with an "intensive twenty-four-week program of ideological training." One of his key talking points was "that most imams ignore discussions of jihad and martyrdom because they want to keep state funding."[30]

Jihadist writers also attempt to convince lay Muslims that insider clerics secretly support jihadism despite publicly opposing it. For example, a document has circulated on Muslim web forums claiming to document statements by various clerics in support of Bin Laden, including prominent members of the Saudi religious establishment: Salih Bin Muhammad al-Luhaydan, Muhammad Ibn al-Uthaymeen, and Ibn Jibreen.[31]

---

28 The breadth of support for jihadist ideas in a series of Pew surveys in the Muslim world is somewhat remarkable (Wike and Samaranayake 2006; Mousseau 2011; Bell et al. 2013).

29 "*Al-Laqāʾ al-Thānī maʿ al-Shaykh al-Mujāhid Abī Yaḥya al-Lībī.*" YouTube. www.youtube.com/watch?v=gMo_DwTuN7k, min. 41:48, accessed March 10, 2012, and archived at http://dx.doi.org/10.7910/DVN/PG4A7K.

30 Taub, Ben. "Journey to Jihad: Why are teen-agers joining ISIS?" *The New Yorker*. www.newyorker.com/magazine/2015/06/01/journey-to-jihad, accessed November 30, 2015.

31 "*Kalām al-ʿUlamāʾ fī al-Shaykh Usāma bin Lādin.*" muslm.org. www.muslm.org/vb/showthread.php?222253, accessed February 10, 2017, and archived at http://dx.doi.org/10.7910/DVN/PG4A7K.

The idea that adopting jihadist ideology signals independence from political authorities resonates with the finding of Zeghal (1999), who traces the effects of the Egyptian regime's attempts to coopt the clerics of al-Azhar from the 1950s onward. She provides anecdotal evidence that when moderate clerics followed the regime's wishes and denounced violent jihad, some nonstate clerics apparently endorsed jihad specifically to show that they were not puppet clerics of the state. I also gain corroborating evidence of the signaling value of jihadism from Wiktorowicz (2005b), who researches Omar Bakri Muhammad, a jihadist cleric based in London. Although many of Omar's peers are supported by Saudi money, he is independently wealthy and has used his financial independence to cultivate an image of theological independence. His willingness to risk deportation or arrest by endorsing violence gives him even more credibility. According to one of Wiktorowicz's respondents, Omar "dares to say things that no one else does. Other religious leaders don't do that. They don't have the guts" (2005b, 144–145). And in a televised debate, a jihadist associate of Omar Bakri Muhammad named Anjem Choudary and an anti-jihadist Muslim commentator named Maajid Nawaz attempted to discredit each other by questioning whether the sources of their salaries were influencing their opinions.[32]

If structure conditions ideology, then do clerics actually believe their theological positions? I expect that virtually all clerics truly believe what they preach. Although material motivations may push clerics to a particular type of ideology, humans are remarkably adept at constructing personal narratives explaining such shifts in more palatable terms. Results from psychology show that individuals can come to believe statements they are induced to recite (Janis and King 1954), meaning that clerics who adopt an ideology for wholly strategic reasons may ultimately come to deeply believe in it. Thus, asking whether jihadists are rational, strategic calculators or fanatical true believers creates a false dichotomy. It is likely that they are both.

That said, the beliefs of a cleric prior to blocked ambition are likely to matter in determining who radicalizes. Because of the ideological affinity between Salafism and Sunni jihadism, it is a smaller step for clerics who already had Salafi orientations to make the move to jihadist ideology than for clerics who were not Salafis. This is because jihadists have constructed their ideology as an outgrowth of Salafi thinking, so a Salafi can become a jihadist while retaining many of his prior ideas. Clerics from other schools of thought will have to revise more ideas to become jihadists. This is not to say that non-Salafis will never become jihadists, but rather that there are more barriers.

It is not the case that all, or even most, outsider clerics will become jihadists. Career options for outsider clerics may be more limited than for insiders, but

---

[32] QuilliamFoundation. "Maajid Nawaz debates Anjem Choudary." YouTube. www.youtube.com/watch?v=2BrueU4xd2w, accessed February 10, 2017, and archived at http://dx.doi.org/10.7910/DVN/PG4A7K.

there are options besides jihadism. In many cases, clerics have nongovernmental options to be preachers or teachers in private mosques and schools or as part of private voluntary organizations. Clerics are also mobile, and some move to other labor markets. However, alternatives to state funding have narrowed for clerics in the Middle East. In Egypt, for example, official reports cited by Gaffney (1994, 47) indicate there were up to six privately run mosques for every state run mosque in Cairo through the 1960s and 1970s. A 1979 report of the Egyptian Ministry of Religious Endowments claimed a total of 34,000 mosques in Egypt, of which only 5,600 were in the orbit of the ministry's official system. However, Taylor (2008, 53, n. 37) reports that 56 percent of Egyptian mosques were state controlled by 1996 and that this increased to 93 percent by 2001 (see also Davis and Robinson 2012, 48). Masoud gives more precise numbers: "As of 2006 there were 71,931 Friday mosques and 21,118 small mosques," with the implication that local imams are all state employees (Masoud 2014, 33, 23). And on June 5, 2014, outgoing interim Egyptian President Adly Mansour signed a law regulating who can preach in mosques, teach religious lessons, or wear the official uniform of a cleric.[33] The situation is similar in Jordan (Wiktorowicz 2001*a*, 53).

It is also important to note the parameters of my argument. Although I argue that blocked ambition is an important factor in the turn of some clerics toward jihadist ideology, it is not the exclusive cause of jihadist radicalization. Multiple factors might explain why a cleric becomes a jihadist, and blocked ambition can have an impact in concert with other factors, at both the individual and group levels. Blocked ambition does not have to explain the radicalization of every cleric who becomes a jihadist, nor does it have to be the sole cause of radicalization in the life of any single cleric, to be relevant as a causal mechanism and hold implications for policy.

An alternative pathway to blocked ambition involves conversion to jihadist ideas later in life for reasons unrelated to a cleric's ambitions. In cases like this, a cleric may have enjoyed a successful insider career that led to a secure position at an Islamic university or government religious institution. The cleric may then become persuaded by jihadi ideology for a number of different reasons, including many of the same reasons that lead lay Muslims to support jihad, such as concern over the plight of oppressed Muslims or theological persuasion that jihadism offers a more correct interpretation of the founding texts of Islam. Under these circumstances, an individual may choose to remain a cleric – meaning that they produce Islamic content for public consumption – but choose to now produce content supporting jihadist ideas. I call individuals who take this path *late-adopting true believers* because they become persuaded

---

[33] "Egypt president Mansour signs law jailing unauthorised Islamic preachers." AhramOnline. http://english.ahram.org.eg/NewsContent/1/64/103020/Egypt/Politics-/Egypt-president-Mansour-signs-law-jailing-unauthor.aspx, accessed December 9, 2015, and archived at http://dx.doi.org/10.7910/DVN/PG4A7K.

to preach violent jihadism after their clerical training for reasons other than blocked ambition. An individual in this position is likely to subsequently lose his career as an insider, leading to blocked ambition that reinforces the idea that the insider-outsider divide is unjust. However, career loss is not the initial spark that turns late-adopting true believers to jihad.

My point is not that all outsider clerics will become jihadists, but that the failure to find an insider job nudges clerics in the direction of jihadism by eliminating the most attractive possible career path. Thus, a failure to break into the insider career track raises the probability of a cleric becoming jihadist, but the rates of jihadism among outsiders may still be low if other career paths are available for outsiders.

3.2.7 Limits of the Theory

My argument adapts ideas from relative deprivation theory to explain the radicalization of jihadist clerics. Like Gurr, I posit that individuals turn to violence when their aspirations do not match their reality. Gurr tends to focus on sources of relative deprivation that affect broad social and ethnic groups, so the specifics of how ambitions are blocked is somewhat different in his account than in mine. Still, my theory can be seen as a direct extension of this earlier work.

As a result, my argument also inherits the key limitation of relative deprivation arguments: many clerics face blocked ambitions and relatively few of them turn to jihadism. It is true that I do not have an adequate theory explaining why some react differently to blocked ambition. My argument is probabilistic, not deterministic. I expect that facing blocked academic ambition will increase the probability that a cleric turns to jihad, but it does not make every disappointed cleric do so. Still, there is clearly variation to be explained among those clerics who face blocked ambitions, and I expect that future research will identify additional causes of cleric radicalization.

However, I have crafted my theory to avoid some limitations of relative deprivation theories. Oberschall (1978, 300–301) criticizes Gurr for being overly vague about the sources of individual frustration. "Gurr's theory is silent on the choice of the comparison group and equity norms. Robbed of this specificity, the relative deprivation notion reduces to little more than that hardship produces discontent and grievances." In contrast, I am very specific about the nature of cleric ambitions and the likely means by which clerics are likely to have these ambitions blocked. This specificity helps make my theory falsifiable because if indicators of the specific types of blocked ambition I posit do not predict radicalization, then my proposed mechanisms of blocked ambition are clearly not operating.

Like the more sociological work on jihadist radicalization of lay Muslims by Sageman (2004), Wiktorowicz (2005b), and Reynolds and Hafez (2017), my theory also incorporates social networks. However, I differ from these sociological theories because I do not argue that network ties pass on radical influences. Clerics are educated enough to know where to find jihadist ideas if they want to seek them out, so I do not think networks play the same role for clerics as they seem to for lay jihadists. Instead, I argue that professional networks provide career opportunities, and that would-be clerics with weak teacher networks are more likely to have their career ambitions blocked. Of course these two possible functions of networks – spreading ideas and helping actors achieve goals – are not mutually exclusive. However, because research on jihadism has focused on how networks spread violent ideas, I think it is important to point out that networks shape the choices of actors in other ways as well.

My argument is also limited in scope, and would require modification to explain radicalization in populations other than Muslims clerics. Although I believe that blocked ambition can motivate extreme behavior in a variety of settings, I focus on the specific ambitions of clerics and the constraints they face as a result of a specific configuration of political and religious institutions in the modern Middle East. These conditions do not hold in many other regions of the world, and I do not expect blocked ambition to have the same results if the conditions are not similar. For example, the relationship between religious institutions and the state is profoundly different in the United States, so I do not expect that clerics in the United States who face blocked ambition are necessarily be at increased risk of turning to jihad.

The argument is also limited to the ambitions created by the culture of modern Islamic legal academia. If this culture were to change, or states in the Middle East were to change their relationship with Islamic academia, the argument I have laid out here might not hold. More generally, although some readers will see parallels between Islamic legal academia and Western academia, the argument requires modification to explain how academics in secular universities in the United States respond to blocked ambition. I do suspect that individuals who are forced out of Western academia when they wanted an academic career are changed as a result, but I doubt that they are at heightened risk of developing antistate ideologies. Because the state is far less involved in Western academia, blocked academic ambitions in that setting do not create grievances against the state (though they can create grievances against the academic system). Also, the outside options for Western academics are substantially better than for Muslim clerics in the Middle East who face blocked ambition.

What is the value of advancing a theory with the limitations I have just listed? I agree with Lakatos (1970) that science advances through "three-cornered fights" between a theory, the best alternative theory, and evidence. Because there is very little existing theory about why some clerics become jihadists, even a limited theory such as mine is a substantial improvement over the alternative of having almost no explanation at all.

3.3 TESTING THE THEORY OF BLOCKED AMBITION

The remaining chapters confront this theory with data. With the arguments fresh in mind, I conclude this chapter with an outline of my strategies for empirical testing and my expectations about what will emerge from the data analysis if the theory is correct.

Providing evidence for the reasons people become jihadist clerics is difficult for a number of reasons. Jihadists, especially jihadist clerics, are not really approachable as research subjects except in exceptional circumstances, so traditional clinical trials that have been used to test the effects of disappointment in the psychological literature are not feasible. This leaves me working with *observational* data – data that I collect from the natural course of events in the world rather than data than I control through experimental manipulation. The statistical tradition of observational research uses the word "control" to refer to factors that are included as conditioning variables in multivariate statistical models, but this sense of control is an analogy and does not carry the same analytical power as clinical trials can provide.

I rely mainly on a combination of quantitative and qualitative observational data analysis to test why some clerics become jihadists while others do not. In the quantitative analysis, I collect information about a large sample of Sunni Muslim clerics (Chapter 4), use their writings to determine which are jihadist (Chapter 5), and then test for statistical associations between indicators of blocked ambition and jihadism (Chapter 6). Identifying blocked ambition is challenging because ambitions can be blocked due to a variety of circumstances, so I focus on two indicators of possible blocked ambition that are generally observable: the strength of a cleric's educational network (an important source of leverage to an insider career track, as described earlier in this chapter) and whether a cleric does, in fact, find employment as an insider imam, professor, or ministry official.

One weakness of this quantitative approach is that finding a correlation between educational networks, career paths, and jihadism does not mean that networks and career paths *cause* jihadism; the correlation could be spurious. Spurious correlation is the main threat to observational data analysis and it is certainly a threat here, not least because the networks and career paths of jihadists-turned-clerics who radicalize for reasons other than blocked ambition might look a lot like the networks and career paths of clerics-turned-jihadists who do radicalize because of blocked ambition.

To see why, consider the correlations I expect to see in the data if blocked ambition pushes some clerics toward jihadism. If strong educational networks help clerics get ahead in their careers, then I expect clerics with many prominent teachers to be unlikely to have their ambitions blocked, while clerics with few connections are more likely to face blocked ambition. In the data, I expect this to manifest as a correlation between the number of teachers a cleric has and their probability of being jihadist: fewer teachers, more likely to be jihadist;

more teachers, less likely to be jihadist. I also expect clerics who obtain an insider career track to be less jihadist because their insider career is evidence that they haven't faced blocked ambitions. Without considering the alternatives below, it might be tempting to see these correlations as evidence of blocked ambition.

The problem is that the same correlations between networks, career paths, and ideology could be true for jihadists-turned-clerics. Consider the path in which a jihadist-turned-cleric might adopt jihadist ideas early in life, choose to become a cleric, and then pursue jihadist ideas throughout his career.[34] Such an individual might go through much of the same training as other clerics, but would already harbor the goal of using their training to support the jihadist movement through their activities as a cleric and apologist. While seeking clerical training, these individuals might hide their true preferences for fear of discrimination against jihadist ideas. After all, clerics in the state-run religious institutions in Egypt, Saudi Arabia, and elsewhere do not generally want to be responsible for training clerics who later reveal themselves to be jihadists. These individuals might be successful in obtaining academic credentials and degrees because they are motivated to pursue these symbols of academic achievement to establish their scholarly authority when they attempt to speak for the jihadist movement. These possibilities mean that associations between networks, career paths, and ideology might arise for reasons other than blocked ambition.

A jihadist-turned-cleric who is obtaining an education for the cause of jihad might be more likely to face blocked ambition than other aspiring clerics. Because prominent teachers in the clerical establishment are not likely to want jihadists as students, if these individuals reveal their true beliefs, they are likely to be excluded from study circles and classes, and even expelled from universities. This would certainly block their ambition to achieve the scholarly credentials they desire and reinforce the alienation that many committed jihadists may feel. However, if an individual already holds jihadist ideas that cause them to face discrimination, blocked ambition cannot be the initial cause of radicalization.

On the other hand, early-adopting true believers may eschew establishment teachers because they view them as morally suspect due to overly cozy relationships with the state. If this is the case, then my observable indicators of likely blocked ambition – weak education networks and a lack of insider career appointments – is in fact the *result* of jihadism rather than the *cause* of it. A jihadist-turned-cleric in this position would not care that they lacked

---

34 Some jihadists-turned-clerics are easy to distinguish from clerics facing blocked ambition because they first become violent activists fighting in jihadist conflicts, and then subsequently parlay their military credentials into scholarly and religious authority and begin writing in cleric genres. These soldiers-turned-clerics are unlikely to have scholarly credentials. Instead, they have experience in conflict zones – the "fields of jihad" – which give their words a certain gravitas with fellow jihadists.

connections to prominent scholars to help launch a successful insider career; such a career was never their desire. Instead, they may pursue Islamic legal training but intentionally remain on the periphery of the networks at their learning institution.

I attempt to account for these possibilities as carefully as possible in my statistical analysis in Chapter 6. However, the analysis has limitations due to data availability, quality, and a lack of experimental control that cannot fully be solved, so I turn to qualitative case studies to complement the weaknesses of the quantitative approach. The purpose of these case studies is not to provide an alternative method for estimating the effect of blocked ambition on cleric radicalization, and because I intentionally select only jihadist clerics for close scrutiny, such an estimate is not possible from the qualitative data. Instead, this exploration of turning points in the lives of jihadist clerics has two purposes: to demonstrate that the pathways I theorize are in fact operating in at least some cases, and then to provide a preliminary estimate of how many jihadist clerics were non-jihadist clerics who radicalized because of blocked ambition and how many began as lay jihadists who later became clerics.

Collectively, the evidence in the remainder of the book provides new data and analysis on who jihadist clerics are, which pathways they are mostly likely to take on their way to preaching jihad, and what differentiates them from other Muslim clerics. It is somewhat remarkable that despite thousands of books that have been written on jihadism since September 11, 2001, not a single one has been able to answer the following foundational questions about the clerics who preach jihad: how many are there, what motivates them, and what proportion of online Islamic discourse do they dominate? In the next three chapters, I provide answers to each of these questions, which I hope will shed new light on why some Muslim clerics turn to preaching violence and what this means for the past and future of the jihadist movement.

4

Meet the Clerics

In Cairene Islamic circles, the appropriate greeting is an upraised right hand that turns and drops to the chest, covering the heart. The head bows slightly, and the words tumble out, seemingly faster than possible, *al-salāmu ᶜalaykum*, "peace be upon you," to which one replies *wa-ᶜalaykum al-salām wa-raḥmatallāhī wa-barakātuh*, "and upon you, peace, and the mercy and blessings of God." The latter is a mouthful, so in many settings, it is shortened to merely *wa-ᶜlaykum al-salām*. Not at al-Azhar. Here, use of the full phrase conveys piety and everyone seems able to reproduce this entire phrase with impossible speed. Despite endless practice, my foreign tongue could not match the cadence of students and sheikhs at al-Azhar. Eventually, I began to cheat by starting with *wa-raḥmatallāhī...* and raising my volume as the phrase progressed so that my interlocutors might be fooled into thinking that I had mumbled the first part. I was always slightly afraid of messing it up. So it was when I finally worked up the courage to knock on the door at the al-Azhar mosque labeled "Office of the Sheikh of al-Azhar."

The sheikh in the office was not Ahmed al-Tayeb, the person most often referred to as the Sheikh of al-Azhar, but rather Barakat Abd al-Fatah Ghoneem, a cleric with a white beard who sometimes led prayer and delivered sermons. It was not easy to get a straight answer from even the mosque regulars about how many sheikhs the al-Azhar mosque really had. There seemed to be three who were often present and rotated Friday sermons, but I was given differing accounts of the authority structure. The cleric in the office was one of the three.

He sat behind a large wooden desk with some papers to one side. Some men sitting at the back of the office, by the door, did not leave when I entered and instead stopped their conversation to listen to ours. As usual, I fumbled the traditional greeting before he asked how he could help. My goal was to secure an interview, so I launched into a short spiel about my general interests.

He listened and then graciously but firmly indicated that he was uninterested in answering my questions, suggesting instead that I could take them to the clerics in the fatwa office. And just like that, my attempt to meet the sheikh was over.

My experience at al-Azhar convinced me that meeting clerics in person was harder than I initially had expected. I never did manage to meet Ahmed al-Tayeb, the head of al-Azhar. Al-Tayeb is a Maliki-school jurist who was appointed in 2010 as the successor to Muhammad Sayyid Tantawy. He is one of approximately fifty imams to have served in this role since the seventeeth century. Dense, long-form biographies and depictions of each of these imams are framed behind glass in an ornate hall situated next to the al-Azhar mosque on the university's campus in the Islamic district of Cairo, where al-Azhar's religious instruction takes place (al-Azhar University also offers secular instruction at a larger campus in Nasser City). A sympathetic doorman at the university campus gate took me in to see them when he learned of my interest in clerics at al-Azhar, but he had limited tolerance for my desire to carefully photograph each one. I made it nine sheikhs back before he asked me to stop. Even in the relative freedom of May 2011 Egypt, taking photographs in government buildings is taboo. This was as close as I came to getting to meet al-Tayeb personally.

I did have a few interviews with sheikhs in the fatwa office, but apart from these, most of my attempts to have nonscripted conversations with clerics failed. Once, I walked into the mushaykha of al-Azhar, which is really the office of the head mufti of Egypt and the Egyptian Dar al-Ifta (the government body that issues official fatwas), and was directed to a side office by the entrance to meet "the sheikh." Again, the sheikh was not the head mufti himself, but a cleric somewhere lower down the chain of authority whose job was to deal with people who came to the mushaykha seeking clerical advice. We had a pleasant, short conversation in which he told me that I was free to wander the building. I walked out of his office and attempted to surreptitiously take a photograph of the sign listing the offices on each floor of the building. This was a mistake. The doorman, who moments before had kindly welcomed me and directed me to the sheikh's office, now became enraged, shouting a phrase that I could not understand at the time but now know (all too well) to be countryside colloquial for "What do you want?" I was hauled back before the sheikh, who looked at me as if I had broken his trust and then asked me to delete the picture.

I did have substantial contact with clerics at al-Azhar, but almost always in the context of group instruction. Class schedules were posted on the walls of the al-Azhar courtyard as well as on Facebook, but I was apparently deficient in reading these because not once did I manage to correctly anticipate when and where a class would take place in the mosque. Instead, I hung around incessantly, attending any class that appeared to be starting. In these settings, other students generally assumed that I was Muslim and I did not challenge this assumption unless asked so as not to change the tenor of instruction.

I did not seem to be the only one with an unrequited desire for more individual conversation. Like clockwork, after teaching a lesson or leading a prayer, the sheikh would be swarmed by attendees kissing their hands, congratulating them on their erudition, and asking questions. In general, clerics seemed to have very little patience for this practice, indulging in perhaps one or two questions only before starting to walk out of the mosque prayer space (where most teaching happened as well), trailing students behind them. From this I learned that clerics manage their time carefully, see themselves as having a lot to do, prefer to talk during "office hours," and tend to prefer formats where they control the message.

In contrast to my experience at the mosque, getting to know clerics in virtual space is surprisingly easy. Clerics increasingly place copious amounts of information about themselves online and engage with their followers through personal websites as well as social media platforms like Facebook, Twitter, and Instagram. In fact, the very sheikh whom I failed to interview in the office at al-Azhar in 2012 has had an active Facebook account since 2013.[1] It is to these sources that I turned to get to know clerics and I use them here to construct a data set of clerics that I will use for analysis in the remainder of the book.

The plan of this chapter is as follows. I first offer a rationale for the construction of a large, representative data set of Muslim clerics. I then describe how I conducted a census of Arabic-speaking Muslim clerics online and how I used this census to collect detailed information on a representative sample of these individuals. I then analyze cleric biographies in order to learn more about who Muslim clerics are, where they live, and how they see themselves. To do so, I employ both quantitative and qualitative methods. To get a general sense of what cleric biographies emphasize, I apply an algorithm from computer science that identifies clusters of clerics with relatively similar biographies. To extract specific information, I read each biography and coded facts about the life path of each cleric. I provide summary statistics of the general characteristics of the clerics in my sample and provide evidence that clerics are overwhelmingly academic in their orientations.

4.1 A WEB CENSUS OF MUSLIM CLERICS

To build my data set, I systematized my exploration of cleric websites and social media such that the resulting data are *representative* of online clerics as a group. I collected representative data for two reasons. First, I wish to confirm the intuition from previous scholarship that clerics are academics, and this claim is best supported with representative data about their backgrounds and activities. Second, representative data about clerics is an essential part of my evidence showing how blocked ambition can be a pathway to jihadism.

---

[1]   www.facebook.com/BarakatAbdelfattahGhoneim, accessed February 10, 2017, and archived.

Existing scholarship illuminates who clerics are, how they see themselves, and how others see them (Zeghal 1996; Zaman 2002; Messick 1996; Wagemakers 2012; Caeiro 2011; Graf and Skovgaard-Petersen 2009; Al-Rasheed 2007; Lacroix 2011; Euben 1999), but most of this research considers only a few individuals or an unrepresentative collection of clerics selected for their historical importance. Many, like Wagemaker's excellent book on Abu Muhammad al-Maqdisi (Wagemakers 2012) or Messick's ethnography of a Yemeni cleric (Messick 1996), unpack the meanings of Muslim clericism by focusing on a single cleric. Others, like Al-Rasheed's or Lacroix's work on religion and rebellion in Saudi Arabia (Al-Rasheed 2007; Lacroix 2011) introduce material on many clerics but primarily those who played an exceptional role in major historical events. Mouline (2015) provides very detailed data on the clerics at the top of the Saudi religious hierarchy, but this is hardly a representative set. Even a work as expansively titled as Zaman's *The Ulama in Contemporary Islam* (2002) turns out to primarily focus on Deobandi clerics in India and Pakistan, with some comparison to specific clerics in Egypt and Saudi Arabia. The work that takes an approach closest to my own is Zeghal (1996), who interviews thirty-seven clerics, both prominent and unknown, at the al-Azhar mosque and university. However, even this admirable sample provides data only about the clerics at al-Azhar and cannot be assumed to generalize to other settings.

Nonrepresentative studies are of limited value when trying to characterize the culture in which the average Muslim cleric resides precisely because they are focused on exceptional cases or particular cases that may not be representative. While nonrepresentative samples of informants can be useful for characterizing some aspects of a culture, they run the risk of failing to faithfully represent that culture in its entirety because many individuals have little or no probability of being included. Making representative statements about a culture can be facilitated by analyzing a representative set of individuals in that culture.

The reason that no prior study of Muslim clerics uses a representative sample is that representative sampling requires a census of a well-defined population from which the sample can be drawn. But tabulating such a census of all Muslim clerics is difficult. The enormity of the task becomes apparent as soon as one hits the ground in any Muslim-majority country. In the old Islamic district of Cairo, for example, mosques adorn every major intersection and each of them is staffed with clerics. Islamic bookstores line the streets behind al-Azhar and are frequented by clerics, and institutes for teaching and proselytizing employ yet more. Generating a census of all of these individuals would most likely require visiting every religious establishment and painstakingly indexing every person. Carrying this out on a global scale would require unimaginable resources.

At least one instance of such a census has occurred on a countrywide level. In the late 1990s, the Iraqi regime decided to keep tabs on dissident clerics and created a set of documents recording the names of clerics, their location of residence, their clerical positions, and information assessing their compliance with regime demands. The files were recovered in the aftermath of the US invasion of Iraq and are now housed at the Hoover Institution, where, with the help of Lisa Blaydes, I examined the records. While there is nothing in the files directly stating that the list is an attempt at a census, it seems to be. Based on the positions recorded for individuals on the list, it seems that the Iraqi government was most concerned about clerics with some stature, suggesting that their implicit definition of a cleric is more restrictive than my own. Still, the number of individuals on this list provides some sense of how many clerics a Muslim-majority country might have.

The Iraqi cleric census contains 3,386 cleric names. The Iraqi population in 1998 was approximately 22.3 million, with roughly 21.5 million Muslims, meaning that there was one cleric for every 6,300 Muslims (this seems a bit low, so I take the Iraqi attempt at a census as a lower bound). If I tenuously posit that this ratio of clerics to lay Muslims is constant throughout all of the Muslim world, then a back-of-the-envelope calculation suggests that there might be approximately 250,000 Muslim clerics serving the global population of approximately 1.6 billion Muslims.

A census such as the one attempted by Saddam Hussein's regime is impractical for research purposes and most likely requires the capacity and coercion of a government. One approach could be to piggyback on governments that comprehensively surveil clerics, but the Iraqi case is the only one I know of where the resulting census has become public, and the documents were not relinquished willingly. Such efforts are rarely public and cooperating with dictatorships that keep tabs on restive clerics seems like an ethical disaster.

Instead, I turn to the Internet, where, since its inception, Muslim clerics have been making information about themselves freely available. My approach is to conduct a global census of Arabic-speaking Muslim clerics with a significant online presence[2] as of April 2015. No such census of Muslim clerics has existed until now. I then sample from this list to create a data set of detailed information on clerics who are representative of online clerics as a whole. This is a practical move; the Internet is the only domain where it is currently feasible to take a census of Muslim clerics. However, the obvious limitation of using the Internet is that any clerics or groups that do not have an Internet presence will be omitted. Investigating only those clerics who have a substantial web presence is a necessary limitation that makes this study tractable without substantially weakening the strength of the findings. Most global conversations about Islam have moved online, and an Internet presence is essentially mandatory for Islamic clerics or groups that wish to spread their opinions or influence. Of course, many clerics are not seeking to join any transnational conversation

---

[2] I consider a cleric to have a "significant online presence" if I can identify their name, distinguish them from other clerics with similar names, find at least some biographical information about them besides their name, and find some type of religious material that they have produced or for which they are responsible.

and are not online. These everyday clerics primarily have local influence – they are the imams who serve the needs of lay Muslims in their immediate neighborhoods. They have no chance of entering my data set because they do not place information on the Internet.

To acknowledge this practical empirical limitation, I limit my argument with the following scope condition: *my theory and evidence apply only to those clerics with the capacity to shape regional, national, or transnational conversations about Islam.* This scope condition is reasonable because the global jihadists I study and their prominent non-jihadist counterparts are certainly engaged in global conversations about the form and content of Islam. As I show below, virtually all such clerics have at least some web presence, whether they create it themselves or others create it for them. The clerics I study are fundamentally trying to promote their ideas, and in the age of the Internet, this means online communication. This scope condition means that my exploration of why elite clerics become jihadist cannot extend to explain why a small-time cleric in the hinterlands of Saudi Arabia might start teaching jihadism in the local mosque. The dynamics may be the same, but the data I collect here can neither support nor reject this possibility.

By focusing on the Internet, I am able to tap into a rich and underutilized wealth of data with immense importance for understanding Muslim clerics. The Internet contains unprecedented amounts of information about these actors and, by virtue of its information-sharing function, encourages those most interested in transnational influence to place the most information online. Clerics and groups create websites and use Facebook, Twitter, and YouTube to spread their opinions. Additionally, information about them is often available on Wikipedia pages, Islamic aggregator sites, and Islamic Internet forums where people post clerics' biographies. Muhammad al-Arayfi, a Saudi cleric known for his exceptional popularity on social media, has a website in Arabic, English, and Farsi, a Facebook page with 12 million "likes," a Twitter feed with 9 million followers, a number of videos on YouTube, and an extensive Wikipedia page. For good measure, an Islamic aggregator site collects his recitations, lessons, video clips, articles, and books. Together, these sources provide rich information about the background and ideology of al-Arayfi. Similar information is available for thousands of Islamic clerics of all sects and ideological persuasions.

I limit my web census to clerics who produce content in Arabic because close reading of website materials proves essential for the analysis that follows, and of the languages preferred by most clerics, I can read Arabic best. Given the primacy of the Arabic language in both Islamic doctrine and practice, this places very little constraint on the analysis. The global Islamic conversation happens largely in Arabic. However, future work could apply the same approach as I use here to study clerics writing in other languages, including Indonesian, Farsi, Turkish, or English.

Using a variety of methods detailed below, I constructed a list of virtually all Arabic-speaking Muslim clerics on the Internet as of April 2015. This census is certainly missing someone – my search methods were extensive but not entirely exhaustive. Moreover, the Internet is a quickly changing space with websites appearing and disappearing daily according to the whims of their owners, so constructing a web census of clerics is difficult and the resulting list may only be a census for a very short period of time. Finally, because of how I constructed the list, a small number of entries are not actually Muslim clerics according to my definition: individuals writing in Islamic genres for public consumption. Still, an approach similar to the one I use here has been shown to recover lists of entities in other online domains (Letham, Rudin, and Heller 2013). Despite the inherent challenges, the resulting list of 10,202 clerics offers the best possible census from which to sample clerics in a representative and transparent way.

Constructing the census was a complicated process, which I describe briefly here. I first employed five methods to comb the Internet to identify entities who might be Muslim clerics: (1) using lists from Islamic aggregator websites, (2) using lists of clerics on the crowd-sourced web-encyclopedia Wikipedia, (3) identifying Wikipedia entries about Muslim clerics, (4) performing Google searches, and (5) exploiting Google autocomplete, a program that recommends search terms.

Islamic aggregator sites are a genre of website that collects Islamic content of interest to Muslims and reposts it, much like news aggregator websites. These websites reproduce content from many clerics and often provide lists of every author with writings on the website. Since many, though not all, of the authors on Islamic aggregator websites fit my definition of a cleric, I collect these lists as a starting point. Many sites have a particular ideological brand or target a particular subgroup of lay Muslims so it is important to examine as many aggregator sites as possible. I tried to be comprehensive in my coverage of existing Islamic aggregator sites, though inevitably I missed some.[3]

Wikipedia – a crowd-sourced online encyclopedia that anyone can edit – is another helpful source of information about clerics because many clerics are the subjects of Wikipedia articles. Despite the fact that all content on Wikipedia is produced for free, and in many cases by nonexperts, the information it

---

3 I collected lists from the following websites: www.al-eman.com (44 entries), www.alifta.net (11 entries), a petition signed by 110 clerics at www.almokhtsar.com/node/165155, www. alsalhenway.com (160 entries), www.alukah.net (18,996 entries), www.anasalafy.com (74 entries), 347 students of Abd al-Aziz Bin Baz listed at www.binbaz.org.sa/mat/21295, islam-call. com (1,330 entries), www.islamlight.net (110 entries), islamport.com (1,742 entries), 268 authors on islamtoday.net/istesharat, www.islamway.com (1,687 entries), 439 likely cleric websites from www.mktba.org/catplay.php?catsmktba=43, www.mohamoon-ksa.com (376 entries, list now defunct), 409 clerics whose phone numbers are listed at www.saaid.net/ Warathah/1/hatif.htm, saaid.net (234 entries), www.sohari.com (11 entries), and www.tawhed. ws (a jihadist web library with 448 listed authors). Not all people listed on these websites are clerics according to my definition, but most are.

contains has proven to be highly reliable in a number of domains (Giles 2005; Brown 2011; Casebourne, Davies, and Fernandes 2012). Wikipedia contains lists of clerics curated by Wikipedia contributors, often grouped into categories such as "Saudi Sunni Religious Scholars." These lists are helpful, but they do not include every Muslim cleric on Wikipedia. To find them all, I designed an algorithm that "crawled" from article to article on Wikipedia, applied a statistical text model to each article, and identified 3,690 articles that were about clerics (details of the algorithm are located in Appendix B).

Yet more names of clerics came from Google searches I conducted for phrases associated with cleric websites, such as "the website of sheikh" (*mawqaᶜ al-shaykh*) and "the website of the honorable sheikh" (*mawqaᶜ faḍīlat al-shaykh*). This resulted in a list of 900 likely cleric websites that I then vetted by hand, resulting in 790 entries.

Finally, I harnessed Google autocomplete, which uses a proprietary algorithm to automatically generate search-term suggestions based on popularity, starting with partial phrases entered by the user into the Google search bar. For example, typing in "fatwa" (in English) into a Google search bar results in the suggestions "fatwa definition," "fatwa meaning," "fatwa Islam," and so on. I use this tool to suggest the names of frequently searched clerics. My strategy was to generate all possible combinations of one and two letters in Arabic, resulting in a set of combinations that is the Arabic equivalent of "aa," "ab," "ac," ... "zz." I then append each combination to the word "al-Shaykh" and a series of common Arabic name prefixes ("al," "abdal," "ibn"). For instance, I entered "al-Shaykh al-aa" and then queried Google autocomplete for each of the results. This mimics the process of someone who wants to search for the name of a particular cleric, with Google helpfully offering suggestions about which cleric they might be searching for based on the letters they have entered so far. Many of the combinations I entered are nonsensical but some are the beginnings of popular clerics' names, and Google autocomplete returned a long list of possible clerics I might be trying to locate via Google search. All told, this method resulted in 12,643 entries.

These search methods provided me with a list with 22,236 entries. Unfortunately, this initial list was marred by the inclusion of many nonclerics and duplicates. For the purposes of random sampling, nonclerics are a nuisance but not a serious problem; if I sample them for further coding, I can simply skip them. In contrast, duplicates create real problems. For example, Abd al-Aziz Bin Baz (the former head mufti of Saudi Arabia) is one of the most famous clerics in recent memory and as a result, variants of his name appear no less than 152 times in this initial list ("Abd al-Aziz Bin Abd Allah Bin Baz, Abd al-Aziz Bin Abdullah Bin Baz, Abd al-Aziz Bin Baz, ... *zawjāt* al-Shaykh Ibn Baz"). A random sample from the list containing duplicates would be unrepresentative because Bin Baz is 152 times more likely to be in the sample than the vast majority of clerics whose names appear only once. Thus, the next step was to disambiguate duplicates in the list and remove as many nonclerics as possible.

First, I disambiguated entries for some well-known clerics such as Abd al-Aziz Bin Baz. Next, I went through the sublists generated by each search method and disambiguated similar names by hand.[4] I then searched the web for each remaining entry and recorded the Internet addresses of websites associated with each cleric. In this search process, I occasionally discovered the web presence of additional clerics who were not originally on the list; I added them. Once I had websites associated with most clerics (some had no results using Google), I merged all entries that had overlapping website addresses, resulting in a final census with 10,202 entries.

This list of 10,202 clerics is too large for me to analyze in its entirety because extracting detailed information for each cleric I analyze is time consuming. Instead, I collected detailed information for a random sample, subject to several criteria. Not all clerics are equally useful for testing arguments about why some clerics become jihadist so I decided to focus my data collection efforts on those clerics to whom my arguments are most likely to apply: clerics who are (1) contemporary (alive after 1980),[5] (2) male,[6] and (3) Sunni.[7] For practical research reasons, I also limit the sampling to clerics who satisfy two more conditions: (4) they have publicly available Arabic-language writing, and (5) I can find sufficient biographical information.[8]

It is very likely that clerics whose online biographies and collections of work are sufficient for my purposes are systematically different from those who are

---

4   For this part of the disambiguation process, I used a name-proximity recommendation system that I designed. For each name, I calculated which other names on the list had similar combinations of letters or shared part of the name verbatim and then checked these names against each other to eliminate any duplicates. Judging duplicates is difficult because names alone do not generally convey the necessary information. In some cases, I was able to quickly identify duplicate entries based on Arab naming conventions. In other cases, I resorted to searching for websites associated with each variant using Google to determine whether there were two clerics with similar names, or if the similar names referred to the same individual. I removed entries that did not refer to clerics when I saw them, but because false positives are not problematic for random sampling, this was a lower priority than removing duplicates.

5   I require that clerics be contemporary, meaning that they were alive at a point in time where they could have participated in the modern jihadist movement had they chosen to do so. Hegghammer (2010a) dates modern jihadism to roughly 1979, so I only include clerics who were alive during or after the year 1980. Twenty-seven percent of clerics on the list are made ineligible by this condition.

6   It is theoretically possible for a female cleric to be a jihadist but to my knowledge there have been none. Approximately two of the clerics in the census are women.

7   I exclude Shia clerics because they are not generally at risk of joining the Sunni jihadist movement. Shia clerics can also endorse political violence, but the dynamics governing Shia extremism are likely to be different from the dynamics among Sunni clerics because the two sects have rather different traditions structuring clerical authority. About 7 percent of clerics online are Shia, notably lower than the 10 to 13 percent of Shia adherents worldwide. Although Shia clerics are not the focus of this study, it is intriguing to entertain the possibility that either there are fewer clerics per layperson in Shi'i Islam or that Shia clerics are less likely than their Sunni counterparts to place material online.

8   Forty-five percent of all entries on the census list fail to meet one or both of these criteria.

not: they are likely to be more famous, more interested in outreach, and perhaps younger (and thus have better facility with the Internet). There is no way around these possible selection effects – it must suffice that my sample will be representative of clerics who meet these criteria, but not representative of the census as a whole. Approximately 1,800 clerics from the census list satisfy these criteria, and I randomly sample 200 for analysis.[9] This is a sufficient sample size for statistical analysis while avoiding the herculean research task of collecting data for *every* eligible cleric in the census.

How representative is my resulting sample of Muslim clerics as a whole? Strictly speaking, the sample is only representative of the approximately 1,800 clerics from the census list who satisfied all of the inclusion criteria listed previously. While this may seem like a small number relative to the 10,000 names I identified in the census, these 1,800 are the clerics who matter most online. They are the clerics who are visible, who are producing content, and about whom people are asking questions and giving answers. Muslim clerics not in this list of 1,800 may be influential in their hometown, or perhaps even in the government of their home country, but they are unlikely to be participating in the global conversation about Islam that has increasingly moved online as the Internet has come of age.

If I had instead used an ad hoc sample, perhaps a list of clerics from a single website, then *sample selection* would be a serious concern for any subsequent analysis. Sample-selection effects can bias statistical results if inclusion in the sample is correlated with the variables of interest. This is less of a concern for my sample because I know how the sample was created, so only a few selection criteria must be considered, rather than a possibly infinite number of confounding possibilities with an ad hoc sample. In Chapter 6, I return to the question of whether sample selection bias is a serious concern for the specific statistical tests described there. The important point for now is that, by carefully constructing the sample, I can be confident of two things: first, that any patterns in the data are not likely due to "sample selection" in which clerics are included in my analysis because of some confounding factor, and second, that the sample is representative of the 1,800 clerics who are most visible online.

4.1.1 Salafi Oversample

Employing a representative random sample in my analysis is important because it allows me to make general claims about clerics that previously were not known. However, random sampling in this setting does come with a limitation. Using methods described in Chapter 5, I find that only 11 percent of the web sample is jihadist, leaving me with a *rare outcome* problem: jihadism is

9 To determine sample eligibility, I work through the randomly ordered census list, starting from the top, and collect biographical information via Google searches to code whether each entry fit the five criteria just listed. I did this until I had 200 clerics who met the criteria.

sufficiently rare in the population of clerics that random sampling does not include enough jihadists for precise analysis. To be clear, the jihadists in my random sample are likely to be representative of the population of jihadist clerics generally because of the sampling procedure, but the problem is there are simply not enough of them. When applying statistical tests to so few cases of the outcome of interest, the results are likely to be too imprecise to reach any conclusions because the analysis lacks sufficient statistical power.

I circumvent this rare outcome problem by collecting an *oversample* of Salafi clerics. The inclusion of these individuals supplements the original sample by increasing the number of certain types of clerics in the data to allow for more precise statistical results. However, these oversampled clerics must be treated with caution because they are not representative of the overall population of clerics. Estimating standard statistical models (such as regression) on the combined web sample and oversample could lead to biased results unless I make appropriate corrections.

My first goal with the oversample is to increase the number of jihadists in my data set. To identify jihadists, I collected the names and biographies of jihadi clerics mentioned in either Brachman (2009) or the "Militant Ideology Atlas" (McCants 2006). My second goal for the oversample is to increase the number of non-jihadists in my data set who share important ideological similarities to jihadists but who do not preach militant jihadism. Sunni jihadism fits within a larger movement called Salafism. While I am not able to directly estimate the rate of Salafism in the web sample, I suspect that it may also be relatively low (though not as low as the rate of jihadism). There are parts of the analysis where it is particularly helpful to compare jihadists to a sufficient number of non-jihadist Salafis. Thus I oversample non-jihadist Salafis from the Salafi aggregator websites islamway.net and saaid.net, both of which curate collections of fatwas and websites from modern Salafi clerics. This search results in an additional 101 clerics, largely from Saudi Arabia (58 percent) and Egypt (22 percent), of whom roughly 27 are jihadist (though this depends on precisely how I detect jihadism, a point I take up in Chapter 5).

To reiterate, this Salafi oversample is not representative because I collect it in a relatively ad hoc manner that is aimed primarily at gathering information on certain types of clerics from sources where I know they are likely to be found. This sample may have the problems of ad hoc samples described in the previous section. However, this oversample can still be valuable if used carefully to complement the representative web sample. When I need to make representative statements about Muslim clerics in general, I rely on the web sample alone. When I need to perform analysis for which a sufficient number of jihadists or non-jihadist Salafis is crucial, I use the oversample, sometimes in combination with the web sample. In the analysis that follows, I will refer to the representative sample as the "web sample" and the oversample as the "Salafi oversample." In places, it is useful to divide the oversample into jihadists and non-jihadists, which I refer to as the "jihadist oversample" and "non-jihadist oversample," respectively.

4.2 CLERIC BIOGRAPHIES

To learn about each cleric in my sample, I rely on biographical information that is publicly available on the Internet. This biographical information can come from a variety of sources: autobiographies and curricula vitae written by clerics themselves, biographies written by others (often by the subject's students), Wikipedia articles (presumably edited by the cleric's followers), biographical information provided by Islamic aggregator sites that host a cleric's works, biographical information posted by users of Islam-oriented Internet message boards, and news articles such as obituaries.

Just as in Western academia, Muslim clerics are often responsible for providing a detailed accounting of their scholarly credentials and pursuits (Zeghal 1996, 53–56). As a result, clerics typically write short biographies describing their religious training, appointments, and scholarly works. Clerics refer to their biographies using several Arabic terms: as an (auto)biography (*sīra (dhātiyya)* or *tarjima*), an "abstract," or a "short description" (*nabdha mukhtaṣara*). On cleric websites, these biographies are often linked from a sidebar or header on the front page of the website with the invitation "Get to Know the Sheikh." In many, perhaps most cases, the biography is written by the cleric himself. In some cases, it is written by his students or other admirers.

These biographies are part of a long tradition of biographical writing in Islam. Since shortly after the time of Muhammad, Muslim scholars have produced biographical writings about prominent religious figures, writers, and clerics, often organized by time period, location, school of Islamic law, or profession. These biographical dictionaries tend to include certain elements that are also included by clerics as they write their own biographies, including full name, education, professional career, scholarly works, and personal characteristics or noteworthy items.[10]

Although the heritage of the genre of cleric biographies primarily derives from the distinctive tradition of Islamic biographical writing in Islam, today many of these biographies resemble curricula vitae common in Western academic settings. This similarity is not accidental. Clerics who hold academic appointments often explicitly label their biographies as an academic curriculum vitae (CV). Tellingly, some cleric websites store the cleric's biography at a web link called "CV," even when the biography is not explicitly labeled as such. Of the 430 web links to biographies for the 200 clerics in my web sample, 35 (8 percent) have "CV" in the URL.

Much like the standardization of academic CVs, a number of common elements appear in these biographies, and formatting is relatively important. Although some biographies are presented in paragraphs, most follow an

---

[10] See Reynolds (2001) for a discussion of historical biographical writing in Islam. See Khalidi (1973) for an introduction to biographical dictionaries, and Bulliet (1970) for some innovative uses of biographical dictionaries in quantitative history.

outlined, bullet-point style of CV with standard categories: lineage, upbringing, education, teachers, employment, scholarly works, students, endorsements by other clerics, and (when relevant) death. There is some variation in the order and emphasis of these categories, but producers and consumers of these biographies appear to agree that these are the important elements to know about a cleric.

The intended purpose of these biographies is to provide information that lay Muslims use to evaluate clerics. Information about clerics is often requested on Muslim web forums. For example, a post on the forum *Muntadiyat ya Hussayn* (www.yahosein.com) has the title "Who is Sheikh al-Ghazi" and asks:

Through my search for information on the sheikh, I did not find much, either because of my ignorance about searching on the internet or because I've found all that is written about the Sheikh.

I would like to find an answer to the subject and on the place of study of the sheikh. Is his exposition correct? And information on him generally.[11]

Another post, on "Forum of the Followers of the Islamic Messengers" (www. ebnmaryam.com), asks a similar question.

Who is Sheikh Imran Hussayn? I heard two lectures by him about the false messiah and Gog and Magog. He is a Sunni, of the people of the Community, trained in political and religious culture, from Indian heritage and born in the country of Trinidad and Tobago. Is there any more information or an opinion of the brothers about this sheikh?[12]

The demand for cleric biographies creates strong incentives for clerics to provide biographical information about themselves. The availability of biographical information about clerics is crucial to my study; without cleric biographies, it would be extremely difficult to measure any of the factors in clerics' lives that I argue increase their risk of radicalization. Through extensive searches, I identified 430 biographies available on the Internet for the 200 clerics in my web sample. Most clerics have only one biography (72 clerics) or two biographies (64 clerics) available, but a few had as many as 6. Some have more than I located; I generally stopped looking for more biographical material once I started finding only reposts of biographies that I had already collected.

To give a sense of how much information these biographies contain, I count the number of words written about each cleric in their online biography (or biographies). Most cleric biographies are under 1,500 words; the median biography is 912 words long and the 75th percentile biography is 1,652 words long. Some are extremely spare (48 words), while the longest in the sample is the length of a short book (16,109 words). As this wide range of lengths suggests,

---

11   "*Man Huwwa al-Shaykh al-Ghazi?*" yahosein.com. www.yahosein.com/vb/showthread.php?
      t=141010, accessed March 23, 2013, and archived.
12   www.ebnmaryam.com/vb/t190707.html, accessed March 23, 2013, and archived.

biographies vary drastically in their scope and attention to details about the life and career of their subjects. I intentionally limited data collection at the outset to only those clerics for whom at least minimal biographical information is available, but even this does not prevent me from running into woefully incomplete biographies.

To give a sense of these biographies as a whole, I use a statistical *topic model* to identify clusters of similar biographies that emerge naturally from the data. I use topic models at multiple points throughout the book, so it is worth introducing them in some detail here.

Topic models are a family of statistical text analysis models introduced by Blei, Ng, and Jordan (2003) and developed by many others; the models I use rely most on work by Porteous et al. (2008), Roberts et al. (2014), and Lucas et al. (2015). A topic model takes raw text as an input and estimates which words are correlated with each other in ways that humans might identify as topics. As with all models, the appropriate standard for evaluating a topic model is not whether it is right or wrong, but whether it is useful.

Often, it is difficult to evaluate the usefulness of statistical models because humans are bad at calculating probabilities and have little inherent sense of what useful results might look like. Evaluating the usefulness of topic models is usually easier because the results can be represented using language. Humans are much better at the task of identifying sensible text than the task of distinguishing sensible probability models from numerical nonsense.

To estimate a topic model, I must first specify the number of topics in advance, potentially raising concerns about how to choose the "correct" number of topics for a particular application. In many applications, this question is as misguided as the parallel question, "How many topics are there in a novel?" In most collections of text, there is probably not an optimal number of topics; estimating a model with five topics is likely to result in broad, high-level themes in a corpus, while estimating a model with 100 smaller topics is likely to result in a more complex, granular view.

Although many clusters of correlated words identified by a topic model will seem like topics to readers, it is important to be aware that not every cluster of correlated words is necessarily useful. The topics in a topic model do not come with labels signifying what they ought to mean; each collection of correlated words must be interpreted by the researcher. This is a deeply subjective task. A significant part of the inference in a topic model occurs at the stage where a researcher looks at a list of correlated words and interprets them substantively as a single concept.

Some "topics" generated by a topic model may not be amenable to interpretation by humans – the features that make these words correlated are not features that humans associate with meaningful "topic-ness." Thus, rather than following the political science literature that engages in substantial hand-wringing about the number of topics, I simply estimate multiple topic models with varying numbers of topics and select the level of granularity that is most useful. Throughout this book, I choose models based on the insights they spark about the data; many but not necessarily all collections of correlated words in these models can be interpreted as topics that humans can recognize.

Turning back to the task of exploring "natural" groupings of similar cleric biographies, I begin by estimating a topic model with fifteen topics using the text of the biographies.[13] The majority of words in the biographies are devoted to two topics that I label *academic lineage* (36 percent of words) and *qualifications/appointments* (33 percent). This result confirms that the main purpose of a biography is to convey information about these two aspects of scholarly qualification. The remaining topics, in order of prevalence, are *narrative recollection* (4.7 percent, common in longer biographies), *places* (4 percent), *metaphysics* (3.3 percent, common in book titles), *fighting* (3.1 percent), *exegesis* (3 percent, from book titles), *media* (2.3 percent), *Saudi Arabia (1)* (2.2 percent), *Egypt* (1.9 percent), *hadith* (1.7 percent), *Saudi Arabia (2)* (1.7 percent), *Africa* (1.4 percent), *Palestine* (1 percent), and an unclear topic that I cannot readily interpret (0.4 percent).[14]

Approximately 66 percent of the words in cleric biographies are assigned to just two topics, *academic lineage* and *qualifications/appointments*, so these topics deserve special attention. The ten most common terms in the academic lineage topic are "the sheikh," "Allah," "Muhammad," "Abd," "book," "was," "knowledge," "have mercy on him," "books," and "the doctor." This list of terms and other words associated with this topic are commonly used by clerics as they list out where they studied and with whom. The names of popular teachers rise to the top of this list – "Allah," "Muhammad," and "Abd," are all popular given names – and there is an emphasis on the titles of these teachers and the scholarship they have produced. Biographies that rely heavily on academic lineage appear to be making an argument for the authority of the subject by highlighting the scholarly authority of their teachers. At the extreme, these biographies are composed almost entirely of lists of teachers.

In contrast, biographies that emphasize the *qualifications/appointments* topic focus on the credentials and career achievements of the subjects themselves, without as much reference to their teachers. The most common words for the *qualifications/appointments* topic are "Islamic," "year," "mosque," "studies," "knowledge," "religion," "Arabic," "preaching," "the sciences," and "*usūl*" (foundations of Islamic jurisprudence). Many of these words are used

---

[13] I looked at results from topic models with more and fewer topics. The two main topics – which I label *academic lineage* and *qualifications/appointments* – persist in models with more topics, while the other topics merge or split.

[14] Two topics list places, people, and institutions related to clerical study and work in Saudi Arabia. I cannot tell precisely why the model fits these words with two distinct topics, so I have labeled them Saudi Arabia 1 and 2. There may be some difference between these topics that is escaping my attention. The unclear topic is concentrated heavily in the biography of Adnan al-Tarsha, who had a career in martial arts as well as a career as a Muslim cleric. I expect that this topic is capturing words that are unusual in cleric biographies.

by clerics to describe their professional appointments; they are employed in departments of Islamic law and religion, they work at mosques, and they teach Arabic, preaching, and the Islamic sciences.

Each cleric's biography can be summarized by the proportion of each topic it contains. To find natural clusters of similar biographies, I use a clustering procedure called *k-means clustering* (MacQueen 1967; Hastie, Tibshirani, and Friedman 2009). This technique involves specifying a desired number of clusters, *k*, into which the model will divide the data. The model then creates clusters that minimize the distance between cases in the same cluster. The algorithm proposes an initial set of case clusters and then evaluates. If a case is close to the center of another cluster, the algorithm tries switching it to see whether the new set of clusters results in better within-cluster similarity. Identifying optimal clusters is tricky because each time a case switches, multiple clusters are affected, which can make other cases switch clusters as well. I run the algorithm from multiple starting points (so that an idiosyncratic initial proposal of clusters does not determine the outcome) and then iterate until the clusters are stable.

As with topics, there is no "right" number of clusters. I check the resulting clusters at different values of *k* and use model fit[15] to arrive at a choice of four clusters: using four clusters improves the fit of the model much more than using three, but a model with five clusters does not perform much better than four.

Examining the resulting four clusters, I find that they mostly capture a trade-off in emphasis on the *academic lineage* and *qualifications/appointments* topics. This can been seen in Figure 4.1, in which I plot the proportion of the *academic lineage* and *qualifications/appointments* topics in each cleric's biography on the x- and y-axes of a scatter plot, using symbols to indicate the cluster to which each cleric is assigned. Three of the clusters, representing 87 percent of the clerics, fall in a diagonal line, indicating a direct trade-off in the biographies between a focus on academic lineage and a focus on qualifications and appointments. In other words, if a cleric's biography devotes 10 percent more of its words to academic lineage, it can be expected to devote 10 percent less to qualifications. Furthermore, it is clear that the topics of academic lineage and qualifications/appointments are the main focus of the biographies in these three clusters, as they devote about 80 percent of their words to just these two topics. Cleric biographies are spread out remarkably evenly along this spectrum: fifty clerics emphasize their academic lineage most, sixty-two emphasize their qualifications most, and sixty-one mention them about equally.

The biographies that stand out are those that I label "Fighting" in Figure 4.1. These twenty-seven clerics write less about both academic lineage

---

[15] Model fit is the degree to which the model is an accurate summary of the data. Here, I evaluate model fit using the *residual sum of squares*: the sum of the squared distance from each data point to the corresponding model prediction. Models with a smaller residual sum of squares fit the data more closely.

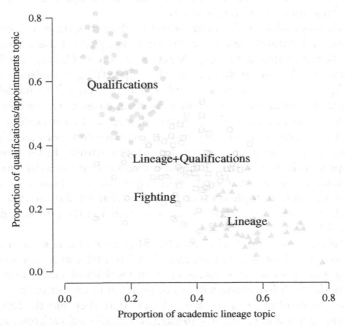

FIGURE 4.1. Four clusters of cleric biographies.

Notes: The average proportion of *academic lineage* and *qualifications/appointments* topics in the biographies of the 200 clerics in the representative web sample. Symbols and labels indicate the four clusters to which cleric biographies are assigned by a k-means clustering algorithm. Approximately 70 percent of words in cleric biographies are devoted to these two topics; the trade-off between them largely defines the clusters to which clerics are assigned.

and qualifications than the others, instead focusing on fighting and places where fighting has occurred. This set of biographies is largely made up of clerics whom I identify as jihadists in the following chapter.

The results of the topic model and clustering algorithm give a broad overview of the content of cleric biographies, but they are not as useful for extracting specific information about clerics. To say more about the characteristics of the clerics in my sample, I thus read their biographies closely. I describe my findings in the following section.

4.3 CHARACTERISTICS OF MUSLIM CLERICS ON THE INTERNET

The biographies of the clerics in my sample allow me to measure information about them that is useful for understanding who these clerics are and how some of them become jihadists. To collect information from the biographies, I read each several times and had a research assistant read them as well for an independent assessment. In this chapter, I use simple analysis such as word counts on key terms to provide summary statistics that give a sense of the themes that emerge from the close reading.

Although they are often highly detailed, there is a certain politics to the writing and circulation of these biographies. It is essential to understand the dynamics governing these writings because the validity of the statistical findings depends on the accuracy of the data derived from the cleric biographies. In particular, clerics sometimes seem to write their biographies in ways that make them appear well educated, influential, and pious (not dissimilar from CVs in other domains, with the exception of piety). It is not likely that clerics will include outright falsehoods in their biographies – there are potentially reputation costs for getting caught with fraudulent credentials – but clerics may embellish the truth in fairly predictable ways. Where relevant below, I discuss how these incentives to embellish aspects of a cleric's biography may affect my ability to measure characteristics of clerics. In most cases, my measurements are still accurate because I intentionally focus on characteristics of clerics that they are unlikely to fabricate.

I use the biographies to collect information for about forty variables relating to clerics' lives and careers. My choices about what to measure are based mostly on considerations related to the demands of my statistical analysis in Chapter 6, though I also collect some other, general information.

4.3.1 How Old Are the Clerics?

My inclusion criteria stipulate that clerics in my sample need to have been alive during or after the year 1980, but I know little else about the age of clerics in my sample until I look at the biographies. One hundred and fifty-one clerics list their date of birth in their biography. Among these, the median cleric was born in 1956, making them about 60 years old at the time of data collection. Two-thirds were born in the 1960s, 1970s, and 1980s, making the majority of clerics between 40 and 70 years old. Only four clerics are younger than 40 at the time I collected data.

To judge when these clerics have been most active, I search each biography for dates and then look at the range of years mentioned. Like Western CVs, cleric biographies generally contain a lot of dates: graduation, years of appointment at academic positions, and date of publication for major works (although in Islamic academia citation often goes by name and book title, rather than name and date). In all, the cleric biographies in my sample mention 4,261 dates by year. Many of these dates are listed according to the Islamic (*hijri*) calendar, so I conduct an approximate conversion (exact conversion is impossible without the day and month because *hijri* and Gregorian years do not correspond one-to-one). I find that 70 percent of dates mentioned in the cleric biographies are after 1980, suggesting that the sample is very much active after the 1980 cutoff I require for inclusion in the sample. Some clerics become inactive or die shortly after 1980 but this is not a substantial portion of the sample. In general, more recent years are listed more often – the sample skews heavily toward clerics who were active between 1980 and 2010, and often up to the time of data collection.

4.3.2 Where Have the Clerics Lived?

Next, I collect information about where clerics are from and where they have lived. Of the 200 clerics in my sample, 182 list their country of birth. Clerics on the Internet come overwhelmingly from a few countries; fully 65 percent are from two countries, Saudi Arabia (74 clerics) and Egypt (45 clerics). The remainder come primarily from countries in the Middle East, but a few come from outside (Nigeria, India, Thailand, and the United States). Within Saudi Arabia, a disproportionate number of clerics comes from what Mouline (2014, 183) calls the "Najdi crescent" – a cluster of cities around and north of Riyadh that constitutes the core of the Najd region and has produced many elite Saudi clerics. Ten of the clerics in my sample are from Burayda, nine from Riyadh, six from al-Zilfi, and three from al-Bukayrira, with a few more from nearby towns like Unayza and Shaqra. Because the sample is representative, this suggests that approximately 15 percent of the Arabic-speaking Sunni Muslim clerics with a substantial online presence come from the Najdi crescent.

Clerics are remarkably mobile. For example, the passage I have translated below from the biography of the late Muhammad Mitwali al-Sha'rawi indicates a substantial amount of travel (marked in boldface).

After graduation he was appointed a teacher of religious institute in **Tanta, Zagazig** and then went to **Alexandria**, and continued teaching for three years. Then he flew to **Saudi Arabia** within the Azhar mission for a professor, Faculty of Law, University of Um Al Qura in 1950. In 1960, Institute of Tanta Azhari appointed him as the Director of the Islamic Call. In 1961, the Ministry of Awqaf appointed him as Inspector of Sciences. In 1963 returned he returned to **Egypt** and served as the Director of the Grand Sheikh of al-Azhar. In 1966, he traveled to **Algeria** as the head of al-Azhar Mission and remained for seven years. He returned to **Egypt** to serve as the Director of Endowment in Al Gharbia and then an agent for al-Azhar. In 1970, he was appointed a visiting professor at King Abdulaziz University Faculty of Sharia in **Mecca**, then President of the Department of Graduate Studies at King Abdul Aziz in 1972. In November of 1976 he was appointed Minister of Endowments and Azhar Affairs, and remained in office until he left the ministry in October 1978. As Minister of Endowments, he was the first to issue a ministerial decision to establish the first Islamic bank in **Egypt**, the Faisal Islamic Bank. Then he flew to **Saudi Arabia** where he taught at the University of King Abdul Aziz for just one year in 1981.[16]

---

[16] www.facebook.com/pg/alsharawy.org/about/?ref=page_internal, accessed February 10, 2017, and archived.

To get a sense of the physical geographies to which clerics have traveled, I searched for the names of countries in their biographies and counted how frequently each country appeared. This method is not a perfect reflection of where clerics have spent time. Clerics may not always mention the names of countries in their biographies, especially when it will be obvious to readers where they were at a given time. For example, clerics studying at al-Azhar may not explicitly list that the university is in Egypt, or may identify it by the city (Cairo) rather than the country. Also, clerics may refer to regions of the Islamic world using traditional regional names, such as *al-shām* for Syria, rather than by the modern country's proper name. Finally, clerics may mention the names of countries for a variety of reasons, including some that do not indicate physical travel – for example, the United States appears in the titles of books on several cleric biographies.

Still, counting the frequency of country references in cleric biographies gives a decent sense of where they have lived and traveled and which countries are of most interest to them. Figure 4.2 shows the results; darker shading indicates a country was mentioned more often than countries with light shading. Saudi Arabia is the country mentioned most frequently, appearing 536 times in 123 of the biographies. Egypt is second (421 mentions), followed by Kuwait (248), Palestine (188), Yemen (139), Algeria (133), Mali (128), Syria (123), Morocco (118), Qatar (115), and Iraq (101). It is not surprising to see that Arab countries and Muslim-majority countries are frequently mentioned in the biographies of Arabic-speaking Muslim clerics. It is more surprising that Western countries like the United States (69) and the United Kingdom (39) are mentioned as frequently as Arab countries in the heart of North Africa, such as Libya (70) and Tunisia (20). Overall, the data support the conclusion that Saudi Arabia and Egypt are far and away the most important countries for Arabic-speaking Muslim clerics but that these clerics do have substantial transnational reach.

Mobility is the norm. Eighty percent of cleric biographies mention more than one country by name, and on average, cleric biographies mention about five countries. Clerics routinely travel for their studies, tapping into a Muslim tradition of "*riḥla*" – travel for seeking knowledge (Touati 2010).

4.3.3 What the Clerics Do

I also make use of the biographies to develop a more nuanced understanding of what clerics do. Notably, I find that the biographies contain many markers of the academic norms and culture. To provide evidence of this, I searched for a number of terms related to academia and recorded the proportion of cleric biographies including these terms. The word "university" appears in 82 percent of biographies; universities are an almost ubiquitous feature of life for Muslim clerics. Titles for academic credentials and rank within universities are also extremely common. A detailed reading of the biographies reveals that 48 percent have a master's degree and 49 percent have a doctorate. Half of

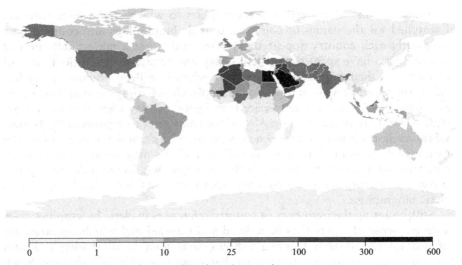

FIGURE 4.2. Countries mentioned in cleric biographies.
Notes: This map shows the number of times the name of each country appears in the cleric biographies of my sample. Countries mentioned more frequently are darker.

all biographies use the word "professor" and close reading reveals that many clerics have held formal teaching titles in a university setting: 13 percent have been lecturers, 14 percent assistant professors, 8 percent associate professors, and 16 percent full professors. Biographies mention a title indicating the cleric was a "dean" or "provost" 14 percent of the time.

More general terms relating to academic research are also common. Clerics frequently mention books (86 percent of biographies), articles (30 percent), theses or dissertations (48 percent), and general terms for academic studies and research (47 percent). They also mention their production of scholarship genres specific to Islamic academia: fatwas (26 percent) and memorization (66 percent). In general, these word searches most likely underestimate the amount and types of scholarship in which clerics engage because clerics may not always mention these terms in their CVs.

Tracking educational attainment of clerics over time shows the rise of academic culture among Muslim clerics. Figure 4.3 shows the relationship between attainment of bachelor's, master's, and doctoral degrees and the year of birth of each cleric. Because of the evolution of Islamic education in the past century, there are temporal trends in this data. The probability of clerics attaining each type of degree is increasing over time for clerics born prior to 1935 (who would have started higher education in approximately 1955). For clerics born after 1935 (educated after 1955), the proportion of clerics attaining each degree appears to stabilize, with about 75 percent of

TABLE 4.1. *Academic terms in cleric biographies.*

Search Term	Percentage of Cleric Biographies with Search Term
university	82
bachelor's [degree]	26
master's [degree]	56
doctorate	57
professor	50
assistant professor	18
associate professor	12
dean/provost	15
book/books	86
article/articles	30
thesis/dissertation	48
fatwa/fatwas	26
study/studies	47
memorization	66

Note: The percentage of cleric biographies that contain particular words related to Islamic academia

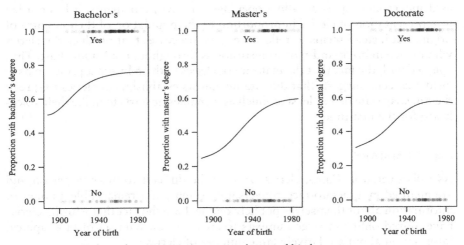

FIGURE 4.3. Higher education attainment and year of birth.
Notes: This figure shows the relationship between attainment of bachelor's, master's, and doctorate degrees and cleric year of birth. A kernel regression fit is shown in black.

clerics gaining a bachelor's degree, 55 percent of clerics gaining a master's degree, and 50 percent going on to obtain a doctorate. This complements and extends the finding of Mouline (2014, 187) that while in 1971 only 50 percent of ʿulamāʾ on the highest religious council in Saudi Arabia, the Committee of Grand ʿUlamāʾ, had received a "modern" education, since 2000 all members have.

To get a clearer picture of the career paths of clerics, I read the appointments and positions listed in each cleric's biography and made a judgment as to whether the cleric was an outsider who had never held any positions funded or controlled by the state, or an insider who had held at least one such position. Of the 200 clerics in my sample, 52 are outsiders. For the rest, I take note of the specific positions they have occupied. Have they worked in a university? As an imam? In a government ministry? I find that 65 percent of insider clerics have spent time in a university, 34 percent have spent time as preachers, and 34 percent have spent time in government. The percentages sum to more than 100 because a number of clerics have held more than one of these roles; 33 percent have worked in two of the three, and 3 percent have worked as preachers, professors, and bureaucrats.

Overall, the data paint a picture of the average Arabic-speaking cleric with an Internet presence as a 60-year-old from Saudi Arabia or Egypt who has traveled a fair amount and probably works as a professor, preacher, or government bureaucrat. What is most surprising about this portrait of clerics with an Internet presence is that, despite their global mobility, clerics come from relatively geographically concentrated origins. While the Internet is often seen as democratizing space to allow openings for new participants, it has not led to representation of clerics in proportion to the population of their country of origin, but instead seems to reflect the same processes that produce the clerics who preach in brick-and-mortar institutions throughout the Middle East. This, coupled with the fact that the majority of clerics with an Internet presence have insider careers, suggests that the Internet allows establishment clerics to spread their messages further at least as much as it enables upstarts to make their voices heard for the first time.

4.4 SUMMARY

As I discovered in Cairo, clerics who can be difficult to meet in person and are guarded in a face-to-face conversation often put a remarkable amount of information about themselves publicly online. I use the fact that Muslim clerics have moved online in large numbers to create a new data set of biographical information about a relatively large number of clerics.

Overall, summary results from the biographies of the clerics in my data set paint a picture of an academic culture with a strong transnational component. In their biographical self-representations, clerics overwhelmingly present themselves as academics: they are assistant professors and deans; they write monographs and publish articles. They are also religious figures, and most clerics see very little friction between these two roles. This is in part because of the nature of Islamic academia and the culture that it fosters.

The feature that distinguishes my analysis of clerics from work by previous researchers is that I have collected a sample of clerics to analyze through methods that are transparent and replicable, and that ensure that the results from the sample are representative to a somewhat broad population of clerics. To be sure, this sample is not representative of the hundreds of thousands of Muslim clerics worldwide who are not posting biographies and writings online, and the sample is not even representative of the 10,000 clerics who are identifiable online, because clerics who provide substantial information about themselves may be quite different than those who do not. However, the key is that this sample of 200 clerics *is* representative of a larger population of about 1,800 clerics with a substantial web presence from which I draw the sample.

Existing work on Muslim clerics has universally relied on nonrepresentative samples of clerics for analysis. Nonrepresentative samples can be informative if used correctly, and this literature has generated many insights about who clerics are and how they behave. Still, the introduction of representative sampling in other areas of social science has greatly expanded our understanding of everything from voting to combat. There is every reason to expect that new, representative data on clerics will offer new findings about Muslim clerics and the worlds they inhabit.

5

Recognizing Jihadists from Their Writings

Who counts as a jihadist? This chapter develops a conceptually grounded, practical approach for detecting which of the many clerics who post writings on the Internet are jihadists. This is a crucial step in my empirical research process because I need to know which clerics in my sample are jihadists in order to test, in the next chapter, whether indicators of blocked ambition predict jihadism.

I define a jihadist cleric as a cleric who produces material expressing jihadist ideology, so the key to identifying jihadists clerics is first to conceptualize jihadist ideology and then find ways to detect which clerics are producing it. I use four different approaches to make my identification process as robust as possible: (1) evaluating the ideological commitments expressed in cleric biographies, (2) evaluating endorsements by actors with known ideological preferences, (3) analyzing expert coding by other scholars, and (4) using statistical text analysis to measure the ideologies expressed in the writings of clerics.

Each of these four approaches has strengths and weaknesses; by using all four, I believe I can distinguish jihadists from non-jihadists with more accuracy than any method could achieve alone. I rely primarily on statistical text analysis to recognize jihadist writing in the documents produced by clerics in my sample, but I evaluate the performance of the statistical model using the cleric biographies, endorsements, and expert coding.

5.1 JIHADIST IDEOLOGY

Since the revelation of the Quran, the concept of jihad has played a prominent and often controversial role in Islamic doctrine and political thought. The term "*jihād*" comes from the Arabic verb "to struggle" and is often roughly translated into English as "holy war," although this translation is inaccurate.

The word "jihad" appears in the Quran, although often with somewhat different connotations than the word carries today (Bonner 2006, 21–22). The concept of Islamic military conflict, both defensive and offensive, was certainly operative in Muhammad's lifetime as evidenced by early conflicts between his followers and the other Arabian tribes. However, ideas of jihad were not fixed at this early date (Mottahedeh and al Sayyid 2001; Mourad and Lindsay 2013).

After the Prophet's death, the responsibility of interpreting Islamic law fell gradually to the ʿulamāʾ – the scholarly religious elite. Islamic jurisprudence covers virtually all aspects of both private and public life, so jihad naturally became subject to interpretation by these clerics. Part of the contest around this term includes a long-standing debate among the clerical elite about the status of the "greater jihad" – the struggle to spiritually purify oneself – and the "lesser jihad" of armed struggle for the cause of Islam. In moderate interpretations of Islam, violent jihad is relatively unimportant and clerics who defend it in principle are unlikely to advocate for it in practice.

The Salafi movement, a conservative Islamist movement arising in the nineteenth century based on the interpretations of Ibn Taymiyya (1263 CE–1328 CE), Muhammad Ibn Abd al-Wahhab (1703 CE–1792 CE), and, according to some, Muhammad Rashid Ridda (1865 CE–1935 CE), is the progenitor of modern Sunni jihadi ideology (Wiktorowicz 2005a, 2006; Meijer 2009; Fuchs 2013; Wiktorowicz 2001a, 113–120). The word "Salafi" is instructive about the nature of the movement: it is derived from the Arabic word salaf, translated as "the pious forefathers," referring to the Companions of the Prophet Muhammad and the first generations of Muslims. Salafis seek to purify Islam from corrupt practices by adhering to a strict interpretation of the faith based on a supposedly unmediated and literal interpretation of the original texts of Islam that mirrors the perceived practices of the first generations of Muslims.

Modern Sunni jihadism, an offshoot of the broader Salafi movement, couples Salafist ideology with a declaration that violence is a legitimate tool for political change. Jihadism is accompanied by an intellectual and religious ideology that dictates a cosmology and belief system for its adherents while offering an ethical system for "right living" (Browers 2005). As an ideology, jihadism provides a "set of fundamental beliefs about how the world works" that "tends to compel its believers into political action" (Hawkins 2009, 1045) and is "the way a system – a single individual or even a whole society – rationalizes itself" (Knight 2006, 619). The ideology of jihadism explains the meaning of events and circumstances in which jihadists find themselves, provides social identity and belonging to those in the movement, and motivates jihadists to act in certain ways while legitimating those actions (see Gerring 1997, 971–972, for a discussion of these functions of ideology).

Jihadist ideology has been described in detail by many scholars; the purpose of my account here is to provide a sufficient conceptual framework in which to situate my measures of jihadist ideology in clerics' writings.[1]

---

[1] See Gerges (2005); Devji (2005); Wiktorowicz (2005c); Bonner (2006); Khosrokhavar (2011); Lav (2012); Brachman (2009); Habeck (2006); Lahoud (2010); Meijer (2007); Fuchs (2013);

Taking the rhetoric of jihadists seriously suggests that the concept of God's oneness (*tawḥīd*) as articulated in Islam and interpreted by jihadists lies at the foundation of jihadist ideology. It is from this concept that jihadist theoreticians elaborate the most distinctive features of jihadist ideology – a dualistic worldview, a utopian outlook, justification of violence, and rejection of democracy.

Tawḥīd is an Arabic word for "the oneness of God," formed from the linguistic combination of the Arabic root w-h-d ("one") and the verb form meaning "to make X occur" so that it literally means "to make something one." Its opposite is *shirk*, which in Arabic means to "ascribe partners to God," and might also be translated as "idolatry" or "polytheism." *Tawḥīd* is foundational to virtually all interpretations of Islam, as expressed in the confession of faith, "(I witness that) there is no god but God. Muhammad is the messenger of God," as well as in *Surah al-Ikhlās*:[2]

> *In the name of Allah, the Most Gracious, the Most Merciful.*
> Say (O Muhammad): "He is Allah, (the) One.
> "*Allah-us-Samad* [Allah the Self-Sufficient Master, Whom all creatures need, (He niether eats nor drinks)].
> "He begets not, nor was He begotten."
> "And there is none co-equal or comparable unto Him."

Jihadists differ from other Muslims in their interpretation of what *tawḥīd* requires. For jihadists, only rules handed down by God can rightfully govern the public and private lives of individuals and groups, so following rules that are not God's is a form of idolatry. Jihadists are typically unreflective about what constitutes "God's law" and write as if these laws are obvious from a straight reading of the Quran and the *sunna* (the received tradition of the behavior and sayings of the Prophet Muhammad and his immediate Companions). Ignoring the potential for contradictions or ambiguities in these texts, jihadists determine whether God's law is in force by looking at both the source of lawmaking and its content. Jihadists are unsatisfied with any rules that claim to be based in any source other than the Quran and the *sunna*, and they are unsatisfied with rules that do not conform to their reading of these texts and traditions.

Deol and Kazmi (2012); Long and Wilner (2014); Aboul-Enein (2010); and Maher (2016) for descriptions and explorations of jihadist ideology. Kepel and Milelli (2005); Euben and Zaman (2009); and Bergesen (2007) provide compilations of jihadist and Islamist texts.

2 This translation and punctuation are from *The Noble Quran in the English Language* translated by Muhammad Taqi-ud-Din al-Halili and Muhammad Muhsin Khan (1996). This translation has been criticized as being "more like a supremacist Muslim, anti-Semitic, anti-Christian polemic than a rendition of the Islamic scripture" (Mohammed 2005). However, it is useful because it is the version promoted by the Saudi Salafi authorities – it "comes with a seal of approval from both the University of Medina and the Saudi Dar al-Ifta" (Mohammed 2005) – and it is perhaps closest to the Quranic interpretation that jihadists themselves might give. For a discussion regarding the importance of choosing appropriate translations of scripture for scholarly work in political science, see Hassner (2013).

There are no limits to the *tawḥīdic* worldview of jihadists – every human action can be interpreted through the lens of *tawḥīd*. For example, cleric Sulayman Bin Nasr al-Ulwan, newly released from the Saudi prison system for involvement in jihadism, ruled in early 2013 that soccer was anti-Islamic. He argued, "There is a serious problem with [soccer] games, which is the refereeing, which follows man-made laws, not Allah's laws."[3] Abu Muhammad al-Maqdisi is equally stringent about the reach of *tawḥīd* into ordinary daily affairs. Citing Sufyan al-Thawri, al-Maqdisi makes the point, "Whoever acquires for them [polytheists] even an ink stand or sharpens for them a pencil or hands them a (piece) of paper" is in danger of hellfire (al-Maqdisi 1984, 68). The demands of *tawḥīd* cannot wait: "The disavowal from the *Tawaghit* [tyrants] and the gods which are worshiped other than Allah the Powerful, the Majestic, along with the disbelief in them; these are never to be delayed or postponed. Rather, these should be openly shown and declared from the outset" (al-Maqdisi 1984, 52).

The most distinguishing feature of jihadists' interpretation of *tawḥīd* is their conclusion that Muslims who do not follow their interpretation are worthy of excommunication. The liberal application of excommunication – *takfīr* in Arabic – is so closely associated with modern jihadists that it has earned them the moniker *takfīrī* (those practicing *takfīr*) among their detractors. Jihadists are not the only clerics who deploy excommunication (Adang et al. 2016), but jihadists are well known for their relatively frequent use of takfir as a legal weapon with which to attack opponents and justify violent actions against the state.

Political leaders who do not enforce jihadists' preferred version of Islamic law are deemed *ṭāghūt*, an Arabic term often translated as "tyrant" or "oppressor," and must be removed. The Quran lists vividly the misdeeds and excesses of *ṭāghūt* political leaders and societies in the past, including the pharaoh of Egypt and the peoples of Ad and Thumud, who are mentioned in *Surah al-Fajr* as "those who transgressed in the land and thus increased the corruption in it." For jihadists, there is no dealing with a ruler who does not meet jihadist standards of *tawḥīd*.

It is not allowed to cozy up to him or to refrain from being hostile toward him or making him (appear) good or honoring him with titles or to greet him during celebrations and events, or to openly show allegiance to him or to his government. Rather, nothing should be said to him except like what Ibrahim and those who were with him said to their people: "Verily, we are free from you and from your constitutions and your laws of *Shirk* and your government of *Kufr*. We have rejected you, and it has become openly seen between us and you, hostility and hatred forever, until you return to Allah and submit and follow His law alone." (al-Maqdisi 1984, 40)

---

3   See a report on the fatwa at www.memri.org/report/en/print6922.htm (accessed February 10, 2017, and archived) and an audio recording of the fatwa at www.youtube.com/watch?v= c45OBkbKQlw (accessed February 10, 2017, and archived).

For jihadists, democracy violates the principle of God's sovereignty by assuming that people are best governed by the laws that a majority approve rather than by laws approved by God. It is not surprising then that Anwar al-Awlaki explained jihad against the United States in terms of *tawḥīd*: "The battle today between the Muslims and the Americans is not merely a battle over oil, over a maritime strait, over a land or a sea, or over Palestine, or Iraq, or Afghanistan. Yes, these are all among the causes of the conflict, but the battle is in its essence, its heart, its foundation, a battle over *tawḥīd*."[4]

Having identified the source of corruption in society as the failure to enact *tawḥīd* by properly following the laws of God, jihadists justify violence as a means for reforming society such that the sovereignty of God will be properly respected.

The reasons for jihad ... are these: to establish God's authority on the earth; to arrange human affairs according to the true guidance provided by God; to abolish all the Satanic forces and Satanic systems of life; to end the lordship of one man over others since all men are creatures of God and no one has the authority to make them his servants or to make arbitrary laws for them. These reasons are sufficient for proclaiming jihad. However, one should always keep in mind that there is no compulsion in religion; that is, once the people are free from the lordship of men, the law governing civil affairs will be purely that of God, while no one will be forced to change his beliefs and accept Islam. (Qutb 2006, 54–55)

Jihadists are utopian, believing that they will ultimately prevail and God's sovereignty will be universally recognized after the defeat of the "Christian" West.

Jihadists have resorted to extreme forms of violence that violate traditional Islamic law and require justification by jihadist clerics. These justifications first categorize the world in terms of good and evil and then explain why killing in a particular situation is permissible because the person to be killed is either evil or is collateral damage in a necessary attack against evil. For many jihadists, killing American soldiers is uncontroversial because the American military presence in the Middle East makes any resistance self-defense. Jihadists invoke this logic to justify attacks, including the Fort Hood shooting in which Nidal Hasan opened fire on unsuspecting and unarmed soldiers in the mess hall of the base where he was stationed. "Glory to God! How can we possibly oppose an operation like that of Nidal Hasan? He targeted American soldiers who were on their way to Iraq and Afghanistan. Who can possibly oppose this? ... Nidal Hasan was Palestinian, from a Palestinian background. He was defending his *umma*."[5]

---

4   www.youtube.com/watch?v=eInGfXV3YvY, min. 19:40, accessed February 25, 2015, and archived.
5   www.youtube.com/watch?v=eInGfXV3YvY, min. 12:00–12:45, accessed February 10, 2017, and archived.

Jihadists recognize that violence against civilians and (especially) lay Muslims requires extraordinary justification. For example, Abdullah Azzam, a prominent jihadist thinker who participated in the Afghan jihad against the Soviets, notes, "The Muslim army is ordinarily prohibited from killing not only Muslims, but also dhimmis (unbelievers living as protected subjects of the Muslim state), as well as old men, women, and children from among the unbelievers" (Azzam 1979, 78). Jihadists, however, justify killing civilians, including Muslims, because (1) they are apostate because of their support for apostate governments, or (2) they are righteous, innocent victims who must be sacrificed for the greater good of the Muslim community. Anwar al-Awlaki articulates these justifications while defending operations he inspired:

With regard to the issue of "civilians," this term has become prevalent these days but we prefer to use the terminology used by our scholars of *fiqh*. They use the terms combatants or non-combatants. A combatant is someone who bears arms, even if they are a woman, and non-combatants are those who have no part in war. The American people as a whole are participants in war because they elected this administration and they finance this war.

If the heroic brother Umar Faruq could have targeted hundreds of soldiers, that would have been wonderful, but we are talking about the practicalities of battle. If the Messenger, peace be upon him, had been able to fight in the daytime only, he would have done so, but there were times he sent battalions at night and due to darkness, women and children were also killed by these battalions.

When the Thaqeef [an Arabian tribe] fortified themselves in Taif, the prophet used catapults against them and these did not distinguish between men, women, and children. This was the reality of the battle.[6]

Suicide attacks too require particular justification because of the prohibition on suicide in Islam. To circumvent this prohibition, jihadists argue that suicide attacks are, in fact, not "suicide attacks" at all, but "martyrdom operations" that bring divine honor upon the perpetrator. Jihadist ideologues have advanced several lines of argument to justify suicide attacks as martyrdom, but perhaps the most important set of ideas is represented by Azzam's writings on the subject. After defending the nobility of martyrdom, Azzam engages in a legalistic debate about the permissibility of a Muslim committing suicide for the good of the faith. In particular, he discusses the legality of a Muslim fighter intentionally plunging into enemy ranks with no hope of survival for the purpose of killing as many enemies as possible. Azzam demonstrates the permissibility of this action by invoking several *hadīth* that purportedly give examples where Muhammad approved of particular individuals intentionally giving their lives in battle. This quote illustrates Azzam's views on the subject:

---

6   "Anwar Al Awlaki Al Malahem Interview FULL ENGLISH Translation," www.youtube.com/watch?v=eInGfXV3YvY, min. 24:00–26:33. Translation by the author to match the Arabic more closely than the al-Qaeda translation.

The name "suicide-operations" used by some is inaccurate, and in fact this name was chosen by the Jews to discourage people from such endeavors. How great is the difference between the one who commits suicide – because of his unhappiness, lack of patience and weakness or absence of Iman [faith] and has been threatened with Hell-Fire – and between the self-sacrificer who embarks on the operation out of strength of faith and conviction. (Azzam 1979, 65)

This sketch of jihadist justifications for extraordinary violence concludes my discussion of jihadist ideology. Armed with an understanding of what makes jihadist ideology distinctive, it is often not difficult to identify jihadist texts, such as this excerpt from Hamud al-Shu'aybi, a prominent Saudi cleric who turned to supporting jihadist positions during the Islamist "awakening" of the 1990s:

Question: The mujahideen in Palestine, Chechnya, and other Muslim countries have carried out their jihad against their enemies using so-called "martyrdom operations." These are operations in which one of the mujahideen puts on a belt of explosives, or puts them in his bag, or his car and then breaks into gatherings of the enemy, and their houses and then detonates himself seeking his own martyrdom and the death of his enemies. What is the ruling of such operations?

Answer: These martyrdom operations are permitted actions when they are done for the sake of jihad in the pathway of God, if the intent of the martyr is pure. These have been one of the most successful jihadi methods and among the most effective against enemies of this religion.[7]

Another example comes from a fatwa issued by extremist cleric Anwar al-Awlaki in the Winter 2010 issue of *Inspire*, an English-language jihadi web magazine:

Muslims are not bound by the covenants of citizenship and visa that exist between them and nations of dar al-harb [the non-Muslim world]. It is the consensus of our scholars that the property of the disbelievers in dar al-harb is halal for the Muslims and is a legitimate target for the mujahidin.[8]

Another jihadist document is similarly recognizable, especially given the prominence of jihadist interpretations of *takfir* and *tawhīd*. This fatwa is from Ali al-Khudayr, a jihadist cleric from Saudi Arabia who was a student of Hamud al-Shu'aybi (quoted above):

---

7 www.tawhed.ws/r?i=dqokvsc5 (link now broken), accessed April 14, 2014, and archived.
8 *Inspire*, Winter 2010, p. 56. Accessing this web magazine is difficult because Western governments have tried to censor it. I accessed it through links provided by Christopher Anzalone at http://occident.blogspot.com/2011/01/4th-issue-of-inspire-magazine-from-al.html (still working as of February 10, 2017). The term *dar al-harb* literally translates as "house of war" and refers to the non-Muslim world; *halal* means "permissible"; *mujahidin* means "jihadi fighters."

Question: Who has the right to declare *takfīr* on someone? Is it permitted for an ordinary person to declare *takfīr* on someone who is in a state of outright disbelief, especially if the person [declaring *takfīr*] is aware of the rulings on *takfīr* and their interpreted meanings? Or is it said to him: Do not do this – leave it to a Judge or a Mufti or the world to come? I would like you to clarify because there is a great deal of confusion about this matter.

Answer: As I have discussed: An ordinary individual who is aware of the rulings on *takfīr* and their expressed meanings; he can declare *takfīr*. It has been working this way since the covenant of the prophet (peace be upon him) until our present time. But to those who do not know, it is not permitted for them because of the *hadīth*: (Whoever says to his brother 'O Apostate,' has become one of them). *Takfīr* is not reserved for a Judge or a Mufti or the world to come; this is a mistake.[9]

Non-jihadist writing, on the other hand, is markedly different in its content, as shown in this this randomly selected fatwa from Abd al-Azim Bin Badawi, an Egyptian preacher who graduated from al-Azhar and has spent his career working in government mosques in Egypt and Jordan:

Question: Awatif and Fardus are sisters. Awatif had two children: Muhammad and Maha, and Fardus had Ahmad, Ala, Ragad, Khaled, Sultan, and Gala. Awatif breastfed Sultan and Fardus breastfed Muhammad, and they each did so for an extended period of time. Is Adel, the husband of Awatif considered the father of all of Fardus' children? Is it permitted for the daughters of Fardus to reveal themselves around Adel or not?

Answer: If a woman breastfeeds a child five different times while it is in the years of breastfeeding, he becomes her son, and she becomes his mother, and her husband becomes a father for him. There is no relationship between the husband of the nurse-mother and her sister, so it is not permitted for them to reveal themselves in front of him.[10]

Another randomly selected example, this time in English from the aggregator site www.islamweb.net, is also readily distinguishable as non-jihadist:[11]

Question (excerpted): [M]y problem is that i really love my husbands family, but they interfer very much in my son and almost dont let me to be mom for him.

Answer (excerpted): Among the most important Islamic objectives is that affection and love should prevail in the Muslim society; this is even more confirmed among those who are related to each other, like the case of the in-laws. Hence, they should close the doors to the devil so that he would not spoil this relationship. Allaah Says (what means): {And tell My servants to say that which is best Indeed, Satan induces [dissension] among them. Indeed Satan is ever, to mankind, a clear enemy.} [Quran 17:53].[12]

---

9 This fatwa is in a document titled, "Who has the Right of *takfīr*," and comes from a jihadist collection called "The Jihadist's Bookbag," described in this chapter. It is archived at http://dx.doi.org/10.7910/DVN/PG4A7K.

10 http://ar.islamway.net/fatwa/13949, accessed March 19, 2013, and archived.

11 To make this random selection, I simply used the most recent fatwa issued in English by www.islamweb.net on April 7, 2011.

12 Fatwa No. 153879. "Her in-laws interfere with the way she brings up her child." April 7, 2011. Accessed at www.islamweb.net/emainpage/index.php?page=showfatwa&Option=FatwaId&Id=153879 on April 7, 2011, and archived. Spelling and grammar mistakes in original.

The literature on jihadism discusses and debates other aspects of jihadist ideology, such as its evolution (Hegghammer 2010*b*), jihadist debates about fighting locally versus fighting the West (Gerges 2005), and the priority of peaceful versus violent jihad, but the foregoing offers enough to proceed with the task of identifying jihadist clerics.

5.2 DETECTING JIHADIST WRITING WITH STATISTICS

I now turn to the task of determining which clerics in my web sample are jihadists. To do so, I first considered what strategy would be most complete and reliable. There are a few promising sources of information about clerics' ideological leanings. Biographies sometimes indicate whether a cleric is jihadist and this information is reliable when it is available, but ideological commitments are not mentioned consistently enough to accurately identify all of the jihadists in my sample. Endorsements by people, groups, or websites associated with jihadism also contain useful information about the ideological leanings of clerics. For example, it is safe to assume that clerics praised by Ayman al-Zawahiri, the head of al-Qaeda, are jihadists. However, only some clerics have been endorsed in this way, making the coverage of clerics in my sample quite spotty. al-Zawahiri may endorse some clerics, but he has not released a definitive list of his opinions on *all* clerics, in part because, prior to this study, no such census of clerics existed.

A third potential source of information comes from scholarly works that mention the ideological orientations of various clerics. For example, Hegghammer (2010*a*) lists a number of jihadist clerics in his book on jihadism in Saudi Arabia, McCants (2006, appendix 2) codes fifty-six individuals as jihadist or not, and the names of other clerics can be culled from the indexes of Lacroix (2011) and Deol and Kazmi (2012). These lists are useful, but they tend to include only relatively prominent clerics and they are often based on unclear coding rules for what counts as jihadist. While biographies, endorsements, and scholarly assessments all contain useful information about cleric ideology, relying solely on these sources will result in missing ideology assessments for many clerics in my sample, reintroducing the problems that motivated me to collect new data in the first place.

Thus, to measure the ideology of the clerics in my data set, I collect the writings of each and use statistical text analysis methods to identify which clerics produce jihadist writing. This method is more thorough than the others described here because it allows me to categorize any cleric that has produced enough public writing to analyze, which in practice means I can estimate the ideology of every cleric in my sample. It has long been common practice for clerics (or their followers) to organize and release collections of writings to illustrate the clerics' scholarly expertise. Increasingly, cleric writings are available online via Internet "fatwa banks" or clerics' own websites. Of course, not every writing by every cleric in my sample will be found online. But in this case, the selection of texts for distribution does not pose a fundamental problem for measuring cleric ideology because the texts that clerics or their followers choose to disseminate widely are perhaps the *best* representation of the ideas for which the cleric would like to be known.

To perform the text analysis, I collect as much writing as I can for each of the 200 clerics in my sample, including books, articles, sermons, and fatwas. Fatwas are ideal for measuring cleric ideology because the broad range of possible topics makes it more likely that a cleric's ideology will be revealed, while the lawlike status of fatwas alleviates my concern that clerics are merely speaking strategically. A cleric has an incentive to say what he really thinks in a fatwa because those are the statements to which his followers will adhere.

An extensive search for Arabic-language writings from each of the 200 clerics in the web sample and the 82 clerics in the Salafi oversample results in 147,605 documents and 97,723,297 words. The distribution of cleric output is skewed. The average cleric has 523 documents, but some clerics are especially prolific – Abdullah Bin Jibreen has written 17,191 documents – and some have only a few.

Ideally, I would determine which clerics are jihadist through a close reading of each document to look for evidence of jihadist ideas, but given the quantity of text, such an approach is infeasible. Instead, I find jihadist ideology in cleric writing using statistical text analysis. There is no evidence that the reason certain types of clerics have fewer documents than others is correlated with an outcome of interest, and thus the skew in documents per cleric should not introduce bias into my analysis. Older clerics have fewer writings available, but the writings that I find for them are longer so I have just as many words to assess.

My approach uses two sets of documents to "train" a statistical model to recognize and distinguish jihadist and non-jihadist writing. As exemplars of jihadist writing, I use "The Jihadist's Bookbag" (*ḥaqībat al-mujāhid*), a collection of 765 documents curated by al-Zubayr al-Ghazi and circulated on jihadist web forums.[13] I select this collection because it was designed by al-Ghazi to be a comprehensive introduction to jihadist ideology and it appears to have circulated widely. As distributed on the Internet, the zipped folder contains 1,029 files, but some of these are unusable either because they are not text documents (the folder contains images, gif animations, etc.), or because the texts are saved in a file format that does not allow extraction of digitized text.[14]

---

13 I accessed "The Jihadist's Bookbag" from the (now-defunct) forum at www.i7ur.com/vb/t9736. html, which pointed me to the zip file at www.megaupload.com/?d=0DXUXL2N on January 27, 2011, (also now defunct). Be aware that the zip file appears to contain at least two computer viruses. The 765 documents in the zip file are not all unique. For example, a fatwa by Hamud al-Shu'aybi titled, "The Legality of Martyrdom Operations," which gives a justification for suicide bombings, appears at least three times in the corpus, filed in different subdirectories. I leave these duplicates because removing them would change the self-representation of jihadist ideology in "The Jihadist's Bookbag."

14 These are primarily pdf files that have not been processed with optical character recognition.

The collection includes works by fifty-three named authors, including current jihadi theorists such as Abu Muhammad al-Maqdisi, operational leaders such as Abu Mus'ab al-Zarqawi, and foundational authors such as Sayyid Qutb and Abdullah Azzam, as well as anonymously authored works. The collection is mostly spiritual instruction and advice, with some political and religious commentary for jihadists and their sympathizers.[15]

Using this collection curated by jihadists helps me avoid the difficult task of deciding which texts are the most authentically jihadist, instead delegating this task to the jihadists themselves. However, selecting any particular collection of jihadist documents to train the statistical text classifier risks bias if the collection is not representative of jihadist ideology. To show that it is, I examine "The Jihadist's Bookbag" to verify that its themes match the outline of jihadist ideology described earlier. My examination of individual documents confirms that they contain jihadist ideas, but carefully examining 765 documents is infeasible. As a result, I turn to the same sort of topic model I used in Chapter 4 to summarize the broad themes in "The Jihadist's Bookbag."

I use a topic model to identify five clusters of correlated words, which I label (1) *Tawhid/Takfir*, (2) *Legal Precedent*, (3) *Conflicts*, (4) *Operations*, and the less informative, catch all category (5) *Mixed*.[16] To convey a sense of the content of each of these topics, I present the top five words associated with each topic in Table 5.1 and the titles of the three documents most associated with each topic in Table 5.2. The words and documents give insights about the nature of each topic: *Tawhid/Takfir* is focused on the centrality of monotheism and excommunication to jihadists, *Legal Precedent* is devoted to styles of proof and citation common in Islamic law, *Conflicts* is about the geopolitical struggles of interest to jihadists, *Operations* discusses tactical specifics such as suicide bombings, and *Mixed* contains an assortment of miscellaneous jihadist writing, including their penchant for poetry.

These five topics vary in their prevalence in "The Jihadist's Bookbag," and authors vary in the extent to which they write about each topic. Figure 5.1 shows the frequency of each topic in the overall corpus (black, at top), and in the writings of each of the twenty-two authors with the most writing in the bookbag. Rather than presenting the authors in haphazard fashion, I group them according to similarity in their topic proportions, using the k-means algorithm (introduced in Chapter 2). Authors in Figure 5.1 who are shown in the same row have similar topic proportions.

Overall, the topic model shows that the core concepts of jihadist ideology are clearly present in "The Jihadist's Bookbag," making it a sound choice as an exemplar corpus of jihadist ideology. The concept of *tawhid* is foundational

---

15   For more analysis, see www.jihadica.com/a-mujahids-bookbag, last accessed February 10, 2017, and archived.

16   Choosing the topic labels in a topic model is both subjective and a substantial part of the inferential process, so I describe my process and rationale in Appendix B.

TABLE 5.1. *Top words for five topics in a jihadist corpus.*

Tawhid/Takfir	Legal Precedent	Conflicts	Operations	Mixed
excommunication	said	America	Jihadis	ten
excommunicate	son	American	martyr	had
tyrant	if	Afghanistan	Afghan	appointed
apostate	Prophet	Afghan	Jihad	big
believe	peace be upon him	United	operation	king

Notes: This table provides the top five words, based on FREX scores, for each of the five topics, estimated using latent Dirichlet allocation on "The Jihadist's Bookbag" corpus. The FREX scores are the harmonic mean of frequency (of the word in a topic) and exclusivity (the extent to which a word is unique to the topic). Each column is a topic; the titles at the top of each column are summary names inferred from the words in the column, not labels provided by the model.

TABLE 5.2. *Texts that are representative of five topics in a jihadist corpus.*

Takfir/Tawhid	1. *This is my creed*, Abu Basir al-Tartusi
	2. *Discussion of the saying of Ibn al-Uthaymeen in which he requires making apostasy permissible instead of following the divine law*, Abu Basir al-Tartusi
	3. *Assorted issues, 601-625*, Abu Basir al-Tartusi
Legal Precedent	1. *The Methodology of the Early Scholars in the Issue of Tadlis*, Nasr al-Fahd
	2. *The ruling about praying for the dead who are missing*, Hamud al-Shu'aybi
	3. *The Response to the Shiites*, Nasr al-Fahd
Conflicts	1. *Informing the Sleepers of the New War Against Islam*, Husayn Bin Mahmoud
	2. *America and the Climb into the Pit of Hell*, Yusuf al-Urayri
	3. *The Jews in America*, Hamid al-Ali
Operations	1. *The Legality of Martyrdom Operations*, Hamud al-Shu'aybi
	2. *The Ruling on Martyrdom Operations*, Sulayman al-Ulwan
	3. *Martyrdom Operations: Jihad in the Pathway of God*, Palestine Scholars Association
Mixed	1. *To My Beloved Mother – Do Not Cry for Me* (poem), Abu Muhammad al-Maqdisi
	2. *The article that made me and most other readers cry concerning Sheikh Yusuf al-Urayri* (blog post), Anonymous on al-Islah forum
	3. *Do You Know My Crimes?* (poem), Abu Muhammad al-Maqdisi

Notes: This table lists the three documents that are most representative of each topic, meaning that they have the highest proportion of words assigned to that topic.

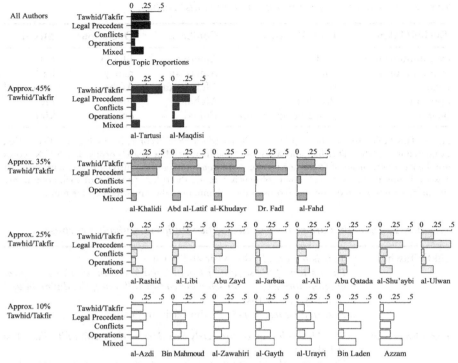

FIGURE 5.1. Proportions of topic use in a jihadist corpus by author.

Notes: This figure shows the proportions of five topics in a jihadi corpus. The top panel shows the overall topic proportions. The remaining panels show the topic proportions of each of the twenty-two named authors with sufficient text for analysis. I group the authors together (in rows and shades of gray) based on the similarity of their topic proportions – authors in the same row and color tend to write about similar things.

for jihadists, so it is reassuring that approximately a third of the words in "The Jihadist's Bookbag" are in the *Tawhid/Takfir* topic. Several authors in the corpus have a particularly strong emphasis on *tawhīd* and *takfīr* in their writings, notably Abu Basir al-Tartusi, Ahmad al-Khalidi, Abd al-Latif, and al-Maqdisi, but virtually every author engages this topic to some degree. Authors differ in their emphasis of other topics: authors in rows three and four write using a substantial amount of legal language, while authors in row five tend to be more focused on politics and the practicalities of violent operations and global struggles than the others. This particular collection of topics and the attention they are accorded by the authors of "The Jihadist's Bookbag" suggests that this corpus is a faithful representation of jihadist ideology.

Still, to be certain that the results below are not dependent on the specific collection of jihadist documents that I use to train my model, I carry out an alternative analysis using documents from an online jihadist library, "Pulpit of Monotheism and Jihad," as the jihadist training set. This website contained the most comprehensive collection of jihadist documents online until it was removed in early 2015, but because it served many purposes, the documents it contained were occasionally less ideologically pure than those in "The Jihadist's Bookbag" (for example, several RAND Corporation reports appeared on the website, apparently for insight into US counter-jihadist strategy). Still, the vast majority of texts were jihadist, and the sheer number of documents – more than 6,000 in all – means that virtually every perspective on jihadist ideology was represented. Using this alternative training source produces essentially identical results to the ones I present in this chapter and in the next chapter.

In order to classify the writing of the clerics in the web sample and Salafi oversample, I need a second set of documents to serve as exemplars of non-jihadist writing. However, I know of no curated, representative set of non-jihadist texts to mirror "The Jihadist's Bookbag." To serve this purpose, I create my own curated set of non-jihadist documents by identifying twelve clerics who are widely acknowledged to be Salafi non-jihadists and collecting 1,004 of their writings.[17]

One downside of using this set of non-jihadist Salafi documents as the exemplar documents for non-jihadist writing is that it risks misclassifying clerics who are not Salafi. There are many non-Salafi clerics in the representative web sample. If their writing is markedly different from both jihadist and non-jihadist Salafis, then the model may have difficulty classifying them. My solution to this is practical: I validate the results of the model to be confident that this possible mismatch between the writing in the training set and the writing from the clerics in the web sample does not result in problematic miscoding. These results are reported in the following section.

I use these jihadist and non-jihadist training documents to inform a statistical model called a naive Bayes classifier, a workhorse text analysis model that has been widely used for spam filtering, among other things. This statistical model uses word frequencies in the training documents to estimate the likelihood that a new document contains jihadist writing. I refer to this likelihood as a *jihad score*; documents that have word frequencies similar to jihadist documents receive higher scores from the model, while documents that have word frequencies dissimilar to jihadist documents have lower scores. Figure 5.2 shows which words the classifier uses to distinguish between jihadi and non-jihadi writing by plotting the difference in frequencies of word use in

---

17 The non-jihadists are Abd al-Aziz Bin Baz, Muhammad Bin Ibrahim Al al-Sheikh, Muhammad Nasr al-Din al-Albani, Muhammad Bin Saleh al-Uthaymeen, Abd al-Aziz Al Abd al-Latif, Ali al-Halibi, Yusuf al-Qaradawi, Salih Bin Muhammad al-Luhaydan, Abd al-Aziz Bin Abdullah Al al-Sheikh, Salih Bin Fawzan al-Fawzan, Salman al-Awda, and Rabi'a Bin Hadi al-Madhkhali. The first seven are coded as non-jihadists by McCants (2006, appendix 2), while the remaining are criticized as non-jihadists by the now-defunct jihadist website Islamic Thinkers Society (see Figure 5.6).

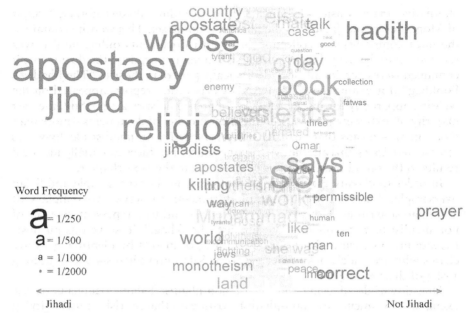

FIGURE 5.2. A word cloud representation of the jihad score classifier.

Notes: This figure shows which words in the training corpus distinguish jihadi documents from non-jihadi documents by plotting jihadi words to the left and non-jihadi words to the right. Words that are used similarly by jihadists and non-jihadists are in the middle and shaded lighter. Word size indicates word frequency in the entire training corpus.

the two sets of training documents. Words that are large and toward the left and right edges are strongly predictive of either jihadi or non-jihadi ideology, respectively. Words in the center of the figure are less predictive of ideology.

Before training the naive Bayes classifier, I reduce the complexity of the training documents through several preprocessing steps that are commonly used in statistical text analysis. First, I "stem" each document, a procedure that trims prefixes and suffixes from words. This procedure is valuable because as long as the resulting stems retain the same general meaning as the original words, it reduces the complexity of the documents without losing relevant information (e.g., "the jihadist" and "jihadists" both become "jihadist"). To perform the stemming, I use a version of Larkey, Ballesteros, and Connell's (2007) "light10" stemmer that I have modified by changing the rules for suffix removal and expanding the lists of suffixes, prefixes, and stop words. This "light stemming" approach has limitations but the size of the corpus leads to reasonable results without aggressive stemming.[18]

---

[18] English-language stemming is well developed (Porter 1980), but there are no industry-standard Arabic-language equivalents. Arabic is a highly inflected language with a high rate of infixing –

Next, I remove stop words – words like "to," "from," "for," and "by," that serve grammatical functions but are not important for identifying the topical content of a document. I also omit words that are too common or too rare across documents to be useful for classification; words that occur in virtually all documents, or in almost none of them, do not provide much information about how a document should be classified. In many text applications, analysts eliminate the 10 percent most common and least common words by default, but this leaves too many stems remaining for feasible computation, so I remove words that occur in less than 10 percent or more than 40 percent of documents. This retains only the words that are most discriminating – those that contain the most information about the meaningful differences between documents.

With the training documents appropriately processed, I "train" the naive Bayes classifier by entering the frequency of each word in the jihadist and non-jihadist documents where required in the model's mathematical representation. I then use the resulting model to produce cleric-level jihad scores. To measure each cleric's ideology, I take all of their texts and perform the same preprocessing, with one additional step: I concatenate them into a single piece of text, one per cleric, so that the model estimates a score for this new composite document. Heuristically, this procedure compares the histogram of word frequencies in the entire public body of work of each cleric and estimates the likelihood that these word frequencies come from the same distribution as the distribution of words found in each of the two training sets. It seems somewhat strange to consider the entire body of work of each cleric as if it were a single document, but in practice, this procedure results in accurate detection of jihadist writers.

Figure 5.3 shows the distributions of cleric jihad scores for the web sample and Salafi oversample. Authors with scores above zero write in a style more like jihadist writing than non-jihadist writing; 11 percent of clerics are classified by the model as more jihadist than not. This is itself worth remarking on because despite years of interest in the phenomenon of jihadism, there have been no reliable estimates of the number of actual jihadists. My data suggest that, of male Sunni clerics on the Internet, approximately one in ten leans jihadist in their writing.

---

speakers of Arabic communicate grammar by modifying the internal syllables of words, as well as prefixes and suffixes – so stemmers designed for other languages cannot be easily repurposed for Arabic. Arabic words are almost always formed from a three-consonant trilateral, called a *root*, and some approaches to Arabic stemming, such as Al-Nashashibi, Neagu, and Yaghi (2010), attempt to identify the root of each word. However, reducing words to their roots leads to inappropriate conflation of terms because words derived from the same root can sometimes have opposite meanings. For example, the triliteral *k-f-r* is the root of the prominent jihadi concepts *takfir* (to excommunicate, declare someone apostate) and *kāfir* (an apostate), but it is also the root of the word *kifāra* (religious atonement). I prefer the "light stemming" approach (Larkey, Ballesteros, and Connell 2007), which ignores infixing and focuses instead on merely removing suffixes and prefixes.

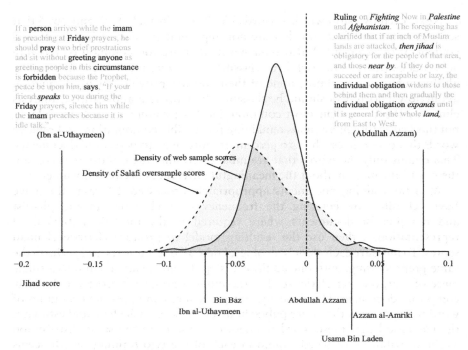

If a person arrives while the imam
is preaching at Friday prayers, he
should pray two brief prostrations
and sit without greeting anyone as
greeting people in this circumstance
is forbidden because the Prophet,
peace be upon him, says, "If your
friend *speaks* to you during the
Friday prayers, silence him while
the imam preaches because it is
idle talk."

(Ibn al-Uthaymeen)

Ruling on *Fighting* Now in *Palestine*
and *Afghanistan*. The foregoing has
clarified that if an inch of Muslim
lands are attacked, *then jihad* is
obligatory for the people of that area,
and those *near by*. If they do not
succeed or are incapable or lazy, the
individual obligation widens to those
behind them and then gradually the
individual obligation *expands* until
it is general for the whole *land*,
from East to West.

(Abdullah Azzam)

Density of web sample scores

Density of Salafi oversample scores

−0.2   −0.15   −0.1   −0.05   0   0.05   0.1

Jihad score

Bin Baz   Abdullah Azzam
Ibn al-Uthaymeen

Azzam al-Amriki

Usama Bin Laden

FIGURE 5.3. Jihad scores for clerics with benchmark texts.

Notes: This figure shows a histogram of the distribution of cleric jihad scores for the web sample of 200 clerics (solid curve) and the oversample of Salafi clerics (dashed curve). For comparison, I indicate the scores for two excerpts from writings by Ibn al-Uthaymeen and Abdullah Azzam (translations from Arabic by me). For each excerpt, black plain type indicates words used more by non-jihadists, black italic type indicates words used more by jihadists, and gray type indicates words omitted from the model because they are too frequent or too rare to be statistically informative.

Because the scores lie on an arbitrary scale, it isn't illuminating to contemplate the raw numbers without some way of benchmarking them. To give a sense of what different scores indicate, I plot the jihad scores for several prominent jihadists, Usama Bin Laden, Abdullah Azzam, and Azzam al-Amriki, as well as two prominent Salafi non-jihadists, Bin Baz and Ibn al-Uthaymeen.

To give some sense of the differences in rhetoric at different ends of the scale, I show two excerpts, one from the writings of Ibn al-Uthaymeen and one from Abdullah Azzam, with the scores *for the excerpts only* (not the writer's overall score for all his writing) indicated by arrows. Note that the scores of these individual excerpts are more extreme than the cleric-level scores because the cleric scores are based on the concatenation of many documents. To show how the words in each excerpt affect the overall excerpt score, I show words that reduce the jihad score in black plain font and words that increase the jihad score with black italic font. Words shown in gray are not included in the classification, either because they are too rare or too common. Highlighting the words in this manner gives a sense of how the text analysis occurs; the excerpt from Ibn al-Uthaymeen is comprised almost entirely of non-jihadist words while all but a few terms in Abdullah Azzam's excerpt lean jihadist.

The jihad scores that come from the naive Bayes classification procedure may seem very precise, but it is important to recognize and account for the uncertainty of these scores. The cleric jihad scores are calculated without error because each score is a deterministic function of the words in the training corpus and the cleric's document. However, this hyper-precision is not quite right. Conceptually, these scores are an estimate of the ideological preference of each cleric with respect to jihadism. Conceivably, the same cleric, with the same ideological preference, could have written each document in somewhat different ways, or produced a slightly different collection of writings.

Overly precise jihad scores can lead to overstated statistical significance in the analysis in Chapter 6, so I account for this uncertainty using a technique called a block bootstrap (Efron and Tibshirani 1993; Lowe and Benoit n.d.). This technique estimates the uncertainty of each cleric's jihad score by resampling the words from each cleric's writings a large number of times – as if the cleric had written the same document but using slightly different words – and calculating the jihad scores for each resample. This gives me a range of plausible jihad scores for each cleric that reflects the uncertainty inherent in the possibility that they could have expressed approximately the same idea but using different words. In general, these ranges are fairly small, but for several clerics who have only a small number of words available online, the range of possible jihad scores is large. I account for this in the statistical analysis in the next chapter and it does not appreciably affect the results.

What do these scores say about the rhetoric of jihadists? To see how my scores rank the clerics, I focus on those clerics with scores above zero – classified as jihadists by the model – in Figure 5.4. I present these thirty-five clerics in order, with the highest jihad scores at the top.

If a cleric has a high jihad score, this means that their writing was much more like the writing in "The Jihadist's Bookbag" than the writing of the non-jihadist portion of the training set. Put differently, those with high scores are not easily mistaken for non-jihadists. The first on the list is Adam Gadahn (1978–2015), an American from Oregon and California who converted to Islam in his teens and then embraced an extreme interpretation of the faith, eventually moving to Pakistan and joining al-Qaeda as a spokesperson and media specialist.[19] His exceptionally high score reflects his singular focus on defending al-Qaeda and taunting its enemies. The others near the top of the list are a mix of relatively famous jihadists – Usama Bin Laden and Abu Bakr al-Baghdadi, the current head of the Islamic State – and others who are less prominent or less well known. Some prominent jihadists appear far down the list. Abu Muhammad al-Maqdisi, who is perhaps the most influential living jihadist thinker, appears

---

[19] www.newyorker.com/magazine/2007/01/22/azzam-the-american, accessed February 11, 2017, and archived.

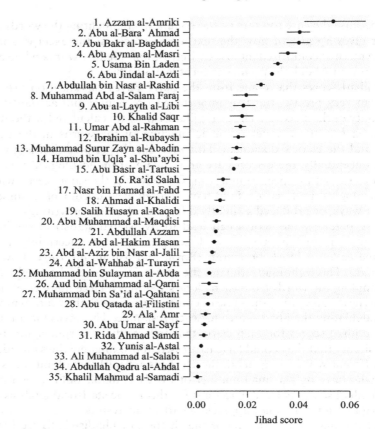

FIGURE 5.4. Jihadist clerics ranked by jihad scores.

Notes: This figure ranks jihadist clerics according to their estimated jihad scores, with the highest scores at the top. Disks represent clerics' scores and bars represent a bootstrapped 95 percent confidence interval around each score.

twentieth on the list. Abdullah Azzam, sometimes called the godfather of jihad, appears twenty-first. And Abu Qatada al-Filistini, a widely read jihadist thinker who was based in London until his deportation and trial in Jordan on terrorism charges, falls to twenty-eighth. This does not mean that these writers are not jihadists, but it does indicate that their writing shares more in common with the writing of non-jihadists than writers like Gadahn, al-Baghdadi, and Bin Laden.

5.3 IS STATISTICAL DETECTION OF JIHADIST WRITING ACCURATE?

The benefit of using statistical text analysis to measure cleric ideology is that I can quickly estimate the ideology of any cleric who produces text. The most serious drawback is that statistical text methods make mistakes that human readers might not. As a consequence, manual validation of the statistical model is crucial in order to build confidence that the results are detecting jihadist ideology in cleric writings with high accuracy.

The most obvious potential for error arises from writing in which removing word ordering might lead to serious problems. This seems most likely in the case of a document that criticizes jihadists or debates jihad from a non-jihadist perspective. In the extreme case, two fatwas might appear very similar when viewed as histograms of word frequencies, but the semantic content could be the opposite of each other. For example, one fatwa might read "jihad in the pathway of God is necessary" while the other reads "jihad in the pathway of God is *not* necessary."

Fatwas such as this exist in my corpus, but they do not appreciably bias my scores for several reasons. First, jihadists and anti-jihadists tend to use different language to talk about the same topics; jihadists write "martyrdom operations" (ʿamaliyyāt al-istishhādiyya) while non-jihadists often write "terrorism" (al-irhāb) to refer to the same acts. Second, because I concatenate all of the documents by a cleric, my scores reflect the complete writings of each cleric. Jihadists tend to focus on jihad much of the time, while non-jihadists may write a small number of documents that frequently reference jihad, but most of their works will be on other different topics. Thus the overall word frequency profiles of the concatenated writings will be very different, even if a single fatwa by a non-jihadist might be mistakenly classified as jihadist by the statistical text model.

To illustrate both the potential problem and the solution, I find examples of the scenarios described earlier. To illustrate the relevance of word order, I find a fatwa that I expect might be misclassified by the naive Bayes classifier because of its frequent use of the word *jihad*. The fatwa comes from Abu Bakr al-Jazairi, and reads:

Question: Is going out in the pathway of God Almighty to do proselyting for God and spending money and bearing hardship ... does this constitute jihad?

Answer: Going out today in the pathway of God and spending money therein would be equivalent to jihad if there was jihad in our day ... but today there is no jihad except for proselyting and preaching because the Muslims do not have an Imam and there is no Islamic state.[20]

This fatwa has a construction that might be problematic – it is a circumstance where the author is clearly writing against militant conceptions of jihad, but the model might mistake this for a militant fatwa by ignoring the word "no" before "jihad." As I expect, the model estimates that this excerpt is jihadist, primarily because of the prevalence of the word "jihad." A similar problem occurs with this document by Salman al-Awda, in which he is writing *against* militant jihad but the model mistakes this as support for jihadism:

---

[20] www.binatiih.com/go/news.php?action=view&id=23, accessed January 27, 2012, and archived.

One time during the situation of internal strife, one of the zealots came to me and said, "Since my childhood, I've always said there is no solution except Jihad!" I said to him, this is a mistake and you should reconsider your view. Maybe it was the first time that he had been contradicted like this, but he was stunned, and I said: "There is no solution but Islam, and Islam is not Jihad. Jihad is just one rite among many."[21]

In both instances, the cleric's overall cleric score is not significantly affected because I consider all of the cleric's writings together.

Overall, these examples demonstrate ways in which my method of calculating scores is largely robust to mistakes introduced by the naive Bayes classifier. However, more sophisticated classification approaches might offer minor improvements to the estimation of cleric ideology scores.

Validating statistical models of text is crucial to make sure they are performing correctly (Grimmer and Stewart 2013). I validate my model by checking the scores it produces against as many alternative sources of information as possible. Each test confirms that the naive Bayes classifier is able to replicate expert judgments about which clerics produce jihadist ideology.

A basic check is to compare my scores to the information in cleric biographies. After coding by hand whether each cleric's biography indicated a jihadist or non-jihadist ideology, I find that clerics with higher jihad scores are more likely to be identified as jihadist in their biographies and that relatively few clerics with low jihad scores have biographies that claim they are jihadists (see the top panel of Figure 5.5). Several of the apparent "mistakes" in the scores make sense once I examine the biographies in question. In a few cases, the clerics have participated in the Algerian independence struggle or the Palestinian-Israeli conflict and refer to themselves as a jihadist (*mujāhid*) in this context. However, this is a different meaning than my understanding of "jihadist" in this book, because the ideologies motivating fighters in these conflicts do not necessarily share the key features of jihadist ideology described earlier in this chapter. For many of these fighters, "jihad" was the struggle against colonial occupation, but not necessarily the struggle to impose a jihadist vision of society.

As a second validation procedure, I ask whether a jihadist cleric would recognize the clerics with positive jihad scores as ideological companions. In March 2008, Ayman al-Zawahiri, the longtime spiritual advisor of Usama Bin Laden and now the leader of al-Qaeda, penned a 188-page document titled *The Exoneration: A Treatise Exonerating the Community of the Pen and the Sword from the Debilitating Accusation of Fatigue and Weakness*. In this document, al-Zawahiri lists nineteen clerics that he believes are supporters of al-Qaeda, including Nasir Bin Hamd al-Fahd, Abd al-Qadr Bin Abd al-Aziz, Umar Abd al-Rahman, Abu Muhammad al-Maqdisi, and Abu Qatada al-Filistini.[22]

---

21   http://islamtoday.net/salman/artshow-28-138026.htm, accessed March 1, 2013, and archived.

22   See a report titled, "Zawahiri tries to clear name, explain strategy," available at www.fas. org/irp/eprint/zawahiri.pdf (accessed February 10, 2017, and archived) that lists the clerics endorsed in *The Exoneration*.

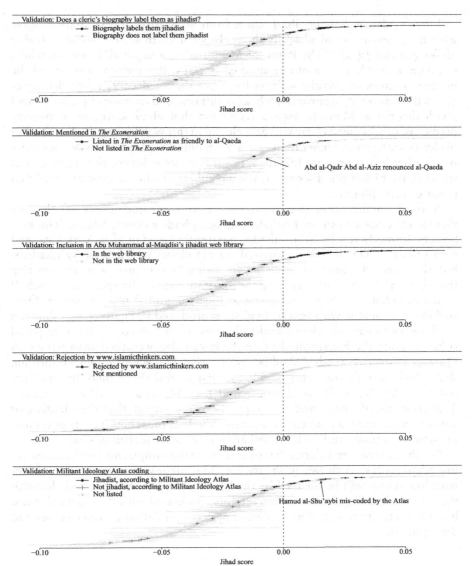

FIGURE 5.5. Validation of jihad scores.

Notes: A comparison of the naive Bayes classifier's jihad score to five expert classifications of clerics as jihadist or not.

Figure 5.5 shows that the clerics endorsed in *The Exoneration* all received high jihad scores from the model, except for Abd al-Aziz, who renounced his full-throated support for militant jihad in 2007.

More evidence that the jihad scores from my statistical text analysis agree with the assessments of jihadists themselves comes from the website *Minbar al-Tawḥīd wal-Jihād* ("The Pulpit of Monotheism and Jihad"), www.tawhed. ws. Although it has been offline since early 2015, this website was one of the premier sources of jihadist writing for more than a decade, more than over 5,000 documents by approximately 400 authors, and overseen by the eminent jihadi theorist al-Maqdisi. Figure 5.5 shows that jihad scores are extremely predictive of whether a cleric will be included in this web library. Only a handful of clerics with scores higher than -.02 are left out of this collection. Some clerics with rather low scores are included, but this is not evidence that these clerics should have higher jihad scores, as the web library includes some material that is not directly jihadist.

A third confirmation that my scores mirror the judgments of jihadists themselves comes from an English-language jihadi website, Islamic Thinkers Society, formerly run by Salafi-jihadis apparently based in New York City, and now offline.[23] This website approved certain clerics as trustworthy jihadists, but also rejected a number of clerics for being "modernists who are twisting the words of Allah" and "favoring the apostate regimes by speaking on behalf of them, defending them, and going against the global jihad front."[24] Most striking is an image with text in English, reproduced in Figure 5.6,[25] showing the faces of twenty-six clerics under the control of George W. Bush, in papal robes, against the background of an American flag wreathed with flames. A Quranic injunction reads, "'And believe in what I have sent down, confirming that which is with you, and be not the first to disbelieve there in, and buy not with My Verses a small price, and fear Me and Me Alone.' -2;41-." This coupling of image and text suggests to the viewer that the jihadists of www.islamicthinkers.com view these individuals as preaching a corrupt version of Islam for money and acclaim and are not properly fearful of God.

For the nine rejected clerics that overlap with my sample, my model estimates low jihad scores, as shown in Figure 5.5. This fits my expectation that clerics with low scores will be disliked by the Islamic Thinkers Society, and although there is a substantial statistical uncertainty associated with this particular test because there are so few clerics, there is perfect correlation between scores and disapproval.

---

23 Their "About Us" page mentions that they proselyte in Times Square and Jackson Heights, NYC (this page was formerly at www.islamicthinkers.com/index/index. php?option=com_content&task=view&id=5&Itemid=57 and can now be viewed at https://web.archive.org/web/20061028125047/http://www.islamicthinkers.com/index/index. php?option=com_content&task=view&id=5&Itemid=57. I have also archived a copy.

24 http://islamicthinkers.com/forum/index.php?showtopic=7211 (link broken). I do not have this page archived.

25 The figure was available at www.islamicthinkers.com/index/index.php?option=com_ content&task=blogcategory&id=86&Itemid=74&limit=9&limitstart=27,   accessed   on March 2, 2013, but has now been removed.

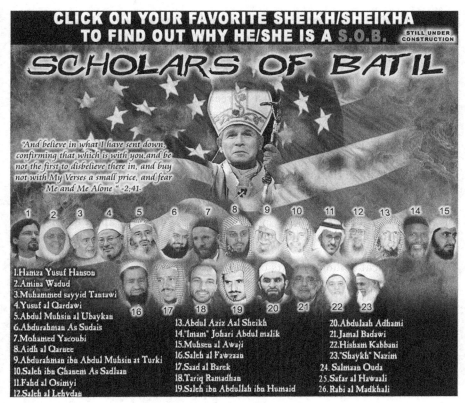

FIGURE 5.6. Jihadist image: scholars of falsehood.

Notes: This is an image created by English-speaking jihadists on the Islamic Thinkers Society website providing images of twenty-six clerics who should be avoided because they oppose jihad.

Finally, I compare my scores to assessments by a group of counterterrorism specialists in appendix 2 of the "Militant Ideology Atlas" (McCants 2006). Comparing the thirty-two clerics that appear in both the atlas list and my Salafi oversample, I find that my cleric-level jihad scores are highly predictive of a "jihadi" designation in the atlas. In fact, my scores reveal a possible mistake in the atlas coding: Hamud al-Shu'aybi is coded in the atlas as a non-jihadi author but his estimated score from my model is high. Based on Hegghammer (2010*a* and 2009, 36), this is probably an error in the atlas coding.

5.4 SUMMARY

In this chapter, I have developed a methodology for measuring jihadi ideology from extremely large collections of cleric-generated texts with relatively minimal assumptions and few of the problems of coding by close reading. My approach offers a new set of tools for analyzing the writing of Muslim clerics. Traditionally, scholars have measured the extent to which clerics adopt jihadist ideology by carefully reading and assessing a cleric's writings. However, this traditional approach is enormously time intensive, and the procedure is not easily replicable. If a scholar decides to change the classification criteria partway through, then each document must be reexamined. In practice, the challenges of manually classifying the writings of jihadists has resulted in scholars basing their assessments on a small number of key texts that are thought to represent the individual's ideology rather than examining all known works.

I present a new approach that leverages the substantive expertise of jihadists themselves through the introduction of training documents that inform a naive Bayes classification model. Because this model can be applied to any number of texts, I am able to assess the ideological commitments of a large number of clerics by considering their entire body of work. My approach is easily replicable, and adjustments to the coding rules do not require rereading a large number of documents.

My statistical coding of texts could probably be marginally improved with more sophisticated methods for stemming and processing Arabic text. There are also more sophisticated statistical models of text that account for elements of language like word order and syntax that might be more accurate. However, extensive validation against a wide array of independent sources shows that the simple methods I use here perform well at correctly estimating the extent to which clerics express jihadist ideology in their writing.

6

Networks, Careers, and Jihadist Ideology

This chapter provides a series of quantitative tests for my argument that blocked ambition is a meaningful factor in the choices of some clerics to preach violent jihadism. The primary data set for testing these propositions comes from the biographies of 200 clerics sampled from the Internet, described in Chapter 4, and the writings produced by these clerics, which I use to measure their rhetorical support for jihadism in Chapter 5. Using a series of statistical models, this chapter demonstrates that there are important correlations between these two data sets.

By combining cleric jihad scores with biographical information about the clerics, I test competing explanations for why some clerics adopt jihadi ideology. My primary focus is on testing whether markers of blocked academic ambition can predict which clerics will adopt jihadist ideology. There are many possible ways that cleric ambitions could be blocked, but I test two especially likely possibilities: that would-be clerics' ambitions are blocked when they lack strong educational networks that will help advance their careers and when they are unable to obtain or maintain insider positions in the state-run religious and educational institutions of the Middle East. I show that there are strong correlations between cleric networks, career paths, and ideology, as my theory predicts.

I use a variety of methods to show that correlations between cleric educational networks, career paths, and ideology are robust. The data allow me to reject some alternative hypotheses about cleric radicalization that are not consistent with the statistical results I present here. However, there remain several different pathways to jihadism that are all consistent with these correlations. I thus employ qualitative case study evidence to further test these competing explanations. To do so, I examine biographies and secondary sources to determine when and why fifteen clerics chose to adopt jihadism.

Finally, I bring evidence to bear on another observable implication of my blocked ambition theory – that jihadist-leaning fatwas are popular with Salafi

Muslim audiences online. This offers one explanation for why a cleric who fails to break into an insider career track, or who is expelled from the ranks of insiders, might to turn to jihadism.

6.1 NETWORKS AND CAREERS ARE CORRELATED WITH JIHADISM

In Chapter 4, I described the process of collecting two data sets that are the basis of my analysis here. The first is the *web sample* of 200 clerics. This data set is valuable because it is the first sample of Sunni Muslim clerics for which the sampling process from the population is known, which means the results from these data are more likely to be representative of trends among Sunni Muslim clerics in general than any previous analysis.

The second data set is a convenience sample of Salafi clerics, some jihadist and some not, which I use to supplement the web sample because the web sample contains relatively few jihadists. I collected this convenience sample of Salafi clerics in an ad hoc way, relying in large part on the clerics who were included on the Islam-oriented website islamway.com and on the lists provided in McCants (2006). This means that the convenience sample needs to be handled with care, because the clerics in it are almost certainly not representative of any larger population.

I have already described some basic characteristics of the clerics in the web sample in Chapter 4. Here, I focus on justifying and measuring the specific variables that need to be included to strengthen the validity of my statistical tests. The main purpose of my statistical analysis is to test observable implications from my theory that blocked ambition makes clerics more likely to become jihadist. The design of my analysis is tightly linked to the theory and potential alternative arguments, so I will recap them here.

I make two main arguments about how individuals come to be jihadist clerics. For individuals who radicalize while they are lay Muslims, prior to pursuing a career as a cleric, I expect that their paths to radicalization will be the same as those of other lay Muslims who never become clerics. Based on insights from the models of Sageman (2004) and Wiktorowicz (2005b), I expect that these individuals will generally be young men, possibly experiencing some challenging or alienating circumstance, who are drawn to jihadism, enter the tutelage of a radicalized mentor, and emerge as proponents of violent jihad. For these individuals, the choice to become a cleric occurs after they adopt jihadist ideology, so their jihadism is likely to shape the way they pursue their career as a cleric. They are unlikely to be interested in the standard insider clerical track, and instead seek to improve their scholarship primarily for the purpose of writing jihadist apologetics. I refer to these individuals as "jihadists-turned-clerics."

The other category of jihadist clerics is made up of individuals who pursue a career as a cleric prior to their radicalization. This pursuit is evidence of their ambition to become clerics – an ambition that can be amplified by the scholarly accolades and monetary compensation that clerics sometimes receive in the Middle East. Some of these individuals will have their ambition blocked, perhaps by accidental circumstances or perhaps by the intentional meddling of the state in the religious and educational spheres. I argue that these blocked ambitions can push some clerics toward jihadism by cutting off their possibility of pursuing a traditional career as a government-funded insider cleric, by inducing anger at the state for their frustrated ambitions, and by creating a need to display theological independence to gain the support and funding of lay Muslims who don't trust insider clerics.

The data in cleric biographies are not ideal for testing arguments about the radicalization of lay Muslims who subsequently pursue a career as a (jihadist) cleric because the focus of cleric biographies is on events that occur after an individual decides to pursue a clerical career. This isn't to say that close inspection of specific biographies can't be informative about the early choices of future clerics, but these types of anecdotes are not common enough in biographies and CVs to be analyzed statistically. Instead, I primarily explore this set of arguments qualitatively later in this chapter. Here, I consider ways to account for this path while testing whether blocked ambition seems to explain the radicalization of clerics-turned-jihadists.

The quantitative data at hand is better for indicating whether certain markers of blocked ambition correlate with jihadism because biographies and CVs tend to cover precisely the periods in time when blocked ambition might occur, as well as the professional aftermath. In a sense, cleric biographies are stories about cleric ambitions – they describe clerics' scholarly mentors, the books they write, the positions they hold, and the careers they ultimately follow. This information can be used to measure the strength of a cleric's educational network and his career path as an insider or outsider.

Before turning to how I make these measurements, it is worth revisiting the question of whether the inclusion criteria for the web sample data, discussed in detail in Chapter 4, create issues of possible sample selection bias for the analysis that follows. Sample selection bias occurs when inclusion in a sample is correlated with the variables in a statistical model applied to the sample. For the purposes of my analysis, the question is whether inclusion in the sample is correlated with the key variables of interest: educational networks, career paths, and jihadist ideology. For example, if my sampling procedures ruled out any clerics with no teachers, then my estimate of the effect of the number of teachers on cleric jihad scores would be biased. However, because my sample was randomly selected from a population of 1,800, there should be no way that my variables of interest are correlated with the random selection process.

More relevant, perhaps, is the question of whether my results are applicable to a population of Muslim clerics that extends beyond the 1,800. Put another way, are the 1,800 a representative sample of the full population of Muslim clerics? It is not possible for me to say. The criteria I used to gather the population of 1,800 clerics exclude clerics about whom little is known and who have little or no influence on transnational Islamic politics. Obviously, this means that my results may provide a biased estimate of the effects of networks and career paths on the ideology of clerics who do not have an online presence. It is possible that the online population I collect excludes some jihadists who avoid posting to the open Internet to hide from surveillance, but it is equally possible that jihadists are overrepresented online (and thus in the web sample) because it provides the best pulpit for spreading their message. Similarly, clerics with insider careers could be underrepresented among clerics with a substantial online presence because their day jobs do not incentivize them to post on the Internet. But it is also possible that insider clerics are more likely to be online because they have the resources to maintain a web page hosted by their institution.

Because there is no evidence with which to adjudicate which of these correlations actually exists, it would be unwise to extrapolate the findings below to clerics beyond the 1,800 that form the population for my web sample. But the results presented here should still be of interest. Notably, it is the largest study to date of jihadi clerics, and thus should provide the best evidence available so far to explain why some individuals choose to become jihadi clerics. Furthermore, there is reason to believe that jihadi clerics with an online presence may be particularly influential in spreading jihadism, thus understanding their path should be relevant for policy-makers and academics alike.

6.1.1 Educational Networks

To assess the extent to which cleric network quality is related to the adoption of jihadi ideology, I use information in the biographies of my web sample of clerics to learn about their educational networks. Connections to individual teachers are very important to clerics, as having famous teachers appears to endow a sense of academic credibility: the perceived quality of a cleric's training depends in part on the perceived quality of his teachers. Teachers, even more than institutions, are the markers of educational prestige in Islamic education. Although there are a number of well-regarded institutions of Islamic higher education – al-Azhar University and the universities in Saudi Arabia among them – it is widely recognized that these universities process a very large number of students and many are not of clerical quality. This creates incentives for clerics to list one or more specific mentors in their biographies.

These connections are typically listed in a distinct section of a cleric's biography, often under the heading "His Sheikhs." In some cases, the section simply provides a bulleted list of teacher names. In others, the description takes a narrative form, describing the nature of their connection to each teacher, such as the subject of study or the time spent, but this practice is not general enough to be useful in my analysis. To code network connections, then, I simply record each of the teacher-student relationships listed in the biography. I call the resulting variable *Number of Teachers*.

One of the functions of the educational networks is to help newly minted clerics obtain academic positions. Thus, I expect that clerics with more teachers will have lower jihad scores than clerics with fewer teachers. However, it is particularly helpful to be connected to well-connected teachers. It is teachers with established networks themselves who can advocate most successfully for their students to be appointed to particular positions. Thus, a young cleric will benefit more from being connected to well-connected teachers. To measure this, I determine whether each cleric has *prominent* teachers by counting the number of students that each teacher has trained in the sample. Because the web sample is representative, this provides an unbiased estimate of the number of students trained by each teacher, which I in turn use as a proxy for the prominence of a teacher; more prominent teachers are those with more students.

In collecting the data on the number of teachers and their prominence, I find that only 113 of the 200 clerics in the web sample list teachers at all. This kind of missing information creates concerns for the analysis of social science data, because missingness may be correlated with the values of the variables in the analysis, inducing spurious correlations. In the analysis that follows, I try several approaches to this problem.

The most basic approach is to assume that when clerics fail to list teachers, this means that they have none to list. After all, individuals rarely enter nonevents in a biography or CV. Under this assumption, it is safe to fill in all of the missing data in number of teachers with zeros and proceed with the analysis, which I do in some of the analysis that follows.

This procedure could be problematic, however, if there are reasons that clerics fail to list teachers even when they have them. Where possible, I simply repeat the analysis, filling in missing data in ways that accord with reasonable alternative assumptions about the reasons that data are missing. A fairly innocuous reason for this missing data arises if biographies are incomplete or very abbreviated, and the biography's author never intended to list teachers. In this case, it seems plausible that missingness is not necessarily related to other relevant characteristics of the cleric. To account for this possibility, I report results from statistical models using only the subset of clerics with detailed biographies and show that the results are the same.

It would be particularly problematic if certain types of clerics systematically failed to list their teachers. Perhaps jihadists are as connected to prominent clerics as non-jihadists but choose not to report these connections because it undermines their jihadi credentials, resulting in missing data and a spurious correlation between the number of teachers and the jihadism of clerics. While it is difficult to be sure that such reporting bias does not exist, I find some evidence against this possibility. At least some jihadist clerics do list their establishment teachers in their biographies, which would be unlikely if doing so were harming their jihadi credentials. Jihadists highlight their connections to prominent teachers even when they disagree with their teachers' ideology because connections to famous clerics offer scholarly legitimacy. For example, in a video urging the release of jihadist cleric Nasr al-Fahd from prison, a supporter attempts to illustrate al-Fahd's position as a serious scholar by saying, "He had many sheikhs, so he's not a drive-by sheikh, the ones who pop up suddenly on YouTube."[1] In an interview about his education and career, prominent jihadist writer Abu Muhammad al-Maqdisi mentions studying with many establishment clerics.[2] And studying *hadith* with Muhammad al-Albani, one of the greatest *hadith* scholars of the last century, endows such credibility that jihadist clerics will mention their studies with him while discussing particular *hadith*, even while criticizing him elsewhere for his counter-jihadi views.

Even when clerics list connections to teachers, it could be that clerics are strategically under- or overreporting their connections. Because Muslim clerics who falsified portions of their CV would face academic consequences, just as academics in other settings would, dramatic overclaiming of connections is unlikely. However, some clerics do apparently feel compelled to "pad" their CVs, mentioning connections to famous scholars despite the actual scholarly interaction being brief and inconsequential. For example, Abd al-Rahman Bin Abdullah al-Suhaym includes the following item at the end of a list of mentors: "I met Abd al-Aziz Bin Baz and asked him questions." Similarly, there is a norm in some biographies to list one's closest advisors first, but other clerics list the most famous clerics first, even when these might not have been their closest advisors. This appears to be another subtle attempt to improve the quality of the CV.[3] My sense from close reading of the biographies is that these attempts to claim tenuous connections with prominent clerics are fairly obvious and generally not consequential for the following analysis.

6.1.2 Career Paths

I expect that clerics who have better networks will be more likely to have successful careers inside the system of state-run religious institutions. As mentioned in Chapter 4, I code clerics as either having "insider" or "outsider" career trajectories based on my holistic reading of the positions they have held. As part of this, I consider the number of "insider" and "outsider" positions listed in each cleric's biography. Clerics who have held prestigious appointments virtually always list them with their biographical information. Knowing which positions are state funded with absolute certainty is impossible, but professorships, positions on religious councils, national ministries for the distribution of *waqfs* (Muslim trusts), national fatwa offices, and the like are almost always controlled by the state. Generally, even one such appointment

---

[1]   www.youtube.com/watch?v=I6zZ5-uJFmY#t=102s, min. 1:45, accessed March 25, 2013, and archived.

[2]   www.youtube.com/watch?v=sFh4R_F5BrE, accessed February 11, 2017, and archived. A longer video was formerly on YouTube at www.youtube.com/watch?v=XQ85NrN9Xh4 but has been removed. Audio of this video is also in the archive.

[3]   www.assuhaim.com/main/pageother.php?catsmktba=15 (link is now broken), accessed January 1, 2012, and archived.

results in coding a cleric as an "insider" because it demonstrates that he was not shut out of positions controlled by the state.

For insider clerics, I also code three subtypes of insider career tracks: academic, religious, and government. Academic insider positions are typically professorships, but other positions at universities or similar institutions also count. Religious insider positions include appointments as an imam, *khatib*, or other religious figure. Government insider positions are generally appointments in a government ministry, such as the Ministry of Religious Affairs. These subcategories are not mutually exclusive. Many clerics have occupied more than one of these types of roles, and a few have occupied all three over the course of their career. Most clerics – 65 percent – have held at least one academic position, while approximately one-third have spent time in religious appointments and one-third have spent time as government officials. These figures are remarkably similar to those presented by Mouline (2014, 193), who uses data from the biographies of the clerics on Saudi Arabia's Council of Grand Ulama to estimate that 65 percent have been professors and 46 percent have been magistrates (15 percent have been both, so the total sums to more than 100 percent), with only 4 percent in other careers.

Missing career information is much less of an issue than missing educational network information. In the representative web sample, 95 percent of clerics report sufficient career information for coding.

Still, the politics of CV writing comes into play when clerics describe their careers. The most prominent dynamic is that clerics sometimes list jobs they were offered but turned down, frequently giving reasons intended to highlight the pious humility of the cleric. For example, a biography of Abd al-Rahman Bin Nasr al-Barak claims that "after the death of Sheikh Bin Baz, the honorable Mufti, Sheikh Abd al-Aziz Al al-Sheikh asked him to become a member of the Ifta, and urged him to do it, but he refused because of the interruption to teaching in his mosque."[4] This job offer is an indicator of access to an insider career, so I generally code clerics who decline some insider positions as insiders nevertheless. The most problematic dynamic would be if jihadists systematically failed to report state-funded appointments because of the jihadist suspicion of clerics who are close to political power. In practice, this does not seem to be the case. Jihadists who are known to have spent time in official positions report these positions in their biographies.

6.1.3 Bivariate Correlations

With information about cleric education networks, career paths, and ideology, it is possible to demonstrate that networks and career paths are statistically related to ideology. To demonstrate that such a relationship exists, I first present unconditional bivariate relationships, which are relationships between two variables that do not take into account potentially confounding

---

4 http://albrrak.net/index.php?option=content&task=view&id=1364&Itemid=45, accessed December 31, 2011, and archived.

factors. To evaluate how robust this relationship is, the next section uses more sophisticated statistical models that incorporate potentially confounding variables.

The first observable implication of the blocked ambition argument is that clerics with fewer teachers will be more likely to express jihadist sentiments in their writing. To see whether the number of teachers predicts cleric jihad scores, I create a scatterplot with the number of teachers a cleric lists on the x-axis and each cleric's jihad score on the y-axis, shown in the left side of Figure 6.1. I overlay a linear regression of these two variables, which calculates the moving average of clerics' jihad scores as their number of teachers increases. Both the scatterplot and the regression show a relationship in the data in which clerics with more teachers generally have lower jihad scores. The scatterplot does show considerable variation in jihad scores no matter how many teachers clerics have, so it is certainly not the case that the number of teachers strictly determines cleric jihad scores. Still, it is clear that only clerics with relatively few teachers are likely to become jihadists – no clerics with more than ten teachers have positive jihad scores.

The bivariate regression tells the same story in slightly different terms. The regression coefficient on the variable *number of teachers* is negative and statistically significant, meaning that the predicted jihad score of a cleric decreases (becomes less jihadist) in the data as his reported number of teachers increases. The size of the predicted decrease in jihad score is easily interpretable from the raw coefficient (one additional teacher changes the predicted jihad

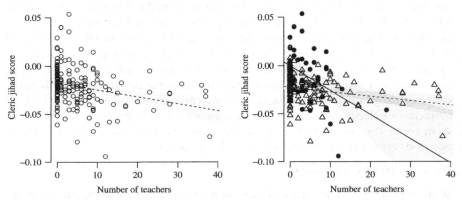

FIGURE 6.1. Correlation between networks, insider appointments, and jihad scores.

Notes: The left panel shows the correlation between the number of teachers a cleric lists (x-axis) and cleric jihad scores (y-axis) with the regression fit and 95 percent confidence interval shown in gray. The right panel shows the same data, but I have divided clerics into outsiders (black discs) and insiders (triangles), with regression lines and 95 percent confidence intervals fit separately to outsiders (solid line) and insiders (dashed line).

score by -0.0007) but this is not really interpretable in substantive terms because the scale of jihad scores is not particularly intuitive. The slope of the regression line in Figure 6.1 is relatively flat compared to the scale of the y-axis, which means that the estimated effect is quite modest. Another way to consider the size of the effect is to take a well-known jihadist, such as Abu Bakr al-Baghdadi (the head of the Islamic State), and evaluate what the model predicts his jihad score would have been if he had had more teachers. His current jihad score is 0.04 and if he had ten additional teachers, his expected score would be 0.032 – smaller, but clearly still on the jihadist end of the scale.

Next, I look at whether clerics with insider careers have lower average jihad scores than clerics with outsider careers by estimating a regression with an indicator variable for an insider career as the only explanatory variable and jihad scores as the outcome variable. The resulting regression coefficient on the variable *insider career* is negative and significant, meaning that insiders have lower scores. To visualize how this variable interacts with the role of teachers in predicting jihad scores, I estimate two additional regressions, the first estimating the relationship between *number of teachers* and *jihad score* for clerics with insider careers, and the second estimating the same relationship for clerics with outsider careers. I plot the results in the right side of Figure 6.1, with the outsider clerics plotted as black discs (with a solid regression line) and the insider clerics plotted as empty triangles (with a dashed regression line).

The combined results of these two regression models suggest that the number of teachers is a stronger predictor of jihad scores for outsider clerics than for insiders.[5] The expected jihad score of both insiders and outsiders decreases detectably as their number of teachers increases, but for outsiders, the decline is about five times as large as the decline of insiders. With zero teachers, the model predicts that the average outsider cleric will have a slightly positive score, putting them on the jihadist side of the scale, but gaining even a single teacher flips them back to the non-jihadist side of the scale, and gaining additional teachers can move them to the low end of the jihad score distribution. For insiders, the effect of teachers on jihad scores is minimal; gaining teachers is only enough to flip a cleric from being jihadist to non-jihadist in the most borderline of cases.

A different way to examine the interaction of teacher connections and career paths is to examine which combinations produce the most jihadists in the data. I do this by coding clerics as having a *limited network* if they have fewer than three teachers and as having an *extensive network* otherwise. I then look at the two-by-two table defined by the interaction of limited versus extensive network and insider versus outsider career to see which cells contain the largest proportion of jihadists. The results, on the left side of Table 6.1, tell the same story as the regressions in Figure 6.1: outsiders with limited networks are the

---

5 Splitting the regression models is equivalent to statistically interacting them. In a combined model, the interaction of *number of teachers* and *insider career* is statistically significant.

TABLE 6.1. *Percentage of jihadi clerics by number of teachers and career path.*

Web Sample Clerics				Clerics with Islamic Degrees		
	Outsider Career	Insider Career			Outsider Career	Insider Career
Limited Network	44% (11/25)	5% (4/80)		Limited Network	45% (5/11)	6.5% (4/61)
Extensive Network	26% (7/27)	1.5% (1/68)		Extensive Network	29% (2/7)	2% (1/51)

Notes: The left panel is a two-by-two table where the cell values are the percentage of jihadist clerics, the rows show whether clerics have limited networks (fewer than three teachers) or extensive networks (three or more teachers), and the columns show outsider career paths versus insider career paths. The right panel shows the same, but for the subset of clerics who have a degree in an Islamic science, suggesting that they pursued Islamic academia at some point.

most likely to be jihadists, outsiders with extensive networks are somewhat likely, and insiders are unlikely to be jihadists. Insiders with extensive networks are slightly less likely to be jihadists than those with limited networks, but this effect is small.

This intriguing interaction of teacher connections and career paths suggests that gaining access to an insider career path can have the same ideological effect on a cleric as having a large number of teachers, or that having many teachers can compensate for failing to break into the insider career track. The clerics most at risk of becoming jihadists are those with both few teachers and an outsider career trajectory.

6.2 ACCOUNTING FOR ALTERNATIVE EXPLANATIONS

The previous section demonstrated that my theory of blocked ambition is consistent with the data. However, it is important to consider whether alternative explanations about the relationship between educational networks, career trajectories, and cleric ideology would produce the same patterns in the data.

Perhaps the most compelling alternative explanation is that the causal relationship is actually the reverse of the one I theorize. In other words, perhaps jihadis never wanted to pursue an insider career in the first place, so the correlation between outsider careers and jihadi scores that I identify occurs because jihadism causes career paths, rather than because closed doors in a career path cause jihadism. The causal variable in this hypothesis requires measuring the inner motivation of would-be clerics, which is virtually impossible, but sometimes people take actions that give some hint about their motivations. One action that clerics are likely to take if they want an insider career is to obtain a degree in the Islamic sciences (foundations of jurisprudence, Quranic exegesis, hadith transmission, and so on). Obtaining a degree is increasingly a prerequisite for advancing as an insider, but is not necessary for would-be clerics who are already sure that they want to be jihadists (in fact, fighting experience would be a better credential in that case). Thus, if I limit the sample of clerics to only those who have a degree in an Islamic science, then I can be more confident that the clerics in the sample did indeed face blocked ambition if they failed to have a career as an insider.

The right side of Table 6.1 shows basically the same results as the left, but for only the 130 clerics with an Islamic degree. This means that the relationship between teacher connections, insider careers, and jihad scores remains virtually unchanged when I control statistically for whether clerics have an Islamic degree. If I am right that obtaining an Islamic degree indicates some intention of pursuing an insider career, then this result casts doubt on the claim that the correlation between career paths and jihadism is driven by the career choices of clerics who decided to be jihadists long before embarking on their clerical careers.

It would be possible to continue to test alternative explanations one by one, in a manner similar to the one I just employed, but this approach is not entirely satisfying because it could be that the alternatives explain away the correlation among networks, career paths, and jihadism in combination, rather than individually. Controlling for many factors at once is not substantially more mathematically complicated than the simple regression models with a few variables that I have just presented, but it is no longer possible to visualize the results as best-fit lines on a scatterplot or counts in the cells of a two-by-two table. Instead, I estimate linear regressions that include a number of control variables to predict cleric jihad scores. I have chosen each control variable with a particular alternative explanation in mind, with the hope that, by conditioning on these variables in a regression model, I can rule out these alternative explanations.

From a statistical point of view, control variables can be grouped into two categories: those that affect all the explanatory variables in my bivariate analysis – networks, career paths, and ideology – and those that are alternative explanations of ideology but do not affect networks or career paths. The first type are called *confounders* in the statistical literature and must be accounted for in order to reach credible causal conclusions. The second type are not essential for causal inference but controlling for them improves the precision of statistical estimates.

Perhaps the most serious threat to statistical inference is some sort of *selection effect*. A "sample selection effect" would occur if clerics were selected into the sample in a way that is correlated with both their academic profiles and their ideology. I have taken great care to avoid this type of sample selection effect by collecting the first representative sample of Sunni Muslim clerics online.

Another type of selection effect might occur if individuals select their values of the "treatment" variables – in this case the educational network and career path variables – about which I would like to make causal inferences.[6] The most obvious selection effect is if the sample contains jihadists-turned-clerics: individuals who become jihadists and then subsequently decide to become clerics. For these jihadist clerics, it cannot be the case that educational networks and career paths caused their turn to violent jihadism because the choice happened far earlier. This is relevant to my analysis because it is likely that jihadists seek out different educational networks and career paths than non-jihadists, meaning that they select the "treatment" that they receive. Jihadists-turned-clerics might make fewer connections to teachers through several selection processes, some of which are difficult to detect with the information available about clerics' backgrounds. It could be the case for some clerics that their jihadi ideology is developed well before the cleric begins to express it in his writing. If future clerics who have already radicalized are less inclined to form connections with teachers, or choose less prominent teachers, this could induce the bivariate correlation between networks and ideology that I have just shown. Alternatively, teachers may choose not to take on students who show early signs of radicalization. All of these alternative mechanisms hinge on the possibility that radicalization happens prior to a future cleric's decision to seek clerical training.

If jihadists-turned-clerics cannot be adequately accounted for, then the correlation between networks, career paths, and jihadism may say more about the impact of jihadism on career trajectories than the effects of career trajectories on jihadism. Both of these possibilities are interesting, but my primary interest is in exploring whether blocked ambition explains why some clerics turn to jihadism, so I would like to account for the alternative explanation that jihadism leads to smaller educational networks and outsider careers.

It is possible that jihadists-turned-clerics account for the correlations I find. It certainly is the case that jihadists are unlikely to seek insider careers because they view governments in the Middle East with distaste and mistrust. Even if they were inclined toward an insider career, governments are generally keen to keep jihadists out of state-funded positions, although a few might get appointed through oversight or because of special connections or circumstances.

It is less likely that jihadists-turned-clerics are impacting the correlation between educational networks and ideology. Jihadists show an ambivalence toward connections with the most prominent clerics. On the one hand, jihadists like Abu Muhammad al-Maqdisi criticize these clerics and those who associate with them. On the other, jihadists treat these clerics with a degree of reverence, and urge their students to read, understand, and follow many of their works.

---

[6] The language of "treatment" variables comes from the statistical literature on analyzing experiments, which provides the philosophical and statistical basis for inferring causation from correlation in nonexperimental studies.

A striking example of this is a syllabus created by jihadist Hamid al-Ali, discussed in Chapter 2. One might expect a jihadist program of study to focus on jihadi authors, but his syllabus includes establishment scholars in the domains where they are recognized experts. The first reading assignment on the syllabus is a book by establishment cleric Ibn al-Uthaymeen, and overall, readings by modern establishment clerics appear to vastly outweigh readings by jihadists. Thus, it is not clear that jihadists intentionally seek out fewer teachers.

This conforms to a broader pattern I sensed, both in reading cleric biographies and while interviewing students at al-Azhar University: students are selective about their teachers, but this selection is based on expertise rather than ideology. For example, Salman, one of the al-Azhar students who was striving to become a cleric, said that he decided fiqh was the best of the Islamic sciences and then sought out the teachers who were best for training in fiqh.[7] Notably, Salman adheres to the Shafa'i school of Islamic law, while his teachers at al-Azhar are Hanafi – a fact that shows that he is willing to cross ideological lines to get the best training.

A different but related observation is that jihadists often try to show that the establishment clerics are actually on their side but cannot admit it publicly. In the introduction to an edition of *The Defense of Muslim Lands*, jihadist Abdullah Azzam (1979, front material) writes of how he presented a draft of the work to a number of establishment scholars:

I wrote this Fatwa and it was originally larger than its present size. I showed it to our Great Respected Sheikh Abdul Aziz bin Bazz. I read it to him, he improved upon it and he said "it is good" and agreed with it.

Then I showed this Fatwa, without the six questions at the end, to the peers of Sheikh Abdullah al Waan, Saeed Hawa, Mohammed Najeeb al Mutyey, Dr. Hassin Hamid Hissan and Umar Sayaf. I read it to them, they agreed with it and most of them signed it. Likewise, I read it to Sheikh Mohammed Bin Salah Bin Uthaimin and he too signed it.

This suggests that jihadists do not avoid connecting to networks of establishment clerics when it suits their purposes. In fact, it seems quite possible that jihadists-turned-clerics might seek out the most prominent teachers possible while hiding their true intentions so that when they reveal themselves as jihadists, they have the credibility of having trained with the very best scholars. This may have been why al-Maqdisi gained personal permission from Bin Baz to study in Saudi Arabia despite the likely fact that he had already turned to a distinctly jihadist ideology (Wagemakers 2012).

Unfortunately for my analysis, it is difficult to measure and control for the possibility that jihadists-turned-clerics are selecting their educational networks and career trajectories because much of the relevant information is

7 Field notes from 2012, pp. 19 and 22, archived at http://dx.doi.org/10.7910/DVN/PG4A7K.

privately held by the individuals involved. Ideally, I would account for early radicalization by conditioning on a baseline measure of the ideology of each cleric prior to their entry into the cleric educational network. Unfortunately, there is no way to systematically measure each cleric's ideology at the start of their education because most had not yet produced texts. Without any certain way to measure early ideology, it is difficult to say whether jihadi clerics might have shown early evidence of radicalization that affected their network connections. It is also difficult to identify clerics who never had academic ambitions (and thus cannot have had them blocked). This problem is at least slightly more tractable because I have information on which clerics have obtained advanced degrees in the Islamic sciences, which I take as an indicator of at least a minimal level of academic ambition. Because of this ambiguity, I first present results that include all of the clerics in the web sample. Then, in subsequent statistical models, I remove those whose biographies indicate clear evidence of a turn to jihadism that preceded their decision to seek training as a cleric.

One related variable that I can measure is the identity of each cleric's teachers. I do not have text for each of the teachers mentioned by the clerics, so I cannot directly test whether more jihadist teachers produce more jihadist students, but I can test whether particular teachers seem to produce jihadist students.

In addition to the selection effects I have just discussed, other factors might simultaneously influence a cleric's networks, career path, and ideology. One of the possible confounding variables is whether a cleric comes from a cleric family, has teachers within his own family, or has some other advantage that gives him both access to a strong educational network at an early age and makes him more likely to hold a particular ideological position. There is evidence that coming from a cleric family gives would-be clerics networking advantages. Mouline (2014, 171–172) examines the social backgrounds of insider clerics who rise to membership in the Committee of Grand Ulama, which sits organizationally atop the hierarchy of clerical institutions in Saudi Arabia, and identifies three categories of clerics: "self-made men," whose families have no connection with the religious establishment, "children of mid-level religious personnel," who have relatives in government religious posts but are not related to "especially renowned Imams or preachers at mosques," and "heirs to the houses of the ulama," who are related to prominent imams and preachers. Individuals in "cleric families" have better networks than others because they inherit the network of their family member rather than having to develop a network on their own (Al-Rasheed 2007, 27–28). According to Mouline (2014, 172), "family background plays a decisive role in their social promotion" because "their family networks allow them to study under the guidance of the most renowned and influential masters and to frequent the best-stocked libraries."[8]

---

[8] Mouline (2014, 198) identifies three particular families – the Al al-Sheikh, the Ibn Humayd, and the al-Shathri – as having particularly advantageous family networks, and recounts several

To account for these factors, I code two indicator variables specifying whether a cleric mentions having a relative who is a cleric, and whether the biography mentions that a cleric took theological instruction from a relative. By my coding, 26 of the 200 clerics come from cleric families, and 22 were taught by relatives at some point.

Whether a cleric attended *religious primary school* is another possible confounding variable. In the Muslim world, religious and secular primary school systems often exist side by side. Parents may have many reasons for enrolling their children in on or the other, but an outcome of enrollment in religious primary school might be that clerics develop better education networks later in life because they are able to forge early connections with clerics in their primary school. I code (to the extent possible) whether each cleric was enrolled in religious or secular primary school. This particular fact is included in many biographies but not all, since it is not particularly central for establishing a cleric's religious authority. This means that the variable *religious primary school* is inevitably measured with some error.

I also account for the educational attainment of clerics. On one hand, failure to attain academic credentials is one way in which ambitions might be blocked. On the other, there is some concern that academic credentials are themselves a confounder because they might be a common cause of both ideology and career paths. I measure whether each cleric has a bachelor's, master's, or doctoral degree and include this information in the main statistical models that follow, but the results are similar if I exclude these variables.

I also try to account for religious expertise, though my measure of expertise is blunt and imperfect. Many clerics list that they have memorized the entire Quran (making them a *ḥāfiẓ* – "one who preserves" the Quran in memory). Complete memorization of the Quran is greatly respected and conveys substantial religious credibility, thus some clerics list this among their religious credentials. In the sample, 44 of the 200 clerics mention memorizing the Quran. Though I suspect that this is undercounting the true rate of Quran memorization by a wide margin, I include the information in the regression models below to demonstrate that reported religious expertise does not somehow explain away the correlations in the data.

Another alternative argument related to educational and religious expertise comes from Gambetta and Hertog (2016), who argue that engineers may be more likely to become jihadists. These individuals may have the vocational training to carry out certain tasks that are useful for terrorism, engineers have faced blocked ambitions of their own in struggling Middle Eastern economies, and engineers lack the traditional religious expertise to join the ranks of insider clerics. I use word searches for the words "engineer" and "engineering" in the biographies of the clerics and control for this in some statistical specifications.

anecdotes of clerics who managed to leverage these family ties for professional advantage as they rose in the Saudi clerical establishment.

Accounting for academic and religious expertise is useful for ruling out some explanations, but it does not entirely disarm an alternative explanation in which jihadist clerics are those who are simply not as smart as their peers, and this makes them more susceptible to jihadist ideology. Measuring the intelligence of clerics is difficult, so I use a rough proxy measure: an estimate of the vocabulary of each cleric. I expect that more intelligent clerics will use a broader vocabulary in their writing, so if jihadists have a very limited vocabulary, perhaps this alternative explanation has some merit. Directly estimating a cleric's vocabulary from the texts I have collected might be problematic because of differences in the variety of document genres and the differing number of documents each cleric has written. Instead, I count how frequently each cleric relies on common words in their writing. I compare the writing of each cleric to a list of the 5,000 most common Arabic words collected by Buckwalter and Parkinson (2011) and calculate the proportion of each cleric's words that are on this list. Clerics whose writing is dominated by common words probably have smaller vocabularies, and by extension, might be considered less intelligent by some standards.

Shifting away from the role of credentials and intelligence, some argue that exposure to Western society was a radicalizing influence on Sayyid Qutb (Wright 2006, 9–23) and other jihadists. I test whether exposure to the West is a plausible explanation for jihadi ideology by coding whether a cleric mentions spending time in one or more of the advanced Western democracies during their formative years and education. I do not include time spent in the West after a cleric has already radicalized, and I also do not include the phenomenon of well-established clerics traveling to Western countries to give lectures or perform *Daʿwa* (missionary work) later in life. Ten clerics have eligible Western exposure according to my definition. Conditioning on time in the West also controls for the possibility that jihadist clerics have disproportionately spent time in the West and been disadvantaged when networking with teachers.

In addition to the control variables I have just mentioned, I also include indicator variables for the country of birth of each cleric and, in alternative specifications, the city of birth of some clerics (for statistical reasons, I can only include cities that are home to more than one cleric). Controlling for the home countries and hometowns of clerics serves a few purposes. For one, there might be unique factors to particular locations that affect the education, careers, and networks of clerics. For example, there might be a radical preacher in a local mosque, a cohort of peers from the same town who take similar paths, or, at the country level, the political culture may tend to produce to particular clerical ideologies. Along these same lines, Hegghammer and Wagemakers (2013) argue that there may be something about Palestine that has made it particularly important in the jihadist movement. And Mouline (2014, 182–184) shows that particular towns in Saudi Arabia that form the Najdi crescent are overrepresented in the Saudi religious establishment. More generally, including country and city variables might account for variation in the local conditions in which clerics were raised, which could help account for difficult-to-measure variables like poverty.

Unfortunately, some likely confounding variables are impossible to measure from the data available. First, it is possible that jihadi clerics share some personality trait that makes them less likely to connect with teachers and more likely to adopt the worldview of militant jihad. Ideally, I might control for personality factors, but I have not identified any way to accurately measure them. Although it might seem intuitive that jihadi ideologues are more inclined to be loners, lack social skills, or have unpleasant personalities, this does not match with anecdotal accounts. For example, Usama Bin Laden was famously charismatic. However, it is currently impossible to systematically measure the personality traits of the clerics in my study.

Should my findings be completely discounted because of possible missing control variables? I argue no. The relationship between networks, career paths, and ideology presented below is substantial and I find additional support for my theory from interviews and observation at al-Azhar University. However, education networks and career paths certainly do not explain all of the variance in cleric jihad scores, so other processes that I cannot measure, including those listed earlier, may be simultaneously shaping cleric ideology.

I now return to estimating the correlation between clerics' educational networks, career paths, and expressions of jihadist ideology, while accounting for the control variables I have just described. I use standard regression techniques except where described as follows. I estimate several variations of the model: using different ways of measuring educational networks and career paths, different versions of some control variables, different samples, and different models of statistical uncertainty. In general, I find similar results from all of these models, so I focus on those that are most informative and simply mention the others as they become relevant.

The first column of Table 6.2 shows the estimated coefficients for the predictors in a model predicting cleric jihad scores for the 200 clerics in the web sample. The coefficients for each variable represent the estimated change in the predicted jihad scores as the variable changes one unit (in the units of each variable). The brackets below each coefficient contain the endpoints of a 95 percent confidence interval, obtained by a bootstrapping procedure, which conveys information about the statistical significance of each coefficient; when this interval does not contain zero, the estimate is statistically significant according to conventional standards, and I indicate this in the table with a star next to the coefficient.

This bootstrapping procedure is only one of several ways I estimate the statistical uncertainty of my results, but I prefer it because it allows me to include uncertainty about the jihad scores themselves, which are otherwise treated as certain by the regression model, even though they are

TABLE 6.2. *Number of teachers and career path predict jihadism.*

	(1) Jihad Score	(2) Jihad Score	(3) Jihad Score	(4) Jihad Score
Number of teachers	-0.0006* [-0.001, -0.0003]			
Insider career	-0.014* [-0.021, -0.006]			
Disconnected outsider		0.024* [0.014, 0.034]	0.027* [0.007, 0.043]	
Connected outsider		0.014* [0.002, 0.027]	0.002	
Disconnected insider		0.008* [0.002, 0.015]	0.008* [0.0009, 0.017]	
Outsider without prominent teachers				0.024* [0.014, 0.034]
Outsider with prominent teachers				0.013* [0.003, 0.024]
Insider without prominent teachers				0.007* [0.001, 0.014]
Family teachers		-0.01 [-0.026, 0.005]	-0.01 [-0.028, 0.003]	-0.009 [-0.026, 0.006]
Clerical family		0.006 [-0.009, 0.02]	0.006 [-0.008, 0.024]	0.005 [-0.01, 0.018]
Religious primary school		-0.003 [-0.01, 0.006]	0.002 [-0.004, 0.012]	-0.004 [-0.01, 0.005]
Bachelor's		0.006 [-0.0003, 0.013]	0.011* [0.0001, 0.022]	0.007* [0.001, 0.014]

TABLE 6.2. *Continued*

	(1) Jihad Score	(2) Jihad Score	(3) Jihad Score	(4) Jihad Score
Master's	−0.0003	−0.001	−0.002	−0.001
	[−0.007, 0.006]	[−0.008, 0.005]	[−0.009, 0.008]	[−0.008, 0.005]
Doctorate	−0.0002	−0.0004	0.002	−0.0008
	[−0.007, 0.006]	[−0.006, 0.007]	[−0.007, 0.011]	[−0.008, 0.006]
Quran memorization	0.003	0.004	0.002	0.003
	[−0.004, 0.009]	[−0.004, 0.011]	[−0.006, 0.011]	[−0.004, 0.01]
Time in the West	−0.002	−0.002	−0.004	−0.002
	[−0.011, 0.006]	[−0.012, 0.006]	[−0.019, 0.008]	[−0.012, 0.007]
Percent common words	−0.088	−0.075	−0.079	−0.079
	[−0.16, 0.001]	[−0.15, 0.009]	[−0.18, 0.017]	[−0.15, 0.007]
Intercept	0.032	0.005	0.002	0.008
	[−0.021, 0.076]	[−0.043, 0.046]	[−0.06, 0.056]	[−0.044, 0.05]
Country of birth fixed effects	✓	✓	✓	✓
Sample	Web sample	Web sample	Islamic degrees	Web sample
Observations	200	200	130	200

Notes: Regression results from four regression models predicting jihad scores as a function of the number of teachers a cleric has, career path, and control variables. Bootstrapped 95 percent confidence intervals are in brackets. * $p < 0.05$.

149

not.[9] Throughout, I mention when alternative approaches for calculating the uncertainty of coefficients give different answers than the bootstrap.

In Model 1, the coefficients on the variables *number of teachers* and *insider career* are negative and statistically significant, meaning that, just like the earlier bivariate models, this model demonstrates a detectable relationship in which well-networked clerics with insider careers have lower jihad scores. The coefficient estimates are similar to those in the bivariate regression, meaning that the magnitude of the estimated effects is, as before, detectable but modest. What is different in this model is that it takes into account alternative explanations using control variables. The fact that networks and career paths remain significant predictors of jihad scores when the controls are included in the model lends empirical support to my argument about blocked ambition and casts doubt on the validity of competing explanations.

It is somewhat risky to interpret the coefficients of the control variables causally because they are, by design, variables that are meant to assist me in interpreting the coefficients on *number of teachers* and *insider career*, so they are often causally prior to and thus confounded by my key variables of interest. Still, the direction and significance (or lack thereof) of a number of the variables is interesting.

Although I was concerned that clerics from well-known cleric families, or who had family teachers, might have lower jihad scores, this doesn't seem to be the case. Along the same lines, I also worried that clerics who went to religious primary schools, rather than secular schools, might have more network connections because of this early interaction with clerics teaching in religious schools. This too does not appear to be the case, as the coefficient on Religious Primary School is not significant. Thus cleric ideology does not seem to be predetermined by one's family or early schooling.

It does seem that clerics with family connections to the cleric profession have better connections and are more likely to have insider careers. In an auxiliary regression predicting *number of teachers* as the outcome, I find that clerics who come from cleric families have four more teacher connections on average than those who do not. Another regression shows that clerics who have family

---

9   Traditionally, the uncertainty of regression coefficients gets calculated by making defensible mathematical assumptions about the variance of the estimates based on the data. Bootstrapping calculates the uncertainty of regression coefficients very differently, by using a resampling scheme to directly estimate the impact of variability in the data on the variability of the regression coefficients (Efron and Tibshirani 1993). The general idea is that by repeatedly drawing samples of the data, with replacement, and estimating the same statistical model, the variation in the estimates over a large number of repeated resampling will begin to converge on the true variability of the estimates if a new sample were in fact drawn from the true population. My specific approach is more complicated, because I first repeatedly resample the words in clerics' texts to get estimates of the variability in their jihad scores, and then subsequently resample the clerics themselves to get an estimate of the variability of the regression coefficients. I use 200 bootstraps at each stage, which is on the low end as explained by Efron and Tibshirani (1993), but saves substantial computing time.

teachers are almost guaranteed to have an insider career, while those without family teachers have only a 75 percent chance of being an insider. And having a family teacher is a significant predictor of jihad scores in a bivariate regression. But controlling for *cleric families* and *family teachers* in Model 1 does not really change the relationship between networks, careers, and jihad scores because, most likely, the relationship of these control variables does not persist when networks and careers are included; *number of teachers* and *insider career* do a better job of accounting for the variation in cleric jihad scores.

Another alternative explanation for the correlation between networks, career paths, and jihad scores is that levels of education might affect all three, leading to a spurious correlation with educational attainment being the culprit. Clerics with a PhD are more likely to be insiders, so these concerns should be taken seriously, but the results from Model 1 suggest that education isn't inducing a spurious correlation. Neither a master's nor doctorate degree appears to matter for predicting jihad scores, and a bachelor's degree is correlated with increased jihad scores but the coefficient is extremely small, meaning that the real-world change in cleric rhetoric associated with a bachelor's degree is miniscule.

My attempt to control for religious expertise is captured by the Quran memorization variable. Its coefficient is not statistically distinguishable from zero, which is some indication that religious expertise is not driving career trajectories, educational networks, and ideology. However, Quran memorization is not a great proxy for religious education because all clerics are expected to memorize the Quran, though some may take more time and have less mastery. In an alternative specification, I include whether a cleric has an Islamic degree as a covariate and also find no result (while the results for networks and career paths stay the same). This lends some additional confidence that some form of religious education is not a confounder, but better data would improve this inference.

The results of Model 1 also lend evidence against an alternative account in which jihadists are less intelligent than their non-jihadist counterparts, which predisposes them somehow toward jihadism as well as toward having more limited academic and professional success. Measuring the intelligence of clerics from afar is tricky, but as a proxy I look at several measures of the vocabulary of clerics, under the assumption that clerics with more diverse vocabularies are probably more intelligent.

In Model 1, I find that my first proxy for intelligence – the proportion of words used by a given cleric that are in the most common 5,000 words in the Arabic language – is negative, large, and almost statistically significant (with robust standard errors, the estimates are significant; with bootstrapped confidence intervals, they miss significance by just a little). This means that clerics with more diverse vocabularies are actually more likely to be jihadists, all else equal, so it is hard to argue that there is any direct evidence that jihadists are less intelligent on average. An alternative measure of vocabulary, the proportion of all of a cleric's words that are unique, gives a similar interpretation when included in the model but is not statistically significant.

Finally, Model 1 includes variables for the country in which each cleric was born as a way to account for a myriad of environmental factors that might lead some places to produce more jihadists than others. Many of these are statistically significant but the coefficients cannot be interpreted as causal effects, especially in light of the other conditioning variables. The purpose of these variables is mostly for statistical adjustment. As such, I omit the details from Table 6.2. In an alternative specification, I also include indicators for every hometown that has three or more clerics in my sample[10] and find that this also does not make the correlations between networks, career paths, and jihad scores go away.

The other models in Table 6.2 reinforce my interpretation of the first model. Model 2 uses the same sample and control variables as Model 1, but this time I look for evidence of the interaction between networks and career paths. I consider a cleric to be disconnected if he lists fewer than three teachers, and to be connected if he lists three or more. To assess the interaction of connectedness and career paths, I multiply the indicator for connected versus disconnected clerics with the indicator for insider versus outsider career paths. This creates four categories of clerics: *disconnected outsiders, connected outsiders, disconnected insiders,* and *connected insiders.* Because of the mechanics of regression, only the first three enter the regression equation, and their effects are estimated relative to the baseline jihad scores of *connected insiders.*

The estimates in Model 2 show that *disconnected outsiders, connected outsiders,* and *disconnected insiders* all have higher expected jihad scores than *connected insiders. Disconnected insiders* get the smallest estimated bump in jihad scores with an increase of 0.008, which is about 40 percent of the standard deviation of jihad scores. *Connected outsiders* get a bigger bump of about three-quarters of a standard deviation, and *disconnected outsiders* have an expected jihad score that is more than a full standard deviation higher than the scores of *connected insiders.* Substantively, this effect size is large enough to flip a relatively large number of clerics from being non-jihadist to jihadist. The control variables behave similarly as in Model 1, so I do not discuss them further.

Model 3 in Table 6.2 estimates the same regression equation as Model 2, but on a subset of clerics that have Islamic degrees, following the logic that clerics with a degree are likely to have pursued an insider career at some point, so the mechanism of blocked ambition is more plausible than for clerics without such a degree. I find somewhat different results than in Model 2. *Connected outsiders* no longer have detectably higher jihad scores than *connected insiders,*

---

[10]   The cities with the most clerics in my sample are, in order: Burayda, Saudi Arabia, 10; Riyadh, Saudi Arabia, 9; al-Zulfi, Saudi Arabia, 6; Mecca, Saudi Arabia, 6; Medina, Saudia Arabia, 6; Damascus, Syria, 6; Cairo, Egypt, 5; Mosul, Iraq, 4; Alexandria, Egypt, 3.

but *disconnected insiders* and *disconnected outsiders* continue to have higher scores. For those with a degree in the Islamic sciences, the key to having a low jihad score is then arguably through connections rather than through an insider career. As another robustness check, not shown in the table, I also estimate the same regression equation as Model 2 but on a larger sample made up of both the web sample and the Salafi convenience sample, reweighted to match the population proportion of jihadists in the web sample. The results are essentially the same as Model 2.

The final column of Table 6.2 reports the results of a regression measuring clerics' network connections in a third way. In the previous models, I measure each cleric's connectedness by simply counting the number of teachers he lists, but this ignores the possibility that some connections are worth more than others. In this regression, I instead measure clerics' connectedness using the prominence of their teachers based on the number of total students their teachers have taught. If teachers with more students are more prominent, then the total number of students that a cleric's teachers have taught will serve as a proxy for the quality of a cleric's connections.

I have collected the names of the clerics, which allows me to see which teachers are responsible for training the most students. The top of the list is dominated by the leading lights of the Saudi establishment in the last half century: Salih bin Fawzan al-Fawzan has eleven students in the sample, Abdullah Bin Jibreen has thirteen, Muhammad Nasr al-Din al-Albani has thirteen, Muhammad Ibn al-Uthaymeen has twenty, and Abd al-Aziz Bin Baz has a remarkable thirty-eight.[11] For each of the 200 clerics in the sample, I calculate the number of students that their teachers have taught and classify clerics who fall above the fiftieth percentile as having prominent teachers and clerics at or below the fiftieth percentile as without prominent teachers. Model 4 in Table 6.2 interacts the variable for prominent teachers with the variable for insider versus outsider careers, similar to Models 2 and 3, and returns estimates that are almost identical to the parallel estimates from Model 2. In a separate regression, not shown in the table, I estimate a regression similar to Model 1, but with the continuous measure of the total number of students taught by each cleric's teachers in place of the variable *number of teachers* and again get similar results.

As is common in applied statistics, I estimate yet more models that probe at various assumptions and modeling choices one by one. In general, the findings I have just presented are robust to these changes, meaning that the estimates of the correlation between cleric networks, career paths, and jihad scores

---

[11] These counts are *not* the full number of students taught by each of these clerics – it is only the count in the sample of 200, which means that because the sample is representative of the approximately 1,800 clerics in the census with enough information that they could have been included, Bin Baz has taught an estimated 342 students. In fact, his website lists 347 students, verifying that the sample is representative.

do not meaningfully change. A few of these changes include: controlling for individual teachers, because teachers influence the jihad scores of their students; reestimating the models using a dichotomous outcome for jihadi or not rather than the continuous jihad scores; using alternative jihad scores estimated with the jihadist web library "Pulpit of Monotheism and Jihad" as the training corpus; interacting *number of teachers* with the indicator for insider versus outsider career; and only including clerics with largely complete biographies.

One alternative specification that deserves mention is a model in which I include indicator variables for the universities that each cleric has attended. Including information about universities does not really change the correlations between the key variables of interest in my analysis, but the Um al-Qura University in Saudi Arabia is associated with slightly higher jihad scores while the Islamic University of Medina is associated with slightly lower scores (the other universities do not have detectable correlations with jihad scores). Two universities, Imam University in Saudi Arabia and al-Azhar University in Cairo, have been attended by enough clerics in my sample that I can estimate the regression models just on the subset from these schools, which holds any school effects constant. I find that the correlations demonstrated above still appear in these two subsets of clerics, even though there are only forty-two clerics from Imam University and only twenty from al-Azhar.[12]

I also test the argument of Gambetta and Hertog (2016) that engineers may be more likely to become jihadists, but find no evidence that this is the case in my sample of clerics.

All told, a large number of statistical models with a variety of controls confirm the same general result: that clerics' educational networks and career trajectories are strongly associated with subsequent jihadist ideology, and that a number of plausible alternative arguments fail to find support.

6.3 TURNING POINTS IN THE LIVES OF JIHADIST CLERICS

Statistical models and quantitative data have clear limitations for exploring why some clerics become jihadists. In this section, I turn to qualitative evidence from the lives of jihadist clerics to complement the statistical findings in two key ways. My first goal is to provide examples of the two broad pathways to becoming a jihadist cleric that I identify in this book: jihadists-turned-clerics who radicalize before embarking on a clerical career path, and clerics who radicalize after facing blocked ambitions. Second, I attempt to estimate the rough proportions of jihadist clerics who have taken each of these two paths, and also explore whether some clerics take other paths to jihad that I have not adequately considered.

---

[12] Regressions on fewer than about thirty observations should be treated with caution because some versions of the central limit theorem that justify regression uncertainty estimates require about thirty observations.

Both of these goals require case selection strategies that intentionally focus on jihadists rather than non-jihadists. Specifically, I select cases at random from the sample of jihadist clerics, so the findings are likely to be representative of the pathways by which clerics become jihadists. Most case study designs rely on only a handful of cases with relatively rich information about each case. However, the paucity of data about some clerics means that this strategy is not ideal for my goal of characterizing how and when academia matters in the lives of jihadists. Instead, I randomly select fifteen jihadists from my combined web sample and oversample. I identify jihadist clerics using the jihad scores developed in the previous chapter; clerics with a positive score are eligible for case study sampling. The benefit of random sampling is that, with enough cases, the results from the case studies provide a representative picture of the mechanisms by which clerics become jihadists (Fearon and Laitin 2008).

Because I intentionally "select on the dependent variable" of jihadism, the resulting cases are *not* useful for estimating the effects of blocked ambition on cleric radicalization.[13] Instead, the purpose is to allow me to classify each case according to the causal mechanism of radicalization that seems most likely and then use the combined information from these cases to estimate the proportion of all jihadists who fit each of the theoretical mechanisms. Thus, it is important that these cases be randomly selected from a representative collection of jihadists so that the results are themselves representative.

These cases cannot definitively substantiate all of the causal claims in my argument, but the information in some of these cases is rich enough that it can rule out some hypotheses and provide evidence for others. Where available, I consult both primary and secondary source materials, starting with the biographies of each cleric and then expanding the search outward for any secondary literature about each person that may give insight into the circumstances of their turn to jihadism. Unfortunately, because of the clandestine nature of jihadists' lives, the level of information differs widely from one case to the next so some are completely uninformative. This uneven quality of case information is a clear cost of using random sampling as a case selection method, but my hope is that the analytic power of examining a representative sample of jihadists compensates.

Table 6.3 summarizes the results of my fifteen randomly selected case studies of jihadists. Summarizing these cases is not an easy task; for the sake of space, I err on the side of reporting only a few details about each case, but

---

[13] This case selection procedure results in a sample that is not useful for estimating the effects of blocked ambition because I look only at jihadists, which is a form of "selection on the dependent variable." As a result, while the cases can inform an estimate of the probability of having faced blocked ambition given that an individual is jihadist, they cannot inform an estimate of the probability of having faced blocked ambition given that someone is not a jihadist, which would be crucial if my goal were to estimate the same quantity of interest above: the probability that someone is jihadist given that they have faced blocked ambitions.

TABLE 6.3. *Summary of case studies of fifteen jihadist clerics.*

Jihadist Cleric	Most Likely Mechanism	Description
1. Nasr Bin Hamad al-Fahd	Blocked ambition	Had an academic career but was imprisoned because of a poem insulting a Saudi prince. With his academic career ruined and bitter from prison, he radicalized.
2. Abu Bakr al-Baghdadi	Blocked ambition	His plans to become a preacher ended when he was kicked out of his mosque by the head imam. Then prison during the US occupation radicalized him further.
3. Faris al-Zahrani (Abu Jindal al-Azdi)	Possible case of blocked ambition	His exact path to radicalization is not clear from his biography, but Hegghammer (2010*a*, 191) describes him as among those with "mediocre resumes or failed careers in the religious sector." Wagemakers (2011, 358) notes that he started a PhD but did not finish, though it is unclear whether this precipitated his turn to jihad.
4. Hamud Bin Uqla' al-Shu'aybi	Blocked ambition and/or late-adopting true believer	He became an outspoken jihadist once he was kicked out of the academy, though Hegghammer (2010*a*) suggests that he might have been encouraged or manipulated by younger jihadists in his orbit.
5. Abdullah Azzam	Late-adopting true believer	He earned a PhD from al-Azhar and then taught in Jordan and Saudi Arabia. He was fired from his position as a lecturer at the University of Jeddah in the repression following the 1979 Grand Mosque seizure in Saudi Arabia. This could qualify as a potential source of blocked ambition, but it seems that Azzam already held jihadist views at this point.
6. Abd al-Hakim Hasan	Jihadist-turned-cleric	Became jihadist while young and then studied at al-Azhar.

Note: Summary of fifteen case studies of mechanisms for cleric adoption of jihadist ideology.

TABLE 6.4. *Summary of case studies of fifteen jihadist clerics (continued).*

Jihadist Cleric	Most Likely Mechanism	Most Likely Path to Jihadism
7. Abu Qatada al-Filistini	Late-adopting true believer	He got clerical training and worked as an imam in the Jordanian Army, but left because his increasingly hardline religious views clashed with his superiors. He eventually went to fight in the Afghan jihad. He was barred from returning to Jordan and emigrated to the United Kingdom, where he became a jihadist preacher.
8. Abu Muhammad al-Maqdisi	Jihadist-turned-cleric	He was radicalized at seventeen by happenstance contact with a radical imam, then sought out more and more radical teachers, and finally decided to become a cleric himself.
9. Abu Basir al-Tartusi	Jihadist-turned-cleric	He radicalized in Hama, Syria, in response to oppression, and then became a cleric.
10. Abu Ayman al-Masri	Jihadist-turned-cleric	He radicalized as a young man and then decided to study with clerics.
11. Muhammad Abd al-Islam Farraj	jihadist-turned-cleric	He radicalized as an engineer, then started preaching jihad as a hobby.
12. Azzam al-Amriki (Adam Gadahn)	Jihadist-turned-cleric	He radicalized as a lay Muslim due to friends, then traveled to fight and started producing Islamic writing.
13. Ibrahim al-Rubaysh	Jihadist-turned-cleric	The causes of his radicalization are unclear, but he graduated with an Islamic sciences degree from al-Imam University and promptly fought in the Afghan jihad. He preached to other detainees while incarcerated in Guantanamo Bay, Cuba. He was subsequently transferred to Saudi Arabia, where he escaped and became a cleric for al-Qaeda.

Note: Summary of fifteen case studies of mechanisms for cleric adoption of jihadist ideology.

TABLE 6.5. *Summary of case studies of fifteen jihadist clerics (continued)*.

Jihadist Cleric	Most Likely Mechanism	Most Likely Path to Jihadism
14. Ra'id Salah	Jihadist-turned-cleric	He was radicalized in childhood and then decided to become a cleric.
15. Salih Hussayn al-Raqab	Insufficient data	He has had an insider career in religious and educational institutions in Gaza, Palestine. The relationship of the ruling authorities to the religious sphere is different in Palestine so it is possible to express jihadist ideas without being forced out of insider positions. His biographies do not elaborate on his early career or the development of his ideas over time, so it is impossible to tell which path to radicalization best fits.

Note: Summary of fifteen case studies of mechanisms for cleric adoption of jihadist ideology.

I have archived more extensive notes and the materials I considered online.[14] Because the cases are randomly selected, the proportion of the cases aligning with each general pathway to jihadism is my best estimate of how prevalent each pathway is in the overall population of jihadist clerics. One of the fifteen cases has insufficient data to reach any conclusion about cleric pathways to radicalization, so the real denominator for estimating the proportion of cases following each mechanism is fourteen.

I find evidence of possibly blocked ambition in two to four of the randomly selected jihadist cases, or between 14 and 28 percent. In most of these cases, it appears that clerics had an insider career, were removed from the academy for political reasons, and then were drawn to jihadist ideas. This evidence is unfortunately highly circumstantial – clerics are unlikely to directly say that their expulsion from academia pushed them toward jihadism.

Because the sample size is small, the uncertainty around these estimates is large. For example, if I consider only the two most clear-cut cases of blocked ambition, when I construct a 95 percent confidence interval around this proportion, I find that it ranges from 2 percent to 40 percent. Similarly, I find that eight of the thirteen clerics are fairly clear cases of jihadists-turned-clerics. A 95 percent confidence interval for this proportion ranges from 28 percent to 82 percent. These confidence intervals are valid because of the random sampling; the problem is that they are rather wide. Still, the results are informative for giving a sense of how frequent different pathways to jihadism might be in the population of jihadist clerics.

One likely case of blocked ambition is that of Nasr al-Fahd, whose turn to jihadism is documented in his own biography as well as in Hegghammer (2010a). Al-Fahd had been producing politically edgy writings for a few years and it is possible that he already had some jihadist leanings before he left the academy. However, he was also welcomed into Saudi academia with prestigious appointments because of his remarkable talent. His undoing was a poem he wrote that insulted the wife of a prince in the royal family. As a result, he was fired from his academic position and put in prison for a remarkably long amount of time – approximately four years.

Hegghammer (2010a) notes that because al-Fahd was imprisoned at about the same time as the leaders of the Sahwa Islamist movement, he received a relatively harsh sentence but because the charges against him were not Sahwa related, he did not experience any of the prestige among the Islamist community that came with being imprisoned. He appears to have become bitter in prison and clashed with the leaders of the Sahwa movement when they were beginning to soften their hardline stances and be reintegrated into the insider cleric institutions. In contrast, al-Fahd was released with no insider career option left and a chip on his shoulder about the moderating Islamists he had fought

---

[14] I archived additional case study materials at http://dx.doi.org/10.7910/DVN/PG4A7K.

with in prison. These factors appear to have pushed him completely over to jihadist ideology.

Was al-Fahd secretly jihadist before losing his academic position? To be confident that this was not the case, I examine his early writings, which are listed in his biography. His first book is *Selections of Sheikh of Islam Ibn Taymiyya and His Determinations on Grammar (ikhtarat shaykh al-islam ibn taymiyya wa taqriratuh fi al-nahu wal-sarf)*, printed in Mecca in 2003 (al-Fahd 2003). When I apply the jihad score model to this book, I get a score of -.068, which places it on the very low end of the scale, quite far away from jihadism. Only later does he turn to titles such as "Clarifying the Apostasy of Those Who Aid the Americans" and "The Ruling on the Use of Weapons of Mass Destruction," for which he is known among jihadist circles.

None of the cases of blocked ambition in the random jihadist case sample appear to be instances where would-be clerics radicalized after being turned away from an insider career because they lacked the connections from graduate school. Instead, it seems that overly harsh repression of modest political dissent among the Islamic professoriate produced an outsized number of today's jihadist clerics. Perhaps if the Saudi government had not imprisoned al-Fahd, but instead insisted that he remain enmeshed in the constraints of insider Islamic academia, he would not have become the jihadist he is today.

Eight out of thirteen clerics in the jihadist case study sample are jihadists-turned-clerics – individuals who became jihadists before the beginning of their clerical careers. One typical example of a true believer is Abu Muhammad al-Maqdisi, whose path to jihadism is well documented by himself[15] and in the secondary literature (Wagemakers 2012). Al-Maqdisi's path to jihadism starts with his apparently random contact with a preacher at his local mosque who happened to be with the Muslim Brotherhood. Al-Maqdisi was persuaded by the politics of the imam's sermons and soon craved more politically activist preaching. He describes how he tried to find a teacher to satisfy his appetite for increasingly jihadist ideology (such as Qutb) while remaining intellectually rigorous within the Salafi method. Eventually, he ended up in Saudi Arabia and was (ironically) permitted by Abd al-Aziz Bin Baz to stay and study in the kingdom for some time. There he found a set of Salafi sources that have heavily informed his theology ever since. About this time, he produced his jihadist masterwork, *The Religion of Abraham*, which was the culmination of his explorations into Salafi jihadism and became widely distributed in jihadist circles.

Several of the jihadists-turned-clerics began as jihadist fighters, so these might be more accurately termed fighters-turned-clerics. A typical example from the sample is Azzam al-Amriki (Adam Gadahn) who became jihadist while living in the United States A following a sequence of ideological shifts well documented in the lay radicalization literature. After traveling to fight, al-Amriki

---

[15] www.youtube.com/watch?v=mFNPBaQ63dw, accessed February 11, 2017, and archived.

eventually decided to write on religious themes. Usama Bin Laden is not in the fifteen randomly selected case studies, but his pathway to jihadism is fairly well documented and he appears to fit the fighter-turned-cleric pattern as well.

Individually, the amount of information about many of these cases is weak because little is known about the clerics besides what is contained in their rather spotty biographies. In a few cases, such as the case of Abu Muhammad al-Maqdisi, there are secondary sources on which to draw that have unearthed a substantial amount of information. In other cases, I find almost no information at all. Case studies of the early lives of clandestine, violent actors are difficult.

Still, the combined information from the fifteen randomly selected cases gives some sense of the pathways that various individuals have taken to becoming jihadist clerics. The majority of clerics – about 60 percent – are jihadists-turned-clerics whose radicalization stories mirror those of other lay Muslims who have become jihadists. A minority – between about 10 and 30 percent have faced some sort of obvious blocked ambition after deciding to become a cleric that seems linked to their turn to jihadism.

6.4 GAINING CREDIBILITY FROM PREACHING JIHAD

This section turns away from the link between educational networks and cleric ideology and instead tests a different part of my argument: that clerics might benefit from preaching jihadism. I argue that clerics may face incentives to start preaching jihad because it is popular and allows them to differentiate themselves in a crowded religious marketplace of clerics, which in turn helps them garner the support necessary to sustain a career without government funding. This section provides evidence to support these claims.

6.4.1 The Popularity of Jihadist Fatwas

Jihadists routinely criticize the insider clerics as sellouts to power who "come and seek the entrance of the Sultan" (al-Maqdisi 1984, 65). As one jihadist writes, "In an age where the Scholars have abandoned the Mujaahideen and have supported the Tawaagheet,[16] the need for true Islamic Scholars has risen to a high degree. Many of the evil things that our Scholars are doing today are either due to love of this world or lack of knowledge."[17]

But do these kinds of arguments resonate with anyone other than those who are already jihadists? If jihadism endows credibility, then I expect that jihadist writing may be more popular with the types of audiences to which

---

[16] "Tawaagheet" is a transliteration of an Arabic word meaning "tyrants" or "oppressors." In this context, the author is referring to the governments of the Middle East, particularly the Saudi government.

[17] https://lyf4hereafter.wordpress.com/2007/10/26/being-practical-about-partaking-in-the-global -jihaad/, accessed September 9, 2016, and archived. I standardized some transliteration of Arabic words.

jihadists might appeal for support. Obviously, jihadist writing is popular with other jihadists, but is it also popular in broader Salafi circles where jihadists are competing for credibility with insider clerics?

To test whether jihadist ideas enjoy broader popularity among Salafis, I turn to a data source that I have not yet used in this book: daily page views of Arabic-language fatwas on the website islamway.com. This website is a large and popular online source of Salafi writing and contains the writing of a broad range of Salafi clerics, but is not aimed particularly at jihadists and only contains a relatively small amount of jihadist content. The documents I use in my analysis are 23,473 fatwas written by seventy-four authors and subsequently posted to the website. Because of a unique feature of the website that tracks page views to each fatwa, I was able to collect the number of page views that each of these fatwas received on a daily basis from February 19, 2011, to August 9, 2011.

My test is simple. I apply the the jihad score model developed in Chapter 5 to score these fatwas from islamway.com to get an estimate of how much each fatwa expresses jihadist ideology. If jihadism is particularly credible to Salafi audiences, then I expect that fatwas expressing jihadist ideology will be more popular than those that do not.

Applying the jihad score model to the fatwas from islamway.com is straightforward; I process each of the texts in the same way as the cleric writings in Chapter 5 and then obtain an individual score for each document. The fatwas on this website are generally not jihadist. Only 3 percent of the approximately 23,000 documents have jihad scores greater than zero, indicating that they are more like the writing of Salafi jihadists than Salafi non-jihadists. Are the 706 documents with positive jihad scores more popular? To test, I add in data on the average page views per day of each document for the 171 days between February 19, 2011, and August 9, 2011. This time window is artificial. Because the daily page-view data must be collected in real time or else the information disappears forever, I cannot go back further in time than February 2011, when I began harvesting the data using a web-scraping program. The website changed its architecture in August 2011 in ways that complicated the collection of page views after that date. Still, this window offers a reasonably good time period in which to test whether jihadist fatwas are more popular with Salafis. The events of the Arabic Spring in 2011 meant that Salafis were particularly engaged in online discussions about politics and if jihadism makes cleric writings more popular, it should be visible in the data. Collectively, these fatwas were viewed an average of 37,500 times per day during the period of observation, meaning that there were approximately 6.4 million page views of these fatwas during the six months that I collected data.

I estimate two linear regressions with *average page views* of each document as the outcome variable. In the first, I use the continuous document jihad scores as a predictor. In the second, I include only an indicator for whether a given document had a jihad score that was positive, which means that it was in the 3 percent of jihadist-leaning fatwas on islamway.com.

TABLE 6.6. *Jihadist fatwas are popular with Salafis.*

	(1) **Avg. Page Views Per Day**	(2) **Avg. Page Views Per Day**
Document jihad score	2.70*	
	(0.40)	
Jihadist-leaning fatwa		0.42*
		(0.17)
Intercept	1.79*	1.51*
	(0.049)	(0.030)
Observations	23,475	23,475

Note: Regression results from two regression models predicting the average page views of fatwas on islamway.com. Standard errors are in parentheses. * $p < 0.05$.

The results in Table 6.6 show that jihadist fatwas are exceptionally popular, on average. The median fatwa on the website is viewed 0.68 times per day, or about two times every three days. As the jihad score of a fatwa increases, the expected number of page views also increases; a two standard deviation increase in jihad score predicts 0.39 additional page views per day (approximately one additional view every three days), which is a substantial effect that effectively increases the popularity of a given fatwa by about one-third. If I instead consider a binary variable indicating whether a fatwa is jihadist leaning or not, I find an effect of similar magnitude. The average jihadist-leaning fatwa on the website can expect to get 0.42 more page views per day than the average non-jihadist fatwa. Both of these effects are statistically significant, as well as substantively meaningful.

From this analysis, I conclude that there is at least some quantitative evidence to suggest that jihadism does indeed help some clerics gain popularity with a broad base of Salafi Muslims. It is perhaps obvious that jihadist documents would be popular with the audiences of jihad-specific websites, but it is more striking that the visitors to a broadly Salafi website with no strong jihadist orientation find jihadist-leaning fatwas particularly interesting and view them more often than others.

6.4.2 Prison as a Jihadist Credential

Additional evidence about the credibility that jihadists derive from their ideological stances comes from the fact that jihadist clerics attempt to highlight their arrests and incarcerations to potential followers as credentials. First, I demonstrate that, instead of garnering prestigious appointments, jihadi clerics tend to go to prison. It is well known that some prominent jihadi clerics have spent significant time in prison because of their ideology, and a number of clerics remain incarcerated. A large number were detained by Saudi Arabia during the

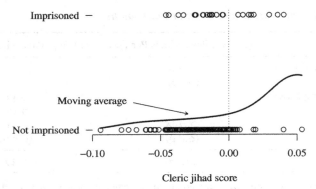

FIGURE 6.2. Cleric jihad scores and imprisonment.

Notes: This figure plots cleric jihad scores on the x-axis and whether each cleric has been imprisoned on the y-axis, with the kernel regression fit between these two variables plotted as a black curve. Higher jihad scores are correlated with a higher probability of imprisonment.

1990s and ultimately released, with some going on to moderate their views and others eventually forming the core of al-Qaeda's current stable of theologians and apologists (Lacroix 2011).

To systematically identify clerics who have spent time in prison, I searched for the words "prison" and "arrest" in cleric bios and coded the variable *prison* as "1" if either of these words appear and "0" otherwise. Twenty-five of the 200 clerics in the web sample have been arrested or spent time in prison. To see if jihadist clerics are more likely to have spent time in jail, I plot the bivariate relationship between jihad score and imprisonment in Figure 6.2, along with the kernel regression estimate of the probability that a cleric will have been imprisoned, given their jihad score. I find that jihad scores are positively correlated with imprisonment and arrest; about 50 percent of the clerics with the highest jihad scores report imprisonment.

This difference in incarceration rates holds when I control for other cleric characteristics. Using a linear probability model, I predict whether a cleric will mention prison time in their biography using cleric jihad scores and the other control variables from the models earlier in this chapter. The model predicts that if a cleric's jihad score increases by two standard deviations, the probability of reporting prison time rises by about 12 percent.[18] The model also predicts that insider clerics are 25 percent less likely to go to prison, holding jihad scores constant.

The costs of incarceration may actually be beneficial to the careers of jihadi clerics. They allow clerics to credibly demonstrate that their rulings are not compromised by allegiance to a political regime but instead represent their

---

[18] I obtain similar findings with logistic regression.

genuine interpretation of Islamic doctrine. This is reflected in the way that jihadi clerics discuss their arrests and incarcerations as credentials. The biographies of jihadi clerics repeatedly stress instances where a cleric's unwillingness to make ideological compromises led to punishment by regime authorities. This credible demonstration of independence may further these clerics' careers by helping them appeal to lay Muslims who prefer independent clerics. For example, the biography of Rafa'i Surur lionizes him for his willingness to go to prison for his jihadi beliefs. "The sheikh was included in the defendants of the case [number; 462, of 1981, Supreme State Security], known by the name 'Case of the Organization of jihad.' He was an example of the Noble Lion and the Patient Sheikh, that does not bend to the tyrants and bows only to God."[19]

Anecdotally, lay jihadists are impressed by the prison "credentials" of clerics. For example, an Islamic State supporter blogging as "Ansaar1" writes of the jihadist cleric Nasr al-Fahd, "The Shaykh is a great scholar jailed in Saudi for speaking the truth," and a video on YouTube decrying his conditions in prison gives the same impression.[20]

I saw evidence of support for imprisoned jihadist clerics while attending Salafi demonstrations in downtown Cairo on April 26, 2012, following the banning of the Salafist presidential candidate. Although the protest was aimed at persuading the military government to step aside and allow the candidates to run freely, I spotted a sign supporting the release of jihadi cleric Umar Abd al-Rahman, who is serving a life sentence in the United States for his role in the 1993 World Trade Center bombing.[21] At the same time, I was having a discussion with a group of approximately fifteen to twenty protesters who assured me that their movement was peaceful and did not support violent tactics to achieve political aims.[22] This apparent contradiction highlights the possibility that Abd al-Rahman's advocacy of militant jihad is primarily viewed as evidence that he is willing to speak truth to power. This buys him support among Salafis in Cairo, even those who are not particularly interested in the jihadi cause that Abd al-Rahman represents.

On the other hand, some clerics renounced their jihadi ideology after being imprisoned. Most notably, three jihadi members of the "awakening" movement – A'id al-Qarni, Safar al-Hawali, and Salman al-Awda – renounced jihadi ideology after spending significant time in Saudi jails during the 1990s. Unlike other clerics who have retained their jihadi orientation, these three clerics have little incentive to play up their incarceration. Rather than being a symbol of theological independence, the prison time of these "reformed" clerics is a reminder that they ultimately gave up jihadi ideology to appease

---

19 www.tawhed.ws/a?a=2ssiuqqb (link now broken), accessed December 30, 2011, and archived.
20 ansaaar1.wordpress.com/2015/08/25/shaykh-nasir-al-fahd-makes-bayah-to-the-islamic
    -state-khilafah, accessed February 11, 2017, and archived; www.youtube.com/watch?v=
    I6zZ5-uJFmY, accessed February 11, 2017, and archived.
21 I've archived this photograph at http://dx.doi.org/10.7910/DVN/PG4A7K.
22 From my 2012 field notes, pp. 29–30, archived at http://dx.doi.org/10.7910/DVN/PG4A7K.

political elites rather than being a symbol of theological independence. I find evidence of this: the biographies of the three clerics do mention their arrests and imprisonment, but often obliquely. Salman al-Awda mentions his prison time in a paragraph at the end of his biography in vague terms that elide his former involvement with jihadism:

The Sheikh was imprisoned for five years, from the year 1415 AH to the end of 1420 AH, due to some lessons and stances. He has been released with his fellow preachers, and resumed his activities in his home, including lessons in the interpretation and ethics and education reform after sunset prayers on Wednesday, Thursday and Friday.[23]

Safar al-Hawali is even more terse, simply mentioning under the heading "Important Events" that he was arrested from 1994 to 1999.[24]

The three "reformed" clerics are in the Salafi oversample, so I can compare their biographies quantitatively to those of other jihadists. Most jihadi clerics who have been to jail mention this fact an average of eight times in their biographies (and as many as twenty-five times), but the three "reformed" clerics mention their prison time an average of only two times. This suggests that clerics who are widely known to be coopted by the state no longer try to use jihadi ideology or the resulting prison time as signals of theological independence.

6.5 SUMMARY

This chapter analyzes data about the lives of Muslim clerics to test competing arguments about why some clerics turn to violent jihadism. My first series of tests was quantitative. I analyzed a sample of Muslim clerics to see whether indicators of possible blocked ambitions – not listing many connections to teachers and not having an insider career – correlate with expressions of jihadist ideology. I find that they do, both in bivariate statistical analysis and multivariate analysis with control variables that account for a number of alternative explanations.

The statistical approach I use was not able to fully distinguish jihadists-turned-clerics from clerics who experienced blocked ambition and radicalized as a result, so I then turned to a series of qualitative examinations of critical periods in the lives of fifteen jihadist clerics. I randomly selected these clerics from the larger set of jihadists, so the proportions of clerics who are jihadists-turned-clerics or who radicalize because of blocked ambition provide an unbiased estimate of the overall prevalence of these two pathways to jihadism in the population of jihadist preachers. I find that approximately 25 percent of jihadist clerics are fairly clear cases of blocked ambition, while about 60 percent appear to have radicalized prior to pursuing a clerical career.

---

[23] http://ar.islamway.com/scholar/1, accessed December 31, 2011, and archived.
[24] http://ar-ar.facebook.com/Dr.safarAlhawali, accessed December 31, 2011, and archived.

The remainder either follow a unique path or are difficult to evaluate because of data constraints. Overall, this suggests that both of the pathways to jihadism I discuss in Chapter 3 are operative, and that together they account for the vast majority of jihadist clerics.

Finally, I turn to evidence on a different question: are there particular incentives for clerics to turn to jihadism? First, I use a unique data set of daily page views on a major Salafi fatwa bank website to show that fatwas that are more jihadist are more popular. Because outsider clerics may rely on popular support for funding, this suggests that there is at least some "jihad" premium that clerics can enjoy if they decide to preach violence.

I then provide some data on how jihadist clerics deploy their stints in prison as credentials. Obviously, spending time in jail is not ideal for clerics, but jihadists make the best of it by using this to convince their followers that they are willing to make substantial sacrifices to speak truth to power. Both qualitative and quantitative evidence suggest that jihadist clerics play up their time in prison in their CVs, unless they have turned away from jihadist preaching, in which case they downplay their prison time.

Pulling back from the specific findings, it is worth reflecting on the benefits and challenges of the statistical analysis of cleric biographies and writings that I have introduced here. My approach is radically different from the approaches of other scholars who have examined the politics of Islamic authority in the Middle East, and there are trade-offs involved in this type of quantitative exercise.

The biggest loss, in my mind, is the nuance and texture that I get from works like that of Zeghal (1996) and Al-Rasheed (2007), which are based entirely on ethnography and related qualitative methods and contain a wealth of information about the histories of specific individuals and institutions. By comparison, the case studies that I include here are much briefer sketches. In some sense, this is because they are designed for the specific purpose of estimating the prevalence of different pathways to becoming a jihadist cleric, and I find that this exercise is not actually very compatible with case studies that provide rich texture. In order to obtain more precise estimates, I selected fifteen cases, a much larger number than I could really dig into with the detail that scholars like Wagemakers (2012) have on just one individual. Also, the random selection of cases meant that not all of them had adequate data for such a detailed analysis.

However, I find that the benefits of my statistical analysis are worth this trade-off in the texture of the qualitative cases. To my knowledge, there has never been an analysis of a sample of clerics for which the findings were applicable to any larger group. Because of my sampling procedures, my findings are applicable to about 1,800 of the most prominent Muslim clerics on the Internet – the movers and shakers of online Islam. The summary statistics about this sample in Chapter 4, the jihad scores estimated in Chapter 5, and the correlations from this chapter all provide new insight about the characteristics and choices of this set of influential religious leaders.

The quantitative analysis is not without its challenges. Measuring data from cleric biographies is frustrating because clerics leave things out without explaining why. Do clerics fail to list teachers in an otherwise detailed biography because they don't have any? Because they are embarrassed to list them? Or because they simply didn't feel like going to the trouble? These questions are hard to answer conclusively and the findings are thus tentative. Still, I believe that the findings significantly increase our understanding of the most likely pathways that lead individuals to become jihadist clerics, and that the analysis represents the current frontier of what can be known given the types of research on jihadism that are feasible and ethical.

My hope is that by presenting these results, and making the data set publicly available, other scholars will be able to make the existing data more accurate, expand it to include other clerics, and extend the findings that I have presented here. I also expect that these data can be used by scholars in a number of fields – Middle East studies, religious studies, and Islamic legal studies, to name a few – that are not currently attuned to statistical approaches or the benefits of representative, transparent sampling procedures. I am confident that in the hands of scholars in these fields, the data and style of analysis that I have presented here will be used to answer important questions that I have not yet even imagined.

7

Conclusion

> Imagine if Shaykh Usama bin Laden (hafidhullah[1]) lived in the
> Arabian Peninsula, received a fixed salary from the Taaghoot,[2] and
> told men to abandon the Jihad and its leadership?[3]

What if Usama Bin Laden had settled down in Saudi Arabia and taken a position as a state-salaried Saudi imam? This question comes from an English-language document that circulated widely on jihadist forums in 2007, urging jihadist readers to consider two alternative histories. The first is the world in which we live, in which militant jihadists such as Bin Laden mounted increasingly lethal attacks on the United States in an attempt to provoke its ire, culminating in the catastrophically violent and destructive attack by al-Qaeda on the World Trade Center in New York City on September 11, 2001. The alternative is a world in which Usama Bin Laden instead cast his lot with the Saudi regime – denoted by the author using the Arabic word for tyrant (*taaghoot*, plural *tawaagheet*) – and joined the cadre of academically oriented, state-funded clerics who urge lay Muslims to avoid global jihadism. This study has examined how modern Muslim clerics navigate the choice between these two paths.

For some jihadist clerics, such as Bin Laden, it isn't obvious what events or actions could have prevented him from embarking on the course that would eventually lead him to create the most widely recognized terrorist franchise of our time (Mendelsohn 2016). Though it is interesting to imagine this alternative outcome, and it appears to deeply move the aforesaid jihadist

---

[1] "Hafidhullah" is a transliteration of an Arabic phrase meaning "may God preserve him."
[2] "Taaghoot" is the singular of "tawaagheet," meaning a "tyrant" or "oppressor."
[3] English-language message board post available at https://lyf4hereafter.wordpress.com/2007/10/26/being-practical-about-partaking-in-the-global-jihaad, accessed September 9, 2016, and archived.

writer, it is difficult to learn from this study what might have turned Bin Laden away from jihad.

Imagine instead a world in which Nasr al-Fahd had kept his academic post and never gone to prison as retribution for having embarrassed a Saudi royal. Would he have ever lent his scholarly expertise to al-Qaeda? Would he have penned a treatise in which he justified the acquisition of weapons of mass destruction by jihadists for use against governments and civilians? It seems more likely that he would have continued with his scholarship in the tradition of his first book, a dense tome on the thinking of a medieval scholar – hardly the stuff of revolution.

Or imagine a world in which Anwar al-Awlaki had not feared that his career as a respected moderate imam in Virginia was about to end, abruptly and with great shame, when whichever agency of the US government that was tracking his movements revealed that he was seeing prostitutes. Would he have nevertheless left his home, traveled to Yemen, and reemerged as a leader of al-Qaeda in the Arabian Peninsula? Would he have directly inspired and mentored individuals who have collectively attempted more than a dozen attacks on US soil? Would his words, immortalized now in the jihadist magazine *Inspire* and on various Internet videos, have urged death and destruction to American citizens? Would he have died in a drone strike?

For Nasr al-Fahd, Anwar al-Awlaki, and other clerics who radicalized after having their ambitions blocked, it is not only possible to imagine a world in which their life paths might have been different. It is also possible to imagine what precisely would have needed to change to prevent their radicalization. These individuals have been crucial to the development of the global jihadist movement, traced in the introductory chapter. If they had not decided to lend their voices to preaching violence, would the jihadist movement be what it is today?

7.1   THE ARGUMENT AND THE EVIDENCE

Why do some Sunni Muslim clerics decide to preach an ideology of militant jihadism? This book explores two main pathways that individuals take to eventually become jihadist clerics. On the one hand, jihadists-turned-clerics are individuals who convert to the ideas of violent jihadism and subsequently decide to become clerics. These individuals become jihadists for the same reasons that any other lay Muslim might find affinity with jihadism. The broad consensus within the scholarship on this phenomenon is that certain sociological factors put individuals at risk of radicalizing. In general, my theory and evidence about these individuals agrees that they are young men, often facing challenges or loneliness, who fall under the sway of a radical teacher, perhaps in the company of friends, and ultimately come to believe in the jihadist cause. The difference for the individuals in my study is that, unlike those who go on to become jihadist fighters, these people become clerics as a way to promote their views after they are convinced of the rightness of a jihadist course. My conclusion from examining jihadists-turned-clerics is that the causes of jihadism among clerics are often the same as the causes of jihadism among lay Muslims.

I also bring to light a less widely recognized path to radicalization for individuals who become clerics first and jihadists second: blocked ambition. The role of blocked academic ambitions in pushing some clerics toward jihadism has been underappreciated. I argue that, in the context of the academic culture of modern Sunni clericism, blocked ambition – the inability of individuals to achieve their deeply held career goals – can make clerics more likely to become jihadist. The academic training for Sunni Muslim clerics helps to create and reinforce an academic culture that fosters their ambitions to achieve a career path within the academic and religious institutions of the states in the Middle East. When would-be clerics maintain their ambitions to seek such a career, they are unlikely to become jihadists because doing so would jeopardize their ambitions. However, if their ambitions are blocked – through poor luck, personal failings, or political meddling – then would-be clerics are at risk of turning to jihadism.

This book has tried to clearly explain the reasons for this study as well as the analysis that led me to these insights. In the introduction, I summarize the rise of global jihadism and argue that understanding the choices of individual religious elites within the jihadist movement was an important part of explaining the rise of the movement as a whole. I then discuss why I chose to gather and analyze evidence through a combination of qualitative and quantitative methods and positivist and interpretive approaches. I also briefly consider the moral and scientific justifications for working on the fraught topic of jihadism.

Chapter 2 lays the groundwork for the rest of the study by introducing my understanding of who Muslim clerics are, who counts as a cleric (a controversial topic), and what it means to be a cleric. I draw on primary sources, my own observations as an ethnographic observer at al-Azhar University, and existing scholarship about Muslim clerics to describe how clerics are trained and the types of writing they produce. The goal of these descriptions is to help the reader identify with the challenges, pressures, feelings, and ambitions that clerics might face.

Chapter 3 lays out my main argument in detail, summarized in the paragraphs at the beginning of this section. The theory that I develop in this chapter is informed directly by data, notably my ethnographic observations of the academic culture and educational institutions of the al-Azhar mosque in Cairo. It was here that I learned to see clerics as academics and gained an appreciation for their academic ambitions and the means through which those ambitions might be blocked.

The remainder of the book, comprising Chapters 4, 5, and 6, builds up a body of empirical evidence in favor of the theoretical propositions. I look for evidence that blocked academic ambitions can turn clerics to violent jihad in a variety of places and using a variety of approaches. In Chapter 4, I turn to the Internet to collect, for the first time, a census of all Arabic-speaking Sunni Muslim clerics online. Using detailed data from a representative sample drawn from my census, I show that the academic culture of Sunni clericism is not confined to al-Azhar where I observed it personally, but is in fact a general feature of modern Sunni Islam. This representative sample then provides a new data source in which to test arguments about why some Muslim clerics become jihadists. The sampling procedures that produced the data are transparent and result in a sample that is representative of a large body of clerics, meaning that my conclusions have broader relevance for the world of Internet clerics as a whole.

Identifying which clerics in my study are jihadists is not an easy task, so in Chapter 5, I consider a number of alternative ways to detect jihadist clerics and ultimately pursue a strategy relying on text analysis of each cleric's collected writings.

In Chapter 6, I combine the biographical data collected in Chapter 4 with the cleric jihadism scores created in Chapter 5 to show that there is a correlation between circumstantial indicators of blocked ambition – weak teacher networks and outsider career paths – and the adoption of jihadist ideology by clerics. I endeavor to rule out a number of alternative arguments about the causes of cleric radicalization by controlling for various factors through statistical means. However, the quantitative results have clear limitations, so I complement the statistical analysis with qualitative evidence from a relatively large number of case studies of jihadist clerics, selected at random from the jihadist clerics in the sample. Information about jihadists is very limited, but within the limits of the available evidence, I find that a majority of jihadist clerics are probably jihadists-turned-clerics. Among clerics-turned-jihadists, I estimate that blocked ambition was probably operative in their path to jihadism for roughly 30 percent.

Chapter 6 also explores whether clerics have an economic incentive to turn to jihadism because it is particularly popular with lay Salafis who might help financially support a clerical career outside of the state-run system of religious and educational institutions. I examine the popularity of clerics' writings on a popular Salafi website and find that jihadist-leaning fatwas are more popular than others.

7.2 WHAT NEXT?

While this study offers and tests a new theory to explain cleric radicalization, it does not provide all the answers to the question of why some Muslim clerics turn to violent jihad. My hope is that the theory, methods, and evidence presented here will inform future work that will deepen our understanding of the jihad movement specifically and the phenomenon of terrorism generally.

One avenue for future research is to build on the theory of blocked ambition to understand when and why it is active. After all, many people face blocked ambitions. Why do some clerics respond to blocked ambition by turning to jihadist ideology while others do not? What factors interact with blocked ambitions to turn previously nonviolent clerics toward violence? While blocked ambition increases the risk that a cleric will become jihadist, there are still many other options they might pursue. I hope that my provocation in this book will spark further work to learn more about what leads clerics to preach violence.

For scholars who continue the study of the radicalization of jihadist clerics, my research offers some guidance as to which avenues will prove difficult and which may be more fruitful. Much of the existing literature focuses on explaining why the jihadist social movement came into being at a particular time and why it evolved as it did (Gerges 2005; Hegghammer 2010a,b). This question is important but very hard to answer because it is difficult to make causal inferences about changes in trends over time when many possible causes are correlated with the rise of modern jihadism and with each other. It will be difficult for future researchers to answer this question more definitively than existing work.

I sidestep the task of explaining the rise of jihadism as a social movement and instead ask about the determinants of individual radicalization among religious elites in the jihadist movement. Research on individual choices has been insightful in the literature on lay Muslim radicalization (see, for example, Drevon 2016), and I expect that further research on clerics will yield important insights as well. Although I faced serious challenges to making credible causal inferences in this study, I expect that the prospects for future research on the question of individual cleric radicalization are promising simply because there is adequate variation and a large enough number of cases for solid inference. I hope that researchers will build upon the analysis here by critiquing it, offering new explanations, and testing them against the data I provide, or perhaps even with improved designs that move more convincingly from correlation to causation.

One possible research design that deserves consideration is a prospective study. My study is retrospective, meaning that I look only at individuals who eventually decide to become clerics. However, a prospective study in this area would be insightful, if it could be designed in a way that made the results informative. Imagine a research project that tracked a cohort of al-Azhar students over time to evaluate whether those who faced challenges on the cleric job market were more likely to become disaffected, hold less conventional ideas, and perhaps endorse jihadism. However, in addition to the obvious logistical challenges of time and access involved in such a project, this study might be inconclusive if not designed carefully because individuals who eventually become full-blown jihadist preachers are relatively rare and the odds that one or more would come out of the cohort under study are slim. This does not mean that researchers shouldn't pursue prospective studies on cleric radicalization, but it does mean that they should consider the challenges carefully.

My work also suggests possible avenues of study for psychological research on terrorism, a field that has faced a number of methodological challenges as described by Crenshaw (2000). Rather than looking for a "terrorist personality," my research suggests that scholars should do more to explore the possibly unexpected effects of apparently ordinary psychological phenomena such as disappointment and resentment. These powerful emotions are clearly on display in the rhetoric of jihadist clerics. Relative deprivation theories of terrorism and political violence are less fashionable today than when they were proposed by Gurr (1970) and others, but I agree with some recent studies, including Canetti et al. (2010) and Gambetta and Hertog (2016), that a second, closer look is now justified by the mounting evidence that blocked ambition seems linked to political violence.

Scholars of terrorism who are not focused on Muslim clerics specifically should still take note of my findings, as blocked ambition may be a factor that influences the turn to political violence for individuals with a variety of backgrounds and careers, not only Muslim religious authorities. This suggests that blocked ambition should be given more attention as a factor in jihadist radicalization of lay Muslims as well. In the models of radicalization proposed by Sageman (2004) and Wiktorowicz (2005b), lay Muslims become open to new ideas about proper faith and worship for a variety of reasons, but one of these reasons is blocked ambition. They cite examples such as losing a job or failing to find employment as circumstances that might precipitate "cognitive opening" that ultimately leads individuals to adopt jihadist ideas. These are likely cases of blocked ambition. As long as the goals of these individuals remained attainable, they did not cast about for violent ideologies to follow. Once it became clear that their ambitions were no longer achievable, they then sought out an ideology or group membership to give new meaning and purpose to their lives.

One clear example of blocked ambition in the radicalization of lay Muslims is the path of Tamerlan Tsarnaev from talented boxer to perpetrator of the 2013 Boston Marathon bombings (Speckhard 2013; Sontag, Herszenhorn, and Kovaleski 2013). In 2010, Tsarnaev faced a crushing blow to his aspirations. According to reporting by *The New York Times*, "After capturing his second consecutive title as the Golden Gloves heavyweight champion of New England in 2010, Tamerlan Anzorovich Tsarnaev, 23, was barred from the national Tournament of Champions because he was not a United States citizen" (Sontag, Herszenhorn, and Kovaleski 2013).[4] Tsarnaev took the news hard: "His aspirations frustrated, he dropped out of boxing competition entirely, and his life veered in a completely different direction." Just three years later, he enlisted his younger brother to detonate bombs built out of pressure cookers, based on instructions in the English-language jihadist magazine *Inspire*, at the finish line of the Boston Marathon. The issue of *Inspire* that the Tsarnaev brothers must have read includes an article by Anwar al-Awlaki that concludes: "The West

---

4   www.nytimes.com/2013/04/28/us/shot-at-boxing-title-denied-tamerlan-tsarnaev-reeled.html, accessed February 21, 2017, and archived.

will eventually turn against its Muslim citizens. Hence, my advice to you is this: you have two choices: either *hijra* or jihād. You either leave or you fight" (al-Awlaki 2010, 58).[5] This suggests that the Boston Marathon bombings were the result of two instances of blocked ambition: the blocked clerical ambitions of al-Awlaki, which led him to preach violent jihad, and the blocked boxing ambitions of Tsarnaev, which made him susceptible to the preaching. It is possible that if either of these individuals had not faced blocked ambition, the attack might not have happened.

7.3 WHAT CAN BE DONE?

What, if anything, can policy-makers in Arab or Western countries do to limit the adoption of jihadi ideology? What can be done to prevent the transformation of individuals into jihadist clerics in the future?

My findings suggest that supporting more clerics in their academic ambitions could prevent some clerics from turning to jihadism when their careers otherwise would have been blocked by, say, their inability to find an academic job. This prescription seems to run counter to current conventional political wisdom; policy-makers and counterterrorism practitioners in the West often seem concerned about the possibly radicalizing effects of Islamic education (Stern 2000; Malik et al. 2007). In 2016, Hillary Clinton was quoted decrying Saudi Arabia's support for "radical schools and mosques around the world that have set too many young people on a path towards extremism."[6] An article by Moeller examining media reporting on the "war on terror" found that commentators from a wide range of political perspectives, including Thomas Friedman and Newt Gingrich, uniformly viewed Islamic education as a radicalizing force.[7] The link between the *madrassa* and terrorism seems firmly entrenched in the minds of policy-makers.[8]

---

[5] Text available at https://archive.org/stream/inspr1to1o/Inspire_1_djvu.txt, accessed February 21, 2017, and archived.

[6] www.nytimes.com/2016/08/26/world/middleeast/saudi-arabia-islam.html, accessed February 21, 2017, and archived.

[7] http://yaleglobal.yale.edu/content/jumping-us-bandwagon-war-terror, accessed February 21, 2017, and archived.

[8] Scholars have also explored the link between Islamic education and radicalization, but the conclusions are circumspect (e.g., Delavande and Zafar 2015; Burde, Middleton, and Wahl 2015). For example, Palmer and Palmer (2008, 202) feel it necessary to address the question in their comprehensive look at Islamism and do posit a link, but they also question whether the substantive impact of Islamic educational institutions on the production of future jihadists is large enough to warrant the blowback that American meddling in Islamic education would cause. Burde (2014) shows that some of the radicalizing effects of religious schooling in Afghanistan were actually the result of aid programs by the United States, such as the USAID-funded (1986–1992) "Alphabet of Jihad Literacy" teaching materials that tried to indoctrinate jihadist anticommunist sentiment while teaching letters.

In contrast, my research questions whether Islamic education causes radicalization, at least for a certain set of schools and students. Although there may be Islamic schools that radicalize students, there is not substantial evidence in my data that school attendance at any level led some clerics to be more radical than their unschooled counterparts. Instead, I find that the *failures* of graduate education are actually highly predictive of future jihadi ideologues. Students who have less access to prominent graduate mentors are the most at risk of turning toward violent extremism, not those with the most access. Rather than adopting the mantra that all Islamic schooling is radicalizing, policy-makers should consider the possibility that more education and improved career prospects might forestall radicalization, even if that education and career are inside of a conservative Islamist environment.

The idea that limited career opportunities may contribute to radicalization aligns with recent work on "overeducation" in the Middle East, which argues that people in the region are gaining high levels of education at a rate exceeding the ability of the various local economies to provide adequate jobs (Haddad and Habibi 2016; Voßemer and Schuck 2016). Gambetta and Hertog (2016) have argued that overeducation helped funnel engineers into the ranks of jihadism by setting their professional expectations high and then dashing them when the struggling economies of the Muslim world could not support consistently high wages for engineers. This book makes a similar argument that graduates of the faculties of Islamic law in the Middle East can be frustrated when they cannot gain employment as insider clerics. These findings suggest that policy-makers should worry less about the content of education in the Middle East and more about the economics of education if they wish to curb pressures encouraging radicalization in the region.

Specifically, my research suggests that programs focused on employment for clerics might be part of the solution to the problem of cleric radicalization. Perhaps simply giving unemployed clerics jobs in religious institutions might reduce their chances of supporting political violence (Berman et al. 2011; Blattman and Annan 2016). And at an earlier stage, mentoring programs that connect students in Islamic law programs in Egypt, Saudi Arabia, and elsewhere to established scholars might also be effective. My results suggest that both insider careers and better connections with teachers help reduce the risk that any individual cleric will decide to preach jihadism.

However, my findings should be taken as the beginning of empirical work on blocked ambition and radicalization, not the definitive word, and these sorts of policies should be tested and evaluated before they are implemented on a large scale. The evidence I can currently provide does not definitively show that a jobs program or mentoring program would necessarily lead to better outcomes, but my findings do suggest that such programs could alleviate a source of jihadism. Interventions of this type are subject to contextual factors and deserve rigorous evaluation before they can be declared successful, but the evidence thus far suggests that such policies deserve more attention from the policy community than they have thus far received.

Another lesson for policy-makers from my research is that when the state intervenes in the academic and religious lives of clerics, it is often overly harsh in ways that can exacerbate the problems of political violence that may have motivated the state to intervene in the first place. Especially in Saudi Arabia, reactions to politically active scholars in the religious and education spheres have been severe. According to reporting by Shane,

Since 2003, when Qaeda attacks in the kingdom awoke the monarchy to the danger it faced from militancy, Saudi Arabia has acted more aggressively to curtail preachers who call for violence, cut off terrorist financing and cooperate with Western intelligence to foil terrorist plots. From 2004 to 2012, 3,500 imams were fired for refusing to renounce extremist views, and another 20,000 went through retraining, according to the Ministry of Islamic Affairs – though the United States Commission on International Religious Freedom expressed skepticism that the training was really "instilling tolerance."[9]

My research suggests that the preferred counterradicalization policy of Arab regimes – arrest and imprisonment, as described by Shane – may be a double-edged sword. Incarcerating jihadi clerics does raise the costs of a career based on jihadi ideology, but it also increases the signaling value of adopting jihadi ideology. Prison may not be an effective deterrent if the most dedicated jihadi clerics are willing to bear the cost of increased repression because it makes them more credible in the eyes of their followers. Even more troubling, the results of my case studies suggest that several prominent jihadist clerics turned to jihadism after their imprisonment for political activism foreclosed any possibility of returning to their prior academic careers. These clerics were not full-blown jihadists when they entered prison and it is likely that, had they remained in the disciplining structures of academia, some of them would not have produced the jihadist material for which they are now known. A punitive strategy on the part of the state, such as the one enacted by Saudi Arabia, is likely to swell the ranks of clerics whose deeply held ambitions are suddenly snatched away. According to my findings, this, in turn, will lead a subset of them to preach jihadism instead of more peaceful philosophies.

Coopting clerics, on the other hand, may be more successful. Doing so in the late stages of cleric ideology development is difficult because clerics who successfully resist "selling out" through cooptation will send the same costly signal about their theological independence as clerics who risk imprisonment. Rather, successful cooptation starts early, by providing more clerics with access to better educational networks and, ultimately, the possibility for fulfilling and secure career prospects.

9 www.nytimes.com/2016/08/26/world/middleeast/saudi-arabia-islam.html, accessed February 21, 2017, and archived.

More broadly, changes in the political institutions of Egypt and other Muslim-majority states after the "Arab Spring" of 2011 could have far-reaching consequences for reducing the future adoption and expression of jihadi ideology. This was not obvious right away; at first, events in Egypt between February 2011 and June 2012 seemed to confirm Western fears that political opening would lead to the rise of militant Islamists throughout the Middle East. For example, Muhammad Mursi, the now-deposed Islamist president of Egypt, publicly declared on June 29, 2012, that he would seek the release of the jihadi cleric Umar Abd al-Rahman, the mastermind of the first World Trade Center bombing, from prison.[10] In the short term, it appeared that democratic opening was making militant Islamist ideologies more mainstream, rather than sidelining them. This was no small part of the reason for the 2013 coup that overthrew Mursi and returned Egypt to official authoritarianism.

However, this opening actually might have eventually undermined the sources of legitimacy upon which jihadi clerics had relied. Jihadist clerics survive in part because of the cooptation of the mainstream clerical elite by the governments of the Middle East. This cooptation fuels jihadi ideology by provoking fears among certain types of lay Muslims that clerics who work for the regime cannot be trusted, making them more likely to listen to and support nonstate clerics, such as jihadis. The 2011 political opening in Egypt temporarily undermined the control of the central government over the religious establishment. For the first time in a half century, the clerics of al-Azhar University contemplated electing their head sheikh rather than accepting a government appointee. Azhari clerics had been more outspoken on political issues in the wake of the January 25, 2011, revolution. As mainstream clerics become more able to speak their minds without fear of reprisal, the credibility value of being a declared jihadi will substantially decrease, draining long-term support among the majority of lay Muslims who do not support militant jihad. This, in turn, might decrease the attractiveness of jihadi ideology as a potential career path for outsider clerics.

Again, the evidence I provide in this study is merely suggestive on this point. I cannot definitively say that, had governments in the Middle East meddled less in the religious sphere, the jihad movement would have developed differently, but that is a possible conclusion from these results and warrants further examination. At least one other recent study has also suggested that heavy-handed state involvement in religious affairs can increase terrorism (Saiya 2016). If governments such as the Saudi monarchy are serious about stopping terrorism within their borders and overseas, then they should be more open to rigorously evaluating and reconsidering long-held policies at the intersection of religion, politics, and public life.

---

[10]   www.foxnews.com/politics/2012/07/03/outrage-builds-as-egypt-presses-for-release-blind-sheik
       -behind-3-wtc-attack, accessed February 21, 2017, and archived.

More generally, when considering how the radicalization of jihadist clerics might be stopped, it is important to realize that preventing every episode of blocked ambition that might lead to future radicalization is impossible. Professional obstacles cannot be entirely removed from the lives of clerics (or boxers, or engineers, or anyone else). Nevertheless, attempting to limit the number of Muslim clerics who feel that their careers have been unjustly sabotaged by government meddling, nepotistic hiring practices, or distortions of the cleric job market seems like a worthy and, to some extent, attainable goal.

7.4 LOOKING FOR BLOCKED AMBITION

What can scholars who do not study jihadism learn from the research in this book? Theoretically, I highlight the concept of blocked ambition, which may have broad applicability in several subfields of political science and beyond, as I describe in this section. The next section turns to what other scholars can learn from the approaches and methods I have used in this study.

In Chapter 3, I describe some of the psychological consequences of blocked ambition, including disappointment and regret, and why those emotions might lead to certain subsequent courses of action. Blocked ambition is not limited to clerics, of course; in fact, it is a near-universal human experience to have an ambition blocked at some point. If blocked ambition is important in the lives of clerics, then it may be an important cause of political action by a wide range of actors. While blocked ambition as a concept has been considered as a possible cause of political violence for a long time (Gurr 1970), I argue that it should be a more widely considered cause of political action across many domains. At times, blocked ambition circulates as a sort of popular psychology explanation for the pathologies of influential political actors. What if Hitler had not been rejected from art school?[11] What if Ted Kaczynski, better known as the "Unabomber," had not been subjected to a series of experiments in which he was told that he was a failure regardless of how well he performed?[12] I believe that these arguments should be moved from the realm of speculation into the mainstream of explanations for extreme social behaviors.

To see how the dynamics of blocked ambition I identify in this study might apply elsewhere, consider the intriguing case of the Taiping Rebellion, started by Hong Xiuquan in 1850s China (Platt 2012). The conflict grew out of the God Worshiping Society, a Christian sect that Hong Xiuquan founded in 1843, and resulted in a decade-long conflict between 10,000 rebels and the ruling Qing dynasty. Intriguingly, Hong Xiuquan appears to have had an early

---

[11] www.telegraph.co.uk/culture/art/art-news/7511134/Hitler-sketches-that-failed-to-secure-his-place-at-art-academy-to-be-auctioned.html, accessed February 21, 2017, and archived.
[12] www.theatlantic.com/magazine/archive/2000/06/harvard-and-the-making-of-the-unabomber/378239, accessed February 21, 2017, and archived.

ambition to attain an official position in the Qing bureaucracy, and he made several attempts to pass the imperial examination that was required to join the "scholar-bureaucrats" that comprised the bureaucracy of the Qing empire. His turn to religion and violence followed shortly after these attempts failed (Yap 1954, 290).

Another example of the radicalizing effects of blocked ambition comes from Menoret's study of why some Saudi youth participate in reckless and occasionally fatal joyriding of stolen cars, which Menoret (2014) identifies as "street revolt." A key to Menoret's insights about the joyriders is the feeling of *tufshan*, a Saudi expression for "the sense of worthlessness that gripped you when you had lived long enough in the capital to have had your efforts and aspirations repeatedly rebuffed" and the condition "when one feels a mismatch between subjective hopes and objective chances" (p. 58). If Menoret is correct that this "awareness of social inadequacy" is "a revolutionary sentiment" that drives youth to joyriding, then the situation is a close parallel to the argument I make that clerics' blocked ambitions can lead them to preach violent, jihadist revolution.

These diverse examples suggest that blocked ambition is universal enough that its consequences for politics deserve more systematic study. Researchers seeking to tease out the psychological mechanisms of blocked ambition will probably have to turn to domains other than jihadism because this research program will require rich data, including perhaps careful experimentation in a lab setting. Getting jihadists into the lab for experimentation is not practical, but if research in other domains can identify the general mechanisms through which blocked ambition operates, this may in turn generate new insights into the radicalization of jihadists as well. Observational data on career advancement and blocked ambition is much easier to collect in other settings (see, for example, Weisman et al. 1976), which may lead to more rapid theory development and testing about when blocked ambition will lead to unexpected, meaningful outcomes.

7.5 NEW WINDOWS, NEW WORLDS

New tools for scientific observation give us new windows through which to examine our world and the possibility of conclusions far outside of anything we had ever before considered. But sometimes, the potential of new scientific tools is hard to recognize at first. The inventors of the telescope, a pair of Dutch eyeglasses makers, never thought to turn the device skyward. It was Galileo who heard of the device, recreated it himself, and used it in his quest to explore the movements of the planets and eventually claim, in agreement with Copernicus, that the earth was not the center of the universe and that the Ptolemaic view of our place in the cosmos was wrong (Drake 1978).

The development of the Internet is causing a revolution in the social sciences, possibly of Copernican proportions (King 2011). In 2010, Eric Schmidt, the

CEO of Google, claimed that humanity was now recording more information every two days than the entire amount of information recorded by all humans from prehistory until the year 2003.[13] Rich new data sources are available on a dizzying array of human behaviors, as the ability of computers to track the flows of information, ideas, and people through physical and virtual spaces becomes ever more sophisticated.

This book is a result of the revolution in data availability about the social world. I have relied so completely on the existence of the Internet, and the fact that Muslim clerics are active on it, that it is not an understatement to say that the project would have been impossible even fifteen years ago, at the turn of the millennium. Having spent a great deal of time thinking about how this wealth of data might be employed to further our understanding of Islam and politics, I can offer some hard-won advice as to how scholars who wish to harness these resources might go about doing so.

To be clear, I am not the first to leverage Internet data sources for the study of Islam and Muslim societies. There have been forays into largescale analysis of the Arabic-language blogosphere (Etling et al. 2010), some exploratory investigation of "online Islam" (Bunt 2003), and efforts to encourage "digital" methods in the study of Islam and the Middle East (Muhanna 2016). Moreover, "big data" approaches to studying Islam predate the Internet; a striking example is Bulliet's (1970) work on the early spread of Islam through a quantitative study of biographical dictionaries. Still, I cannot escape the feeling that this is only the beginning and that the majority of researchers are not aware of how data from the Internet, and new tools for analyzing it, could revolutionize their work.

Perhaps the largest gains to be had for most researchers are in the area of text analysis, which facilitates the analysis and interpretation of large volumes of text. Even if we confine ourselves to Muslim clerics, the subjects of this study, the amount of text they are posting online is accumulating faster than any researcher could read. Moreover, resources are coming online that allow researchers more access to texts of the past than ever before, through such online repositories as "The Complete Library" (shamela.ws), which stores the works of 2,793 Muslim authors as of this writing. To researchers who sift through the materials in the traditional way, this onslaught of text can be overwhelming, but with new tools, the data can provide a virtual observatory for understanding the Islamic world.

In this book, for example, text analysis tools allow me to analyze the works of a large number of Muslim clerics comprehensively. Working with traditional methods would have been almost impossible. I would have needed to identify representative works from each cleric for closer analysis rather than use each cleric's full canon, but even if I had selected only one piece of writing from which to estimate each cleric's ideology, I still would have had to read almost

[13] https://techcrunch.com/2010/08/04/schmidt-data, accessed February 21, 2017, and archived.

300 texts to carry out the statistical analysis in Chapter 6. As my study shows, statistical text analysis can facilitate text-based research on a scale that is simply impossible otherwise.

Obviously, statistical text analysis can miss much of the nuance in a text, so I am not calling for "digital methods" to replace close reading. In fact, my method of detecting jihadists using text in Chapter 5 relies heavily on my own close reading of jihadist materials to understand the texture of jihadist ideology and make sure the model is identifying jihadist ideology accurately. I also rely on the expert reading of the jihadist who compiled "The Jihadist's Bookbag" collection that I use to "train" the statistical model to recognize jihadist writing. Statistical text analysis is not a replacement for close reading, but a complement to it that allows the insights from close reading to scale up. Researchers who decide to apply statistical text analysis in their own research can expect to do the same amount of reading as they would have needed to in the absence of such methods, and perhaps more. The difference is that, at the end of the process, they may be able to make sense of 5 million documents, instead of 5, or even 500.

Researchers who are inspired to see what statistical text analysis methods have to offer should begin by consulting resources such as Grimmer and Stewart (2013) and Lucas et al. (2015), which give an overview of the process and map out what different text analysis methods can do. From there, it is often most helpful to work through examples from published research to understand precisely how the models work and learn the practical aspects of statistical programming. All of the analyses in this book can be replicated with code and explanations that I have placed online; these might provide a starting point for researchers working with similar materials.

For researchers who would like to work with Arabic-language texts, there is an extra layer of complexity involved in using statistical text analysis tools because these tools were developed primarily for English. As part of the research underlying this book, I developed my own set of tools for working with Arabic text that are freely available online. The most notable of these is a statistical tool for processing Arabic text that performs "stemming" (which removes some grammatical constructions from the text) and transliteration (which converts Arabic letters into Roman characters that are compatible with existing text analysis software).[14]

The Internet does not only make more text available to researchers than ever before. In addition, the structure of the Internet means that every item of text exists within a network of relationships to other text. There is exciting new work on Muslim networks (Cooke and Lawrence 2005), but more could be done to understand how these networks are changing as a result of the Internet. I have used some tools for social network analysis in this book, but I have only

---

[14] This tool is available online as the "arabicStemR" package, written for the R statistical computing language, https://cran.r-project.org/web/packages/arabicStemR/index.html.

scratched the surface of what might be possible with the data available on the networks linking clerics to each other, to their followers, to their works and citations, and ultimately to the effects that their preaching brings about in the world. Scholars who are looking for ideas about how the study of networks might enhance their research should read Watts (2004), while those looking for a rigorous introductory treatment might consider Jackson (2008).

In addition to making new texts available and revealing network connections, the Internet also allows researchers to observe how users interact with texts in the digital environment. In Chapter 6, I use the fact that islamway.com records the number of visitors to each document on its website to show that jihadist-leaning fatwas are more popular than non-jihadist fatwas, at least in terms of daily page views. This type of data is not always publicly available because it relies on information provided by website administrators, but where available, information about page views, Facebook "likes," Twitter "retweets," and similar forms of user interaction can reveal new information about how users engage with texts. This could open up vast new areas of research on Islamic thought. Until now, the study of Islamic thought has been primarily confined to the study of intellectual elites because these are the people whose interactions with text can be traced through traditional methods, such as citations. Now, for the first time, it is possible to get fine-grained, real-time data on how Islamic texts are received by their intended audiences.

For researchers interested in the activity of individuals on the Internet, the failure of the Internet to be fully self-archiving presents a serious challenge. For example, the analysis of daily page views on islamway.com is only possible because I wrote a series of computer programs to capture the data each day and then set it up to run without interruption. When the website architecture changed, I had to change the computer programs as well. Any day that the program failed to run was a day of data lost. And to be frank, I began collecting the data without a clear research question in mind. Rather, I had the sense that data was slipping away forever and that it might be worth trying to capture some of it.

Similarly, when I began collecting data from the websites of Muslim clerics, I realized that if I didn't act quickly, some of their websites would go down, removing the information forever. Another example is the case of Abu Muhammad al-Maqdisi's jihadist web library, "The Pulpit of Monotheism and Jihad" (formerly at www.tawhed.ws), which served as a major source of primary source documents for scholarly writing on jihadism until it abruptly disappeared from the web in early 2015. I use an archived copy for access to some of the documents in this book, but many of the footnotes in works such as Hegghammer (2010a) are now obsolete because of the changing nature of the Internet.

My advice for researchers in this area is that if you know of potentially interesting information available online, start collecting it now, even if the end goal is not immediately clear. It is relatively cheap to store data these days, while if the history of the rise of digital Islam is not adequately archived, it will be lost to scholarship forever.

Although these tools open exciting new vistas for scholarship, researchers will want to keep research ethics clearly in mind when deciding how best to use the Internet observatory for studying the politics, culture, and practices of Muslim societies. Scholars can now listen in on conversations that had been private for centuries, such as the process of giving and receiving fatwas. Even the public sphere of Islam has expanded. Sermons that in the past would have been heard by a few hundred worshipers at a mosque can now be viewed remotely across the world. In addition to listening in, researchers can participate in these conversations, often anonymously. Participation is crucial to many forms of research, from ethnographic participant observation to experimental studies. However, the ethics of intervening in a religious training environment should be considered seriously, and many interventions that become possible in the world of digital Islam may be unethical (Nielsen 2015). With the capacity to digitally eavesdrop and intervene on these relatively intimate conversations, researchers should carefully consider how their observations might affect the lives of those they observe.

My invitation for scholars of Islam and the Middle East to employ new methods should not be mistaken for a call that all scholars do work in a particular way, or an endorsement of quantitative methods over qualitative approaches. In this study, I have intentionally combined analysis of "big data" with interpretive ethnographic methods, and I am confident that the research is richer and more insightful as a result. One underappreciated aspect of working with large data sets is that a great deal of interpretation is necessary to make any sense of the data. Perhaps the most obvious example occurs in statistical text analysis with topic models, in which a researcher tries to interpret what the authors under study might have meant when they produced the words that the model has identified as having similar usage patterns. More broadly, the Internet produces data of such scale that without insights into the meaning that other humans intended when they produced the data, quantitative methods alone would make almost no headway. My research implicitly advocates for more collaborations between those who analyze data quantitatively and ethnographically (Ford 2014).

The transformative effect of the Internet is not limited to data availability, of course. The Internet has also had a dramatic and disruptive effect on traditional structures of Islamic authority. It has been called a "crisis of authority in Islam" by Bulliet (2002), and in fact, this may be understating the scope and scale of upheaval in the religious authority that binds together the world's 1.6 billion Muslims. This crisis of authority has already gifted the world with al-Qaeda and the Islamic State, and the crisis seems far from concluded.

In this new world of digitally mediated Islamic authority, powerful institutions such as al-Azhar are struggling to remain relevant with slow, clunky websites, while social-media-savvy clerics can send their thoughts to millions of followers at any moment (in catchy memes of 140 characters or less). The need to understand and analyze the dynamics of Islamic authority in this new, digitally mediated, hyper-connected world is only growing, and so are the size of the data sets available to do so. This study provides one template for how this research could be done, though it is certainly not the only one. In so doing, it opens new and exciting avenues of inquiry in a number of fields, and hopefully new avenues for incremental progress toward achieving a more just, safe world in which the preaching of violence is increasingly rare.

Appendix A

Syllabus of Hamid al-Ali

Detailed Program for the Seeker of Knowledge
By: Hamid Abdullah al-Ali

In the name of Allah, Most Gracious, Most Merciful.
Praise be to Allah, the Cherisher and Sustainer of the worlds and may his peace and blessings be upon our Prophet Muhammad and upon his family and his companions. To continue:

This is a small thesis which can place in the hands of the student of religious knowledge, with blessings from God, a complete curriculum for learning how to seek knowledge of Sharia Studies based on the Salafi school of thought. I have provided this hastily, based on the desires of students from about nine years ago. It found, with God's grace, wide approval from students, and many of them have informed me that they have benefited from it. Then, when the first edition copies ran out, some students urged me to re-publish it with edits, additions, and re-structuring so that the program becomes more clear and easy in organization. So I did as they asked me, while seeking God's aid and relying on him.

And here is the second edition in the hands of the students of Sharia, in its new format with its important additions.

I provided this publication to the student with the purpose that the student may increase his knowledge by studying it and so that he might rise in the levels of Sharia Studies. Perhaps someone else is more knowledgeable than him, I might have not known this or have forgotten this, but I hope that what I have provided for the student can help him achieve his purpose and reach his goals. And this will happen for him if he keeps to righteousness and belief because they are the most important things, the light of this world. If a student loses them, then he will not be blessed in his work and God will only distance him. As the Sheikh of Islam, Ibn Taymiyya, may God have mercy on his soul said "The Muslim Community has immersed itself in every art of the arts of knowledge, he who God has put light into his heart, God has granted him his share of it, and he who God has blinded, his accumulation of books will not give him more than confusion and darkness."

I ask God, in His glorious names, and His great and elevated attributes, that he accept our actions and make them pure only for his gracious face. So that He might write for us good things in His House of Dignity, in the day when no money or children can help, only those who come to God with a clean heart, and may God bless our prophet Muhammad and his family and his companions.

Hamid Abdullah al-Ali
Kuwait, Safar 1422 Hijri

FIRSTLY: GENERAL ADVICE FOR STUDENTS

These are ten pieces of advice that it is incumbent upon the student to follow in his path of seeking knowledge. In making these, I have benefited from the book *Huliyat Talib al-ᶜIlm* (*The Adornments of the Seeker of Knowledge*) by the scholar Bakr Abu Zayd as well as other scholars, with some additions.

1. It is necessary for the student who is on the road to knowledge to be loyal to God. He must have the intention of being near to God and asking Him for the rewards of the afterlife. He must give up false allegiance, the love for display, the desire to overcome colleagues, or asking for worldly things like money or prestige or placement or a confession with which to reach material benefits. All of these things remove the blessings of knowledge. As Bashr Bin al-Harith, may God have mercy upon him, said "I've seen great scholars seek knowledge for the world but they were exposed, and others who sought knowledge and placed it in its appropriate place and acted upon it and those are the ones who survived, God has blessed them. I've seen people who have only heard little of knowledge, act on it and I've seen others who have heard much but God did not let them benefit from it." (*The Adornments of the Followers* 349/8)

2. He should adopt the manners of modesty, and he should be opposed to the arrogant gait, self-admiration, disrespecting the teacher, boasting to people about his criticism of his opponents and colleagues, and arrogance to admit mistakes.

3. He should be of good character, he should not play around, or waste time, or raise his voice with trivial things or laugh too much. He should not gossip about his opponents and colleagues in order to appear better than them.

4. He should act with kindness, and he should be opposed to critical words, stubbornness of opinion, and stubbornness despite being in the wrong when he is dealing with people and judging them.

5. He should take very good care of the Quran and increase his recitation and memorization of it. He should follow the paths of remembrance [of God], prayer, fasting, and non-obligatory prayers because these are amongst the greatest things that can aid a student in his path of seeking knowledge with God's blessings.

6. He should rise through the curriculum so he should memorize a summary of every art if possible and master it with a smart teacher, then he should move on to something higher, and so on. He should avoid preoccupation with long-winded issues and books from different disciplines before he masters the Usul. It is not right in asking for knowledge for the student to hurry to arrive at a highly conflicted issue before the principles and Usul that are contained within summaries, because that divides his attention and decreases from the benefits of seeking knowledge. Like Sufyan al-Thawi, may God grant him mercy said, "If a man rushes, he is harmed with too much knowledge but if he asks and asks, then he arrives." (*The Adornment of the Followers* 081/7).

7. For his mentor Sheikh, he should pick a man who speaks carefully and morally, who has good manners, who is above engaging in suspicious activities, and above petty behavior. He should treat him well by only asking [questions] at the appropriate times, and listening carefully and making sure to be in attendance and to study.

8. He should also pick a good colleague who is careful about seeking knowledge, who is opposed to seeking conflict, to chit chat, preoccupied with what does not concern him and does not confront big issues before mastering knowledge, do not befriend someone of this type for he will waste your life without benefit.

9. He should be particularly careful about choosing his books, especially the books of the Sunna and the remnants of the past, and the books of Ibn al-Qayyim and Ibn Taymiyya, and the publications of the scholars of the doctrines of the renewer Imam Muhammad Ibn Abd al-Wahhab may God grant him mercy. As well as other Salafi books that strive to present the book [the Quran] and the Sunna and the artifacts from the forbears and to emulate their doctrine and to hold on to the principles that they agreed upon, because God has placed within them goodness and blessings.

10. The student should make himself a guide for the people. His tongue should not criticize those who are busy with calling the people [to Islam], advising people, who are busy with Jihad, or who have made themselves free to worship, or with an art other than the one revealed to him and liked by him, because things are made for certain people. The student should make himself an extension of his brothers who have placed themselves in Islam's other openings.

The compilation of all good is in supplication. If the student prays to God insistently, asking God to open his great door of his mercy, God will open for him what he likes and all grace is in God's hands, He gives it to who He wills, and God is of the greatest grace and God is the one who helps.

A DETAILED PROGRAM FOR THE STUDENT

The duration of this program is ten years after which the student graduates with a specialty in Sharia Studies, with God granting success. In it, the student passes five levels which increase him in devotion and piety.

I. The first level lasts one and a half years.

   a. In it he memorizes the last six parts of the Quran.
   b. In Theology, he should read:

      i. The Scholar al-Uthaymeen's *explanation of the three Principles of Jurisprudence and the four Rules.*
      ii. *The book of the Doctrine of Oneness with the Right Opinion.*
      iii. Imam Muhammad Bin Abd al-Wahhab's *Uncovering Suspicions.*

   c. In Jurisprudence, he should read: *An Easy Explanation of the Most Important Laws* by al-Bassam, with it he should learn the the proper way to pray from the contemporary, summarized publications like the scholar Abd al-Aziz Bin Baz (may God grant him mercy) or the scholar al-Uthaymeen or *The Characteristics of Prayer* by the scholar al-Albani, may God grant him mercy.
   d. In Hadith, he should read:

      i. The 40 hadiths from al-Nawwawi's book.
      ii. *The Gardens of the Good*
      iii. *The Brightest Lantern*

   e. In the Study of Hadith: the book *Explaining Hadith*
   f. In Disciplining Behavior, he should read:

      i. *The Sufficient Answer* by Ibn al-Qayyim
      ii. The summary of *The Curriculum of the Seekers*
      iii. *Knowledge that you have to Act on* by al-Hafeth al-Baghdadi

   g. In Language Studies, he should read: *Al-Igrumiya and Its Explanation The Sunni Treasure.*
   h. In Biography and History, he should read: *The Sealed Honey*

II. The second level which lasts two and a half years

    a. In it he should memorize parts 19-24 of the Quran.
    b. In Theology, he should read:

        i. Ibn Qasim's *Annotation of the Book of the Oneness of God*
        ii. Al-Salman's *explanation of The Middle*
        iii. *Ascension of Acceptance* by al-Hakmi

    c. In Jurisprudence, he should read: The student's guidebook with its explanation *The Lantern of the Way or The Guidance of the Desirer*
    d. In Quranic Studies and Exegesis, he should read:

        i. Al-Sadi's *Exegesis*
        ii. *The Principles of Exegesis* by Ibn Taymiyya
        iii. *Research in Quranic Studies* by al-Qattan

    e. In Hadith, he should read:

        i. The 40 Hadith in al-Nawawi's book
        ii. *Sahih al-Bukhari*
        iii. *Sahih Muslim*
        iv. *The Clear Light in Valid and Weak Hadiths*

    f. In the Study of Hadith, he should read:

        i. *The Selected Thoughts* by Ibn Hijr
        ii. *The Principles of Extraction and Validation* by Mahmud Talhan
        iii. *In Remembrance of the Six Valid Hadiths*

    g. In Principles of Jurisprudence and the Purpose of Sharia, he should read:

        i. *The Papers* by al-Jawayny
        ii. *The Principles of the Study of Principles* by al-Uthaymeen
        iii. *The Clear in Principles of Jurisprudence* by al-Ashqar

    h. In Behavior and Discipline, he should read:

        i. *The Torrential Rain* by Ibn al-Qayyim
        ii. *The Toolkit of the Patient* by Ibn al-Qayyim
        iii. *The introduction to Rescuing the Compelled* by Ibn al-Qayyim

    i. In Language Studies, he should read:

        i. *Drops of Dew* by Ibn Hisham

    ii. *The Clear Eloquence* by al-Jaram

  j. In Prophetic Biography, he should read:

    i. *The Biography by Ibn Hisham*
    ii. *The Sustenance of the Day of Judgment* by Ibn al-Qayyim

  k. In the general principles and manners of Proselytizing , he should read:

    i. *Instructions for Wakefulness* by al-Uthaymeen

  l. In Fatwas , he should read: the fatwas of the Permanent Committee on Issuing Fatwas in the Kingdom of Saudi Arabia

    i. *The Warnings of the Prostrates* by al-Albani
    ii. *The Types and Laws of Entreaties* by al-Albani
    iii. *Entreaties and Methods* by Ibn Taymiyya
    iv. *Single Source Supported Narrated Hadiths* by al-Albani
    v. *The Sunna and its Place Within Islam* by al-Albani
    vi. *The Purification of Gardens and Corners* by al-Tami
    vii. *The Openness of the Hearts of the Good* by al-Sadi
    viii. *Seeking Knowledge and the Levels of the Educated* by al-Shawkani
    ix. *One Souled* by al-Qayyim
    x. *The Methods and Studies of Names and Adjectives* by al-Shanqiti

III. The third phase, which lasts two years.

  a. In which he memorizes the Quran from the beginning of the Chapter of the Cow to the end of the sixth part.
  b. In Theology, he should read:

    i. *The Call of Muhammad Ibn Abd al-Wahhab and its Effects* by Salih al-Abud
    ii. *The Creed for the People of Hama by Ibn Taymiyya and The Optimal Rules* by al-Uthaymeen.
    iii. *The Explanation of Imam al-Tahawi's book* by Ibn Abi al-Iz
    iv. *The Sunna* by Ibn Abi Asim

  c. In Jurisprudence, he should read:

    i. *Zad al-Mustaqna' and The Garden* with Ibn Hashem's *Explanation*

    ii. Al-Uthaymeen's *Explanation of Zad,* with *The Guidance* by al-Sadi

    iii. *The explanation of Attaining Desires* by al-Basam

d. In Exegesis, he should read: Ibn Kathir's *Exegesis*

e. In Hadith, he should read:

    i. *The Six Books*

    ii. *The Series of True Hadiths* by al-Albani

    iii. *The Sahih of Small Collections* by al-Albani

    iv. *The Good Purposes* by al-Sakhawi

f. In Studies of Hadith, he should read:

    i. *The Opening of the Rescuer* by al-Sakhawi

    ii. *The Compilation of the Manners of the Narrator* by al-Baghdadi

    iii. *Studies in Critiquing and Acceptance of Hadith Narrators* by al-Athami

    iv. *The Writing of the Prophetic Biography* by Muhammad al-Zahrani

g. In Principles of Jurisprudence and the Purpose of Sharia, he should read:

    i. *The Viewer's Garden* with al-Shanqiti's memo

    ii. *The Brief of Jurisprudence Principles* by Muhammad Sidqi al-Barnu

h. In Behavior and Discipline, he should read:

    i. *The Paths of the Travelers* by Ibn al-Qayyim

    ii. The thesis, *Acts of the Hearts* by Ibn Taymiyya

    iii. *The Manners of Scholars* by Ibn al-Agri

    iv. *The Adornment of the Seeker of Knowledge* by Bakr Abu Zayd

i. In Language Studies, he should read:

    i. Ibn Aqil's *explanation of Ibn Malek's Alfeya*

j. In History he should read:

    i. *The Beginning and the End*

    ii. *The Debates on Infallibility* by Ibn al-Arabi

k. In the general principles and manners of Proselytizing , he should read:

    i. *The Principles of Preaching* by Zaydan
    ii. *The Death of Polytheism and Superstition* by al-Hajjaj
    iii. *Innovations and their Laws* by al-Ghamidi
    iv. *The Crisis of the Age* by Mohammad Mohammad Hussayn

l. In Fatwas, he should read the fatwas of the scholar Muhammad al-Uthaymeen
m. In Completion and Miscellaneous things, he should read:

    i. *Preferring the Truth over the People* by al-Murtatha al-Yamani
    ii. *Faith* by al-Shatibi
    iii. *What Iblis has Hidden* by Ibn al-Jawzi
    iv. *The Collection of Bright Theses* [from various scholars]
    v. *The Smiling Garden* by Ibn al-Wazir
    vi. *Introduction to the Study of Sharia* by Zaydan
    vii. *The Introduction to the Ibn Hanbal School of Thought* by Ibn Badran
    viii. *The Detailed Introduction to Imam Bin Hanbal's Principles of Jurisprudence* by Bakr Abu Zayd
    ix. *The Standards of Knowledge* by al-Midani
    x. *On the Necessity of the Straight Path* by Ibn Taymiyya

IV. The fourth phase lasts two years

a. During which he should memorize the Quran from the beginning of the seventh part to the end of the twelfth part
b. In Theology, he should read:

    i. *The Claims of the Opponents of the Call* of Ibn Abd al-Wahhab
    ii. *The summary of The Sent Lighting Bolts*
    iii. *The Sunnah* by al-Kay'iy and *The Oneness of God* by Ibn Khuzayma and *The Sharia* by al-Ijri and *The Sunnah* by Abdullah Bin Ahmed and *The Clarification* by Ibn Bata
    iv. *The Answer to al-Jahmiya and al-Marisi* by Al-Darami
    v. *The Healing of the Ailing* by Ibn al-Qayyim
    vi. *The End of Upheaval and Battles* by Ibn Kathir

c. In Principles of Jurisprudence, he should read:

    i. *Al-Kafi* by Ibn Qidama

d. In Quranic Studies and Exegesis, he should read:

    i. *The Lights of Truth* by al-Shanqiti

    ii. *The Aid of the Subtle Benefactor [God], the summary of Quranic Exegesis* by al-Sadi

e. In Hadith, he should read:

    i. Imam Malik's *Muti'*, and Imam Ahmad's *Book of Supported Hadith*, and *The Chosen* by Ibn al-Jarud, and *The Traditions* of al-Durami, and *The Musannaf* of Ibn Abi Shubaya and *The Musannaf* of Abd al-Razaq

    ii. *The Series of Weak and Inserted Hadith* by al-Albani

f. In Studies of Hadith, he should read:

    i. *The Focus Points on Ibn Salah* by Ibn Hijr
    ii. *Explaining Al-Tirmithi's Reasons* by Ibn Rajab
    iii. *Raising and Completing* by al-Kanawi

g. In Principles of Jurisprudence and the Purpose of Sharia, he should read:

    i. *The Guidance of Males* by al-Shawkani
    ii. *The Exceptional Scholars*
    iii. *Removing Blame from the Exceptional Imams* by Ibn Taymiyya
    iv. *Youth and the Curriculum of Jurisprudence* by Muhammad al-Ashqar

h. In Behavior and Discipline, he should read:

    i. *Asceticism* by Hinad Bin al-Siri
    ii. *Asceticism* by Waki' Bin al-Jarah
    iii. *Asceticism* by Ahmad Bin Hanbal
    iv. *Capturing Epiphanies* by Ibn al-Jawzi

i. In Language Studies, he should read:

    i. *Principles of Grammar* by al-Sayuti
    ii. *The Rational Singer* by Ibn Hisham
    iii. *Poetry and Poets* by Ibn Qutayba

j. In History, he should read:

    i. *The Organized* by Ibn al-Jawzi

k. In the general principles and manners of Proselytizing, he should read:

    i. *Fundamentals of Enjoining Good and Forbidding Evil* by Ibn Taymiyya
    ii. *Secularism* by al-Hawali
    iii. *An Islamic Vision in our Contemporary Reality* by Muhammad Qutb
    iv. *Necessary Standards before Judging Groups and Communities* by Hamid al-Ali

l. In Fatwas, he should read:

    i. *The Great Fatwa* by Ibn Taymiyya
    ii. *The Fatwas of Muhammad Bin Ibrahim al-Sheikh*

m. In Completion and Miscellaneous things, he should read:

    i. *Degrading* by al-Mu'alimi
    ii. *The Measure* by al-Ashqar
    iii. *The Innovation of Doctrinal Extremism* by al-Abasi
    iv. *Complete Giving in Commentary on Sunni Principles of Jurisprudence* by al-Albani
    v. *The History of the Principles of Jurisprudence* by Omar al-Ashqar
    vi. *The Bright Standards of Principles of Jurisprudence* by Ibn Taymiyya
    vii. *Achieving Desires from Interpretation of Law Verses* by Sadiq Khan
    viii. *The Path of Reaching the Desired Knowledge* by al-Sadi
    ix. *Principles of Understanding Heritage* by al-Shaybani
    x. *The Beauties of the Heart* by Ibn al-Qayyim
    xi. *Ibn Taymiyyah's Stance on Abu Musa Al-Ashari's Group* by Abd al-Rahman al-Mahmoud
    xii. *The Summary of Egyptian Jurisprudence* by Ibn Taymiyya

V. The fifth level which lasts two years

a. In which he memorizes from the 13th to the 18th part of the Quran
b. In Theology, he should read:

    i. *Explanation of al-Nawnawiya*
    ii. *The Chosen from the Moderation Approach*
    iii. *The Publications of Theology from the Collection of Jurisprudence*
    iv. *The Prophecies by Ibn Taymiyya*
    v. *Sufi Thought* by Abd al-Rahman Abd al-Khaliq
    vi. *The Sunna and the Shia* by Ihsan Alha Dhahir
    vii. *The Guidance of the Confused* by Ibn Al-Qayyim

    viii. *The Secret Societies of the Islamic World* by Muhammad al-Khatib

    ix. *The Dogmatic and Scientific Deviations in the 3rd and 4th Centuries Hijri and their Effect on the Life of the Muslim Community* by Al al-Zahrani

    x. *Contemporary Groups that Claim Islam* by Ali al-Awaji

    xi. *The Phenomenon of not following Religion and its Effects on the Islamic World* by al-Hawali

c. In Principles of Jurisprudence, he should read:

    i. *The Enricher* by Ibn Qidama

d. In Quranic Studies and Exegesis, he should read:

    i. *Mastering Quranic Studies* by al-Sayuti

e. In Hadith, he should read:

    i. *The Hadith's Parts*

f. In Studies of Hadith, he should read:

    i. He should read a book about extraction and judging sources like *The Narrator's Ghalil* by al-Albani with practice on Hadith extraction and routes of transmission, he should read the introduction to *The Opening of the Doer of Good* and the introductions of the books of narrators.

g. In Principles of Jurisprudence and the Purpose of Sharia, he should read:

    i. *The Explanation of The Bright Planet* by Ibn al-Najjar al-Fituhi

    ii. *The Agreements* by al-Shatibi

    iii. *The Shared Issues Between the Principles of Jurisprudence and Religion* by al-Arusi

h. In Behavior and Discipline, he should read:

    i. The biographies of the forbearers like *The Adornment of the Followers* and *The Virtues of the Chosen* and *The Traits of the Chosen*

i. In Language Studies, he should read:

    i. *The Particularities* by Ibn Jini

    ii. *The Secrets of Eloquence and the Proof of Miracles* by al-Jarjani

    iii. *The Collection of Popular Poems of the Arabs* by Ibn Zayd
       al-Qurayshi

  j. In Prophetic Biography and History, he should read:

    i. *The Biographies of the Exceptional Prophets* by al-Dhahbi

  k. In the general principles and manners of Proselytizing, he should
    read:

      i. *The Three Wings of Deception* by al-Maydani
     ii. *Uncovering the False in Contemporary Ideological Doctrines* by
       al-Maydani
    iii. *The Protocols of the Zionist Leaders* by Ajaj Nuwayhidh
    iv. *Articles About the Curriculum* by Salman al-Awda

  l. In Fatwas, he should read:

    i. The research of the Committee of Great Scholars
    ii. *The Principles of Jurisprudence of Calamities* by Bakr Abu Zayd

  m. In Completion and Miscellaneous things, he should read:

      i. *The Statement of Talbis al-Jihmiya* by Ibn Taymiyya
     ii. *The Collection of Issues and Statements* by Ibn Taymiyya
    iii. *The House of Two Migrations* by Ibn al-Qayyim
    iv. *The Key to the House of Happiness*
     v. *The Actions of the Prophet Peace be upon him* by Muhammad
      al-Ashqar
    vi. *The Great Imamate* by al-Dumayji
    vii. *The Goals of the Entrusted* by Omar al-Ashqar
  viii. *Removing Shame in Sharia* by Ibn Hamid
    ix. The publications of Imam Muhammad Bin Abd al-Wahhab may
      God have mercy upon him.
     x. *The Sunni Pearls in the Proselytizing messages of Najd*
    xi. *The Compilation of Fatawa* by Ibn Taymiyya

THE STUDENT'S LIBRARY

It is incumbent upon the student to own a library which contains the most
important books in every art, and the following is a list of some of the most
important books:

The Greatest in Knowledge:

  1. The publications of Ibn Taymiyya, the Sheikh of Islam and his student
    Ibn al-Qayyim, may God have mercy upon them. It is incumbent upon

the student to collect any of their work that he lays his eyes on. For in them there is so much blessings for knowledge, only God knows how great. Whomever is diligent in reading these publications, then God will put light in his heart and open his eyes and bless him in his work.

2. The books of the Salafi movement that have been transmitted by the predecessors with validity, like *The Sunnah* by Ibn Abi Asim and by al-Khilal and Abdullah Bin al-Imam Ahmad, and *The Oneness of God* by Ibn Khuzayma and *The Principles of Sunni Beliefs* by al-Lakayky, and *The Clarification* by Ibn Batta and *Al-Sharia* by al-Ijri and others.

3. The books and publications of the renewer Imam Muhammad Bin Abd al-Wahhab may God grant him mercy, and his students and the scholars of the Salafi message who followed him: like, *The Collection of Issues* and *Letters of Najd* and *The Sunni Pearls* and others.

4. The four Sahihs and four schools of thought and their explanation. Especially *Fatih al-Bari*, it is necessary that the student's library not be without it. If a student doesn't read this book, then his knowledge is empty.

5. The books of Ibn Hijr al-Asqalany in Hadith Studies.

6. The great books of Islam like *The Enricher* by Ibn Qudama and *The Introduction* by Ibn Abd al-Bar and al-Tubari's interpretation of the Quran and its history. And al-Nawwawi's collection of Hadith and *The Adorner* by Ibn Hazam, *The Scattered Pearls in Interpretation of Known Narrations* by al-Sayuti and the introduction to *Mastering Quranic Studies*, al-Qurtubi's exegesis, *The Compilation of Collections* by al-Sayuti, and *The End* by Ibn Athir, *The Rising Lights in Strange Hadiths* by al-Qadhi Iyath, and *The Beginning and the End* by Ibn Kathir, and *The Organized* by Ibn al-Jawzi.

7. The exegesis of the Quran by Ibn Kathir and Shawkani and al-Baghwi and *The Lights of Truth* by al-Shanqiti.

8. From the principles of jurisprudence books, *The Garden of the Observer* by Ibn Qidama and al-Shanqiti's commentary on it, and a summarized explanation of *The Garden* by al-Tufi, and the explanation of *The Bright Planet* by Ibn al-Najjar.

9. From the useful books of contemporary scholars we have the books of the scholar, al-Shanqiti who is the author of *The Lights of Truth*. And the publications of the scholar Abd al-Rahman al-Sadi, and the scholar Abd al-Aziz Bin Baz and the scholar Muhammad al-Salih al-Uthaymeen and the publications of the renewer al-Albani in Hadith and its studies and the books and letters of the great scholar, Bakr Bin Abdullah Abu Zayd.

10. From the books of the school of thought of imam Ahmed Bin Hanbal, among the most important is *The Ultimate Desires* by al-Fatawhi and *Persuasion* by al-Hajawi. The cycle of jurisprudence and the sources of law revolve around them. If they are in opposition then you can go back

to *The Ultimate Goals in Joining Persuasion and Desires* by Shaikh Muri al-Karmi.

Amongst the most useful books of the school of thought is *The Branches* by al-Shams Bin Muflih and *The Innovator* by al-Barhan Ibn Muflih and the *Remover of the Mask* by al-Bahuti and *The First Demands in Explaining the Ultimate Goals* by al-Rayhabani.

Among texts, the most important is *The Pillars* by Ibn Qidama and *Zad Al-Mustaqna*, the summary of *Zad Al-Muqana* by al-Hajawi and this summary (*Zad*) is one of the most important of the Ibn Hanbal School of thought for historians until it was said: The text of Zad and Bilugh are sufficient for maturity, by which he means the texts of *Zad al-Mustaqna* and *Achieving Desires* by Ibn Hijr. And amongst its most important explanations is *the Square Garden* by al-Bahuti.

Other important texts include *The Student's Guide* by al-Mari al-Karmi and *The Pillars of the Student* by al-Bahuti printed with its explanation *The Guidance of the Desirer* and *The Sufficient for Introduction* and *The Summary of Summaries* which belong to Ibn Balban. The latter has a useful explanation by the name of *Unveiling the Veiled* and *the Flower Gardens* in *Explaining the Summary of Summaries* by al-Bayli al-Halbi and God knows best.

THE LETTER OF REFORM

If God aids the student in attaining Sharia knowledge and his breast maintained it and his heart understood it, then his duty becomes to preach and inform and to enjoin good and forbid evil as much as he can. This duty requires him to be aware of the societal situation and knowledgeable of what violations of Sharia occur within it. He should be aware of the reality of his Muslim Community and the Islamic World and the most important problems that Muslims face in this world. Similarly, it is necessary for him to be aware of the deception of enemies of Islam, and how to face their deception and their hatred with typical contemporary tools.

This is because Sharia knowledge is entrusted to us by God, we cannot be true to it unless we act in its rights. Its rights are loyalty to God and opposition to seeking the favor of sultans, and to treat it with grace so that the soul does not ask for the material goods of this world.

Amongst its other rights is to be taught to the people and to be made accessible to general Muslims, and to struggle in preaching it and to have patience in the face of harm for the sake of learning it and teaching it as we have inherited it from our Prophet peace be upon him, to the best of our abilities. "Allah does not charge a soul except with that within its capacity." A scholar is not a person who memorizes knowledge then closes his door to the faces of the people who need him, the scholar is not the person who doesn't care about Muslims' situation, and who doesn't care about their calamities and who does not strive to better their worldly situation and guides to what has in store for them their safety in this world and the hereafter.

Whomever takes God's knowledge and acts upon it in God's sake and supports with it God's religion will enter with God's blessings as God had said "Allah will raise those who have believed among you and those who were given knowledge, by degrees." Only God knows, may God's blessings be upon our Prophet Muhammad and his family and companions.

Appendix B

Technical Appendix

B.1 ALGORITHM FOR WIKIPEDIA SPIDER

Wikipedia lists can be used to identify Wikipedia articles about clerics. Inspired by Gong (n.d.), I implement an automated search through Wikipedia that simultaneously finds candidate entries and classifies whether each entry is the biography of a cleric. This methodology allows me to identify all of the Wikipedia articles about clerics. For this approach, I train a statistical text classification model to distinguish articles about clerics from other types of articles. I develop a program called a "spider" that moves from link to link within Wikipedia. The program starts by visiting a set of initial Wikipedia entries that I specify (I start with a list of approximately forty clerics from my data set). The program uses a statistical text classifier called a random forest (Breiman 2001) to classify each page it visits as "cleric" or "not." For each of the Wikipedia entries classified as "cleric," the program then follows every hyperlink from that entry, visits each of them, and repeats the same classification process on the resulting pages' links. The program continues until all links in the resulting network have been visited.

The statistical text classifier is key to the success of this procedure so it is worth explaining a few of the details. The classifier is trained on a training corpus that I generated from the Wikipedia pages about clerics in my data set. I went to each of these pages, collected all of the links, and classified 727 outgoing links to other Wikipedia articles by hand as either pointing to an article about a cleric or not. I use the text of these hand-coded pages as the training set. This has some practical limitations – because the training set is derived from the entries of clerics, it is most accurate when the links it is classifying come from a cleric entry. However, if the classifier mistakenly classifies an entry as a cleric biography when in fact it is not, then the next set of articles that the classifier faces comes from a different distribution than the training set, making misclassification more likely. For example, a primary feature that distinguishes cleric from noncleric entries in the classifier are markers of biographical entries: names, words about birth, childhood, education, and careers. Upon implementing the search procedure, I found many instances where the classifier mistakenly coded noncleric entries as being about clerics: entries about singers, television shows, and Companions of the Prophet. The reason is clear – these entries also have many names, words about birth, childhood, education, and careers. To improve the classification, I added a step to the classifier in which I compare the title of the Wikipedia page to a predetermined dictionary of words. This ensures that articles with titles including "singer" or "actress" are automatically classified as "noncleric." I also automatically omit articles that have no dates after 1900 to avoid articles about classical scholars.

Assuming each Wikipedia article about a cleric can be reached via a hyperlink from another page about a cleric, this procedure will produce a list of all articles about Muslim clerics on Wikipedia. Automated classification may slightly reduce list accuracy, but this procedure produces a list of candidate entities that are very likely to be Muslim clerics. I improved the accuracy by having a (Muslim) research assistant visit 1,500 pages that were classified as clerics by an initial version of the search algorithm to code whether each result was in fact a Wikipedia article about a cleric. This allowed me to improve the algorithm until it achieved 90 percent agreement with the research assistant, a remarkably high level of accuracy for automated text classification. I then searched through Wikipedia using the final version of this Wikipedia snowball census to recover articles about 3,690 unique clerics.

Algorithmically, the procedure is this:

Algorithm 1 Classify Wikipedia Pages as "Cleric" or "Not"

1: **procedure**
2:     begin with a *seed list* of links to hand-selected Wikipedia pages of likely clerics
3:     **while** length of *seed list* > 0 **do**
4:         follow the first link in *seed list* and remove it from *seed list*
5:         classify the link text using a text classifier
6:         **if** link is of class "cleric" **then**
7:             save the link and html
8:             gather all new links from the html
9:             **if** new links have not been visited **then**
10:                 add new links to *seed list*
11:         **else**
12:             continue to next link of *seed list*

B.2 ASSIGNING TOPIC LABELS TO A TOPIC MODEL OF "THE
JIHADIST'S BOOKBAG"

When labeling each topic in the topic model of the texts in "The Jihadist's Bookbag," I attempt to summarize the most important semantic content of each cluster of words. These clusters are large – every single word in the 765-document corpus is assigned to one of the five clusters – so there is substantial semantic heterogeneity within the clusters. The purpose of affixing a label, and of a topic model more generally, is dimension reduction. The process of fitting a topic model reduces the dimensionality of the corpus dramatically. In my implementation, word order is discarded, similar words are combined through stemming, and then the five estimated topics are summarized by probability distributions over the vocabulary. However, even this amount of dimension reduction does not render the topic model output intelligible, so analysts typically reduce the dimensionality further by (a) looking only at lists of words that are most "representative" of each topic (usually because these words occur most frequently in a given topic) or (b) assigning labels to each topic, usually based on lists of most frequent words. When looking at lists, the dimensionality of the corpus is reduced to the length of the list (typically less than twenty words per topic) and with a single label, the dimensionality of the corpus is fully reduced to the number of topics. The loss of complexity is obvious. The benefit is that extreme parsimony can allow analysts to see previously hidden trends and roughly describe the contours of a corpus to audiences that are not able to carefully digest each of the texts.

I infer topic labels by first generating lists of words that summarize the content of each topic. Typically, analysts summarize topics from topic models using the most frequent terms in each topic. However, in practice this often leads to confusing lists of words that seem unrelated because the most frequent words in a topic are not necessarily the words that best distinguish one topic from another. For example, in the five-topic model that follows, "Allah" is the most frequent term in both the *Legal Precedent* and *Operations* topics, but "Allah" provides little semantic content to distinguish these topics from each other unless the analyst has more context. This is because the word is used for different reasons in these two topics. In the *Legal Precedent* topic, "Allah" is prominent because of frequent usage of legally valid *hadith*, which almost always include the phrase "The messenger of Allah said...." In the *Operations* topic, "Allah" is frequent because of the phrase "jihad in the pathway of Allah." Recent work by Bischof and Airoldi (2016) and Roberts, Stewart, and Airoldi (2016) suggests that topics can be better summarized by using the exclusivity of words – how exclusive a word is to a particular topic – to infer the best semantic label for each topic.[1]

---

[1] Specifically, I follow Roberts, Stewart, and Airoldi (2016) by generating three lists of words for each topic: the most frequent words, the most exclusive words, and the words that score highest on the geometric mean of frequency and exclusivity (denoted FREX scores).

TABLE B.1. *Top words for five topics in a jihadist corpus.*

Tawhid/Takfir	Legal Precedent	Conflicts	Operations	Mixed
excommunication	said	America	Jihadis	ten
excommunicate	son	American	martyr	had
tyrant	if	Afghanistan	Afghan	appointed
apostate	Prophet	Afghan	Jihad	big
believe	peace be upon him	United	operation	king
loyalty	peace be upon him	region	Russia	mosque
legislation	book	organization	enemy	country
come down	science	movement	Azzam	four
categorized	hadith	government	Russian	was
apostates	command	Pakistan	leader	house/stanza
ignorance	mercy	leader	martyrs	begin
Murjites	Sahih	president	martyrdom	knots
apostates	remember	dollar	Communist	five
prohibitions	theology	leadership	fighter	sir
suspicion	issue	Saudi	invasion	woman
apostate	narrated	Iraq	sword	city
make halal	do	West	kill	thousand
excommunicate	book/volume	front	battles	nights
Polytheism	imam	politics	battle	law
Khawarij	books	East	horses	news
read	rulings	States	airplane	head
Jahmi	Ahmad	countries	Persians	wife
Most High	leave	peninsula	factions	mosque
faith	good	million	blood	hour
outright disbelief	original	Bin Laden	arms	Communist
tyrants	evidence	brothers	family	return
sovereignty	Taymiyya	center	spite	Emir
democracy	Companions	years	fighters	prison
excused	house	Crusaders	kill	where?
legislation	meaning	decision	invaders	Hajj

This table provides the top thirty words, based on FREX scores, for each of five topics estimated using latent Dirichlet allocation on "The Jihadist's Bookbag" corpus. The FREX scores are the harmonic mean of frequency (of the word in a topic) and exclusivity (the extent to which a word is unique to the topic). Each column is a topic; the titles at the top of each column are summary names inferred from the words in the column, not labels provided by the model.

In Table B.1, I show the FREX scores for each of the five topics. In practice, I use all three lists of words to infer topic labels, but I present only the top words according to FREX scores. This is partly because of space, but in general, the FREX scores were the most important list as I inferred topic labels, while the exclusivity and frequency lists were a distant second and third. I use lists of fifty words for each topic, but I only display the top thirty here for space considerations.

I also use information about representative documents to infer the most appropriate labels for each topic. Specifically, I find the five documents that have the largest proportion of words assigned to a particular topic by the topic model and consider the title, author, and text (limited in most cases to a quick skimming of the first few pages, although I read some shorter documents entirely). The representative titles for each topic are listed in Table B.2.

Tawhid/Takfir: I label the first topic *Tawhid/Takfir*. It is not hard to see the *takfīrī* component of this topic in the list of words with the highest FREX scores. The first two words on the list are the Arabic word *takfīr*, which I translate as "excommunication," and the word *yukāffir*, which is a verb meaning "to excommunicate." The remainder of the list includes many terms connected to *tawhīd* that are familiar to the reader from the foregoing discussion of jihadist ideology: "tyrants," (referring to oppressive governments that do not enforce tawhid), "legislation" (the illegitimacy of earthly legislation), "ignorance" (Sayyid Qutb's concept of Jahiliyya), *shirk* (polytheism), and "democracy," among others. The list also includes words related to discussions about the use of excommunication by jihadists – the words *Murjites* and *Khawārij* are the names of historical groups within Islam connected with opposite positions on the excommunication of supposedly heretical Muslims.

The five titles in the corpus that most represent this topic confirm that this topic is about *tawhīd* and *takfīr*. Four of the works are by the (in)famous jihadist *takfīrī* Abu Basir al-Tartusi: a treatise on *tawhīd*, a collection of fatwas about *takfīr*, and two criticisms of the positions of prominent establishment scholars on *takfīr*. The final document in the list of five is by Ali al-Khudayr and is a *takfīrī* fatwa.

It is encouraging that the topic model corroborates my foregoing analysis and identifies issues of *tawhīd* and *takfīr* as a coherent topic within the jihadist corpus.

Legal Precedent: The second topic primarily relates to legal precedent within Islamic law. This is not a topic in the sense that the correlated words are not about a specific subject. Rather, these words are the collection of terms that accompanies legalistic reasoning in Islamic law, regardless of content. Thus, this topic represents a trend that might have been overlooked by a human reader, but nevertheless gives insight into the nature of the corpus.

The top five documents are extremely legalistic, and in at least one case, are actually treatises on legal theory. Although it may not be immediately obvious, five of the first six terms in this topic all draw on the science of *hadith*, by which legal precedent is determined in Islamic law. To see how these terms are about precedent, consider the classic form of an introduction to a *hadith* (called an *isnād*). I have underlined occurrences of the first six words in the selection.

TABLE B.2. *Texts that are representative of five topics in a jihadist corpus.*

Takfir/Tawhid	1. *This is my creed*, Abu Basir al-Tartusi
	2. *Discussion of the saying of Ibn al-Uthaymeen in which he requires making apostasy permissible instead of following the divine law*, Abu Basir al-Tartusi
	3. *Assorted issues, 601-625*, Abu Basir al-Tartusi
	4. *Ruling about one who defends the Tyrants*, Ali Khudayr
	5. *Discussion of the saying of Ibn Baz*, Abu Basir al-Tartusi
Legal Precedent	1. *The Methodology of the Early Scholars in the Issue of Tadlis*, Nasr al-Fahd
	2. *The ruling about praying for the dead who are missing*, Hamud al-Shu'aybi
	3. *The Response to the Shiites*, Nasr al-Fahd
	4. *The Ruling Upon Alcohol Based Perfumes*, Nasr al-Fahd
	5. *The book of principles for discovering the opposing viewpoints on evidence and practice from the words of the salafi Imams*, Ali Khudayr
Conflicts	1. *Informing the Sleepers of the New War Against Islam*, Husayn Bin Mahmoud
	2. *America and the Climb into the Pit of Hell*, Yusuf al-Urayri
	3. *The Jews in America*, Hamid al-Ali
	4. *The Presence of the Americans in the Arabian Peninsula: Their Accomplishments and Aims*, Yusuf al-Urayri
	5. *The Opium War*, Husayn Bin Mahmoud
Operations	1. *The Legality of Martyrdom Operations*, Hamud al-Shu'aybi
	2. *The Ruling on Martyrdom Operations*, Sulayman al-Ulwan
	3. *Martyrdom Operations: Jihad in the Pathway of God*, Palestine Scholars Association
	4. *The Way to the Battlefield*, Yusuf al-Urayri
	5. *Martyrdom Operations: the Pinnacle of Martyrdom*, Abu Sa'ad al-Amali
Mixed	1. *To My Beloved Mother – Do Not Cry for Me* (poem), Abu Muhammad al-Maqdisi
	2. *The article that made me and most other readers cry concerning Sheikh Yusuf al-Urayri* (blog post), Anonymous on al-Islah forum

TABLE B.2. *Continued*

---

3. *Do You Know My Crimes?* (poem), Abu Muhammad
   al-Maqdisi
4. *Papers From the Prisoner's Notebook,* 2 (prose and poetry),
   Abu Muhammad al-Maqdisi
5. *The Preachers at the Gates of Heaven* (poem), Abu
   Muhammad al-Maqdisi

This table lists the five documents that are most representative of each topic, meaning that they have the highest proportion of words assigned to that topic. In some cases, documents that appear more than once in the corpus were in the top five – when this occurred I skipped repeated documents as the purpose of this list is to give the reader a sense of the topic and new titles are more informative than repeats.

Abu Abdullah <u>son</u> of Sahnun <u>said</u>: Abi Sahnun related to me, by way of Abdullah <u>son</u> of Wahhab, by way of Sufyan al-Thawri, by way of Ilqima <u>son</u> of Marthud (?), by way of Abi Abd al-Rahman al-Salami (?), by way of Uthman <u>son</u> of Afan – may god be pleased with him – that the <u>prophet</u> of God – <u>peace be upon him</u> – <u>said</u>: ...[2]

Five of the six top words on the list occur in this *isnād*, several repeatedly, demonstrating that these words are intimately linked to the establishment of legal precedence in Islam. Note that the honorific for the Prophet Muhammad – peace be upon him – appears twice in Table B.1, but these are two distinct parts of the honorific. For semantic clarity, I translate the entire honorific each time.

The other words further down the list corroborate my assessment that this topic is about legal precedent. The topic is related to the science of *hadith* ("hadith," "science," "narrated," the "Companions" of the Prophet), collections of prophetic sayings (including *Sahih Muslim, Sahih al-Bukhari,* and the collection of Ibn Taymiyya), and issues of Islamic rulings more generally ("book," "books," "rulings," "book volume," "evidence").

Conflicts: I label the third topic *conflicts* because of its focus on past and present jihadist political conflicts with the United States, Russia, and Saudi Arabia, with fighting in the theaters of Afghanistan, Pakistan, and Iraq. The top five words for this category all relate to America and the Afghan war. Other political entities are also prominent, including generic terms for political entities ("leader," "government," "president," "leadership"). Al-Qaeda is typically referred to as "the organization of Al-Qaeda" by jihadists, so the fact that the words "organization" and "Bin Laden" both appear indicates a focus on al-Qaeda and its role in conflicts with the West. The top documents for the topic further suggest that this topic is really about jihadist conflicts – all five exemplar

---

[2] Taken from p. 69 of *Kitāb ᵓAdab al-Muᶜallimīn li-Muḥammad bin Saḥnūn,* photocopy provided by William Granara.

texts are works explaining the evils of the United States and its supposed plans for domination and humiliation of Muslims and their lands.

Operations: The fourth topic is about operations, and the exemplar documents suggest that it may even be more tightly focused on "martyrdom operations," or suicide attacks. Four of the five exemplar documents are fatwas defending the legality of suicide attacks. The focus on suicide is less clear in the top words of the topic, although words directly related to martyrdom occur in positions two, eleven, and twelve on the list, suggesting that, with more accurate stemming to combine these similar words, the term "martyrdom" might in fact define the topic. Regardless, the topic remains clearly centered on violent operations in a variety of contexts.

Mixed: The last topic is difficult to summarize. The list of top words is perplexing, regardless of whether I use word frequency, exclusivity, or the combination FREX scores. The most frequent term in the topic is the Arabic preposition *ilā* meaning "to." The most exclusive words are those for "marriage" and "wife," but the list quickly turns into a list of verbs with no apparent semantic connection. The list of top words by FREX score does not overlap either the frequency or exclusivity lists, suggesting that this topic has no words that are both frequent and exclusive.

Inspection of the top documents for this topic begins to clarify the puzzle: the top documents are poetry or mixed poetry and prose. Further investigation of the corpus reveals that poetry is a major feature of jihadist rhetoric. Within "The Jihadist's Bookbag," Abu Muhammad al-Maqdisi has an entire subdirectory containing nineteen pieces of poetry. Verse and rhyme also appear frequently in other genres, including some of the most foundational texts.

B.3 NAIVE BAYES CLASSIFIER FOR TEXT

I am interested in estimating the probability that a new document S belongs to the jihadi class (J), given the words in S. From Bayes' rule we know that:

$$P(J|S) = \frac{P(S|J)P(J)}{P(S)}$$

Take $P(S|J)$ to be the independent[3] product over all words in the document S and denoting the i-th word in S as w_i, we can write

$$P(S|J) = \prod_i P(w_i|J)$$

---

[3] This independence assumption is clearly violated because words are correlated within documents (hence the "naive" in naive Bayes). There are other more complex options, but I find that the naive Bayes classifier works well in practice. Also, like most classification models, the naive Bayes classifier relies on the assumption that the proportions of the classes are the same in the training set and the overall population of documents. This is clearly not satisfied because I am not even able to characterize the total population of texts. Recently developed methods relax this assumption (Hopkins and King 2010; King and Lu 2008) and could offer an alternative solution.

$$P(J|S) = \frac{P(J)}{P(S)} \prod_i P(w_i|J)$$

I use the frequency of word w_i in the combined jihadi corpus, J as my estimate of $P(w_i|J)$.[4] I assume that a text is either jihadi or not, which allows a symmetrical equation for the probability that a text is not jihadi.

$$P(J'|S) = \frac{P(J')}{P(S)} \prod_i P(w_i|J')$$

These two quantities can be combined and simplified to produce a logged likelihood ratio, which I use as the document-level jihad score:

$$Jihad\ Score = \sum_i log \frac{P(w_i|J)^{w_i}}{P(w_i|J')^{w_i}}$$

I estimate the uncertainty of my jihad scores using a block bootstrap of each document. In general, bootstrapping procedures estimate uncertainty by treating the observed data as the population, and resampling the data with replacement to get an estimate of the variability inherent in the data (Efron and Tibshirani 1993). In the case of text, Lowe and Benoit (n.d.) find that a block bootstrap – sampling sequences of words together rather than individually – performs well for quantifying the uncertainty of a corpus while retaining the correlations between words that arise because of the structure of written communication. For each cleric, I resample each document in overlapping blocks of length 10, creating 200 bootstrapped versions of each document. I then concatenate these into a single document, as with the original corpus, and calculate new scores for each of the bootstrapped versions. The 2.5th and 97.5th percentiles of these scores provide a 95 percent confidence interval around each cleric's jihad score.

As an alternative to concatenating the documents into a single document, I also calculate document-level jihad scores for 27,142 documents produced by the 101 prominent clerics and then aggregate these document-level scores to produce cleric-level jihad scores. Because clerics can write about many things, not all of their writing is relevant to estimating their ideal point on the issue of militant jihad. I argue that an adequate conceptual definition of a cleric's jihad score is the *the most extreme statement by a cleric that is not an error* (either an error of speech by the cleric or an error of classification by my model). To operationalize this, I identify the top 10 percent of document-level jihad scores for each cleric and then use the median score of these documents as the

---

4   The maximum likelihood estimate is $P(w_i|J) = \frac{W_i}{\sum_{i' \in J} W_{i'}}$, where W_i is the sum of total occurrences of word w_i in J. This creates problems because terms that do not appear at all in J automatically make $\prod_i P(w_i|J) = 0$. I use the standard solution of Laplace smoothing, so the actual calculation is $P(w_i|J) = \frac{W_i+1}{\sum_{i' \in J}(W_{i'}+1)}$.

cleric-level jihad score. This ensures that (1) a cleric's jihad score is determined by their most extreme statements, and (2) the scores will be relatively robust to any mistaken classification of individual documents. Note, however, that this procedure potentially builds bias into my estimates because clerics with more documents are more likely to have extreme documents, given identical ideologies. However, in practice I find that this procedure produces a similar ranking of clerics from least to most jihadist.

Bibliography

Abadie, Alberto. 2006. "Poverty, Political Freedom, and the Roots of Terrorism." *American Economic Review* 96(2):50.

Aboul-Enein, Youssef H. 2010. *Militant Islamist Ideology: Understanding the Global Threat.* Annapolis, MD: Naval Institute Press.

Abu-Zahra, Nadia. 1997. *The Pure and the Powerful: Studies in Contemporary Muslim Society.* Reading, Berkshire: Ithaca Press.

Adang, Camilla, Hassan Ansari, Maribel Fierro, and Sabine Schmidtke, eds. 2016. *Accusations of Unbelief in Islam: A Diachronic Perspective on Takfir.* Leiden: Brill.

Adena, Maja, Ruben Enikolopov, Maria Petrova, Veronica Santarosa, and Ekaterina Zhuravskaya. 2015. "Radio and the Rise of The Nazis in Prewar Germany." *The Quarterly Journal of Economics* 130(4):1885–1939.

Agrama, Hussein Ali. 2010. "Ethics, Tradition, Authority: Toward an Anthropology of the Fatwa." *American Ethnologist* 37(1):2–18.

Ahmed, Amel and Rudra Sil. 2012. "When Multi-Method Research Subverts Methodological Pluralism – or, Why We Still Need Single-Method Research." *Perspectives on Politics* 10(4):935–953.

Airoldi, Edoardo M., and Jonathan M. Bischof. 2016. "Improving and Evaluating Topic Models and Other Models of Text." *Journal of the American Statistical Association* 111(516):1381–1403.

Al Aswany, Alaa. 2011. *On the State of Egypt: What Made the Revolution Inevitable.* New York: Vintage Books.

al-Awlaki, Anwar. 2010. "Shaykh Anwar's Message to the American People and Muslims in the West." (Winter) *Inspire.*

al-Fahd, Nasr. 2003. *Ikhtarat shaykh al-islam ibn taymiyya wa taqriratuh fi al-nahu wal-sarf.* Mecca: Dar 'ilm al-fawa'id.

al-Halili, Muhammad Taqi ud-Din, and Muhammad Muhsin Khan. 1996. *The Noble Quran in the Englis Language.* Madina, Saudi Arabia: King Fahd Complex for the Printing of the Holy Quran.

Alimi, Eitan Y., Lorenzo Bosi, and Chares Demetriou. 2015. *The Dynamics of Radicalization: A Relational and Comparative Perspective.* Oxford: Oxford University Press.

al-Jazairi, Abd al-Malik al-Ramadani. 2007. "The Savage Barbarism of Aboo Qataadah." SalafiManhaj. Available at http://download.salafimanhaj.com/pdf/ SalafiManhajQataadah.pdf, accessed February 9, 2017.

al-Maqdisi, Abu Muhammad. 1984. *Millat Ibrahim (The Religion of Abraham)*. At-Tibyan Publications. Available at www.e-prism.org/images/Millat_Ibrahim_-_ English.pdf, accessed March 18, 2013.

Al-Nashashibi, May Y., D. Neagu, and Ali A. Yaghi. 2010. "An Improved Root Extraction Technique for Arabic Words." In *2nd International Conference on Computer Technology and Development*.

al-Qarni, Aaidh. 2005. *Don't Be Sad*, 2nd edition. Riyadh: International Islamic Publishing House.

Al-Rasheed, Madawi. 2007. *Contesting the Saudi State: Islamic Voices from a New Generation*. New York: Cambridge University Press.

Al-Rasheed, Madawi. 2013. *A Most Masculine State: Gender, Politics, and Religion in Saudi Arabia*. New York: Cambridge University Press.

Al-Rasheed, Madawi. 2015. *Muted Modernists: The Struggle Over Divine Politics in Saudi Arabia*. London: C. Hurst & Co.

Ansari, Hamied N. 1984. "The Islamic Militants in Egyptian Politics." *International Journal of Middle East Studies* 16(01):123–144.

Antoun, Richard T. 1989. *Muslim Preacher in the Modern World*. Princeton: Princeton University Press.

Antoun, Richard T. 2006. "Fundamentalism, Bureaucratization, and the State's Co-optation of Religion: A Jordanian Case Study." *International Journal of Middle East Studies* 38(3):369–393.

Ayubi, Nazih. 2003. *Political Islam: Religion and Politics in the Arab World*. New York: Routledge.

Azzam, Abdullah. 1979. *Defense of the Muslim Lands*. London: Azzam Publications.

Bagader, Abubaker A. 1983. *The Ulama in the Modern Muslim Nation-State*. Malaysia: Polygraphic Press.

Bell, James et al. 2013. "The World's Muslims: Religion, Politics and Society." In *The Pew Forum on Religion and Public Life*. Washington, DC: Pew Research Center.

Benmelech, Efraim and Claude Berrebi. 2007. "Human Capital and the Productivity of Suicide Bombers." *Journal of Economic Perspectives* 21(3):223–238.

Bergesen, Albert J., ed. 2007. *The Sayyid Qutb Reader*. New York: Routledge.

Berkowitz, Leonard. 1962. *Aggression: A Social Psychological Analysis*. New York: McGraw-Hill.

Berkowitz, Leonard. 1978. "Whatever Happened to the Frustration-Aggression Hypothesis?" *American Behavioral Scientist* 21(5):691–708.

Berkowitz, Leonard. 1989. "Frustration-Aggression Hypothesis: Examination and Reformulation." *Psychological Bulletin* 106(1):59.

Berman, Eli and David Laitin. 2008. "Religion, Terrorism and Public Goods: Testing the Club Model." *Journal of Public Economics* 92(10–11):1942–1967.

Berman, Eli, Michael Callen, Joseph H. Felter, and Jacob N. Shapiro. 2011. "Do Working Men Rebel? Insurgency and Unemployment in Afghanistan, Iraq, and the Philippines." *Journal of Conflict Resolution* 55(4):496–528.

Bernard, H. Russell. 1995. *Research Methods in Anthropology*. Walnut Creek, CA: AltaMira Press.

Blattman, Christopher and Jeannie Annan. 2016. "Can Employment Reduce Lawlessness and Rebellion? A Field Experiment with High-Risk Men in a Fragile State." *American Journal of Political Science* 110(1):1–17.

Blau, Peter Michael. 1994. *The Organization of Academic Work*. New Brunswick, NJ: Transaction Publishers.

Blaydes, Lisa and Drew A. Linzer. 2008. "The Political Economy of Women's Support for Fundamentalist Islam." *World Politics* 60(04):576–609.

Blei, David M., Andrew Y. Ng, and Michael I. Jordan. 2003. "Latent Dirichlet Allocation." *Journal of Machine Learning Research* 3:993–1022.

Blyth, Mark. 1997. "Any More Bright Ideas? The Ideational Turn of Comparative Political Economy." *Comparative Politics* 29(1):229–250.

Blyth, Mark. 2001. "The Transformation of the Swedish Model: Economic Ideas, Distributional Conflict and Institutional Change." *World Politics* 54(1):1–26.

Blyth, Mark. 2003. "Structures Do Not Come with an Instruction Sheet: Interests, Ideas and Progress in Political Science." *Perspectives on Politics* 1(4):695–703.

Boellstorff, Tom, Bonnie Nardi, Celia Pearce, and T. L. Taylor. 2012. *Ethnography and Virtual Worlds: A Handbook of Method*. Princeton: Princeton University Press.

Bonner, Michael. 2006. *Jihad in Islamic History*. Princeton: Princeton University Press.

Bourdieu, Pierre. 1984. *Homo Academicus*. Stanford: Stanford University Press.

Boyle, Helen N. 2004. *Quranic Schools: Agents of Preservation and Change*. New York: RoutledgeFalmer.

Brachman, Jarret M. 2009. *Global Jihadism*. Abingdon, Oxford: Routledge.

Breiman, Leo. 2001. "Random Forests." *Machine Learning* 45(1):5–32.

Brinton, Jaquelene. 2016. *Preaching Islamic Renewal: Religious Authority and Media in Contemporary Egypt*. Oakland: University of California Press.

Browers, Michaelle L. 2005. "The Secular Bias in Ideology Studies and the Case of Islamism." *Journal of Political Ideologies* 10(1):75–93.

Brown, Adam R. 2011. "Wikipedia as a Data Source for Political Scientists: Accuracy and Completeness of Coverage." *PS: Political Science and Politics* 44:339–343.

Brown, Nathan. 2012. *When Victory Is Not an Option: Islamist Movements in Arab Politics*. Ithaca, NY: Cornell University Press.

Buckwalter, Tim and Dilworth Parkinson. 2011. *A Frequency Dictionary of Arabic*. Abingdon, Oxford: Routledge.

Bueno de Mesquita, Ethan. 2005. "The Quality of Terror." *The American Journal of Political Science* 49(3):515–530.

Bulliet, Richard W. 1970. "A Quantitative Approach to Medieval Muslim Biographical Dictionaries." *Journal of the Economic and Social History of the Orient* 13:195–211.

Bulliet, Richard W. 2002. "The Crisis of Authority in Islam." (Winter) *Wilson Quarterly*.

Bunt, Gary R. 2003. *Islam in the Digital Age: E-jihad, Online Fatwas and Cyber Islamic Environments*. London: Pluto Press.

Burde, Dana. 2014. *Schools for Conflict or for Peace in Afghanistan*. New York: Columbia University Press.

Burde, Dana, Joel A. Middleton, and Rachel Wahl. 2015. "Islamic Studies as Early Childhood Education in Countries Affected by Conflict: The Role of Mosque Schools in Remote Afghan Villages." *International Journal of Educational Development* 41:70–79.

Byman, Daniel L. and Kenneth M. Pollack. 2001. "Let Us Now Praise Great Men: Bringing the Statesman Back In." *International Security* 25 (4):107–146.

Caeiro, Alexandre. 2011. Transnational Ulama, European Fatwas, and Islamic Authority. In *Producing Islamic Knowledge: Transmission and Dissemination in Western Europe*, ed. Martin van Bruinessen and Stefano Allievi. New York: Routledge.

Cammett, Melani and Pauline Jones Luong. 2014. "Is There an Islamist Political Advantage?" *Annual Review of Political Science* 17.

Campante, Filipe R. and Davin Chor. 2012. "Why Was the Arab World Poised for Revolution? Schooling, Economic Opportunities, and the Arab Spring." *The Journal of Economic Perspectives* 26(2):167–187.

Canetti, Daphna, Stevan E. Hobfoll, Ami Pedahzur, and Eran Zaidise. 2010. "Much Ado about Religion: Religiosity, Resource Loss, and Support for Political Violence." *Journal of Peace Research* 47(5):575–587.

Carpenter, Charli. 2012. "You Talk of Terrible Things So Matter-of-Factly in This Language of Science: Constructing Human Rights in the Academy." *Perspectives on Politics* 10(2):363–383.

Casebourne, Imogen, Chris Davies, Michelle Fernandes, and Naomi Norman. 2012. "Assessing the Accuracy and Quality of Wikipedia Entries Compared to Popular Online encyclopaedias: A Comparative Preliminary Study across Disciplines in English, Spanish and Arabic." Wikimedia Foundation. Retrieved from http://commons.wikimedia.org/wiki/File:EPIC_Oxford_report.pdf.

Chaney, Eric. 2013. "Revolt on the Nile: Economic Shocks, Religion and Political Power." *Econometrica* 81(5):2033–2053.

Cherribi, Sam. 2010. *In the House of War: Dutch Islam Observed*. Oxford: Oxford University Press.

Chiozza, Giacomo and Hein E. Goemans. 2011. *Leaders and International Conflict*. New York: Cambridge University Press.

Chwieroth, Jeffrey M. 2007. "Testing and Measuring the Role of Ideas: The Case of Neoliberalism in the International Monetary Fund." *International Studies Quarterly* 51:5–30.

Clark, Burton R. 1983. *The Higher Education System: Academic Organization in Cross-national Perspective*. Berkeley: University of California Press.

Clingingsmith, David, Asim Ijaz Khwaja, and Michael Kremer. 2009. "Estimating the Impact of The Hajj: Religion and Tolerance in Islam's Global Gathering." *Quarterly Journal of Economics* 124(3).

Commins, David. 2015. From Wahhabi to Salafi. In *Saudi Arabia in Transition*, ed. Bernard Haykel, Thomas Hegghammer, and Stephane Lacroix. Cambridge: Cambridge University Press.

Cooke, Miriam and Bruce B. Lawrence, eds. 2005. *Muslim Networks from Hajj to Hip Hop*. Chapel Hill: University of North Carolina Press.

Cosgel, Metin M., Thomas J. Miceli, and Jared Rubin. 2012. "The Political Economy of Mass Printing: Legitimacy, Revolt, and Technology Change in the Ottoman Empire." *Journal of Comparative Economics* 40(3):357–371.

Cottee, Simon. 2017. "'What ISIS Really Wants' Revisited: Religion Matters in Jihadist Violence, but How?" *Studies in Conflict & Terrorism* 40(6):439–454.

Crecelius, Daniel Neil. 1967. "The Ulama and the State in Modern Egypt," PhD thesis, Princeton University.

Crecelius, Daniel. 1972. "Nonideological Responses of the Egyptian Ulama to Modernization." In *Scholars, Saints, and Sufis: Muslim Religious Institutions in the*

Middle East since 1500, ed. Nikki R. Keddi. Berkeley, CA: University of California Press.

Crenshaw, Martha. 1981. "The Causes of Terrorism." *Comparative Politics* 13(4):379–399.

Crenshaw, Martha. 1993. "Book Review: The Mind of the Political Terrorist." *Political Psychology* 14(1):169–171.

Crenshaw, Martha. 2000. "The Psychology of Terrorism: An Agenda for the 21st Century." *Political Psychology* 21(2):405–420.

Culpepper, Pepper D. 2008. "The Politics of Common Knowledge: Ideas and Institutional Change in Wage Bargaining." *International Organization* 62:1–33.

Davies, James C. 1969. "The J-Curve of Rising and Declining Satisfaction as a Cause of Some Great Revolutions and a Contained Rebellion." In *Violence in America*, ed. Hugh Davis Graham and Ted Robert Gurr. New York: Signet.

Davis, Nancy Jean and Robert V. Robinson. 2012. *Claiming Society for God: Religious Movements and Social Welfare*. Indiana: Indiana University Press.

Dawson, Lorne L. and Amarnath Amarasingam. 2017. "Talking to Foreign Fighters: Insights into the Motivations." *Studies in Conflict & Terrorism* 40(3):191–210.

Delavande, Adeline and Basit Zafar. 2015. "Stereotypes and Madrassas: Experimental evidence from Pakistan." *Journal of Economic Behavior & Organization* 118:247–267.

Della Porta, Donatella. 2013. *Clandestine Political Violence*. Cambridge: Cambridge University Press.

Deol, Jeevan and Zaheer Kazmi, eds. 2012. *Contextualising Jihadi Thought*. New York: Columbia University Press.

Devji, Faisal. 2005. *Landscapes of the Jihad*. Ithaca, NY: Cornell University Press.

Dollard, John, Neal E. Miller, Leonard W. Doob, Orval Hobart Mowrer, and Robert R. Sears. 1939. *Frustration and Aggression*. New Haven, CT: Yale University Press.

Dolnik, Adam, ed. 2013. *Conducting Terrorism Field Research: A Guide*. New York: Routledge.

Drake, Stillman. 1978. *Galileo at Work: His Scientific Biography*. Chicago: University of Chicago Press.

Drevon, Jerome. 2016. "Embracing Salafi Jihadism in Egypt and Mobilizing in the Syrian Jihad." *Middle East Critique* 25(4):1–19.

Efron, Bradley and Robert Tibshirani. 1993. *An Introduction to the Bootstrap*. Boca Raton, FL: Chapman & Hall/CRC.

El-Ghobashy, Mona. 2005. "Metamorphosis of the Egyptian Muslim Brothers." *International Journal of Middle East Studies* 37:373–395.

Enders, Walter, Gary A. Hoover, and Todd Sandler. 2014. "The Changing Nonlinear Relationship between Income and Terrorism." *Journal of Conflict Resolution* 60(2):195–225.

Etling, Bruce, John Kelly, Robert Faris, and John Palfrey. 2010. "Mapping the Arabic Blogosphere: Politics and Dissent Online." *New Media & Society* 12(8):1225–1243.

Euben, Roxanne. 1999. *Enemy in the Mirror*. Princeton: Princeton University Press.

Euben, Roxanne L. and Muhammad Qasim Zaman, eds. 2009. *Princeton Readings in Islamist Thought: Texts and Contexts from al-Banna to Bin Laden*. Princeton: Princeton University Press.

Fabbe, Kristin. 2012. "Disciples of the State: Secularization and State Building in the Former Ottoman World," PhD thesis, Massachusetts Institute of Technology.

Fair, C. Christine, Jacob S. Goldstein, and Ali Hamza. 2017. "Can Knowledge of Islam Explain Lack of Support for Terrorism? Evidence from Pakistan." *Studies in Conflict & Terrorism* 40(4):339–355.

Fair, C. Christine, Rebecca Littman, Neil Malhotra, and Jacob N. Shapiro. 2013. "Relative Poverty, Perceived Violence, and Support for Militant Politics: Evidence from Pakistan." *Political Science Research and Methods*: 1–25.

Faraj, Muhammad Abd al-Islam. 1981. *Al-Jihad: al-farida al-gha'iba [Jihad: The Forgotten Duty]*.

Fearon, James D. and David D. Laitin. 2008. "Integrating Qualitative and Quantitative Methods." In *The Oxford Handbook of Political Methodology*, ed. Janet M. Box-Steffensmeier, Henry E. Brady, and David Collier. Oxford: Oxford University Press.

Flowerdew, John. 2002. *Academic Discourse*. London: Taylor and Francis.

Ford, Heather. 2014. "Big Data and Small: Collaborations between Ethnographers and Data Scientists." *Big Data & Society* 1(2):1–3.

Fox, Jonathan. 2000. "Is Islam More Conflict Prone Than Other Religions? A Cross-Sectional Study of Ethnoreligious Conflict." *Nationalism and Ethnic Politics* 6(2):1–24.

Fox, Jonathan. 2003. "Religion as an Overlooked Element of International Relations." *International Studies Review* 3(3):53–73.

Fuchs, Simon Wolfgang. 2013. "Do Excellent Surgeons Make Miserable Exegetes? Negotiating the Sunni Tradition in the ğihādī Camps." *Die Welt des Islams* 53(2):192–237.

Gaffney, Patrick D. 1991. "The Changing Voices of Islam: The Emergence of Professional Preachers in Contemporary Egypt." *Muslim World* 81(1):27–47.

Gaffney, Patrick D. 1994. *The Prophet's Pulpit: Islamic Preaching in Contemporary Egypt*. Berkeley: University of California Press.

Gambetta, Diego and Steffen Hertog. 2016. *Engineers of Jihad: The Curious Connection betwen Violent Extremism and Education*. Princeton: Princeton University Press.

Gerges, Fawaz A. 2005. *The Far Enemy: Why Jihad Went Global*. New York: Cambridge University Press.

Gerring, John. 1997. "Ideology: A Definitional Analysis." *Political Research Quarterly* 50 (4):957–994.

Giles, Jim. 2005. "Internet Encyclopaedias Go Head to Head." *Nature* 438:900–901.

Gill, Anthony. 1998. *Rendering unto Caesar: The Catholic Church and the State in Latin America*. Chicago: University of Chicago Press.

Goldstein, Judith and Robert O. Keohane, eds. 1993. *Ideas and Foreign Policy: An Analyitical Framework*. Ithaca, NY: Cornell University Press.

Gong, Abe. n.d. "An Automated Snowball Census of the Political Web." Accessed at http://papers.ssrn.com/sol3/papers.cfm?abstract_id=1832024.

Graf, Bettina and Jakob Skovgaard-Petersen, eds. 2009. *Global Mufti*. London: C. Hurst & Company.

Grimmer, Justin and Brandon Stewart. 2013. "Text as Data: The Promise and Pitfalls of Automatic Content Analysis Methods for Political Texts." *Political Analysis* 21(3):267–297.

Gurr, Ted. 1968a. "A Causal Model of Civil Strife: A Comparative Analysis Using New Indices." *American Political Science Review* 62(04):1104–1124.

Gurr, Ted. 1968*b*. "Psychological Factors in Civil Violence." *World Politics* 20(02):245–278.

Gurr, Ted Robert. 1970. *Why Men Rebel*. Princeton: Princeton University Press.

Gurr, Ted Robert. 2010. *Why Men Rebel*, Fortieth Anniversary Edition. Princeton: Princeton University Press.

Gurr, Ted Robert and Raymond Duvall. 1973. "Civil Conflict in the 1960s: A Reciprocal Theoretical System with Parameter Estimates." *Comparative Political Studies* 6(2):135–169.

Habeck, Mary R. 2006. *Knowing the Enemy: Jihadist Ideology and the War on Terror*. New Haven, NJ: Yale University Press.

Habibi, Nader. 2017 "Higher Education Policies and Overeducation in Turkey." *European Journal of Higher Education* 1–10.

Haddad, Gholamreza Keshavarz and Nader Habibi. 2016. "Vertical Skill Mismatch Incidence and Wage Consequences in Low-Skill Jobs: Evidence from Iran's Labor Market." *International Labour Review*.

Hafez, Mohammed M. 2003. *Why Muslims Rebel: Repression and Resistance in the Islamic World*. Boulder, CO: Lynne Rienner Publishers.

Hall, Peter A., ed. 1989. *The Political Power of Economic Ideas: Keynesianism across Nations*. Princeton: Princeton University Press.

Harmon-Jones, Cindy, Brandon J. Schmeichel, and Eddie Harmon-Jones. 2009. "Symbolic Self-Completion in Academia: Evidence from Department Web Pages and Email Signature Files." *European Journal of Social Psychology* 39(2):311–316.

Hasenclever, Andreas and Volker Rittberger. 2000. "Does Religion Make a Difference? Theoretical Approaches to the Impact of Faith on Political Conflict." *Millenium: Journal of International Studies* 29(3):641–674.

Hassner, Ron E. 2009. *War on Sacred Grounds*. Ithaca, NY: Cornell University Press.

Hassner, Ron E. 2011. "Blasphemy and Violence." *International Studies Quarterly* 55(1):23–45.

Hassner, Ron E. 2013. "How to Cite a Sacred Text." *Politics and Religion* 6(4):844–861.

Hassner, Ron E. 2016. *Religion on the Battlefield*. Ithaca, NY: Cornell University Press.

Hassner, Ron E. and Michael C Horowitz. 2010. "Debating the Role of Religion in War." *International Security* 35(1):201–208.

Hastie, Trevor, Robert Tibshirani and Jerome Friedman. 2009. *Elements of Statistical Learning: Data Mining, Inference, and Prediction*. New York: Springer.

Hatina, Meir. 2010. *Ulama, Politics, and the Public Sphere: An Egyptian Perspective*. Salt Lake City: University of Utah Press.

Hawkins, Kirk. 2009. "Is Chavez Populist? Measuring Populist Discourse in Comparative Perspective." *Comparative Political Studies* 42(8):1040–1067.

Haykel, Bernard, Thomas Hegghammer, and Stéphane Lacroix. 2015. *Saudi Arabia in Transition: Insights on Social, Political, Economic and Religious Change*. New York: Cambridge University Press.

Hegghammer, Thomas. 2009. "Jihadi-Salafis or Revolutionaries? On Religion and Politics in the Study of Militant Islamism." In *Global Salafism: Islam's New Religious Movement*, ed., R. Meijer. New York: Columbia University Press.

Hegghammer, Thomas. 2010*a*. *Jihad in Saudi Arabia: Violence and Pan-Islamism Since 1979*. Cambridge: Cambridge University Press.

Hegghammer, Thomas. 2010*b*. "The Rise of Muslim Foreign Fighters: Islam and the Globalization of Jihad." *International Security* 35(3):53–94.

Hegghammer, Thomas. 2013. "Should I Stay or Should I Go? Explaining Variation in Western Jihadists' Choice between Domestic and Foreign Fighting." *American Journal of Political Science* 107(1):1–15.

Hegghammer, Thomas and Joas Wagemakers. 2013. "The Palestine Effect: The Role of Palestinians in the Transnational Jihad Movement." *Welt des Islams* 53(3-4):281–314.

Hermassi, Abdelbaki. 1994. "The Political and Religious in the Modern History of the Maghrib." In *Islamism and Secularism in North Africa*, ed. John Reudy. New York: St. Martin's Press.

Hopkins, Daniel and Gary King. 2010. "A Method of Automated Nonparametric Content Analysis for Social Science." *American Journal of Political Science* 54(1):229–247.

Horgan, John. 2003. "The Search for a Terrorist Personality." In *Terrorists, Victims, and Society: Psychological Perspectives on Terrorism and Its Consequences*, ed. A. Silke. Chichester, West Sussex: Wiley.

Horowitz, Michael C. 2009. "Long Time Going: Religion and the Duration of Crusading." *International Security* 34(2):162–193.

Horowitz, Michael C., Allan C. Stam, and Cali M. Ellis. 2015. *Why Leaders Fight*. New York: Cambridge University Press.

Iannaccone, Laurence R. 1988. "A Formal Model of Church and Sect." *The American Journal of Sociology* 94:s241–s246.

Iannaccone, Laurence R. 1994. "Why Strict Churches Are Strong." *American Journal of Sociology* 99(5):1180–1211.

Iannaccone, Laurence R. 1995. "Voodoo Economics? Defending the Rational Choice Approach to Religion." *Journal for the Scientific Study of Religion* 34:76–88.

Iannaccone, Laurence R. 1998. "The Economics of Religion: A Survey of Recent Work." *Journal of Economic Literature* 36:1465–1496.

Iannaccone, Laurence R. and Eli Berman. 2006. "Religious Extremism: The Good, the Bad, and the Deadly." *Public Choice* 128(1-2):109–129.

Jackson, Matthew O. 2008. *Social and Economic Networks*, Vol. 3. Princeton: Princeton University Press.

Jacobs, Alan M. 2009. "How Do Ideas Matter? Mental Models and Attention in German Pension Politics." *Comparative Political Studies* 42(2):252–279.

Janis, Irving L. and Bert T. King. 1954. "The Influence of Role Playing on Opinion Change." *The Journal of Abnormal and Social Psychology* 49(2):211–218.

Jones, Calvert. 2017. *Bedouins into Bourgeois: Remaking Citizens for Globalization*. New York: Cambridge University Press.

Jones, Seth G. 2014. A Persistent Threat: The Evolution of al Qa'ida and Other Salafi Jihadists. Santa Monica, CA: RAND Corporation. www.rand.org/pubs/research_reports/RR637.

Judge, Timothy A. and John D. Kammeyer-Mueller. 2012. "On the Value of Aiming High: the Causes and Consequences of Ambition." *Journal of Applied Psychology* 97(4):758.

Jungert, Tomas. 2013. "Social Identities among Engineering Students and through Their Transition to Work: A Longitudinal Study." *Studies in Higher Education* 31(1):39–52.

Keefer, Philip and Norman Loayza, eds. 2008. *Terrorism, Economic Development, and Political Openness*. Cambridge: Cambridge University Press.

Kenney, Jeffrey T. 2015. "Selling Success, Nurturing the Self: Self-help Literature, Capitalist Values, and the Sacralization of Subjective Life in Egypt." *International Journal of Middle East Studies* 47(4):663–680.

Kepel, Gilles. 1984. *Muslim Extremism in Egypt: The Prophet and the Pharaoh.* Berkeley and Los Angeles: University of California Press.

Kepel, Gilles and Jean-Pierre Milelli, eds. 2005. *Al-Qaida Dans la Texte.* Cambridge, MA: Harvard University Press.

Khalidi, Tarif. 1973. "Islamic Biographical Dictionaries: A Preliminary Assessment." *The Muslim World* 63(1):53–65.

Khosrokhavar, Farhad. 2011. *Jihadist Ideology: The Anthropological Perspective.* Aarhus, Denmark: Centre for Studies in Islamism and Radicalization.

King, Gary. 2011. "Ensuring the Data-Rich Future of the Social Sciences." *Science* 331(6018):719–721.

King, Gary and Ying Lu. 2008. "Verbal Autopsy Methods with Multiple Causes of Death." *Statistical Science* 23(1):78–91.

King, Michael and Donald M. Taylor. 2011. "The Radicalization of Homegrown Jihadists: A Review of Theoretical Models and Social Psychological Evidence." *Terrorism and Political Violence* 23(4):602–622.

Knight, Kathleen. 2006. "Transformations of the Concept of Ideology in the Twentieth Century." *American Political Science Review* 100(4):619–626.

Krueger, Alan B. 2007. *What Makes a Terrorist: Economics and the Roots of Terrorism.* Princeton: Princeton University Press.

Krueger, Alan B. and Jitka Maleckova. 2003. "Education, Poverty and Terrorism: Is There a Causal Connection?" *Journal of Economic Perspectives* 17(4):119–144.

Kruglanski, Arie W., Xiaoyan Chen, Mark Dechesne, Shira Fishman, and Edward Orehek. 2009. "Fully Committed: Suicide Bombers' Motivation and the Quest for Personal Significance." *Political Psychology* 30(3):331–357.

Kuran, Timur. 2011. *The Long Divergence: How Islamic Law Held Back the Middle East.* Princeton: Princeton University Press.

Lacroix, Stephane. 2011. *Awakening Islam: The Politics of Religious Dissent in Contemporary Saudi Arabia.* Cambridge, MA: Harvard University Press.

Lahoud, Nelly. 2010. *The Jihadis' Path to Self-Destruction.* London: C. Hurst & Co. Ltd.

Lakatos, Imre. 1970. Falsification and the Methodology of Scientific Research Programs. In *Criticism and the Growth of Knowledge,* ed. I. Lakatos and A. Musgrave. Cambridge: Cambridge University Press.

Larkey, Leah S., Lisa Ballesteros, and Margaret E. Connell. 2007. "Light Stemming for Arabic Information Retrieval." In *Arabic Computational Morphology,* Vol. 38, ed. Abdelhadi Soudi, Antal van den Bosch, and Günter Neumann. Dordrecht: Springer.

Lav, Daniel. 2012. *Radical Islam and the Revival of Medieval Theology.* New York: Cambridge University Press.

Lee, Alexander. 2011. "Who Becomes a Terrorist? Poverty, Education, and the Origins of Political Violence." *World Politics* 63(2):203–245.

Lester, David, Bijou Yang, and Mark Lindsay. 2004. "Suicide Bombers: Are Psychological Profiles Possible?" *Studies in Conflict & Terrorism* 27(4):283–295.

Letham, Benjamin, Cynthia Rudin, and Katherine A. Heller. 2013. "Growing a List." *Data Mining and Knowledge Discovery* 27(3):372–395.

Lia, Brynjar. 2008. *Architect of Global Jihad: The Life of Al Qaeda Strategist Abu Mus'ab Al-Suri.* New York: Columbia University Press.

Lockman, Zachary. 2004. *Contending Visions of the Middle East: The History and Politics of Orientalism.* New York: Cambridge University Press.

Long, Jerry Mark and Alex S. Wilner. 2014. "Delegitimizing al-Qaida: Defeating an 'Army Whose Men Love Death.'" *International Security* 39(1):126–164.

Lowe, William and Kenneth Benoit. n.d. "Estimating Uncertainty in Quantitative Text Analysis." Unpublished manuscript, prepared for the 2011 Midwest Political Science Association.

Loza, Wagdy. 2007. "The Psychology of Extremism and Terrorism: A Middle-Eastern Perspective." *Aggression and Violent Behavior* 12(2):141–155.

Lucas, Christopher, Richard Nielsen, Margaret Roberts, Brandon Stewart, Alex Storer, and Dustin Tingley. 2015. "Computer Assisted Text Analysis for Comparative Politics." *Political Analysis* 23(3):254–277.

MacQueen, J. B. 1967. Some Methods for Classification and Analysis of Multivariate Observations. In *Proceedings of 5th Berkeley Symposium on Mathematical Statistics and Probability*. Berkeley: University of California Press.

Maher, Shiraz. 2016. *Salafi-Jihadism: The History of an Idea*. New York: Oxford University Press.

Maleckova, Jitka. 2005. Impoverished Terrorists: Stereotype or Reality? In *Root Causes of Terrorism: Myths, Reality and Ways Forward*, ed. Tore Bjorgo. London: Routledge.

Malik, Jamal et al. 2007. *Madrasas in South Asia: Teaching Terror?* Abingdon, Oxford: Routledge.

Martens, Willem H. J. 2004. "The Terrorist with Antisocial Personality Disorder." *Journal of Forensic Psychology Practice* 4(1):45–56.

Masoud, Tarek. 2014. *Counting Islam: Religion, Class, and Elections in Egypt*. New York: Cambridge University Press.

Masoud, Tarek, Amaney Jamal, and Elizabeth Nugent. 2016. "Using the Qur'ān to Empower Arab Women? Theory and Experimental Evidence From Egypt." *Comparative Political Studies* 49(12):1555–1598.

Masud, Muhammad Khalid, Brinkley Messick, and David S. Powers, eds. 1996. *Islamic Legal Interpretation: Muftis and Their Fatwas*. Cambridge, MA: Harvard University Press.

Mazawi, Andre Elias. 2005. "The Academic Profession in a Rentier State: The Professoriate in Saudi Arabia." *Minerva* 43:221–244.

McCants, William. 2006. "Militant Ideology Atlas." West Point, NY: Combating Terrorism Center, U.S. Military Academy.

McCants, William. 2015. *The ISIS Apocalypse: The History, Strategy, and Doomsday Vision of the Islamic State*. New York: Macmillan.

McClendon, Gwyneth and Rachel Beatty Riedl. 2015. "Religion as a Stimulant of Political Participation: Experimental Evidence from Nairobi, Kenya." *The Journal of Politics* 77(4):1045–1057.

Mehta, Jal. 2011. "The Varied Roles of Ideas in Politics: From 'Whether' to 'How.'" In *Ideas and Politics in Social Science Research*, ed. Daniel Béland and Robert Henry Cox. New York: Oxford University Press.

Meijer, Roel. 2007. "Yūsuf al-'Uyairī and the Making of a Revolutionary Salafi Praxis." *Die Welt des Islams* 47(3–4):422–459.

Meijer, Roel, ed. 2009. *Global Salafism: Islam's New Religious Movement*. New York: Columbia University Press.

Mendelsohn, Barak. 2009. *Combating Jihadism: American Hegemony and International Cooperation in the War on Terrorism*. Chicago: University of Chicago Press.

Mendelsohn, Barak. 2016. *The Al-Qaeda Franchise: The Expansion of Al-Qaeda and Its Consequences.* New York: Oxford University Press.

Menoret, Pascal. 2014. *Joyriding in Riyadh: Oil, Urbanism, and Road Revolt.* New York: Cambridge University Press.

Messick, Brinkley. 1996. "Media Muftis: Radio Fatwas in Yemen." In *Islamic Legal Interpretation: Muftis and Their Fatwas*, ed. Muhammad Khalid Masud, Brinkley Messick, David Powers. Cambridge, MA: Harvard University Press.

Milgram, Stanley. 1975. *Obedience to Authority: An Experimental View.* New York: Harper & Row.

Miller, Flagg. 2015. *The Audacious Ascetic: What the Bin Laden Tapes Reveal about Al-Qa'ida.* Oxford: Oxford University Press.

Miller, Neal E. 1941. "I. The Frustration-Aggression Hypothesis." *Psychological Review* 48(4):337.

Mironova, Vera, Loubna Mrie, and Sam Whitt. 2014. "Voices of Syria Project," https://harvardgazette.files.wordpress.com/2015/04/islamists1-read-only.pdf.

Moghadam, Assaf and Brian Fishman, eds. 2011. *Fault Lines in Global Jihad: Organizational, Strategic, and Ideological Fissures.* New York: Routledge.

Moghaddam, Fathali M. 2005. "The Staircase to Terrorism: A Psychological Exploration." *American Psychologist* 60(2):161–169.

Mohammed, Khaleel. 2005. "Assessing English Translations of the Qur'an." *Middle East Quarterly* 12(2):58–71.

Mottahedeh, Roy Parviz and Ridwan al Sayyid. 2001. "The Idea of the Jihad in Islam before the Crusades." In *The Crusades from the Perspective of Byzantium and the Muslim World*, ed. Angeliki E. Laiou and Roy Parviz Mottahedeh. Washington, DC: Dumbarton Oaks.

Mouline, Nabil. 2015. "Enforcing and Reinforcing the State's Islam: The Functioning of the Senior Committee of Scholars." In *Saudi Arabia in Transition*, ed. Bernard Heykal, Thomas Hegghammer, and Stephane Lacroix. Cambridge: Cambridge University Press.

Mouline, Nabile. 2014. *The Clerics of Islam: Religious Authority and Political Power in Saudi Arabia.* New Haven: Yale University Press.

Mourad, Suleiman A. and James E. Lindsay. 2013. *The Intensification and Reorientation of Sunni Jihad Ideology in the Crusader Period.* Leiden: Brill.

Mousseau, Michael. 2011. "Urban Poverty and Support for Islamist Terror: Survey Results of Muslims in Fourteen Countries." *Journal of Peace Research* 48(1):35–47.

Muhanna, Elias, ed. 2016. *The Digital Humanities and Islamic & Middle East Studies.* Berlin: Walter de Gruyter.

Naroll, Raoul. 1962. *Data Quality Control.* New York: Free Press.

Nasr, Vali. 2007. *The Shia Revival: How Conflicts within Islam Will Shape the Future.* New York: W. W. Norton & Company.

Nelson, Stephen C. 2014. "Playing Favorites: How Shared Beliefs Shape the IMF's Lending Decisions." *International Organization* 68(2):297.

Nielsen, Richard A. 2015. "Ethics for Experimental Manipulation of Religion." In *Ethics and Experiments: Problems and Solutions for Social Scientists and Policy Professionals*, ed. Scott Desposato. London: Routledge.

Nielsen, Richard A. 2017. "Replication Data for: Deadly Clerics (CUP 2017)." http://dx.doi.org/10.7910/DVN/PG4A7K.

Nisbett, Richard and Timothy DeCamp Wilson. 1977. "Telling More Than We Can Know: Verbal Reports on Mental Processes." *Psychological Review* 84(3):231–260.

Oberschall, Anthony. 1978. "Theories of Social Conflict." *Annual Review of Sociology* 4(1):291–315.

O'Mahoney, Joseph. 2015. "Why Did They Do That? The Methodology of Reasons for Action." *International Theory* 7(2):231–262.

Orsi, Robert A. 2005. *Between Heaven and Earth: The Religious Worlds People Make and the Scholars Who Study Them*. Princeton: Princeton University Press.

Palmer, Monte and Princess Palmer. 2008. *Islamic Extremism: Causes, Diversity, and Challenges*. Lanham, MD: Rowman & Littlefield Publishers Inc.

Pastore, Nicholas. 1952. "The Role of Arbitrariness in the Frustration-Aggression Hypothesis." *Journal of Abnormal and Social Psychology* 47(3):728.

Patel, David. 2012. "Concealing to Reveal: The Informational Role of Islamic Dress." *Rationality and Society* 24(3):295–323.

Pearlman, Wendy. 2015. "Puzzles, Time, and Ethnographic Sensibilities: Research Methods after the Arab Spring." *Middle East Law and Governance* 7(1):132–140.

Pearlstein, Richard M. 1991. *The Mind of the Political Terrorist*. Wilmington, DE: Scholarly Resources Inc.

Pepinsky, Thomas B., R. William Liddle, and Saiful Mujani. 2012. "Testing Islam's Political Advantage: Evidence from Indonesia." *American Journal of Political Science* 56(3):584–600.

Pezzo, Mark V. and Jason Beckstead. 2008. "The Effects of Disappointment on Hindsight Bias for Real-world Outcomes." *Applied Cognitive Psychology* 22(4):491–506.

Philpott, Daniel. 2000. "The Religious Roots of Modern International Relations." *World Politics* 52(2):206–245.

Philpott, Daniel. 2001. *Revolutions in Sovereignty: How Ideas Shaped Modern International Relations*. Princeton: Princeton University Press.

Piazza, James A. 2006. "Rooted in Poverty? Terrorism, Poor Economic Development, and Social Cleavages 1." *Terrorism and Political Violence* 18(1):159–177.

Platt, Stephen R. 2012. *Autumn in the Heavenly Kingdom: China, the West, and the Epic Story of the Taiping Civil War*. New York: Vintage Books.

Porteous, Ian, David Newman, Alexander Ihler, Arthur Asuncion, Padhraic Smyth, and Max Welling. 2008. "Fast Collapsed Gibbs Sampling for Latent Dirichlet Allocation." *SIGKDD*.

Porter, Martin. F. 1980. "An Algorithm for Suffix Stripping." *Program* 14(3):130–137.

Post, Jerrold M., Farhana Ali, Schuyler W. Henderson, Stephen Shanfield, Jeff Victoroff, and Stevan Weine. 2009. "The Psychology of Suicide Terrorism." *Psychiatry* 72(1):13–29.

Qutb, Sayyid. 2006. *Ma'alim fi'l-Tareeq [Milestones]*. Birmingham: Maktabah Booksellers and Publishers.

Reich, Robert B., ed. 1988. *The Power of Public Ideas*. Cambridge, MA: Harvard University Press.

Reynolds, Dwight F., ed. 2001. *Interpreting the Self: Autobiography in the Arabic Literary Tradition*. Berkeley: University of California Press. Full text available at http://ark.cdlib.org/ark:/13030/ft2c6004x0.

Reynolds, Sean C. and Mohammed M. Hafez. 2017. "Social Network Analysis of German Foreign Fighters in Syria and Iraq." *Terrorism and Political Violence*: 1–26.

Richardson, Laurel. 1997. *Fields of Play: Constructing an Academic Life*. New Brunswick, NJ: Rutgers University Press.

Roberts, Margaret E., Brandon M. Stewart, Dustin Tingley, Christopher Lucas, Jetson Leder-Luis, Shana Kushner Gadarian, Bethany Albertson, and David G. Rand. 2014. "Structural Topic Models for Open-Ended Survey Responses." *American Journal of Political Science* 58(4):1064–1082.

Roberts, Margaret E., Brandon M. Stewart, and Edoardo M. Airoldi. 2016. "A Model of Text for Experimentation in the Social Sciences." *Journal of the American Statistical Association* 111(515):988–1003.

Sageman, Marc. 2004. *Understanding Terror Networks.* Philadelphia: University of Pennsylvania Press.

Sageman, Marc. 2014. "The Stagnation in Terrorism Research." *Terrorism and Political Violence* 26(4):565–580.

Said, Edward. 1978. *Orientalism.* New York: Pantheon Books.

Saiya, Nilay. 2016. "Religion, State, and Terrorism: A Global Analysis." *Terrorism and Political Violence*: 1–20.

Schwedler, Jillian. 2007. *Faith in Moderation: Islamist Parties in Jordan and Yemen.* New York: Cambridge University Press.

Schwedler, Jillian. 2011. "Can Islamists Become Moderates? Rethinking the Inclusion-Moderation Hypothesis." *World Politics* 63(2):347–376.

Shane, Scott. 2015. *Objective Troy: A Terrorist, a President, and the Rise of the Drone.* New York: Tim Duggan Books.

Shapiro, Jacob. 2013. *The Terrorist's Dilemma: Managing Violent Covert Organizations.* Princeton: Princeton University Press.

Silke, Andrew. 2003. "Becoming a Terrorist." In *Terrorists, Victims, and Society: Psychological Perspectives on Terrorism and Its Consequences*, ed. A. Silke. Chichester, West Sussex: Wiley.

Skocpol, Theda. 1979. *States and Social Revolutions: A Comparative Analysis of France, Russia and China.* Cambridge: Cambridge University Press.

Smith, Adam and Joseph Shield Nicholson. 1887. *An Inquiry Into the Nature and Causes of the Wealth of Nations.* Edinburgh: T. Nelson and Sons.

Sontag, Deborah, David M. Herszenhorn, and Serge F. Kovaleski. 2013. "A Battered Dream, Then a Violent Path." *The New York Times* (April 27).

Speckhard, Anne. 2013. "The Boston Marathon Bombers: The Lethal Cocktail that Turned Troubled Youth to Terrorism." *Perspectives on Terrorism* 7(3).

Stern, Jessica. 2000. "Pakistan's Jihad Culture." *Foreign Affairs* (Nov–Dec):115–126.

Stern, Jessica. 2014. "Response to Marc Sageman's 'The Stagnation in Terrorism Research.'" *Terrorism and Political Violence* 26(4):607–613.

Sullivan, Daniel P. 2007. "Tinder, Spark, Oxygen, and Fuel: The Mysterious Rise of the Taliban." *Journal of Peace Research* 44(1):93–108.

Tarrow, Sidney G. 2011. *Power in Movement: Social Movements and Contentious Politics.* Cambridge: Cambridge University Press.

Taylor, Julie. 2008. "Prophet Sharing: Strategic Interaction Between Muslim Clerics and Middle Eastern Regimes." *Journal of Islamic Law and Culture* 10(1):41–62.

Tilly, Charles. 1978. *From Mobilization to Revolution.* Boston: Addison-Wesley Publishing Company.

Tilly, Charles. 2003. *The Politics of Collective Violence.* Cambridge: Cambridge University Press.

Tilly, Charles, Douglas McAdam, and Sidney Tarrow. 2001. *Dynamics of Contention.* Cambridge: Cambridge University Press.

Toft, Monica Duffy. 2007. "Getting Religion? The Puzzling Case of Islam and Civil War." *International Security* 31(4):97–131.

Toft, Monica Duffy, Daniel Philpott, and Timothy Samuel Shah, eds. 2011. *God's Century: Resurgent Religion and Global Politics*. New York: W. W. Norton & Company.

Touati, Houari. 2010. *Islam and Travel in the Middle Ages*. Chicago: University of Chicago Press.

Trejo, Guillermo. 2009. "Religious Competition and Ethnic Mobilization in Latin America: Why the Catholic Church Promotes Indigenous Movements in Mexico." *American Political Science Review* 103(03):323–342.

Trejo, Guillermo. 2012. *Popular Movements in Autocracies: Religion, Repression, and Indigenous Collective Action in Mexico*. Cambridge: Cambridge University Press.

Trotsky, Leon. 1932. *The History of the Russian Revolution, Volume 2: The Attempted Counter-Revolution*. Prinkipo.

Tuastad, Dag. 2003. "Neo-Orientalism and the New Barbarism Thesis: Aspects of Symbolic Violence in the Middle East Conflict(s)." *Third World Quarterly* 24(4):591–599.

van Dijk, Wilco W., Joop van der Pligt, and Marcel Zeelenberg. 1999. "Effort Invested in Vain: The Impact of Effort on the Intensity of Disappointment and Regret." *Motivation and Emotion* 23(3):203–220.

Victoroff, Jeff. 2005. "The Mind of the Terrorist: A Review and Critique of Psychological Approaches." *The Journal of Conflict Resolution* 49(1):3–42.

Voßemer, Jonas and Bettina Schuck. 2016. "Better Overeducated than Unemployed? The Short- and Long-Term Effects of an Overeducated Labour Market Re-entry." *European Sociological Review* 32(2):251–265.

Wagemakers, Joas. 2011. "Al-Qa'ida's Editor: Abu Jandal al-Azdi's Online Jihadi Activism." *Politics, Religion & Ideology* 12(4):355–369.

Wagemakers, Joas. 2012. *A Quietist Jihadi: The Ideology and Influence of Abu Muhammad al-Maqdisi*. Cambridge: Cambridge University Press.

Waltz, Kenneth. 1979. *Theory of International Politics*. New York: McGraw-Hill.

Watts, Duncan J. 2004. *Six Degrees: The Science of a Connected Age*. W. W. Norton & Company.

Wedeen, Lisa. 2010. "Reflections on Ethnographic Work in Political Science." *Annual Review of Political Science* 13:255–272.

Weisman, Carol S, Laura L. Morlock, Diana G. Sack, and David M. Levine. 1976. "Sex Differences in Response to a Blocked Career Pathway among Unaccepted Medical School Applicants." *Work and Occupations* 3(2):187–208.

Wendt, Alexander. 1999. *Social Theory of International Politics*. Cambridge: Cambridge University Press.

Wickham, Carrie. 2002. *Mobilizing Islam: Religion, Activism, and Political Change in Egypt*. New York: Columbia University Press.

Wickham, Carrie Rosefsky. 2013. *The Muslim Brotherhood*. Princeton: Princeton University Press.

Wicklund, Robert A. and Peter M. Gollwitzer. 1981. "Symbolic Self-Completion, Attempted Influence, and Self-Deprecation." *Basic and Applied Social Psychology* 2(2):89–114.

Wike, Richard and Nilanthi Samaranayake. 2006. "Where Terrorism Finds Support in the Muslim World." Washington, DC: Pew Research Center.

Wiktorowicz, Quintan. 2001*a*. *The Management of Islamic Activism*. Albany, New York: State University of New York Press.

Wiktorowicz, Quintan. 2001*b*. "The New Global Threat: Transnational Salafis and Jihad." *Middle East Policy* 8(4):18–38.

Wiktorowicz, Quintan. 2005*a*. "A Genealogy of Radical Islam." *Studies in Conflict & Terrorism* 28(2):75–97.

Wiktorowicz, Quintan. 2005*b*. *Radical Islam Rising: Muslim Extremism in the West*. Lanham, MD: Rowman & Littlefield.

Wiktorowicz, Quintan. 2005*c*. "The Salafi Movement: Violence and Fragmentation of Community." In *Muslim Networks from Hajj to Hip Hop*, ed. Miriam Cooke and Bruce B. Lawrence. Chapel Hill: University of North Carolina Press.

Wiktorowicz, Quintan. 2006. "Anatomy of the Salafi Movement." *Studies in Conflict & Terrorism* 29:207–239.

Wood, Elisabeth Jean. 2003. *Insurgent Collective Action and Civil War in El Salvador*. Cambridge: Cambridge University Press.

Wood, Graeme. 2015. "What ISIS Really Wants." *The Atlantic* 315(2):78–94.

Wright, Lawrence. 2006. *The Looming Tower: Al-Qaeda and the Road to 9/11*. New York: Alfred A. Knopf.

Yanagizawa-Drott, David. 2014. "Propaganda and Conflict: Evidence from the Rwandan Genocide." *The Quarterly Journal of Economics* 129(4):1947–1994.

Yap, P. M. 1954. "The Mental Illness of Hung Hsiu-Ch'uan, Leader of the Taiping Rebellion." *The Far Eastern Quarterly* 13(3):287.

Zaman, Muhammad Qasim. 2002. *The Ulama in Contemporary Islam*. Princeton: Princeton University Press.

Zaman, Muhammad Qasim. 2005. "The Scope and Limits of Islamic Cosmopolitanism and the Discursive Language of the 'Ulama.'" In *Muslim Networks from Hajj to Hip Hop*, ed. Miriam Cooke and Bruce B. Lawrence. Chapel Hill: University of North Carolina Press.

Zaman, Muhammad Qasim. 2012. *Modern Islamic Thought in a Radical Age*. New York: Cambridge University Press.

Zeelenberg, Marcel and Rik Pieters. 1999. "On Service Delivery that Might Have Been." *Journal of Service Delivery* 2(1):86–97.

Zeelenberg, Marcel, Wilco W. van Dijk, Antony Manstead, and Joop van der Pligt. 1998. "The Experience of Regret and Disappointment." *Cognition & Emotion* 12(2):221–230.

Zeelenberg, Marcel, Wilco W. van Dijk, Antony S. R. Manstead, and Joop van der Pligt. 2000. "On Bad Decisions and Disconfirmed Expectancies: The Psychology of Regret and Disappointment." *Cognition and Emotion* 14(4), 521–541.

Zeelenberg, Marcel, Wilco W. van Dijk, Joop van der Pligt, Antony S. R. Manstead, Pepijn van Empelen, and Dimitri Reinderman. 1998. "Emotional Reactions to the Outcomes of Decisions: The Role of Counterfactual Thought in the Experience of Regret and Disappointment." *Organizational Behavior and Human Decision Processes* 75(2):117–141.

Zeghal, Malika. 1996. *Gardiens De L'Islam: Les Oulémas D'Al Azhar dans L'Egypte Contemporaine*. Paris: Presses de Sciences Po.

Zeghal, Malika. 1999. "Religion and Politics in Egypt: The Ulema of Al-Azhar, Radical Islam, and the State (1952-1994)." *International Journal of Middle East Studies* 31(3):371–399.

Index

Abd al-Rahman, Umar, 70n25, 165, 178
Abu-Zahra, Nadia, 58–59
academe, 13–14, 14n21
academic freedom, 16
academic research, by clerics, 102
academic writing, by clerics, 38–39
academics, and insider careers, 61–62
ad hoc sampling, 24
Afghanistan war, 5
Agrama, Hussein Ali, 42, 49
Ahmed, Amel, 19–20
Airoldi, Edoardo M., 203
al-Albani, Muhammad, 35, 136
Al Abd al-Latif, Abd al-Aziz, 118, 119n
al-Ali, Hamid
    syllabus of, 31–35, 143, 187–201
        detailed program for student, 190–194
            first level, 1.5 years, 190
            fourth phase, 2 years, 194–196
            fifth level, 2 year, 196–198
            second level, 2.5 years, 191–192
            third phase, 2 years, 192–194
        general advice for students, 188–190
        letter of reform, 200–201
        student library, 198–200
        topics of fatwas, 45–46
Al al-Sheikh, Abd al-Aziz Bin Abdullah, 29
Al al-Sheikh, Muhammad Bin Ibrahim, 69
al-Amriki, Azzam (Adam Gadahn), 122f, 157t,
    160–161
al-Arayfi, Muhammad, 87
Al Aswany, Alaa, 70
al-Awda, Salman, 37, 125, 165–166
al-Awlaki, Anwar, 170

counterterrorist officials on, 9
educational attainment, 1, 1n3
and Fort Hood shooting, 1
as inspirational, 174–175
on jihad against US, 110
path to jihadism, 51–52
on violence, 112
al-Azdi, Abu Jindal (Faris al-Zahrani), case
    study on, 127, 156t
al-Azhar University, Cairo, 17–18,
    19, 20
    becomes state university, 59–60
    as deterrent to jihadism, 70n25
    library at, 39
    study circles at, 66
    study lesson at, 41–42, 83–84
al-Baghdadi, Abu Bakr, 2, 5, 13, 124f, 139,
    156t
al-Banna, Hassan, 4
al-Barak, Abd al-Rahman Bin Nasr, 34, 62,
    137
al-Dawsary, Abd al-Rahman, 33–34
al-Fahd, Nasr, 12–13, 135–136, 156t, 170
    case study on, 156t, 159–160
al-Filistini, Abu Qatada, 30, 124f, 157t
al-Funaysan, Saud Bin Abdullah, 63
al-Ghazi, al-Zubayr, 115
al-Hawali, Safar, 165–166
al-Ibad, Abd al-Muhsin bin Hamad, 62,
    68–69
alim, definition of, 29n2 (See also cleric(s))
al-Khalidi, Ahmad, 118
al-Khudayr, Ali, 112–113
al-Libi, Abu Yahya, 74

al-Maqdisi, Abu Muhammad, 2, 10, 142
    case study on, 157t, 160, 161
    criticism of modern academic system, 74
    education and career of, 136
    emphasis on tawdid/takfir, 118
    jihad score for, 123–124f
    pathway to jihadism, 12
    web library of, 119, 128, 154, 183
    works in The Jihadist's Bookbag, 116
al-Masri, Abu Ayman, case study on, 157t
al-Masri, Abu Umar, 46
al-Masari, Nufal Abd al-Hadi, 31
al-Muhajiroun, 56
al-Qa'ida, 5, 123, 126
al-Qarni, A'id, 38, 165–166
al-Raqab, Salih Hussayn, case study on, 158t
Al-Rasheed, Madawi, 85, 167
al-Riyan, Ahmad, 27, 69, 70
al-Rubaysh, Ibrahim, case study on, 157t
al-Sabr, Sa'ad, 38
al-Sha'rawi, Muhammad Mitwali, 100
al-Shanqiti, Muhammad al-Amin, 68
al-Shu'aybi, Hamud bin Uqla', 7, 67–68, 112,
    129,
    case study on, 156t
al-Suhaym, Abd al-Rahman Bin Abdullah,
    136
al-Tarsha, Adnan, 30
al-Tartusi, Abu Basir, 118, 157t
al-Tayeb, Ahmed, 83
al-Thawri, Sufyan, 109
al-Ulwan, Sulayman Bin Nasr, 34, 63, 109
al-Wada'i, Muqbil Bin Hadi, 29
al-Zahrani, Faris (Abu Jindal al-Azdi), case
    study on, 156t
al-Zawahiri, Ayman, 2
    clerics praised by, as jihadists, 114
    The Exoneration, 126–127f
    path to jihadism, 52
    works in The Jihadist's Bookbag, 116
Amarasingam, Amarnath, 56n1
Ansari, Hassan, 6, 54–55
Arab Spring, 55, 178
authority, clerical, 28
"awakening" movement, 71, 112,
    165–166
Ayubi, Nazih, 6, 54–55
Azzam, Abdullah, 4, 7–8, 143
    case study on, 156t
    jihad score for, 122f, 123, 124f
    on justification of violence, 111–112
    works in The Jihadist's Bookbag, 116

Bagader, Abubaker A., 28, 29n2
Ballesteros, Lisa, 120
Bayes classifier, 209–211
Belkacem, Fouad, 74
Benoit, Kenneth, 210
Berkowitz, Leonard, 54
Bernard, H. Russell, 19, 20, 21
bias
    hindsight, 72
    in present study, 22
Bin Badawi, Abd al Azim, 113,160
Bin Baz, Abd al-Aziz, 29, 35, 60, 68, 89, 122f
Bin Jibreen, Abdullah, 115
Bin Laden, Usama, 2, 4, 7–8, 34, 169–170
    fatwas of, as illegitimate, 29
    jihad score for, 122f, 123, 124f
    path to jihadism, 52, 161
    personality traits, 147
Birhami, Yasir, 63
Bischof, Jonathan M., 203
Blaydes, Lisa, 86
Blei, David, 95
block bootstrap, 123
blocked ambition, 5–6
    definition of, 2, 13, 171
    future research needs, 174–175
    See also under clerics who become jihadists;
        educational networks and career paths,
        correlation with jihadism
bootstrapping, 123, 210–211
Boston Marathon bombings (2013),
    174–175
Bourdieu, Pierre, 14
Brinton, Jaquelene, 29n2
Bulliet, Richard W., 181, 184
Bunzel, Cole, 46–47
bureaucrats, government, 62
Bush, George W., 5

Canetti, Daphna, 174
Cherribi, Sam, 58
Choudary, Anjem, 75
Clark, Burton R., 13
cleric(s)
    academic identity, symbols of, 14
    clerical production, 35–49
        academic writing, 38–39
        fatwas, 42–49
        lessons, lectures, recordings, 41–42
        popular writing, 38–39
        sermons, 39–41
        websites, 36–37

definition of, 1n2, 24, 28–31
importance to jihadist movements, 8–9
knowledge needed by, 31–35
monitoring/punishment of insider clerics,
71–72
state cooptation of, 60, 70, 177, 178
cleric(s), present study
biographies of, 93–98, 133
common elements of, 93–94
curriculum vitae (CV), 93, 133, 136, 137
demand for, 94
k-means clustering, 97, 98f
length of, 94–95
purpose of, 94
topic model of, 95–97
characteristics on Internet, 98–104
age, 99–100
educational attainment, 102–104, 103f
place of birth/mobility, 100–101, 102f
what they do, 101–104
academic credentials/rank, 101–102, 103f
academic research, 102
where they are from/where they live,
100–101
educational attainment, 102–104, 103f
web census of, 84–92
empirical limitations of, 87
methodology, 88–91
number of clerics worldwide, 86
sampling
ad hoc sampling, 91
random sampling, 90–91
rare outcome problem, 91–92
Salafi oversample, 88, 92
sample size, 91
significant online presence of clerics,
86–87, 86n2
clerics who become jihadists, 57–81, 132–133
ambitions of clerics, 58–59
blocked ambitions theory, 2–3, 57–58, 64,
69–70
and cleric prior beliefs, 75
and disappointment, 72–73
and hindsight bias, 72
and late-adopting true believers, 75–77,
156t, 157t
limits of theory, 77–78
as not only factor in radicalization, 76
and signaling value of jihadism, 75
and social networks, 77–78
and sociological mechanisms, 73–74

testing theory of blocked ambitions,
79–81
career paths and radicalization, 70–72
insider careers, 61–63
academic, 61–62
government bureaucrat, 62
sharia consultants, 62–63
lay theories on radicalization as not
applicable to, 24
outsider careers, 63, 75–76
professional networks and academic careers,
64–70
informal study circles, 65–67
mentoring relationships, 66–69
and state control of clerical careers, 59–61
testing theory of blocked ambitions, 79–81
See also jihadists who become clerics
Clinton, Hillary, 175
Committee of Grand Ulama, 144
conclusions, present study
argument and evidence, 170–172
future research, 172–175
lessons learned, 179–180
policy making, 175–178
revolution in data availability, 180–185
role of educational attainment, 176
role of insider career, 176
Conflicts topic, 116, 208–209
Connell, Margaret E., 120
cooptation, state, of clerics, 60, 70, 177, 178
counterradicalization policy of Arab regimes,
177
counterterrorism, 9
credibility of clerics, 74, 143, 145, 178
gaining from preaching jihad
popularity of jihadist fatwas, 161–163t,
167
prison as jihadist credential, 163–166
Crenshaw, Martha, 174
curriculum vitae (CV), clerics in present study,
93, 133, 136, 137

Dar al-Ifta (House of Fatwa-giving), 47–48,
48n39, 83
data collection, 16–21
biographies, 24
ethnographic approach to, 17–20
Internet, 180–185
mixed methods, 16, 20
observational data, 79, 180
participant observation, 16, 19, 20, 184
primary source material, 20–21

data collection (*cont.*)
    revolution in data availability, 180–185
    social network analysis, 182–183
    statistical approach to, 17, 19–20
    statistical text analysis (*See* text analysis,
        statistical)
    See also sampling
Dawson, Lorne L., 56n1
Deol, Jeevan, 114
Dollard, John, 54

educational attainment
    of Abu Muhammad al-Maqdisi, 136
    of Anwar al-Awlaki, 1, 1n3
    cleric(s), present study, 102–104, 103f, 145
    role of, 176
educational networks and career paths,
    correlation with jihadism, 132–140
    theory of blocked ambition
        bivariate correlations, 137–140
            extensive network, 139, 140t
            interaction of teacher connection to
                career path, 138f–140
            limited network, 139–140t
        career paths, 136–137
        educational networks., 134–136
        incentives for preaching jihad, 161–166
        popularity of jihadist fatwas, 161–163,
            167
            application of jihad score model to
                fatwas, 162–163t
        prison as jihadist credential, 163–166,
            164f, 167
    insider career paths, coding, 136–137
    qualitative evidence in jihadist case studies,
        154–161, 166–167
        challenges to qualitative analysis, 168
        jihadism as dependent variable, 155
        jihadist-turned-cleric, 160
        random sampling, 155, 159
        sample size, 159
        source materials, 155, 161
        summary of case studies, 156t–158t
    quantitative evidence for alternative
        explanations, 140–154, 166
        academic expertise, 145–146
        control variables, 141, 145–146
        educational attainment of clerics, 145
        engineers as, 145–146, 154
        exposure to Western society, 146
        indicator variables, 143, 146–147
            country/city of birth of clerics, 146–147

jihadists-turned-clerics, 142–144,
    148t–149t
regression techniques to estimate
    correlations between networks,
    paths, and jihadism, 147–154
    bootstrapping procedure, 147, 150,
        150n9
    Model 1 (number of teachers), 150–152
        cleric families, 150–151
        country in which cleric born, 152
        education levels, 151
        family teachers, 151
        insider career, 150–151
        intelligence of clerics, 146, 151–152
        number of teachers, 150–151
    Model 2 (networks and career paths),
        152
        connected insiders, 152
        connected outsiders, 152
        disconnected insiders, 152
        disconnected outsiders, 152
    Model 3 (cleric with Islamic degree),
        152–153
    Model 4 (prominence of teachers),
        153–154
    religious expertise, 145, 146
    religious primary school variable, 145
    selection effects, 141–144
    treatment variables, 142, 142n6
    universities cleric attended, 154
    statistical analysis, benefits and challenges
        of, 167–168
ethics, and present study, 3, 17, 22, 184
excommunication, 109

Facebook, 28, 37, 42, 83, 84, 87, 111, 183
Fahmi (informant), 21–22
    on definition of cleric, 29, 30
Farraj, Muhammad Abd al-Islam, case study
    on, 157t
fatwas, 42–49
    Dar al-Ifta (House of Fatwa-giving), 47–48,
        48n39, 83
    fatwa-giving process, 47–49
    illegitimate, 29
    popularity of, 161–163, 167
    topics of, 44f–47
fiqh (jurisprudence), 27, 39, 39n24, 111, 143
Fort Hood shooting (2009), 1, 110
Foust, Joshua, 9
Friedman, Thomas, 175
frustration-aggression hypothesis, 54

Gadahn, Adam (Azzam al-Amriki), 123
case study on, 157t, 160–161
Gaffney, Patrick D., 76
Gambetta, Diego, 55, 145, 174, 176
Ghoneem, Abd al-Fatah Barakat, 82–83
Gingrich, Newt, 175
God, sovereignty of, 3, 25
Gomaa, Ali, 70, 70n25
Gong, Abe, 202
Google, 28, 88, 89
Google autocomplete, 88, 89
Google n-grams project, 4, 4n6
government bureaucrats, 62
greater jihad, 107
Grimmer, Justin, 182
Gurr, Ted, 6, 54, 55, 57n2, 77, 174

hadith, 34, 36, 39, 42, 111, 113, 136, 208
Hafez, Mohammed M., 7, 77
Hasan, Abd al-Hakim, case study on, 156t
Hasan, Nidal, 1, 110
Hegghammer, Thomas, 1n1, 4, 7, 129,
    159–160, 183
Hermassi, Abdelbaki, 59
Hertog, Steffan, 55, 145, 174, 176
hindsight bias, 72
Hong Xiuquan, 179–180
Horgan, John, 53
Hussein, Saddam, 5

Ibn Abd al-Wahhab, Muhammad, 107
Ibn al-Qayyim, 35
Ibn al-Uthaymeen, Muhammad, 35, 122t, 123
Ibn Taymiyya, 32, 35, 45–46, 107, 160
informal study circles, 65–67
insider careers, 15
    clerics who become jihadists, 61–63
        academics, 61–62
        government bureaucrats, 62
        sharia consultants, 62–63
    connected insiders, 152
    disconnected insiders, 152
    educational networks and career paths,
        correlation with jihadism
        coding of career paths, 136–137
        theory of blocked ambition
            bivariate correlations of teacher
                connection to career path,
                138f–140
            quantitative alternative explanations,
                regression techniques

Model 1 (number of teachers),
    150–152
Model 2 (networks and career paths),
    152
Model 3 (clerics with degree),
    152–153
Model 4 (prominence of teacher),
    153
monitoring/punishment of insider clerics,
    71–72
role of, 176
See also outsider careers
Instagram, 84
intelligence of clerics, 146, 151–152
Internet, and data availability, 180–185
interpretive orientation, 19, 20, 171
Iraq war, 5
Islamic leaders, crackdown on, in Saudi
    Arabia, 12–13
Islamic Thinkers Society, 128, 129f
Islamist, meaning of, 8n10

jihad
    appearance in Quran, 106–107
    greater, 107
    increased usage of term, 4
jihadism
    reasons to study, 21–23, 171
    rise of modern, 3–11
    signaling value of, 75
jihadist clerics, detecting from writings on
    Internet
    information sources
        biographies, 114
        endorsements, 114
        scholarly assessments, 114
    jihadist ideology, 106–114
    non-jihadist writing, 113–114
    using statistics, 25, 114–124
        accuracy of, 124–129
            relevance of word order, 125–126
            validation procedures, 126–129f, 127f
        jihad scores for clerics, 121–124, 122f
        statistical significance, 123
        statistical text analysis (*See* text analysis,
            statistical)
jihadist cleric(s)
    definition of, 106
    radicalization of, 11–16
jihadist ideology, 1n1, 106–114
    on democracy, 110
    justification of violence, 110–113

jihadist ideology (*cont.*)
   ṭāghūt (tyrant/oppressor, 109
   takfīr (excommunication), 109, 112–113
   tawḥīd (oneness of God), 108–109, 110,
      112–113
The Jihadist's Bookbag topics
   Conflicts, 208–209
   Legal Precedent, 206, 208
   Mixed, 209
   Operations, 209
   summary of, 207t–208t
   Tawhid/Takfir topic, 206
jihadists who become clerics, 2, 53–57, 132
   conclusions on, 170–171
   psychological theories on, 53–54
   sociological theories on, 53, 55–56
   See also clerics who become jihadists
Jordan, Michael I., 95

Kaczynski, Ted, 179
Kazmi, Zaheer, 114
Kepel, Gilles, 6
Khomeini (Ayatollah), 43
k-means clustering, 97, 98f

Lacroix, Stephane, 85, 114
Lakatos, Imre, 78
Larkey, Leah, 120
late-adopting true believers, 76–77, 156t, 157t
Legal Precedent topic, 116, 206, 208
lesser jihad, 107
light stemming approach, 120
Lowe, William, 210
Lucas, Christopher, 182

Mansour, Adly, 76
Masoud, Tarek, 76
Mawdudi, Abu al-Ala, 4
McCants, Will, 9, 114, 132
memorization, role in Islamic education,
   65–66, 65n15
Menoret, Pascal, 19n24, 180
mentors/mentoring, 11–12, 63, 66, 132, 134,
   176
Messick, Brinkley, 85
Milgram, Stanley, 21
"Militant Ideology Atlas," 92, 127f, 129
Miller, Flagg, 4
Miller, Neal E., 54
mixed methods, 16, 20
Mixed topic, 116, 209

model fit, 97n15
mosques in Egypt
   funding of, 76
   numbers of state *vs.* private, 76
Mouline, Nabile, 66, 85, 103–104, 144,
   144n8–145n8, 146
Muhammad, Omar Bakri, 75
Muslim Brotherhood, 160

naive Bayes classifier, 209–211
name proximity recommendation system, 90n4
Nawaz, Maajid, 75
neo-Orientalism, 22
Ng, Andrew Y., 95
Nisbett, Robert, 21

Obama, Barack, 51
Oberschall, Anthony, 7, 77
observational data, 79, 180
Operations topic, 116, 209
Orsi, Robert, 23
outsider careers, 15
   clerics who become jihadists, 63, 75–76
   connected outsiders, 152
   disconnected outsiders, 152
   jihad score for, 138f–140
   See also insider careers
overeducation, 176

participant observation, 16, 19, 20, 184
Pearlman, Wendy, 16
policy making, 175–178
political economy of religion, 14–15
popular writing, by clerics, 38–39
positivist orientation, 19, 20, 171
prospective studies, 173
psychological research, 173–174
Pulpit of Monotheism and Jihad, 119, 128,
   154, 183

qualitative approach, 26, 79, 172. *See also*
   under educational networks and career
   paths, correlation with jihadism
quantitative approach, 26, 79. *See also under*
   educational networks and career paths,
   correlation with jihadism
Quran
   appearance of word *jihad* in, 106–107
   memorization of, 18, 33–34, 145, 151
   talawiyyat (recitations), 36
Qutb, Sayyid, 4, 29, 34, 52, 116, 146

Ramadan, Tariq, 42–43
random sampling, 24, 155, 159
rapid assessment, 19
relative deprivation theory, 5–6, 54–55, 57n2, 77
residual sum of squares, 97n15
Reynolds, Sean C., 77
Ridda, Muhammad Rashid, 107
Roberts, Margaret E., 203
Rushdie, Salman, 43

Sadat, Anwar, 6
Sageman, Marc, 8, 55–56, 77, 132, 174
Sahwa Islamism, 12
Said (student at al-Azhar), 21–22
Said, Edward, 14
Salafi jihadism, 12
Salafi movement, 107
Salafism, 12n17
Salah, Ra'id, case study on, 158t
sampling
  ad hoc, 24
  random, 24, 155, 159
  rare outcome problem, 91–92
  Salafi oversample, 88, 92
  sample size, 91
Schmidt, Eric, 180–181
sermons, by clerics, 39–41
Shane, Scott, 51–52, 177
Sharia4Belgium, 74
sharia consultants, 62–63
shaykh, 28
Shia clerics, 90n7
Shi'i sect, 12n17
signaling value of jihadism, 75
Sil, Rudra, 19–20
Silke, Andrew, 55
Smith, Adam, 63n14
social network analysis, 77–78, 182–183
social network theory, 53
sociological factors, 170
sociological theory, 73–74, 78
statistical text analysis. *See* text analysis, statistical
Stewart, Brandon, 182, 203
street revolt, 180
suicide attacks, 111–112
Sullivan, Daniel P., 54–55
sunna, 73, 108
Sunni ideology, 107
Sunni sect, 12n17
Surur, Rafa'i, 165

ṭāghūt (tyrant/oppressor), 109, 161, 161n16
takfīr (excommunication), 109, 112–113
Taiping Rebellion, 179–180
tawḥīd (oneness of God), 108–109, 110, 112–113
talawiyyat (recitations of Quran), 36
Tantaway, Muhammad Sayyid, 83
Taub, Ben, 74
Tawhid/Takfir topic, 116–117, 118, 206
Taylor, Julie, 76
text analysis, statistical, 114–124
  conclusions about, 182
  light stemming approach, 120
  naive Bayes classifier as statistical model, 119–120f, 121
  removal of least/most common words, 121
  removal of stop words, 121
  topic model, 116, 117t
    Conflicts, 116
    Legal Precedent, 116
    Mixed, 116
    Operations, 116
    proportions of topic use in jihadist corpus by author, 118f
    Tawhid/Takfir, 116–117, 118
    texts representative of topics, 117t
  using documents from online jihadist library, 119
  using "The Jihadist Bookbag," 115–116, 118, 119
  using non-jihadist documents, 119–120f
Tilly, Charles
Tsarnaev, Tamerlan, 174–175
Twitter, 28, 84, 87, 183

ulama *(See also cleric(s))*
  definition of, 28, 29n2
  as interpreters of Islamic law, 107
umma, 110

Wagemakers, Joas, 10, 85, 146, 167
Wahhabism, 7, 7n9
war on terror, 5, 175
Watts, Duncan, 183
websites, cleric, 36–37
Wedeen, Lisa, 20, 21
Western society, exposure to, 146
Wickham, Carrie, 21
Wikipedia, 87, 88–89, 93
Wikipedia spider, algorithm for, 202–203

Wiktorowicz, Quinton, 8, 55–56, 75, 77, 132, 174
Wilson, Timothy D., 21
Wood, Graeme, 9, 54
World Trade Center attacks, 4, 23, 165, 169, 178
writings by clerics
    popular/academic, 38–39
    See also jihadist clerics, detecting from
        writings on Internet

wuḍū (ritual cleansing), 18, 40

YouTube, 28, 87, 136, 165

Zakaria, Yemni, 30–31
Zaman, Muhammad Qasim, 29n2, 85
Zeelenberg, Marcel, 72
Zeghal, Malika, 2, 60, 72, 85, 167

Other Books in the Series *(continued from page ii)*

Laia Balcells, *Rivalry and Revenge: The Politics of Violence during Civil War*
Lisa Baldez, *Why Women Protest? Women's Movements in Chile*
Kate Baldwin, *The Paradox of Traditional Chiefs in Democratic Africa*
Stefano Bartolini, *The Political Mobilization of the European Left, 1860–1980: The Class Cleavage*
Robert Bates, *When Things Fell Apart: State Failure in Late-Century Africa*
Mark Beissinger, *Nationalist Mobilization and the Collapse of the Soviet State*
Pablo Beramendi, *The Political Geography of Inequality: Regions and Redistribution*
Nancy Bermeo, ed., *Unemployment in the New Europe*
Nancy Bermeo and Deborah J. Yashar, eds., *Parties, Movements, and Democracy in the Developing World*
Carles Boix, *Democracy and Redistribution*
Carles Boix, *Political Order and Inequality: Their Foundations and their Consequences for Human Welfare*
Carles Boix, *Political Parties, Growth, and Equality: Conservative and Social Democratic Economic Strategies in the World Economy*
Catherine Boone, *Merchant Capital and the Roots of State Power in Senegal, 1930-1F985*
Catherine Boone, *Political Topographies of the African State: Territorial Authority and Institutional Change*
Catherine Boone, *Property and Political Order in Africa: Land Rights and the Structure of Politics*
Michael Bratton and Nicolas van de Walle, *Democratic Experiments in Africa: Regime Transitions in Comparative Perspective*
Michael Bratton, Robert Mattes, and E. Gyimah-Boadi, *Public Opinion, Democracy, and Market Reform in Africa*
Valerie Bunce, *Leaving Socialism and Leaving the State: The End of Yugoslavia, the Soviet Union, and Czechoslovakia*
Daniele Caramani, *The Nationalization of Politics: The Formation of National Electorates and Party Systems in Europe*
John M. Carey, *Legislative Voting and Accountability*
Kanchan Chandra, *Why Ethnic Parties Succeed: Patronage and Ethnic Headcounts in India*
Eric C. C. Chang, Mark Andreas Kayser, Drew A. Linzer, and Ronald Rogowski, *Electoral Systems and the Balance of Consumer-Producer Power*
José Antonio Cheibub, *Presidentialism, Parliamentarism, and Democracy*
Ruth Berins Collier, *Paths toward Democracy: The Working Class and Elites in Western Europe and South America*
Daniel Corstange, *The Price of a Vote in the Middle East: Clientelism and Communal Politics in Lebanon and Yemen*

Pepper D. Culpepper, *Quiet Politics and Business Power: Corporate Control in Europe and Japan*

Sarah Zukerman Daly, *Organized Violence after Civil War: The Geography of Recruitment in Latin America*

Christian Davenport, *State Repression and the Domestic Democratic Peace*

Donatella della Porta, *Social Movements, Political Violence, and the State*

Alberto Diaz-Cayeros, *Federalism, Fiscal Authority, and Centralization in Latin America*

Alberto Diaz-Cayeros, Federico Estévez, Beatriz Magaloni, *The Political Logic of Poverty Relief*

Jesse Driscoll, *Warlords and Coalition Politics in Post-Soviet States*

Thad Dunning, *Crude Democracy: Natural Resource Wealth and Political Regimes*

Gerald Easter, *Reconstructing the State: Personal Networks and Elite Identity*

Margarita Estevez-Abe, *Welfare and Capitalism in Postwar Japan: Party, Bureaucracy, and Business*

Henry Farrell, *The Political Economy of Trust: Institutions, Interests, and Inter-Firm Cooperation in Italy and Germany*

Karen E. Ferree, *Framing the Race in South Africa: The Political Origins of Racial Census Elections*

M. Steven Fish, *Democracy Derailed in Russia: The Failure of Open Politics*

Robert F. Franzese, *Macroeconomic Policies of Developed Democracies*

Roberto Franzosi, *The Puzzle of Strikes: Class and State Strategies in Postwar Italy*

Timothy Frye, *Building States and Markets After Communism: The Perils of Polarized Democracy*

Geoffrey Garrett, *Partisan Politics in the Global Economy*

Scott Gehlbach, *Representation through Taxation: Revenue, Politics, and Development in Postcommunist States*

Edward L. Gibson, *Boundary Control: Subnational Authoritarianism in Federal Democracies*

Jane R. Gingrich, *Making Markets in the Welfare State: The Politics of Varying Market Reforms*

Miriam Golden, *Heroic Defeats: The Politics of Job Loss*

Jeff Goodwin, *No Other Way Out: States and Revolutionary Movements*

Merilee Serrill Grindle, *Changing the State*

Anna Grzymala-Busse, *Rebuilding Leviathan: Party Competition and State Exploitation in Post-Communist Democracies*

Anna Grzymala-Busse, *Redeeming the Communist Past: The Regeneration of Communist Parties in East Central Europe*

Frances Hagopian, *Traditional Politics and Regime Change in Brazil*

Mark Hallerberg, Rolf Ranier Strauch, Jürgen von Hagen, *Fiscal Governance in Europe*

Henry E. Hale, *The Foundations of Ethnic Politics: Separatism of States and Nations in Eurasia and the World*

Stephen E. Hanson, *Post-Imperial Democracies: Ideology and Party Formation in Third Republic France, Weimar Germany, and Post-Soviet Russia*

Michael Hechter, *Alien Rule*

Timothy Hellwig, *Globalization and Mass Politics: Retaining the Room to Maneuver*

Gretchen Helmke, *Institutions on the Edge: The Origins and Consequences of Inter Branch Crises in Latin America*

Gretchen Helmke, *Courts Under Constraints: Judges, Generals, and Presidents in Argentina*

Yoshiko Herrera, *Imagined Economies: The Sources of Russian Regionalism*

Alisha C. Holland, *Forbearance as Redistribution: The Politics of Informal Welfare in Latin America*

J. Rogers Hollingsworth and Robert Boyer, eds., *Contemporary Capitalism: The Embeddedness of Institutions*

John D. Huber, *Exclusion by Elections: Inequality, Ethnic Identity, and Democracy*

John D. Huber and Charles R. Shipan, *Deliberate Discretion? The Institutional Foundations of Bureaucratic Autonomy*

Ellen Immergut, *Health Politics: Interests and Institutions in Western Europe*

Torben Iversen, *Capitalism, Democracy, and Welfare*

Torben Iversen, *Contested Economic Institutions*

Torben Iversen, Jonas Pontussen, and David Soskice, eds., *Unions, Employers, and Central Banks: Macroeconomic Coordination and Institutional Change in Social Market Economics*

Thomas Janoski and Alexander M. Hicks, eds., *The Comparative Political Economy of the Welfare State*

Joseph Jupille, *Procedural Politics: Issues, Influence, and Institutional Choice in the European Union*

Stathis Kalyvas, *The Logic of Violence in Civil War*

Stephen B. Kaplan, *Globalization and Austerity Politics in Latin America*

David C. Kang, *Crony Capitalism: Corruption and Capitalism in South Korea and the Philippines*

Junko Kato, *Regressive Taxation and the Welfare State*

Orit Kedar, *Voting for Policy, Not Parties: How Voters Compensate for Power Sharing*

Robert O. Keohane and Helen B. Milner, eds., *Internationalization and Domestic Politics*

Herbert Kitschelt, *The Transformation of European Social Democracy*

Herbert Kitschelt, Kirk A. Hawkins, Juan Pablo Luna, Guillermo Rosas, and Elizabeth J. Zechmeister, *Latin American Party Systems*

Herbert Kitschelt, Peter Lange, Gary Marks, and John D. Stephens, eds., *Continuity and Change in Contemporary Capitalism*

Herbert Kitschelt, Zdenka Mansfeldova, Radek Markowski, and Gabor Toka, *Post-Communist Party Systems*

David Knoke, Franz Urban Pappi, Jeffrey Broadbent, and Yutaka Tsujinaka, eds., *Comparing Policy Networks*

Ken Kollman, *Perils of Centralization: Lessons from Church, State, and Corporation*

Allan Kornberg and Harold D. Clarke, *Citizens and Community: Political Support in a Representative Democracy*

Amie Kreppel, *The European Parliament and the Supranational Party System*

David D. Laitin, *Language Repertoires and State Construction in Africa*

Fabrice E. Lehoucq and Ivan Molina, *Stuffing the Ballot Box: Fraud, Electoral Reform, and Democratization in Costa Rica*

Mark Irving Lichbach and Alan S. Zuckerman, eds., *Comparative Politics: Rationality, Culture, and Structure, 2ⁿᵈ edition*

Evan Lieberman, *Race and Regionalism in the Politics of Taxation in Brazil and South Africa*

Richard M. Locke, *The Promise and Limits of Private Power: Promoting Labor Standards in a Global Economy*

Julia Lynch, *Age in the Welfare State: The Origins of Social Spending on Pensioner's Workers and Children*

Pauline Jones Luong, *Institutional Change and Political Continuity in Post-Soviet Central Asia*

Pauline Jones Luong and Erika Weinthal, *Oil is Not a Curse: Ownership Structure and Institutions in Soviet Successor States*

Doug McAdam, John McCarthy, and Mayer Zald, eds., *Comparative Perspectives on Social Movements*

Lauren M. MacLean, *Informal Institutions and Citizenship in Rural Africa: Risk and Reciprocity in Ghana and Côte d'Ivoire*

Beatriz Magaloni, *Voting for Autocracy: Hegemonic Party Survival and its Demise in Mexico*

James Mahoney, *Colonialism and Postcolonial Development: Spanish America in Comparative Perspective*

James Mahoney and Dietrich Rueschemeyer, eds., *Historical Analysis and the Social Sciences*

Scott Mainwaring and Matthew Soberg Shugart, eds., *Presidentialism and Democracy in Latin America*

Melanie Manion, *Information for Autocrats: Representation in Chinese Local Congresses*

Isabela Mares, *From Open Secrets to Secret Voting: Democratic Electoral Reforms and Voter Autonomy*

Isabela Mares, *The Politics of Social Risk: Business and Welfare State Development*

Isabela Mares, *Taxation, Wage Bargaining, and Unemployment*

Cathie Jo Martin and Duane Swank, *The Political Construction of Business Interests: Coordination, Growth, and Equality*

Anthony W. Marx, *Making Race, Making Nations: A Comparison of South Africa, the United States, and Brazil*

Bonnie M. Meguid, *Party Competition between Unequals: Strategies and Electoral Fortunes in Western Europe*

Joel S. Migdal, *State in Society: Studying How States and Societies Constitute One Another*

Joel S. Migdal, Atul Kohli, and Vivienne Shue, eds., *State Power and Social Forces: Domination and Transformation in the Third World*

Scott Morgenstern and Benito Nacif, eds., *Legislative Politics in Latin America*

Kevin M. Morrison, *Nontaxation and Representation: The Fiscal Foundations of Political Stability*

Layna Mosley, *Global Capital and National Governments*

Layna Mosley, *Labor Rights and Multinational Production*

Wolfgang C. Müller and Kaare Strøm, *Policy, Office, or Votes?*

Maria Victoria Murillo, *Political Competition, Partisanship, and Policy Making in Latin American Public Utilities*

Maria Victoria Murillo, *Labor Unions, Partisan Coalitions, and Market Reforms in Latin America*

Monika Nalepa, *Skeletons in the Closet: Transitional Justice in Post-Communist Europe*

Ton Notermans, *Money, Markets, and the State: Social Democratic Economic Policies since 1918*

Aníbal Pérez-Liñán, *Presidential Impeachment and the New Political Instability in Latin America*

Roger D. Petersen, *Understanding Ethnic Violence: Fear, Hatred, and Resentment in 20th Century Eastern Europe*

Roger D. Petersen, *Western Intervention in the Balkans: The Strategic Use of Emotion in Conflict*

Simona Piattoni, ed., *Clientelism, Interests, and Democratic Representation*

Paul Pierson, *Dismantling the Welfare State?: Reagan, Thatcher, and the Politics of Retrenchment*

Marino Regini, *Uncertain Boundaries: The Social and Political Construction of European Economies*

Kenneth M. Roberts, *Changing Course in Latin America: Party Systems in the Neoliberal Era*

Marc Howard Ross, *Cultural Contestation in Ethnic Conflict*

Roger Schoenman, *Networks and Institutions in Europe's Emerging Markets*

Ben Ross Schneider, *Hierarchical Capitalism in Latin America: Business, Labor, and the Challenges of Equitable Development*

Lyle Scruggs, *Sustaining Abundance: Environmental Performance in Industrial Democracies*

Jefferey M. Sellers, *Governing from Below: Urban Regions and the Global Economy*

Yossi Shain and Juan Linz, eds., *Interim Governments and Democratic Transitions*

Beverly Silver, *Forces of Labor: Workers' Movements and Globalization since 1870*

Theda Skocpol, *Social Revolutions in the Modern World*

Prerna Singh, *How Solidarity Works for Welfare: Subnationalism and Social Development in India*

Austin Smith et al, *Selected Works of Michael Wallerstein*

Regina Smyth, *Candidate Strategies and Electoral Competition in the Russian Federation: Democracy Without Foundation*

Richard Snyder, *Politics after Neoliberalism: Reregulation in Mexico*

David Stark and László Bruszt, *Postsocialist Pathways: Transforming Politics and Property in East Central Europe*

Sven Steinmo, *The Evolution of Modern States: Sweden, Japan, and the United States*

Sven Steinmo, Kathleen Thelen, and Frank Longstreth, eds., *Structuring Politics: Historical Institutionalism in Comparative Analysis*

Susan C. Stokes, *Mandates and Democracy: Neoliberalism by Surprise in Latin America*

Susan C. Stokes, ed., *Public Support for Market Reforms in New Democracies*

Susan C. Stokes , Thad Dunning , Marcelo Nazareno , and Valeria Brusco, *Brokers, Voters, and Clientelism: The Puzzle of Distributive Politics*

Milan W. Svolik, *The Politics of Authoritarian Rule*

Duane Swank, *Global Capital, Political Institutions, and Policy Change in Developed Welfare States*

Sidney Tarrow, *Power in Movement: Social Movements and Contentious Politics*

Sidney Tarrow, *Power in Movement: Social Movements and Contentious Politics, Revised and Updated Third Edition*

Tariq Thachil, *Elite Parties, Poor Voters: How Social Services Win Votes in India*

Kathleen Thelen, *How Institutions Evolve: The Political Economy of Skills in Germany, Britain, the United States, and Japan*

Kathleen Thelen, *Varieties of Liberalization and the New Politics of Social Solidarity*

Charles Tilly, *Trust and Rule*

Daniel Treisman, *The Architecture of Government: Rethinking Political Decentralization*

Guillermo Trejo, *Popular Movements in Autocracies: Religion, Repression, and Indigenous Collective Action in Mexico*

Rory Truex, *Making Autocracy Work: Representation and Responsiveness in Modern China*

Lily Lee Tsai, *Accountability without Democracy: How Solidary Groups Provide Public Goods in Rural China*

Joshua Tucker, *Regional Economic Voting: Russia, Poland, Hungary, Slovakia and the Czech Republic, 1990-1999*

Ashutosh Varshney, *Democracy, Development, and the Countryside*

Yuhua Wang, *Tying the Autocrat's Hand: The Rise of The Rule of Law in China*

Jeremy M. Weinstein, *Inside Rebellion: The Politics of Insurgent Violence*

Stephen I. Wilkinson, *Votes and Violence: Electoral Competition and Ethnic Riots in India*

Andreas Wimmer, *Waves of War: Nationalism, State Formation, and Ethnic Exclusion in the Modern World*

Jason Wittenberg, *Crucibles of Political Loyalty: Church Institutions and Electoral Continuity in Hungary*

Elisabeth J. Wood, *Forging Democracy from Below: Insurgent Transitions in South Africa and El Salvador*

Elisabeth J. Wood, *Insurgent Collective Action and Civil War in El Salvador*

Daniel Ziblatt, *Conservative Parties and the Birth of Modern Democracy in Europe*